THE SHORT PROSE READER

THE SHORT PROSE READER

THIRTEENTH EDITION

Gilbert H. Muller
The City University of New York
LaGuardia

Harvey S. Wiener
The City University of New York
LaGuardia

The McGraw·Hill Companies

THE SHORT PROSE READER, THIRTEENTH EDITION

Published by McGraw-Hill, a business unit of The McGraw-Hill Companies, Inc., 1221 Avenue of the Americas, New York, NY 10020.

Some ancillaries, including electronic and print components, may not be available to customers outside the United States.

This book is printed on acid-free paper.

1 2 3 4 5 6 7 8 9 0 DOC/DOC 1 0 9 8 7 6 5 4 3 2

ISBN 978-0-07-338393-4
MHID 0-07-338393-7

Vice President & Editor-in-Chief: *Michael Ryan*
Vice President & Director Specialized Publishing: *Janice M. Roerig-Blong*
Publisher: *David Patterson*
Senior Sponsoring Editor: *Debra B. Hash*
Director of Marketing & Sales: *Jennifer J. Lewis*
Senior Project Manager: *Joyce Watters*
Design Coordinator: *Margarite Reynolds*
Cover Designer: *Mary-Presley Adams*
Cover Image: *Diana Ong*
Buyer: *Susan K. Culbertson*
Media Project Manager: *Sridevi Palani*
Compositor: *MPS Limited, a Macmillan Company*
Typeface: *10/12 Times Roman*
Printer: *R. R. Donnelley*

Library of Congress Cataloging-in-Publication Data

The short prose reader / [compiled by] Gilbert H. Muller, Harvey S. Wiener. -- 13th ed.
p. cm. -- (The short prose reader)
ISBN 978-0-07-338393-4 (acid-free paper) 1. College readers.
2. English language--Rhetoric--Problems, exercises, etc. 3. Report writing--Problems, exercises, etc. I. Muller, Gilbert H., 1941- II. Wiener, Harvey S.
PE1417.S446 2012
808'.0427--dc23

2011025424

www.mhhe.com

ABOUT THE AUTHORS

Gilbert H. Muller, who received a PhD in English and American literature from Stanford University, is currently professor emeritus of English at the LaGuardia campus of the City University of New York. He has also taught at Stanford, Vassar, and several universities overseas. Dr. Muller is the author of the award-winning study *Nightmares and Visions: Flannery O'Connor and the Catholic Grotesque, Chester Himes, New Strangers in Paradise: The Immigrant Experience and Contemporary American Fiction,* and *William Cullen Bryant: Author of America.* His essays and reviews have appeared in *The New York Times, The New Republic, The Nation, The Sewanee Review, The Georgia Review,* and elsewhere. He is also a noted author and editor of textbooks in English and composition, including *The McGraw-Hill Reader* and, with John Williams, *The McGraw-Hill Introduction to Literature.* Dr. Muller has received awards from the National Endowment for the Humanities, Fulbright Commission, and the Ford and Mellon foundations.

Harvey S. Wiener, professor emeritus at LaGuardia Community College of the City University of New York, served as Vice President of Adult Programs and Community Outreach at Marymount Manhattan College. Previously University Dean for Academic Affairs at the City University of New York, he was founding president of the Council of Writing Program Administrators. Dr. Wiener is the author of many books on reading and writing for college students and their teachers, including *The Writing Room* (Oxford,

1981). He is coauthor of *The McGraw-Hill College Handbook,* a reference grammar and rhetorical text. Dr. Wiener has chaired the Teaching of Writing Division of the Modern Language Association (1987). He has taught writing at every level of education from elementary school to graduate school. A Phi Beta Kappa graduate of Brooklyn College, he holds a PhD in Renaissance literature from Fordham University. Dr. Wiener has won grants from the National Endowment for the Humanities, the Fund for the Improvement of Postsecondary Education, and the Exxon Education Foundation. His book *Any Child Can Write* was an alternate selection of the Book of the Month Club and was featured on the *Today* show. His writing has appeared in *Anglia, College English, College Composition and Communication,* and *WPA Journal,* as well as in the London *Times,* the New York *Daily News,* and *Gentleman's Quarterly.*

To the memory of George Groman

CONTENTS

CHAPTER 2

CHAPTER 3

CHAPTER 4

CHAPTER 5

CHAPTER 6

CHAPTER 7

CHAPTER 8

CHAPTER 9

CHAPTER 10

CHAPTER 11

THEMATIC CONTENTS

Scenes and Places

Childhood and Family

Cultures and Ethnicities

School and Education

Gender Issues

Nature and the Environment

Social and Political Issues

Science and Technology

Psychology and Behavior

Language and Identity

Humor and Satire

PREFACE

The thirteenth edition of *The Short Prose Reader* maintains the best features of the earlier editions: lively reading selections supported by helpful apparatus to integrate reading and writing in college composition and reading courses. In working through the text, the student progresses from key aspects of the writing and reading processes to chapters on the essential patterns of writing and then to more rigorous forms of analysis and argument. Each chapter provides diverse and lively prose models suited for discussion, analysis, and imitation.

New features of the thirteenth edition include:

- **Many new reading selections,** with essays by John Grisham, Anna Quindlen, Richard Rodriguez, Barry Lopez, Andrew Lam, and Deborah Tannen. We balance these contemporary readings—all published since 2000—with favorites from earlier editions of *The Short Prose Reader,* such as Langston Hughes's "Salvation," George Orwell's "A Hanging," Amy Tan's "Mother Tongue," and Rachel Carson's "A Fable for Tomorrow."
- **New topics and issues** that will appeal to students, among them texting from an automobile, Internet privacy, the Facebook phenomenon, and Muslim identity.
- **A revised table of contents** that lets students move from easier rhetorical strategies to more challenging ones (like classification and definition) that stress synthetic and higher-order cognitive abilities.
- **New units in the thematic table of contents,** including Scenes and Places, Cultures and Ethnicities, Nature and the Environment, and Language and Identity.

- **A major revision of Chapter 11, Argumentation and Persuasion,** with a fresh pro/con pair on social networking and new selections on the "Perspectives on Ethnicity" Unit.
- **New visuals** throughout *The Short Prose Reader* that encourage students to move from seeing to writing.
- **A Guide to Research and Documentation,** which follows the most recent MLA guidelines.
- **Links to the online learning center (OLC)** integrated throughout the text. The OLC provides students with links to more information about some of the writers in this collection.

These features enhance the key elements of *The Short Prose Reader* that have made the previous twelve editions so enduringly popular.

ORGANIZATION

The organization of *The Short Prose Reader* is one of its major strengths. Chapter 1, On Writing, and Chapter 2, On Reading, offer students brief overviews of these two interdependent skills; each chapter offers four unique views on the crafts of writing or reading by well-known writers. Each of the following eight chapters contains four short essays that illustrate clearly a specific pattern or technique—description, narration, process analysis, illustration, comparison and contrast, causal analysis, classification, or definition. The final chapter is on argumentation. Students learn to build upon earlier techniques and patterns as they progress through the book.

READABILITY

From the beginning, we have chosen selections for *The Short Prose Reader* that are readable yet substantial and representative of many different types of writers. The essays, which range typically between 300 and 1,200 words, achieve their goals succinctly and clearly and are easy to understand. They exemplify both the types of college writing expected of students and the length of essay that is frequently assigned. The detailed questions that follow each essay can be used in reading as well as writing classes, since they ask the student to analyze both the content and the form of the prose selections.

APPARATUS

The questions and activities we have included for each piece are comprehensive and integrated—designed to develop and reinforce the key critical-thinking skills required in college writing.

- **Extensive biographical notes:** The headnotes preceding the selections provide valuable information about each writer, giving students more tools for reading the essays critically.
- **Prereading questions:** Before each essay, students encounter an activity called Prereading: Thinking About the Essay in Advance, which encourages them to think and talk about the topic before reading what the writer says about it. Studies show that such prior discussion arouses interest and holds the reader's attention.
- **Vocabulary exercises:** Each selection includes two vocabulary exercises. Words to Watch alerts students to words they will read in context, and Building Vocabulary uses other effective methods of teaching vocabulary, including attention to prefixes and suffixes, context clues, synonyms and antonyms, and abstract versus concrete words.
- **Questions that emphasize critical thinking:** To emphasize critical thinking as the main reason for questioning and discussion, we have grouped our conversational prods and probes under the heading Thinking Critically About the Essay. The questions titled Understanding the Writer's Ideas reinforce reading comprehension. The questions titled Understanding the Writer's Techniques and Exploring the Writer's Ideas provide excellent bases for class discussion and independent reading and analysis.
- **Prewriting prompts:** These sections help students record informal thoughts for writing in advance of producing an essay.
- **Guided Writing Activities:** A key exercise for each essay and a novel feature of *The Short Prose Reader,* the Guided Writing activities offer a dynamic approach to writing projects. These activities tie the writing project to the reading selection, but instead of simply being told to write an essay on a certain topic, students can use the Guided Writing segment to move from step to step in the composing process.
- **Collaborative activities:** Thinking and Writing Collaboratively activities encourage students to work together in groups on essays and ideas for writing.

- **Reader response activities:** Writing About the Text asks students to examine closely the language and ideas in each selection and to write thoughtfully about them.
- **Additional writing projects:** More Writing Projects provides students with additional ideas for writing on the topic of the selection.

At the end of each chapter is a **Summing Up** section, a means for students to focus their attention on issues raised by several of the chapter's selections and on more writing topics, and a **From Seeing to Writing** activity, an engaging visual assignment that gives students another means of coming up with ideas for writing. And at the end of the text is an **appendix on research and documentation,** including a step-by-step guide to the research process, a section on using MLA style to document sources, and a sample student research paper on body image and advertising that uses a visual as support.

FLEXIBILITY

Students and teachers alike can use *The Short Prose Reader* flexibly and effectively. An alternate table of contents suggests thematic groupings of readings. The text is simple yet sophisticated, inviting students to engage in a multiplicity of cultural and traditional topics through essays and exercises that are easy to follow but never condescending. Weighing the needs and expectations of today's first-year students, we have designed a rhetoric/reader that can serve as the primary text for almost any composition course.

The Option of a Custom Text. It's Your Course; Make It Your Text With Create. Craft your teaching resources to match the way you teach! With McGraw-Hill Create, you can easily rearrange chapters and add material from other content sources. Create even allows you to personalize your book's appearance by selecting the cover and adding your name, school, and course information. Order a Create book and you'll receive a complimentary print review copy in 3-5 business days or a complimentary electronic review copy (eComp) via email in about one hour. Go to www.mcgrawhillcreate.com and register today.

ANCILLARIES

- **The Instructor's Manual** provides teaching approaches for each chapter and essay, along with answers to the vocabulary and critical-thinking questions that follow each essay.

- **The text's companion Web site at www.mhhe.com/shortprose13e** offers three types of links—cultural, bibliographical, and biographical—to further information on selected authors within *The Short Prose Reader*.

ACKNOWLEDGMENTS

For this edition of *The Short Prose Reader,* we enjoyed the support of John Kindler, our sponsoring editor, who has brought a fresh perspective and calm persistence to the project. We are also deeply grateful for the patient and extraordinary efforts of Janice Wiggins-Clarke, our development editor.

We wish to thank our colleagues across the country for their support:

Andrew Tomko, *Bergen Community College*
Brett Bodily, *North Lake College*
David-Michael Allen, *Donnelly College*
Ellen Laird, *Hudson Valley Community College*
Kathryn Lacey, *Cincinnati State University*
Magdalena Aquilar, *El Paso Community College*
Marina Gore, *Hudson Valley Community College*
Mary B. Caldwell, *El Paso Community College*
Matthew Goldstein, *Laney College*
Rachel Bornn, *Hudson Valley Communite College*
Sara Tedesco, *Hudson Valley Community College*
Theodore Johnston, *El Paso Community College*

Gilbert H. Muller
Harvey S. Wiener

CHAPTER 1

On Writing

WHAT IS WRITING?

Writing helps us to record and communicate ideas. It is a definitive and essential part of daily human experience. Whether we write a shopping list or a great novel, we use a tool without which we would find ourselves isolated. Without writing we cut ourselves off from vital processes like the expression of political opinions, the description of medical emergencies, and the examination of our feelings in diaries and letters.

Writing crosses many cultures. Whether we consider historic cave drawings or the transmission of fax messages after the World Trade Center disaster, we find evidence of the human instinct to communicate ideas to other people.

In the past, writing brought about change. African American slaves were frequently forbidden to learn to read or write, but some managed to find ways to gain literacy anyway. Their narratives of slave life helped fire the abolition movement. Women in the nineteenth century used writing to advance the cause of suffrage, winning votes with passionate speeches and articles in newspapers. Immigrants struggled to learn English in order to find a better life in the New World.

Writing celebrates human achievement. In religion, in love, in wartime and in peace, in astronomy and medicine and archaeology, in the arts and humanities, writing reminds us of our shared human identity. From the Song of Solomon in the Bible to the words of Martin Luther King Jr.'s "I Have a Dream," from the Declaration of Independence to song lyrics by Bruce Springsteen or Alicia Keys, writing helps us to come to terms with who we are and what we want.

What is writing, exactly? For most of us, writing is so familiar that the question seems silly. We all know what writing is. Yet when we try to write ourselves, we may find that asking and answering the question are vital.

Writing is both a product and a process. Writing is, of course, *what* we write: a letter, a law brief, a term paper, an inaugural address. Since it is a product, we must think of writing as having a public as well as a private purpose. While some writing, like shopping lists or a diary, may be meant only for our own eyes, most writing is intended for an audience. In learning what writing is, we need to think about who the audience is, and what the purpose of the writing is.

Writing is also a process; it is *how* we write. In learning to write well, we examine the process of transferring ideas from head to hand. We realize that the actual, mechanical practice of writing out ideas helps us to think more carefully, to plan and arrange ideas, to analyze our vague thoughts into solid words on a page.

HOW DO WE WRITE?

The process of writing is not absolute; there is no one sure way to learn to write well. However, there are some common elements in this process that will help anyone getting started as a writer.

Warming Up: Prewriting

Like an athlete, the writer benefits from warm-up exercises. Usually called prewriting, these steps help a writer prepare gradually and thoughtfully for the event of writing a long essay. Writers stretch their intellectual muscles by thinking about a topic before they write about it. They talk to friends and colleagues. They visit a library and flip through reference books, newspapers, magazines, and books. Sometimes, they make notes and lists as a way of putting pen to paper for the first time. Some writers brainstorm: they use free association to jot down ideas as thoroughly as possible in an unedited form. Others use "timed writing": they write nonstop whatever comes to mind in a set time period—fifteen or twenty minutes, say. Freewriting like this loosens up ideas without the worry of correctness in language too early in the writing process. After these preliminary warm-ups, many writers try to group or classify ideas by making a rough outline or drawing boxes or making lists to try to bring some plan or order to their rough ideas.

Once the writer has a rough topic area outlined, he or she may return to the audience and purpose for the essay. Who will read the essay? What material would best suit this audience? What language would be most appropriate for this audience? What is the purpose of the essay? A thesis sentence is important here. The thesis is your main point, the essential idea you want to assert about your subject. It's always a good idea to write out your thesis whether or not you ultimately use it in your essay.

Often the purpose or intent becomes clearer as the writer continues to think and write. Choosing the audience and purpose carefully—and stating the thesis succinctly—make the writer's as well as the reader's task easier.

Look at the following prewriting by a student who wanted to write about her impressions of a hospital. She made a list of free associations with the intent of using her notes to prepare the draft of an essay.

Roller skating accident
Go to the hospital for tests
My mother drops me off and has to go to work in the supermarket
I'm alone, I never stayed in a hospital before
I did visit my aunt in Atlanta when she was in the hospital and I was
there for the summer
Doctors and nurses whispering
Tray drops suddenly and scares me out of my wits
A nurse helps a girl but she pulls the curtain & I can't see
My third grade class wrote letters to one of the children who was in
the hospital but we never saw the hospital room
I can't sleep, there's too much noise
The nurse takes my temperature, I have 102 she gives me pills
Nobody tells me anything about what's happening or what to expect
they just do things to me
The nurse's heels squeak on the floor and give me the shivers
A red lite goes on and off in the opposite room

As she reviewed her prewriting list, the student realized that her purpose was to write about her own short stay in the hospital after an accident. Most of the items recorded relate directly to that incident. She saw that she had included on the list a number of impressions that, although hospital related, did not suit her purpose for this essay. She wanted to write about her own particular experiences, and so she ultimately rejected the items about her aunt in Atlanta, her mother going to work, and the third-grade classmate. With a clearer sense of how to proceed, she thought about a thesis sentence. The essay needed focus: exactly what point did she want to make in her essay? Simply presenting descriptive details might give readers a picture of the hospital but would not make an assertion about the experience. In fact she intended to write about how uncomfortable she felt and how the sights and sounds of the hospital contributed to that discomfort. She developed this thesis sentence:

I was uncomfortable in the hospital after my accident.

This thesis states an opinion, and so it helps the writer narrow her topic. Yet it is very broad, and some of the details on the list suggest a thesis that could more accurately express the writer's main point. After several more tries, she developed the thesis which includes, as you can see, an error in spelling and verb use, that appears in the draft:

> There I layed stiff and silent in the night listening to the noises outside my room in the long corridors and watching everything that went on around me.

First Draft

Prewriting leads to the first draft. Drafts are usually meant for the writer's eyes only; they are messy with rethinking, rewriting, and revision. Drafts help the writer figure out what to write by giving him or her a place to think on paper before having to make a public presentation of the writing. Everyone develops a personal style of draft writing, but many writers find that double-spacing, leaving wide margins, and writing on only one side of the paper are steps that make rewriting easier. If you write on a computer, you'll find you can easily revise and produce several drafts without discarding earlier versions of the essay.

In a first draft, a writer begins to shape paragraphs, to plan where to put each piece of the essay for maximum effect.

Sometimes, a first draft doesn't have an introduction. The introduction can be written after the writer has finished the draft and has a better sense of what the essay is about. The audience will see only the final draft, after all, and will never know when the writer wrote the introduction.

Having finished the first draft, the writer tries to become the audience. How will the essay sound to someone else? Does it make sense? Are the ideas and expression clear? Is there a main point? Do all the ideas in the essay relate to this main point? Is there a coherent plan to the essay? Do ideas follow logically one from the next? Would someone unfamiliar with the topic be able to follow the ideas? Should more information be added? What should be left out?

In attempting to answer these questions, writers often try to find a friendly reader to look over the draft and give advice. Whatever else they may look for at this stage, they do not pay too much attention to spelling or grammar. A helpful reader will enable the writer to see the essay as the audience will see it, and suggest ways to reorganize and clarify ideas.

Here is an early draft of the essay written from the prewriting sample you observed on page 3.

DRAFT

ALL ALONE

There I sat all alone in my hard bed at the hospital. This was the place I most definitely did not want to be in. But because of my rollerskating accident I had no choice. I had to listen to the doctors and go for the necessary tests. There I layed stiff and silent in the night
5 listening to the noises outside my room in the long corridors and watching everything that went on around me.

As I layed there bundled up in my white sheets and the cold, hard steel bars of the bed surrounding me. I could hear everything that was happening on my ward. Nurses would pass up and down the corridor
10 with their white rubber heal shoes squeeking on the white freshly polished floors. The squeaking would send shrieking chills up my spin. Soft whispers were heard as doctors and nurses exchanged conversations. If they only knew how disturbing it was for me to hear these slight mutters. The most startling noise, though, was when a
15 tray must have accidentally slipped out of a nurses hand. The clatter of the tray echoed down the long, endless white corridors setting

my nerves on end, I must have sat there shaking for at least five minutes.

Watching what was going on outside and inside my room was no picnic either. In the hall a bright light shown enabling me to 20 view the room next door. As I was peering out my door, I noticed the little red light above the opposite door light flash along with a distantly faint ringing of a bell down the hall. The nurse, in a clean white uniform, was there in an instant to help the young curly haired girl. With a sturdy thrust of her hand the nurse pulled the 25 white cloth divider across the room concealing the two of them in the corner.

Two other nurses were making their rounds when they noticed I was awake. One was in her mid forties, had brown hair, brown eyes and was slim. The other nurse looked slightly older, taller than 30 the first one, had white streaks throughout her dark hair and was of medium build. The first nurse said to me, "What are you doing up at this hour." I told her I could not sleep. They noticed that I was perspiring and decided to take my temperature. The first nurse left and returned with the thermometer. She placed the cold, thin piece of 35 glass into my warm mouth and put her cool fingers around my wrist to take my pulse. They discovered I had a fever of a hundred and two. The second nurse disappeared this time and returned holding a little silver packet with two tylonal aspirins in it. I took out the two white tablets and swallowed them with water. Every so often until 40 the following morning either one of the nurses would saunter into my room to check on me. All this happened in one night.

Hospital visits can be very frightening. Nobody realizes the trauma patients go threw.

After discussing her draft with students in the class and with her teacher, the writer of the hospital essay knew how to make revisions. As she weighed her options, she knew that an even more clearly stated thesis would help her readers understand what she was trying to accomplish, and so she revised it further. The thesis from the revised draft appears below:

> I was supposed to be in the hospital to recuperate; instead of sleeping, though, I lay there all night stiff and silent, uncomfortably listening to the noises outside my room off the long hallway and watching everything that happened around me.

Friendly readers suggested further that the writer needed to fill in more information about the reason for her hospital stay and also to provide more snapshots of the scene around her. If in fact her objective was to portray the hospital as producing further discomfort, she needed to offer more sensory details than she had presented to her readers. (See pages 5–6.) Some readers felt that the writer should better organize these details, perhaps considering the sights and the sounds separately or pointing out first the activity in the room and then the activity in the hallway, both places apparently contributing to the writer's unhappiness. And to improve the coherence of the essay, the writer knew that in revising she should look carefully at sentence transitions, particularly from paragraph to paragraph.

Several readers felt that the conclusion was flat and that somehow the writer had to figure out a way to raise the issue of the hospital's indifference to her discomfort. It was not enough to record the unpleasantness; she also wanted to recommend some ways hospitals could avoid distressing their patients, and she decided that the conclusion might be a good place to raise those issues.

Errors distracted readers even at the draft stage. These included the sentence fragment on lines 7 and 8 and the comma splice on line 17. Some spelling, usage, and grammar errors needed attention—*layed* in line 7 (the correct verb form needed here is *lay*) and *squeeking* for *squeaking* in line 10, for example. The use of the passive voice in line 12 does not help the descriptive and narrative flow, and the writer knew to change the passive to active as she revised. Simply by revising sentences some errors vanish and others appear, and attentive writers know that a careful editing prior to producing the final draft is critical.

Additional Drafts

After getting responses from a reader, the writer begins the second draft. And the third. And maybe the fourth. No one can predict how many drafts are necessary for a final essay, but very few writers get by with fewer than two or three drafts. Revision usually involves working first on the clear expression of ideas and later on editing for spelling, grammatical correctness, and good sentence structure.

Here is a revised draft of the essay "All Alone." Note the comments in the margin.

REVISED DRAFT

Introductory paragraph: fills in accident details; leads comfortably to the thesis.

Thesis: last sentence of the first paragraph.

Concrete sensory details ("white sheets," "cold steel bars," "rubber heels squeaking," etc.): heighten readers' awareness of hospital room scene.

Frustration at disturbing room noises now clear; readers perceive essay's unity with repeated references to sounds.

"Perhaps the most startling noise"—effective link to thesis.

Transition from paragraph 2 to paragraph 3: "All the noises aside" links the topic of paragraph 3 to the topic of paragraph 2 and to the thesis.

ALL ALONE

I spent a long, unpleasant weekend in a bed at University Hospital, the result of a bad roller skating accident I had one Saturday afternoon last October. There might be a concussion; there might he broken bones—and so I had no choice but to listen to the doctors and go for necessary tests. I was supposed to be in the hospital to recuperate; instead of sleeping, though, I lay there all night, stiff and silent, uncomfortably listening to the noises outside my room off the long hallway and watching everything that happened around me.

Bundled up in my white sheets and surrounded by the cold steel bars of my bed I heard every little sound in my ward all night long. Nurses, their rubber heels squeaking on the freshly polished floors, passed up and down the corridor. I heard soft whispers as one doctor in a green shirt spoke to two orderlies leaning against the wall with their arms folded. Occasionally one of them would laugh and the other two would giggle and say, "Sh! Sh!" If they only knew how disturbing it was for me to hear their muttering! At one point I almost shouted "Would you all get out of here!" but I didn't have the courage, and I pulled the blanket over my head instead. Perhaps the most startling noise, though, was the sound of a tray that must have accidentally slipped out of a nurse's hand far beyond my view. I jumped up as the clatter echoed down the long, endless white corridors, setting my nerves on end. Perspiration streaming down my face, I must have sat there in my bed shaking for at least five minutes.

All the noises aside, watching the activity outside and inside my room disturbed me, too. Across the hall a little red light above the door of the opposite room suddenly flashed on and off. A nurse in a clean white uniform was there in an instant to help a young, curly haired girl twisting and crying on her bed. A bright light in the hall enabled me to see the actions clearly. With a sturdy thrust of her hand the nurse pulled the white cloth divider across the room, concealing the two of them in the corner. However, I saw the nurse's shadow moving up and down, back and forth, until the child quieted down.

Soon after I noted all this, two other nurses making their rounds saw that I was still awake. One, a slim woman in her mid forties with brown eyes, said in a loud voice, "What are you doing up at this hour, dear? It's after two AM." When I said I couldn't sleep, they saw how clammy I was, and the one who spoke to me rushed off for a thermometer. Placing the rigid glass rod in my mouth, she took my pulse with cool fingers at my wrist. "A hundred and two," she said. "Wanda, bring this girl something for her fever." The second nurse disappeared this time and returned holding a silver packet of Tylenol, and I swallowed the pills with water from the drinking glass on my bedstand. Every so often until morning one of the nurses would saunter in, touch my brow, and make cheerful but noisy conversation. I knew they were trying to help, but all this activity did not make me feel any better. It made me feel worse.

Because hospital stays can be very frightening, hospital employees must realize the trauma patients go through just lying in their beds wondering what will happen to them next. The slightest sound, the barest visible action magnifies a million times in a tense person's mind. Couldn't the admitting clerk, a floor nurse, or an intern explain to patients about what to expect at the hospital? I would have liked knowing all about the tests I'd have to go through, but also would have liked knowing not to expect much sleep. If I knew in advance of all the noise and activity I might have relaxed.

The words "watching the activity outside and inside my room disturbed me, too" set the topic of the next part of the essay.

Concrete sensory detail holds readers' interest and brings scene to life: "red light above the door"; "clean white uniform"; "curly haired girl twisting and crying on her bed"; "nurse's shadow moving up and down, back and forth."

Clear connection to previous paragraph; "Soon after I noted all this" provides transition, helping to build essay's coherence.

Nurses' spoken words add life to the essay.

Short, succinct final sentence very effective in this paragraph.

Conclusion adds depth to the essay; it places narrative and descriptive details in a larger, more profound framework.

We call attention particularly to the greatly improved last paragraph in the revised draft, the writer's conclusion. This is no mere restatement of the topic. The writer has used the experience that she revealed in the rest of the essay to establish a new context for the topic. What did her unpleasant stay in University Hospital tell her? Hospitals don't realize the trauma even a short stay can produce in a patient, and if only hospital staff would explain what to expect in advance, patients might not have such a rough time. We can see how the body paragraphs lead her to reach this conclusion and feel satisfied that the writer has led us to new insights based on her experiences.

Throughout the revised essay, the writer has tightened her sentences by combining a number of them and by eliminating unnecessary words and phrases. In addition, we note a reduction of distracting errors in sentence structure and spelling. Efforts to eliminate errors and improve language and sentences will continue as the writer moves toward producing a final draft and formally edits her paper.

Final Draft

The final draft is intended for public, rather than private, reading. It must be the writer's best effort. Most editors and teachers require final drafts to be double-spaced, with wide margins, and printed by means of a computer; and clearly identified with the writer's name, the date, and information to locate the writer (such as class code or home address). The four writers in this chapter represent a variety of approaches to both the craft and the inspiration of writing. Jennifer Lee investigates the relation between standard written English and instant-messaging language created by the online population of computer users. John Grisham shows us the dead-end jobs he took as he evolved into a successful writer. Amy Tan finds her writer's voice when she realizes that her mother is the ideal audience. Like William Zinsser pleading for the preciseness that comes only with simplicity, Tan advises us to aim for direct and simple language instead of academic jargon or pretentious style.

The four writers represented here also introduce expository techniques discussed in subsequent chapters. Careful examination of their sources of inspiration *and* their revelations about the nuts and bolts of how to get the writing done prepares the way for later chapters and writing assignments.

Finally, though the Internet and CD-ROMs increasingly replace the printed page, the basic medium of communication is still words. Whether we scratch them onto stone tablets, draw them on parchment with turkey feathers, or type them into a computer, we still use words. Without writing, we risk the loss of our political freedom and our personal history. With words, we pass ideas and values on from one generation to the next. The words of Henry Miller will always ring true: "Writing, like life itself, is a voyage of discovery."

USING AND MIXING PATTERNS

Essay writing presents a challenge to beginning writers. Even for an accomplished and experienced writer, facing a blank page can be scary. However, attention to the writing process and some careful thought about what you are trying to accomplish can make the task more manageable. Discovering and exploring the purpose for a piece of writing will help you decide what your essay should be and what organizing techniques you can use.

We call these organizing techniques *patterns,* or rhetorical modes. The four major modes, or patterns, of writing are narration, description, exposition, and argumentation-persuasion. To tell a story, a writer uses narration. To bring to life a situation or scene, a writer draws on description, vivid words, and phrasing that "paint a picture" for the reader. To explain an idea or situation, a writer uses exposition.

We can further break exposition down into six different writing patterns: illustration, in which the use of examples makes an idea clearer; comparison and contrast, which exposes two or more objects or ideas in relation to each other; definition, which explains the meaning of certain words; classification, which establishes categories for a subject; process analysis, which outlines the methods for doing or making something; and cause-and-effect analysis, which examines a subject for its origins or results.

The final, and perhaps most important, writing pattern is argumentation-persuasion, in which a writer makes a claim concerning a controversial topic and/or encourages the reader to engage in a course of action. The following chart gives an overview of these rhetorical modes, what purpose they serve in an essay, and an example of what kind of essay you might find them in.

Rhetorical Mode	*Purpose*	*Example*
Description	To give the reader the texture of reality, to evoke images and other sensations through words	A travel essay
Narration	To tell a story	A personal essay recounting an important event from one's childhood
Process Analysis	To show how something is done or how something happens	Written instructions for how to create a movie on your computer
Illustration	To give examples to support an important idea	An essay about victims of drug abuse in a community
Comparison/ Contrast	To set two or more subjects side by side to show their similarities or differences	A critical article explaining why one movie is better than another movie
Cause-and-Effect Analysis	To explain the reason for an event or the effects of an event	An essay about the effects of the 2004 tsunami on tourism in Southeast Asia
Classification	To categorize information to show relationships between items or concepts	A humorous essay about the many kinds of men women meet when Internet dating
Definition	To explain the meaning of a word or concept	An essay exploring the various meanings of the word *bad* in slang
Argumentation and Persuasion	To convince readers to change their views or to act in a certain way	An opinion piece in a newspaper about drug sentencing legislation before Congress

Choosing a mode of writing can help you focus your thoughts, but essays would be impoverished if you were forced to choose just one of these patterns and stick to it. Thus, writers often choose a dominant mode for an essay but then draw on other modes to achieve their goals. For example, suppose you want to write an essay about the time your girlfriend or boyfriend broke up with you. You would use narration as the dominant mode, unfolding the events as they occurred. But your essay would be ineffective if you didn't at least include some physical description of your lost love, and to explain what went wrong and why your relationship fell apart, you'd need to draw on cause-and-effect analysis. Or imagine that you want to write a persuasive essay to convince your readers to adopt a pet from an animal shelter. Your essay would fall flat without an emotional appeal, so in addition to drawing on persuasion, you'd also want to describe a cute puppy or kitten; you might also want to lead your reader through the process of adopting an animal, classify the kinds of animals that end up in shelters, analyze the causes of pet abandonment, or tell a personal narrative based on your own experience adopting a pet.

Mixing rhetorical modes can improve any essay. Consider this paragraph by acclaimed essayist Scott Russell Sanders. The dominant mode in Sanders's essay is classification, but there are several patterns at work here.

Sanders is using narration here. This is an event that happened, and he is going to tell it as it happened.

The author uses vivid description, pointing out visual images that will make this scene more real in the mind's eye of the reader.

Comparison and contrast will be an important part of any classification essay, and this is true of Sanders's essay as well.

The author's main idea is dependent on a certain definition of manhood, and here he offers a couple of preliminary definitions—he will offer more later.

The first men, besides my father, I remember seeing were black convicts and white guards, in the cottonfield across the road from our farm on the outskirts of Memphis. I must have been three or four. The prisoners wore dingy gray-and-black zebra suits, heavy as canvas, sodden with sweat. Hatless, stooped, they chopped weeds in the fierce heat, row after row, breathing the acrid dust of boll-weevil poison. The overseers wore dazzling white shirts and broad shadowy hats. The oiled barrels of their shotguns flashed in the sunlight. Their faces in memory are utterly blank. Of course, those men, white and black, have become for me an emblem of racial hatred. But they have also come to stand for the twin poles of my early vision of manhood—the brute toiling animal and the boss.

We present all major rhetorical patterns at length in subsequent chapters. Moreover, the last essay in each chapter in this book demonstrates a blending of patterns and is followed by a "Mixing Patterns" assignment that asks you to identify how the writer of that essay combines the various rhetorical modes. Use the questions to develop your understanding of the importance and power of drawing on a range of strategies and staying flexible after you ask yourself that original question—What is this essay for?

This overview sketches in some of the important steps and strategies in the writing process. But you don't want to lose the idea that writing is a process both of inspiration and of craft. Many writers have tried to explain how the two connect in their own particular efforts to create. The novelist and short story writer Katherine Anne Porter, for example, tells how inspiration becomes communication in her writing: "Now and again thousands of memories converge, harmonize, and arrange themselves around a central idea in a coherent form, and I write. . . ." Jean Cocteau, the playwright, asserts the need to shape inspiration into language for a page of writing: "To write, to conquer ink and paper, accumulate letters and paragraphs, divide them with periods and commas, is a different matter from carrying around the dream of a play or a book." The point made by Porter and Cocteau is that writing emerges from both creativity and skill, instruction and technique, talent and effort. As we said, writing is a process *and* a craft.

I Think, Therefore IM

Jennifer Lee

Jennifer Lee was born in New York City in 1976 and grew up there. Lee attended Harvard University, where she majored in applied mathematics and economics, but she developed an interest in current affairs while working with low-income students. After graduation in 1999, Lee became a reporter for the *New York Times,* covering the metropolitan desk and cultural affairs. Her book, *The Fortune Cookie Chronicles* (2008), explores the history of Chinese food as well as its role in American culture. In the following selection, which appeared in the September 19, 2002, issue of the *New York Times,* Lee examines the impact of instant-messaging shorthand on students' writing styles.

PREREADING: THINKING ABOUT THE ESSAY IN ADVANCE

Reflect on your online writing habits. Does online writing have a style of its own? How does online writing differ from "standard" writing that appears in newspapers, magazines, and books—as well as essays you compose for college courses?

Words to Watch

lingua franca (par. 8) a hybrid or mixed language used for communication
errant (par. 12) straying from what is right; wrong
riddled (par. 15) shot through; made holes in
milieu (par. 19) surroundings; environment

1 Each September Jacqueline Harding prepares a classroom presentation on the common writing mistakes she sees in her students' work.

2 Ms. Harding, an eighth-grade English teacher at Viking Middle School in Gurnee, Ill., scribbles the words that have plagued generations of schoolchildren across her whiteboard:

3 There. Their. They're.

4 Your. You're.

5 To. Too. Two.

6 Its. It's.

7 This September, she has added a new list: u, r, ur, b4, wuz, cuz, 2.

When she asked her students how many of them used shortcuts like these in their writing, Ms. Harding said, she was not surprised when most of them raised their hands. This, after all, is their online lingua franca: English adapted for the spitfire conversational style of Internet instant messaging. 8

Ms. Harding, who has seen such shortcuts creep into student papers over the last two years, said she gave her students a warning: "If I see this in your assignments, I will take points off." 9

"Kids should know the difference," said Ms. Harding, who decided to address this issue head-on this year. "They should know where to draw the line between formal writing and conversational writing." 10

As more and more teenagers socialize online, middle school and high school teachers like Ms. Harding are increasingly seeing a breezy form of Internet English jump from e-mail into schoolwork. To their dismay, teachers say that papers are being written with shortened words, improper capitalization and punctuation, and characters like &, $ and @. 11

Teachers have deducted points, drawn red circles and tsk-tsked at their classes. Yet the errant forms continue. "It stops being funny after you repeat yourself a couple of times," Ms. Harding said. 12

But teenagers, whose social life can rely as much these days on text communication as the spoken word, say that they use instant-messaging shorthand without thinking about it. They write to one another as much as they write in school, or more. 13

"You are so used to abbreviating things, you just start doing it unconsciously on schoolwork and reports and other things," said Eve Brecker, 15, a student at Montclair High School in New Jersey. 14

Ms. Brecker once handed in a midterm exam riddled with instant-messaging shorthand. "I had an hour to write an essay on Romeo and Juliet," she said. "I just wanted to finish before my time was up. I was writing fast and carelessly. I spelled 'you' 'u.'" She got a C. 15

Even terms that cannot be expressed verbally are making their way into papers. Melanie Weaver was stunned by some of the term papers she received from a 10th-grade class she recently taught as part of an internship. "They would be trying to make a point in a paper, they would put a smiley face in the end," said Ms. Weaver, who teaches at Alvernia College in Reading, Pa. "If they were presenting an argument and they needed to present an opposite view, they would put a frown." 16

17 As Trisha Fogarty, a sixth-grade teacher at Houlton Southside School in Houlton, Maine, puts it, today's students are "Generation Text."

18 Almost 60 percent of the online population under age 17 uses instant messaging, according to Nielsen/NetRatings. In addition to cellphone text messaging, Weblogs and e-mail, it has become a popular means of flirting, setting up dates, asking for help with homework and keeping in contact with distant friends. The abbreviations are a natural outgrowth of this rapid-fire style of communication.

19 "They have a social life that centers around typed communication," said Judith S. Donath, a professor at the Massachusetts Institute of Technology's Media Lab who has studied electronic communication. "They have a writing style that has been nurtured in a teenage social milieu."

20 Some teachers see the creeping abbreviations as part of a continuing assault of technology on formal written English. Others take it more lightly, saying that it is just part of the larger arc of language evolution.

21 "To them it's not wrong," said Ms. Harding, who is 28. "It's acceptable because it's in their culture. It's hard enough to teach them the art of formal writing. Now we've got to overcome this new instant-messaging language."

22 Ms. Harding noted that in some cases the shorthand isn't even shorter. "I understand 'cuz,' but what's with the 'wuz'? It's the same amount of letters as 'was,' so what's the point?" she said.

23 Deborah Bova, who teaches eighth-grade English at Raymond Park Middle School in Indianapolis, thought her eyesight was failing several years ago when she saw the sentence "B4 we perform, ppl have 2 practice" on a student assignment.

24 "I thought, 'My God, what is this?'" Ms. Bova said. "Have they lost their minds?"

25 The student was summoned to the board to translate the sentence into standard English: "Before we perform, people have to practice." She realized that the students thought she was out of touch. "It was like 'Get with it, Bova,'" she said.

26 Ms. Bova had a student type up a reference list of translations for common instant-messaging expressions. She posted a copy on the bulletin board by her desk and took another one home to use while grading.

27 Students are sometimes unrepentant.

28 "They were astonished when I began to point these things out to them," said Henry Assetto, a social studies teacher at Twin

Valley High School in Elverson, Pa. "Because I am a history teacher, they did not think a history teacher would be checking up on their grammar or their spelling," said Mr. Assetto, who has been teaching for 34 years.

29 But Montana Hodgen, 16, another Montclair student, said she was so accustomed to instant-messaging abbreviations that she often read right past them. She proofread a paper last year only to get it returned with the messaging abbreviations circled in red.

30 "I was so used to reading what my friends wrote to me on Instant Messenger that I didn't even realize that there was something wrong," she said. She said her ability to separate formal and informal English declined the more she used instant messages. "Three years ago, if I had seen that, I would have been 'What is that?'"

31 The spelling checker doesn't always help either, students say. For one, Microsoft Word's squiggly red spell-check lines don't appear beneath single letters and numbers such as u, r, c, 2 and 4. Nor do they catch words which have numbers in them such as "l8r" and "b4" by default.

32 Teenagers have essentially developed an unconscious "accent" in their typing, Professor Donath said. "They have gotten facile at typing and they are not paying attention."

33 Teenagers have long pushed the boundaries of spoken language, introducing words that then become passe with adult adoption. Now teenagers are taking charge and pushing the boundaries of written language. For them, expressions like "oic" (oh I see), "nm" (not much), "jk" (just kidding) and "lol" (laughing out loud), "brb" (be right back), "ttyl" (talk to you later) are as standard as conventional English.

34 "There is no official English language," said Jesse Sheidlower, the North American editor of the Oxford English Dictionary. "Language is spread because not anyone dictates any one thing to happen. The decisions are made by the language and the people who use the language."

35 Some teachers find the new writing style alarming. "First of all, it's very rude, and it's very careless," said Lois Moran, a middle school English teacher at St. Nicholas School in Jersey City.

36 "They should be careful to write properly and not to put these little codes in that they are in such a habit of writing to each other," said Ms. Moran, who has lectured her eighth-grade class on such mistakes.

37 Others say that the instant-messaging style might simply be a fad, something that students will grow out of. Or they see it as an opportunity to teach students about the evolution of language.

38 "I turn it into a very positive teachable moment for kids in the class," said Erika V. Karres, an assistant professor at the University of North Carolina at Chapel Hill who trains student teachers. She shows students how English has evolved since Shakespeare's time. "Imagine Langston Hughes's writing in quick texting instead of 'Langston writing,'" she said. "It makes teaching and learning so exciting."

39 Other teachers encourage students to use messaging shorthand to spark their thinking processes. "When my children are writing first drafts, I don't care how they spell anything, as long as they are writing," said Ms. Fogarty, the sixth-grade teacher from Houlton, Maine. "If this lingo gets their thoughts and ideas onto paper quicker, the more power to them." But during editing and revising, she expects her students to switch to standard English.

40 Ms. Bova shares the view that instant-messaging language can help free up their creativity. With the help of students, she does not even need the cheat sheet to read the shorthand anymore.

41 "I think it's a plus," she said. "And I would say that with a + sign."

BUILDING VOCABULARY

Lee sprinkles her article with words, abbreviations, and terms drawn from online communication. Prepare a list of the "instant communication" forms that appear in the essay, and offer definitions or explanations for them.

THINKING CRITICALLY ABOUT THE ESSAY

Understanding the Writer's Ideas

1. In what ways, according to Lee, do instant messaging and other forms of social communication on the Internet affect students' classroom writing?
2. How do teachers respond to student writing that shows the effects of online communication? Do all teachers respond the same way? Justify your response.
3. What does Lee mean by "language evolution"? Where does this term appear in the essay? What is the effect of technology on this evolution?
4. Why do some students resist teachers' attempts to purge their essays of online writing styles?

5. According to some observers, how might online writing styles influence critical and creative thinking?

Understanding the Writer's Techniques

1. What is the thesis of Lee's essay? Does she state her main idea or imply it? Explain your response.
2. Lee jumps right into her subject without any formal introduction. Do you find this opening effective? Why or why not?
3. What elements of a journalistic style do you detect in this essay? How do these features make the article accessible to a reading audience or literate public? What assumptions does Lee make about her audience?
4. Why does Lee use so many examples drawn from online communication? What is the effect?
5. What comparisons and contrasts does Lee draw between students' online communication styles and teachers' expectations? What tone or attitude does she adopt? What is her purpose? What does she hope to accomplish?
6. How does the conclusion of the essay affect your overall response to the article?

Exploring the Writer's Ideas

1. Lee suggests that the connections between online writing and school writing are more complicated than one might originally think. What do you think about this issue?
2. The writer focuses, in large part, on the responses of teachers to student writing that is "riddled," as one instructor contends, with terrible forms of online style. What is your opinion of such teachers? Do they have a valid concern?
3. Based on your reading of Lee's essay, what is the best approach to the implicit clash between instant online writing styles and the expectations of teachers that their students compose essays in standard English?

IDEAS FOR WRITING

Prewriting

Spend a few minutes jotting down abbreviations and images (for example, *OMG, btw,* ☺) that you or friends use when communicating online. Share these abbreviations and their meanings during classroom discussion.

Guided Writing

Write your own essay titled "I Think, Therefore IM."

1. Begin briskly, as Lee does, by reciting some of the online abbreviations that you use when blogging, instant messaging, or employing other online communication styles. Establish your thesis based on these examples.
2. Next, recount the ways in which you think these online communication forms help or hinder students when writing for courses.
3. As you develop the essay, support your own observations by referring to some of the teachers and experts who appear in Lee's article.
4. Throughout the essay, try to maintain a balanced tone, laying out the pros and cons of online communication styles.
5. Write a conclusion that circles back to your introduction and adds substance to it.

Thinking and Writing Collaboratively

In groups of three or four, combine your lists of online abbreviations from the prewriting exercise, and then compose (like Ms. Bova in Lee's essay) a reference list of translations for common instant-messaging expressions.

Writing About the Text

Write an essay in which you analyze Lee's journalistic style. Explain the ways she develops her article and tries to appeal to a specific audience of *New York Times* readers. What assumptions does she make about her primary audience?

More Writing Projects

1. In a journal entry, recount your online social interactions for the day and the ways you communicated with various people.
2. In an extended paragraph, write about one blog that you find appealing for its style and format.
3. Write an essay in which you argue for or against the idea that instant-messaging styles can enhance a student's critical thinking and writing ability.

Boxers, Briefs, and Books

John Grisham

Born on February 8, 1955, in Jonesboro, Arkansas, John Grisham is one of America's best-selling authors. His immensely popular novels, mostly legal thrillers, also have served as the basis of successful films. *The Firm* (1991), for example, topped the *New York Times* Best Seller List for forty-seven weeks, sold to Paramount Pictures for $600,000, and starred Tom Cruise in the acclaimed film. Other successful novels turned into movies include *The Pelican Brief* (1992), *The Client* (1993), and *The Rainmaker* (1995). Grisham attended Northwest Junior College in Senatobia, Mississippi, and ultimately entered Mississippi State University, where he majored in accounting. He then attended law school at the University of Mississippi. After he graduated in 1981, he worked for a small Mississippi law firm, specializing in criminal defense and personal injury litigation. In 1983 he was elected to the state House of Representatives, where he served for seven years. In this 2010 selection, Grisham provides insights into how and why he became a writer after trying many "hard, dead-end jobs."

PREREADING: THINKING ABOUT THE ESSAY IN ADVANCE

What are the various jobs—paying or nonpaying—that you have held in your life so far? In what ways do you think they have influenced your current career plans?

Words to Watch

inspiration (par. 2) stimulation; bright idea
repentant (par. 3) regretful, sorry
honky-tonk (par. 4) cheap and often disreputable nightclub
humiliating (par. 5) embarrassing
indigent (par. 9) poor; impoverished, penniless
riveting (par. 11) fascinating

I wasn't always a lawyer or a novelist, and I've had my share of hard, dead-end jobs. I earned my first steady paycheck watering rose bushes at a nursery for a dollar an hour. I was in my early teens, but the man who owned the nursery saw potential, and he promoted me to his fence crew. For $1.50 an hour, I labored 1 like a grown man as we laid mile after mile of chain-link fence. There was no future in this, and I shall never mention it again in writing.

2 Then, during the summer of my 16th year, I found a job with a plumbing contractor. I crawled under houses, into the cramped darkness, with a shovel, to somehow find the buried pipes, to dig until I found the problem, then crawl back out and report what I had found. I vowed to get a desk job. I've never drawn inspiration from that miserable work, and I shall never mention it again in writing, either.

3 But a desk wasn't in my immediate future. My father worked with heavy construction equipment, and through a friend of a friend of his, I got a job the next summer on a highway asphalt crew. This was July, when Mississippi is like a sauna. Add another 100 degrees for the fresh asphalt. I got a break when the operator of a Caterpillar bulldozer was fired; shown the finer points of handling this rather large machine, I contemplated a future in the cab, tons of growling machinery at my command, with the power to plow over anything. Then the operator was back, sober, repentant. I returned to the asphalt crew.

4 I was 17 years old that summer, and I learned a lot, most of which cannot be repeated in polite company. One Friday night I accompanied my new friends on the asphalt crew to a honky-tonk to celebrate the end of a hard week. When a fight broke out and I heard gunfire, I ran to the restroom, locked the door and crawled out a window. I stayed in the woods for an hour while the police hauled away rednecks. As I hitchhiked home, I realized I was not cut out for construction and got serious about college.

5 My career sputtered along until retail caught my attention; it was indoors, clean and air-conditioned. I applied for a job at a Sears store in a mall. The only opening was in men's underwear. It was humiliating. I tried to quit, but I was given a raise. Evidently, the position was difficult to fill. I asked to be transferred to toys, then to appliances. My bosses said no and gave me another raise.

6 I became abrupt with customers. Sears has the nicest customers in the world, but I didn't care. I was rude and surly and I was occasionally watched by spies hired by the company to pose as shoppers. One asked to try on a pair of boxers. I said no, that it was obvious they were much too small for his rather ample rear end. I handed him an extra-large pair. I got written up. I asked for

lawn care. They said no, but this time they didn't offer me a raise. I finally quit.

Halfway through college, and still drifting, I decided to become a high-powered tax lawyer. The plan was sailing along until I took my first course in tax law. I was stunned by its complexity and lunacy, and I barely passed the course. 7

Around the same time, I was involved in mock-trial classes. I enjoyed the courtroom. A new plan was hatched. I would return to my hometown, hang out my shingle and become a hotshot trial lawyer. Tax law was discarded overnight. 8

This was 1981; at the time there was no public-defender system in my county. I volunteered for all the indigent work I could get. It was the fastest way to trial, and I learned quickly. 9

When my law office started to struggle for lack of well-paying work—indigent cases are far from lucrative—I decided to go into yet another low-paying career: in 1983, I was elected to a House seat in the Mississippi State Legislature. The salary was $8,000, which was more than I made during my first year as a lawyer. Each year from January through March I was at the State Capitol in Jackson, wasting serious time, but also listening to great storytellers. I took a lot of notes, not knowing why but feeling that, someday, those tales would come in handy. 10

Like most small-town lawyers, I dreamed of the big case, and in 1984 it finally arrived. But this time, the case wasn't mine. As usual, I was loitering around the courtroom, pretending to be busy. But what I was really doing was watching a trial involving a young girl who had been beaten and raped. Her testimony was gut-wrenching, graphic, heartbreaking and riveting. Every juror was crying. I remember staring at the defendant and wishing I had a gun. And like that, a story was born. 11

Writing was not a childhood dream of mine. I do not recall longing to write as a student. I wasn't sure how to start. Over the following weeks I refined my plot outline and fleshed out my characters. One night I wrote "Chapter One" at the top of the first page of a legal pad; the novel, "A Time to Kill," was finished three years later. 12

The book didn't sell, and I stuck with my day job, defending criminals, preparing wills and deeds and contracts. Still, something about writing made me spend large hours of my free time at my desk. 13

14 I had never worked so hard in my life, nor imagined that writing could be such an effort. It was more difficult than laying asphalt, and at times more frustrating than selling underwear. But it paid off. Eventually, I was able to leave the law and quit politics. Writing's still the most difficult job I've ever had—but it's worth it.

BUILDING VOCABULARY

Use *context clues* (see *Glossary*) to determine the meanings of the words below. Use a dictionary to check your definitions.

a. sauna (par. 3)
b. contemplated (par. 3)
c. sputtered (par. 5)
d. surly (par. 6)
e. ample (par. 6)
f. lunacy (par. 7)
g. lucrative (par. 10)
h. loitering (par. 10)

THINKING CRITICALLY ABOUT THE ESSAY

Understanding the Writer's Ideas

1. What kind of work does Grisham characterize as dead end?
2. What event turned the writer against construction work?
3. How did working in the men's underwear department influence Grisham's behavior toward customers? Why wouldn't his bosses grant him a transfer?
4. What law-based careers did Grisham see for himself? How did the early plans turn out?
5. What was the other "low-paying career" that the writer took on? Why did he take notes on that job?
6. How, according to the writer, was "a story born"? What was that story?
7. How long did it take the writer to finish *A Time to Kill*? What happened to Grisham's writing career after the novel didn't sell well?

Understanding the Writer's Techniques

1. What is the thesis of this selection?
2. What is Grisham's purpose in this piece? Who do you think is his audience?
3. Why does the writer repeat in paragraph 2 the words from paragraph 1, "I shall never mention it in writing"?
4. What does each of the words in the title refer to in terms of Grisham's various iobs?
5. What are the various *transitions* (see Glossary) that Grisham uses in this piece? How do they help smooth the flow of ideas?
6. How would you characterize Grisham's style in this selection? Would you call it simple or complex? Why? Given Grisham's audience, why do you think that he has adopted the style that he has?
7. How does the last paragraph serve as an effective conclusion of this piece?

Exploring the Writer's Ideas

1. The writer clearly finds construction work unappealing. Why? How do you think people who take on construction work manage to do their jobs and find fulfillment in them?
2. Regarding the novel he decided to write, Grisham says, "I refined my plot outline and fleshed out my characters." Why might these steps be important for a novelist? How would other novelists feel about this strategy?
3. In general, Grisham's writing technique calls attention to advanced planning. How might this strategy be useful for any kind of writing—even for papers in college?
4. Why do you think Grisham says that despite the fact that writing was "the most difficult job" he'd ever had, "it's worth it"? Is he talking about the huge financial rewards his writing brought him? Or do you think that something else attracted him? Why do you feel as you do?
5. Why do you think Grisham says that being at the State Capitol in Jackson, Mississippi, was "wasting serious time"? Why did he stick to the job as legislator? What did the job offer him?

IDEAS FOR WRITING

Prewriting

Make a list of the various jobs or careers that interest you at this point in your life, jobs you might like to have in the future. In what ways do you think that you are prepared, or are preparing, for some of them? Unprepared?

Guided Writing

Write an essay about the various dead-end, unappealing, or difficult jobs that you have held. Consider nonpaying (such as unwanted babysitting responsibilities or cleaning rooms at home, for example) as well as paying jobs.

1. Open with a sentence that indicates your thesis as being about bad jobs you had.
2. Identify at least two or three jobs that you didn't like and give reasons for your distaste for them.
3. Write about them in chronological order—earliest job first, most recent job last.
4. Use transitions to connect the job experiences thoughtfully.
5. Be sure to explain why the jobs were unappealing or "dead end" and how you behaved on the job as a consequence of your unhappiness. Grisham, for example, tells how he behaved toward Sears customers.
6. Write in a simple, direct style.
7. Create a two- or three-word title, each word reflecting an aspect of one of the jobs you wrote about in your essay.

Thinking and Writing Collaboratively

According to Grisham, writing is an effort "more difficult than laying asphalt and at times more frustrating than selling underwear." In small groups discuss this observation. Do you agree? What difficult or frustrating experiences have you had in writing something—an essay, a research paper, a story, a poem?

Writing About the Text

Grisham's critics often view his writing as simplistic and formulaic. Do you find any traces in this essay of elements that you could criticize? Or, do you find the style here appropriate for the audience? Explain your responses in a brief essay.

More Writing Projects

1. In your journal write an entry about the various jobs that a senior member of your family had held before finding the work that would become the person's career. If possible, interview your relative for valuable information.
2. Write a paragraph or two about the popularity of courtroom dramas and legal-themed television programming. Why do these kinds of presentations continue in popularity and hold the attention of large elements of today's society?
3. Read any of John Grisham's novels or see one of the films based on them, and write an essay about why it has achieved the level of popularity that it has.

Simplicity

William Zinsser

This selection is a chapter from one of the most successful books about writing, titled *On Writing Well.* The *New York Times* has compared William Zinsser's book, first published in 1976, with the classics in the field, saying it "belongs on any shelf of serious reference works for writers." From 1959 to 1987 Zinsser, the author of fifteen books, was general editor of the Book-of-the-Month Club. He now teaches in New York City at the New School and the Columbia University Graduate School of Journalism. In this selection, Zinsser begins with a fairly pessimistic analysis of the clutter that pervades and degrades American writing, and he offers many examples to prove his point. Zinsser deals with almost all major aspects of the writing process—thinking, composing, awareness of the reader, self-discipline, rewriting, and editing—and concludes that simplicity is the key to them all.

To learn more about Zinsser, click on **More Resources > Chapter 1 > William Zinsser**

PREREADING: THINKING ABOUT THE ESSAY IN ADVANCE

Do you find writing difficult or easy? Why? What is there about the act of writing that annoys, frustrates, or satisfies you?

Words to Watch

decipher (par. 2) to make out the meaning of something obscure
adulterants (par. 3) added substances that make something impure or inferior
mollify (par. 4) to appease; to soothe
spell (par. 4) a short period of time
assailed (par. 8) attacked with words or physical violence
tenacious (par. 10) stubborn; persistent
rune (par. 10) character in an ancient alphabet
bearded (par. 12) approached or confronted boldly

Clutter is the disease of American writing. We are a society strangling in unnecessary words, circular constructions, pompous frills and meaningless jargon. 1

Who can understand the clotted language of everyday American commerce: the memo, the corporation report, the business letter, the notice from the bank explaining its latest "simplified" statement? What member of an insurance or medical plan can decipher the brochure explaining his costs and benefits? What father or mother can put together a child's toy from the instructions on the box? Our national tendency is to inflate and thereby sound important. The airline pilot who announces that he is presently anticipating experiencing considerable precipitation wouldn't think of saying it may rain. The sentence is too simple—there must be something wrong with it. 2

But the secret of good writing is to strip every sentence to its cleanest components. Every word that serves no function, every long word that could be a short word, every adverb that carries the same meaning that's already in the verb, every passive construction that leaves the reader unsure of who is doing what—these are the thousand and one adulterants that weaken the strength of a sentence. And they usually occur in proportion to education and rank. 3

During the 1960s the president of my university wrote a letter to mollify the alumni after a spell of campus unrest. "You are probably aware," he began, "that we have been experiencing very considerable potentially explosive expressions of dissatisfaction on issues only partially related." He meant that the students had been hassling them about different things. I was far more upset by the president's English than by the students' potentially explosive expressions of dissatisfaction. I would have preferred the presidential approach taken by Franklin D. Roosevelt when he tried to convert into English his own government's memos, such as this blackout order of 1942: 4

> Such preparations shall be made as will completely obscure all Federal buildings and non-Federal buildings occupied by the Federal government during an air raid for any period of time from visibility by reason of internal or external illumination.

"Tell them," Roosevelt said, "that in buildings where they have to keep the work going to put something across the windows." 5

6 Simplify, simplify. Thoreau said it, as we are so often reminded, and no American writer more consistently practiced what he preached. Open *Walden* to any page and you will find a man saying in a plain and orderly way what is on his mind:

> I went to the woods because I wished to live deliberately, to front only the essential facts of life, and see if I could not learn what it had to teach, and not, when I came to die, discover that I had not lived.

7 How can the rest of us achieve such enviable freedom from clutter? The answer is to clear our heads of clutter. Clear thinking becomes clear writing; one can't exist without the other. It's impossible for a muddy thinker to write good English. He may get away with it for a paragraph or two, but soon the reader will be lost, and there's no sin so grave, for the reader will not easily be lured back.

8 Who is this elusive creature, the reader? The reader is someone with an attention span of about 30 seconds—a person assailed by many forces competing for attention. At one time those forces were relatively few: newspapers, magazines, radio, spouse, children, pets. Today they also include a galaxy of electronic devices for receiving entertainment and information—television, VCRs, DVDs, CDs, video games, the Internet, e-mail, cell phones, BlackBerries, iPods—as well as a fitness program, a pool, a lawn and that most potent of competitors, sleep. The man or woman snoozing in a chair with a magazine or a book is a person who was being given too much unnecessary trouble by the writer.

9 It won't do to say that the reader is too dumb or too lazy to keep pace with the train of thought. If the reader is lost, it's usually because the writer hasn't been careful enough. The carelessness can take any number of forms. Perhaps a sentence is so excessively cluttered that the reader, hacking through the verbiage, simply doesn't know what it means. Perhaps a sentence has been so shoddily constructed that the reader could read it in several ways. Perhaps the writer has switched pronouns in midsentence, or has switched tenses, so the reader loses track of who is talking or when the action took place. Perhaps Sentence B is not a logical sequel to Sentence A; the writer, in whose head the connection is clear, hasn't bothered to provide the missing link. Perhaps the writer has used a word incorrectly by not taking the trouble to look it up.

Faced with such obstacles, readers are at first tenacious. They blame themselves—they obviously missed something, and they go back over the mystifying sentence, or over the whole paragraph, piecing it out like an ancient rune, making guesses and moving on. But they won't do this for long. The writer is making them work too hard, and they will look for one who is better at the craft. 10

Writers must therefore constantly ask: what am I trying to say? Surprisingly often they don't know. Then they must look at what they have written and ask: have I said it? Is it clear to someone encountering the subject for the first time? If it's not, some fuzz has worked its way into the machinery. The clear writer is someone clearheaded enough to see this stuff for what it is: fuzz. 11

I don't mean that some people are born clearheaded and are therefore natural writers, whereas others are naturally fuzzy and will never write well. Thinking clearly is a conscious act that writers must force on themselves, as if they were working on any other project that requires logic: making a shopping list or doing an algebra problem. Good writing doesn't come naturally, though most people seem to think it does. Professional writers are constantly bearded by people who say they'd like to "try a little writing sometime"—meaning when they retire from their real profession, like insurance or real estate, which is hard. Or they say, "I could write a book about that." I doubt it. 12

Writing is hard work. A clear sentence is no accident. Very few sentences come out right the first time, or even the third time. Remember this in moments of despair. If you find that writing is hard, it's because it *is* hard. 13

is too dumb or too lazy to keep pace with the ~~writer's~~ train
of thought. My sympathies are ~~entirely~~ with him. ~~He's not~~
~~so dumb~~. If the reader is lost, it is generally because the
writer ~~of the article~~ has not been careful enough to keep
him on the ~~proper~~ path.

This carelessness can take any number of ~~different~~ forms.
Perhaps a sentence is so excessively ~~long and~~ cluttered that
the reader, hacking his way through ~~all~~ the verbiage, simply

doesn't know what it ~~the writer~~ means. Perhaps a sentence has been so shoddily constructed that the reader could read it in any of several ~~two or three different~~ ways. ~~He thinks he knows what the writer is trying to say, but he's not sure.~~ Perhaps the writer has switched pronouns in mid-sentence, or ~~perhaps he~~ has switched tenses, so the reader loses track of who is talking ~~to whom,~~ or ~~exactly~~ when the action took place. Perhaps Sentence B is not a logical sequel to Sentence A — the writer, in whose head the connection is ~~perfectly~~ clear, has not bothered to provide ~~given enough thought to providing~~ the missing link. Perhaps the writer has used an important word incorrectly by not taking the trouble to look it up. ~~and make sure.~~ He may think that "sanguine" and "sanguinary" mean the same thing, but ~~I can assure you that~~ the difference is a bloody big one. ~~to the reader.~~ The reader ~~He~~ can only ~~try to~~ infer ~~what~~ (speaking of big differences) what the writer is trying to imply.

Faced with these ~~such a variety of~~ obstacles, the reader is at first a remarkably tenacious bird. He ~~tends to~~ blames himself. He obviously missed something, ~~he thinks,~~ and he goes back over the mystifying sentence, or over the whole paragraph, piecing it out like an ancient rune, making guesses and moving on. But he won't do this for long. ~~He will soon run out of patience.~~ The writer is making him work too hard, ~~— harder than he should have to work —~~ and the reader will look for one ~~a writer~~ who is better at his craft.

The writer must therefore constantly ask himself: What am I trying to say? ~~in this sentence?~~ Surprisingly often, he doesn't know. ~~And~~ Then he must look at what he has ~~just~~ written and ask: Have I said it? Is it clear to someone encountering ~~who is coming upon~~ the subject for the first time? If it's not, ~~clear,~~ it is because some fuzz has worked its way into the machinery. The clear writer is a person ~~who is~~ clear-headed enough to see this stuff for what it is: fuzz.

I don't mean ~~to suggest~~ that some people are born
clear-headed and are therefore natural writers, whereas
others ~~other people~~ are naturally fuzzy and will ~~therefore~~ never write
well. Thinking clearly is a ~~an entirely~~ conscious act that the
writer must force ~~keep forcing~~ upon himself, just as if he were
embarking ~~starting out~~ on any other ~~kind of~~ project that requires ~~calls for~~ logic:
adding up a laundry list or doing an algebra problem. ~~or playing
chess~~. Good writing doeesn't ~~just~~ come naturally, though most
people obviously think it does. ~~it's as easy as walking~~. The professional

Two pages of the final manuscript of this chapter from the first edition of *On Writing Well*. Although they look like a first draft, they had already been rewritten and retyped—like almost every other page—four or five times. With each rewrite I try to make what I have written tighter, stronger and more precise, eliminating every element that is not doing useful work. Then I go over it once more, reading it aloud, and am always amazed at how much clutter can still be cut. (In later editions I eliminated the sexist pronoun "he" denoting "the writer" and "the reader.")

BUILDING VOCABULARY

1. Zinsser uses a number of words and expressions drawn from areas other than writing; he uses them to make interesting combinations or comparisons in such expressions as "elusive creature" (par. 8) and "hacking through the verbiage" (par. 9). Find other such expressions in this essay. Write simple explanations for the two above and the others that you find.
2. List words or phrases in this essay that pertain to writing—the process, the results, the faults, the successes. Explain any with which you are unfamiliar.

THINKING CRITICALLY ABOUT THE ESSAY

Understanding the Writer's Ideas

1. State simply Zinsser's meaning in the opening paragraph. What faults of "bad writing" does he mention in this paragraph?
2. To what is Zinsser objecting in paragraph 2?
3. What, according to the author, is the "secret of good writing" (par. 3)? Explain this "secret" in a few simple words of your

own. What does Zinsser say detracts from good writing? Why does Zinsser write that these writing faults "usually occur, in proportion to education and rank"?

4. What was the "message" in the letter from the university president to the alumni (par. 4)? Why does the writer object to it? Was it more objectionable in form or in content?
5. Who was Thoreau? What is *Walden?* Why are references to the two especially appropriate to Zinsser's essay?
6. What, according to Zinsser, is the relation between clear thinking and good writing? Can you have one without the other? What is meant by a "muddy thinker" (par. 7)? Why is it "impossible for a muddy thinker to write good English"?
7. Why does the author think most people fall asleep while reading? What is his attitude toward such people?
8. Look up and explain the "big differences" between the words *sanguine* and *sanguinary; infer* and *imply.* What is the writer's point in calling attention to these differences?
9. In paragraph 11, Zinsser calls attention to a writer's necessary awareness of the composing process. What elements of the *process* of writing does the author include in that paragraph? In that discussion, Zinsser speaks of *fuzz* in writing. What does he mean by the word as it relates to the writing process? To what does Zinsser compare the writer's thinking process? Why does he use such simple comparisons?
10. Explain the meaning of the last sentence. What does it indicate about the writer's attitude toward his work?

Understanding the Writer's Techniques

1. What is the writer's thesis? Is it stated or implied?
2. Explain the use of the words *disease* and *strangling* in paragraph 1. Why does Zinsser use these words in an essay about writing?
3. For what purpose does Zinsser use a series of questions in paragraph 2?
4. Throughout this essay, the writer makes extensive use of examples to support general opinions and attitudes. What attitude or opinion is he supporting in paragraphs 2, 4, 5, 6, and 9? How does he use examples in each of those paragraphs?
5. Analyze the specific structure and organization of paragraph 3:
   a. What general ideas about writing does Zinsser propose?
   b. Where does he place that idea in the paragraph?

   c. What examples does he offer to support his general idea?
   d. With what new idea does he conclude the paragraph? How is it related to the beginning idea?
6. Why does Zinsser reproduce exactly portions of the writings of a past president of a major university, President Franklin D. Roosevelt, and Henry David Thoreau? How do these sections make Zinsser's writing clearer, more understandable, or more important?
7. What is the effect on the reader of the words "Simplify, simplify," which begin paragraph 6? Why does the writer use them at that particular point in the essay? What do they indicate about his attitude toward his subject? Explain.
8. Why does the author begin so many sentences in paragraph 9 with the word "Perhaps"? How does that technique help to *unify* (see Glossary) the paragraph?
9. For what reasons does the writer include the two pages of rough manuscript as a part of the finished essay? What is he trying to show the reader in this way? How does seeing these pages help you to understand better what he is writing about in the completed essay?
10. Overall, how would you describe the writer's attitude toward the process and craft of writing? What would you say is his overall attitude toward the future of American writing? Is he generally optimistic or pessimistic? On what does his attitude depend? Refer to specifics in the essay to support your answer.
11. Do you think Zinsser expected other writers, or budding writers, to be the main readers of this essay? Why or why not? If so, with what main ideas do you think he would like them to come away from the essay? Do you think readers who were not somehow involved in the writing process would benefit equally from this essay? Why?

Exploring the Writer's Ideas

1. Do you think that Zinsser is ever guilty in this essay of the very "sins" against writing about which he is upset? Could he have simplified any of his points? Select one of Zinsser's paragraphs in the finished essay and explain how you might rewrite it more simply.
2. In the reading that you do most often, have you noticed overly cluttered writing? Or, do you feel that the writing is at its clearest level of presentation and understanding for its

audience? Bring to class some examples of this writing, and be prepared to discuss it. In general, what do you consider the relation between the simplicity or complexity of a piece of writing and its intended readership?

3. In the note to the two rough manuscript pages included with this essay, the writer implies that the process of rewriting and simplifying may be endless. How do you know when to stop trying to rewrite an essay, story, or poem? Do you ever really feel satisfied that you've reached the end of the rewriting process?
4. Choose one of the rough manuscript paragraphs, and compare it with the finished essay. Which do you feel is better? Why? Is there anything Zinsser deleted from the rough copy that you feel he should have retained? Why?
5. Comment on the writer's assertion that "Thinking clearly is a conscious act that writers must force upon themselves" (par. 12). How does this opinion compare with the opinions of the three other writers in this chapter?
6. Reread John Grisham's essay "Boxers, Briefs, and Books" (pages 22–25). What similarities and differences do you note in Zinsser's and Grisham's approaches to writing and language?

IDEAS FOR WRITING

Prewriting

For the most part, teachers have called upon you to put your thoughts in writing from your elementary school days onward. Make a list of your writing "problems"—the elements of writing or the elements of your personality that create problems for you whenever you try to produce something on paper.

Guided Writing

In a 500- to 750-word essay, write about what you feel are some of the problems that you face as a writer.

1. In the first paragraph, identify the problems that you plan to discuss.
2. In the course of your essay, relate your problems more generally to society at large.
3. Identify what, in your opinion, is the "secret" of good writing. Give specific examples of what measures to take to achieve that secret process and thereby to eliminate some of your problems.
4. Try to include one or two accurate reproductions of your writing to illustrate your composing techniques.

5. Point out what you believe are the major causes of your difficulties as a writer.
6. Toward the end of your essay, explain the type of writer that you would like to be in order to succeed in college.

Thinking and Writing Collaboratively

Form groups of two and exchange drafts of your Guided Writing essay. Do for your partner's draft what Zinsser did for his own: edit it in an effort to make it "stronger and more precise, eliminating every element that is not doing useful work." Return the papers and discuss whether or not your partner made useful recommendations for cutting clutter.

Writing About the Text

Teachers of writing tend to stress two, apparently contradictory, philosophies about writing. The first is that clear thinking makes for clear writing. This point of view assumes that thinking precedes writing, that you need to get your thoughts in order before you can write. The second is that you don't really know what you think until you write it down. This point of view assumes that writing is a process of discovery and that thinking and writing occur more or less simultaneously. Write an essay to explain which position you think Zinsser would take. What evidence does he present to support this position? Then explain your position on the matter. Draw on your own experience as a writer.

More Writing Projects

1. Over the next few days, listen to the same news reporter or talk-show host on television or radio. Record in your journal at least ten examples that indicate the use of "unnecessary words, circular constructions, pompous frills, and meaningless jargon." Or compile such a list from an article in a newspaper or magazine you read regularly. Then write an essay presenting and commenting on these examples.
2. Respond in a paragraph to Zinsser's observation, "Good writing doesn't come naturally."
3. In preparation for a writing assignment, collect with other class members various samples of junk mail and business correspondence that confirm Zinsser's statement that these tend to be poorly written. Write an essay describing your findings. Be certain to provide specific examples from the documents you have assembled.

Mixing Patterns

Mother Tongue

Amy Tan

Amy Tan is a fiction writer and essayist who was born in California several years after her parents emigrated from China to the United States. Her first book, *The Joy Luck Club* (1989), is a collection of related short stories (often assumed to be a novel) that depicts the conflicted relationship of Chinese mothers and their American-born daughters. This extremely popular book was followed by *The Kitchen God's Wife* (1991), *The Hundred Secret Senses* (1995), *The Bonesetter's Daughter* (2001), *The Opposite of Fate* (2003), and, most recently, *Saving Fish from Drowning* (2005), a novel about a group of American tourists lost in the jungles of Burma. Like *The Joy Luck Club,* the first three books explore intercultural relationships between Chinese-born mothers and their American-born daughters, or, in the case of *The Hundred Secret Senses,* between Chinese- and American-born half sisters. *The Opposite of Fate,* Tan's first work of nonfiction, collects essays about Tan's life and experience and provides rich detail of her personal challenges and triumphs.

Although she is a writer whose work has enjoyed impressive commercial success, Tan chose to publish this selection in 1990 in a small West Coast literary magazine, *The Threepenny Review,* edited by the writer Wendy Lesser. You might want to ask why she made this choice. The essay's title is a pun, referring at once to the language that nurtures us and, literally, to the language spoken by Tan's mother. Tan presents herself here as a writer and not a student of language, although she holds an MA in linguistics from San Jose State University. Speaking and writing in standard English is essential, Tan argues, but the diversity of cultures in America requires that we acknowledge the different "Englishes" spoken by immigrants. As you read her essay, think about your own experience in learning English and about how you respond to the other Englishes you may have heard spoken by your family or neighbors. Consider why Tan chooses to write in standard English.

www.mhhe.com/
shortprose13e

To learn more about Tan, click on
More Resources > Chapter 1 > Amy Tan

PREREADING: THINKING ABOUT THE ESSAY IN ADVANCE

What varieties of English do you speak? In other words, do you speak different kinds of English in different situations and to different individuals or groups of people? Why or why not?

Words to Watch

intersection (par. 3) crossroad
wrought (par. 3) made; worked
belies (par. 7) misrepresents; disguises
wince (par. 8) cringe; shrink
empirical (par. 9) relying on observation
guise (par. 10) outward appearance
benign (par. 14) not harmful
insular (par. 15) like an island; isolated

I am not a scholar of English or literature. I cannot give you much more than personal opinions on the English language and its variations in this country or others. 1

I am a writer. And by that definition, I am someone who has always loved language. I am fascinated by language in daily life. I spend a great deal of my time thinking about the power of language—the way it can evoke an emotion, a visual image, a complex idea, or a simple truth. Language is the tool of my trade. And I use them all—all the Englishes I grew up with. 2

Recently, I was made keenly aware of the different Englishes I do use. I was giving a talk to a large group of people, the same talk I had already given to half a dozen other groups. The nature of the talk was about my writing, my life, and my book, *The Joy Luck Club*. The talk was going along well enough, until I remembered one major difference that made the whole talk sound wrong. My mother was in the room. And it was perhaps the first time she had heard me give a lengthy speech, using the kind of English I have never used with her. I was saying things like, "The intersection of memory upon imagination" and "There is an aspect of my fiction that relates to thus-and-thus"—a speech filled with carefully wrought grammatical phrases, burdened, it suddenly seemed to me, with nominalized forms, past perfect tenses, conditional phrases, all the forms of standard English that I had learned in 3 school and through books, the forms of English I did not use at home with my mother.

4 Just last week, I was walking down the street with my mother, and I again found myself conscious of the English I was using, the English I do use with her. We were talking about the price of new and used furniture and I heard myself saying this: "Not waste money that way." My husband was with us as well, and he didn't notice any switch in my English. And then I realized why. It's because over the twenty years we've been together I've often used that same kind of English with him, and sometimes he even uses it with me. It has become our language of intimacy, a different sort of English that relates to family talk, the language I grew up with.

5 So you'll have some idea of what this family talk I heard sounds like, I'll quote what my mother said during a recent conversation which I videotaped and then transcribed. During this conversation, my mother was talking about a political gangster in Shanghai who had the same last name as her family's, Du, and how the gangster in his early years wanted to be adopted by her family, which was rich by comparison. Later, the gangster became more powerful, far richer than my mother's family, and one day showed up at my mother's wedding to pay his respects. Here's what she said in part:

6 "Du Yusong having business like fruit stand. Like off the street kind. He is Du like Du Zong—but not Tsung-ming Island people. The local people call putong, the river east side, he belong to that side local people. That man want to ask Du Zong father take him in like become own family. Du Zong father wasn't look down on him, but didn't take seriously, until that man big like become a mafia. Now important person, very hard to inviting him. Chinese way, came only to show respect, don't stay for dinner. Respect for making big celebration, he shows up. Mean gives lots of respect. Chinese custom. Chinese social life that way. If too important won't have to stay too long. He come to my wedding. I didn't see. I heard it. I gone to boy's side, they have YMCA dinner. Chinese age I was nineteen."

7 You should know that my mother's expressive command of English belies how much she actually understands. She reads the *Forbes* report, listens to *Wall Street Week,* converses daily with her stockbroker, reads all of Shirley MacLaine's books with ease—all kinds of things I can't begin to understand. Yet some of my friends

tell me they understand 50 percent of what my mother says. Some say they understand 80 to 90 percent. Some say they understand none of it, as if she were speaking pure Chinese. But to me, my mother's English is perfectly clear, perfectly natural. It's my mother tongue. Her language, as I hear it, is vivid, direct, full of observation and imagery. That was the language that helped shape the way I saw things, expressed things, made sense of the world.

Lately, I've been giving more thought to the kind of English my mother speaks. Like others, I have described it to people as "broken" or "fractured" English. But I wince when I say that. It has always bothered me that I can think of no way to describe it other than "broken," as if it were damaged and needed to be fixed, as if it lacked a certain wholeness and soundness. I've heard other terms used, "limited English," for example. But they seem just as bad, as if everything is limited, including people's perceptions of the limited English speaker. **8**

I know this for a fact, because when I was growing up, my mother's "limited" English limited *my* perception of her. I was ashamed of her English. I believed that her English reflected the quality of what she had to say. That is, because she expressed them imperfectly her thoughts were imperfect. And I had plenty of empirical evidence to support me: the fact that people in department stores, at banks, and at restaurants did not take her seriously, did not give her good service, pretended not to understand her, or even acted as if they did not hear her. **9**

My mother has long realized the limitations of her English as well. When I was fifteen, she used to have me call people on the phone to pretend I was she. In this guise, I was forced to ask for information or even to complain and yell at people who had been rude to her. One time it was a call to her stockbroker in New York. She had cashed out her small portfolio and it just so happened we were going to go to New York the next week, our very first trip outside California. I had to get on the phone and say in an adolescent voice that was not very convincing, "This is Mrs. Tan." **10**

And my mother was standing in the back whispering loudly, "Why he don't send me check, already two weeks late. So mad he lie to me, losing me money." **11**

And then I said in perfect English, "Yes, I'm getting rather concerned. You had agreed to send the check two weeks ago, but it hasn't arrived." **12**

13 Then she began to talk more loudly. "What he want, I come to New York tell him front of his boss, you cheating me?" And I was trying to calm her down, make her be quiet, while telling the stockbroker, "I can't tolerate any more excuses. If I don't receive the check immediately, I am going to have to speak to your manager when I'm in New York next week." And sure enough, the following week there we were in front of this astonished stockbroker, and I was sitting there red-faced and quiet, and my mother, the real Mrs. Tan, was shouting at his boss in her impeccable broken English.

14 We used a similar routine just five days ago, for a situation that was far less humorous. My mother had gone to the hospital for an appointment, to find out about a benign brain tumor a CAT scan had revealed a month ago. She said she had spoken very good English, her best English, no mistakes. Still, she said, the hospital did not apologize when they said they had lost the CAT scan and she had come for nothing. She said they did not seem to have any sympathy when she told them she was anxious to know the exact diagnosis, since her husband and son had both died of brain tumors. She said they would not give her any more information until the next time and she would have to make another appointment for that. So she said she would not leave until the doctor called her daughter. She wouldn't budge. And when the doctor finally called her daughter, me, who spoke in perfect English—lo and behold—we had assurances the CAT scan would be found, promises that a conference call on Monday would be held, and apologies for any suffering my mother had gone through for a most regrettable mistake.

15 I think my mother's English almost had an effect on limiting my possibilities in life as well. Sociologists and linguists probably will tell you that a person's developing language skills are more influenced by peers. But I do think that the language spoken in the family, especially in immigrant families which are more insular, plays a large role in shaping the language of the child. And I believe that it affected my results on achievement tests, IQ tests, and the SAT. While my English skills were never judged as poor, compared to math, English could not be considered my strong suit. In grade school I did moderately well, getting perhaps B's, sometimes B-pluses, in English and scoring perhaps in the sixtieth or seventieth percentile on achievement tests. But those scores were not good enough to override the opinion that my true abilities lay

in math and science, because in those areas I achieved A's and scored in the ninetieth percentile or higher.

16 This was understandable. Math is precise; there is only one correct answer. Whereas, for me at least, the answers on English tests were always a judgment call, a matter of opinion and personal experience. Those tests were constructed around items like fill-in-the-blank sentence completion, such as, "Even though Tom was ____________, Mary thought he was ____________." And the correct answer always seemed to be the most bland combinations of thoughts, for example, "Even though Tom was shy, Mary thought he was charming," with the grammatical structure "even though" limiting the correct answer to some sort of semantic opposites, so you wouldn't get answers like, "Even though Tom was foolish, Mary thought he was ridiculous." Well, according to my mother, there were very few limitations as to what Tom could have been and what Mary might have thought of him. So I never did well on tests like that.

17 The same was true with word analogies, pairs of words in which you were supposed to find some sort of logical, semantic relationship—for example, "*Sunset* is to *nightfall* as ____________ is to ____________." And here you would be presented with a list of four possible pairs, one of which showed the same kind of relationship: *red* is to *stoplight, bus* is to *arrival, chills* is to *fever, yawn* is to *boring*. Well, I could never think that way. I knew what the tests were asking, but I could not block out of my mind the images already created by the first pair, "*sunset* is to *nightfall*"—and I would see a burst of colors against a darkening sky, the moon rising, the lowering of a curtain of stars. And all the other pairs of words—red, bus, stoplight, boring—just threw up a mass of confusing images, making it impossible for me to sort out something as logical as saying: "A sunset precedes nightfall" is the same as "a chill precedes a fever." The only way I would have gotten that answer right would have been to imagine an associative situation, for example, my being disobedient and staying out past sunset, catching a chill at night, which turns into feverish pneumonia as punishment, which indeed did happen to me.

18 I have been thinking about all this lately, about my mother's English, about achievement tests. Because lately I've been asked, as a writer, why there are not more Asian Americans represented in American literature. Why are there few Asian Americans enrolled

in creative writing programs? Why do so many Chinese students go into engineering? Well, these are broad sociological questions I can't begin to answer. But I have noticed in surveys—in fact, just last week—that Asian students, as a whole, always do significantly better on math achievement tests than in English. And this makes me think that there are other Asian-American students whose English spoken in the home might also be described as "broken" or "limited." And perhaps they also have teachers who are steering them away from writing and into math and science, which is what happened to me.

19 Fortunately, I happen to be rebellious in nature and enjoy the challenge of disproving assumptions made about me. I became an English major my first year in college, after being enrolled as pre-med. I started writing nonfiction as a freelancer the week after I was told by my former boss that writing was my worst skill and I should hone my talents toward account management.

20 But it wasn't until 1985 that I finally began to write fiction. And at first I wrote using what I thought to be wittily crafted sentences, sentences that would finally prove I had mastery over the English language. Here's an example from the first draft of a story that later made its way into *The Joy Luck Club,* but without this line: "That was my mental quandary in its nascent state." A terrible line, which I can barely pronounce.

21 Fortunately, for reasons I won't get into today, I later decided I should envision a reader for the stories I would write. And the reader I decided upon was my mother, because these were stories about mothers. So with this reader in mind—and in fact she did read my early drafts—I began to write stories using all the Englishes I grew up with: the English I spoke to my mother, which for lack of a better term might be described as "simple"; the English she used with me, which for lack of a better term might be described as "broken"; my translation of her Chinese, which could certainly be described as "watered down"; and what I imagined to be her translation of her Chinese if she could speak in perfect English, her internal language, and for that I sought to preserve the essence, but neither an English nor a Chinese structure. I wanted to capture what language ability tests can never reveal: her intent, her passion, her imagery, the rhythms of her speech and the nature of her thoughts.

22 Apart from what any critic had to say about my writing, I knew I had succeeded where it counted when my mother finished reading my book and gave me her verdict: "So easy to read."

BUILDING VOCABULARY

Tan uses technical words to distinguish standard English from the English her mother speaks. Investigate the meanings of the following terms, and find examples to illustrate them for your classmates.

a. scholar (par. 1)
b. nominalized forms (par. 3)
c. transcribed (par. 5)
d. imagery (par. 7)
e. linguists (par. 15)
f. semantic opposites (par. 16)
g. word analogies (par. 17)
h. freelancer (par. 19)
i. quandary (par. 20)
j. nascent (par. 20)

THINKING CRITICALLY ABOUT THE ESSAY

Understanding the Writer's Ideas

1. Why does Tan start her essay by identifying who she is *not?* What does she see as the difference between a scholar and a writer?
2. What does Tan mean when she says, "Language is the tool of my trade"? What are the four ways she says language can work?
3. Tan speaks of "all the Englishes I grew up with" in paragraph 2, and later of the "different Englishes" she uses. Why does her mother's presence in the lecture room help her recall these Englishes? Why does she give us examples of what was "wrong" with her talk in paragraph 3?
4. In paragraph 4, Tan recognizes that she herself shifts from one English to another. Which English is "our language of intimacy"? Why?
5. Tan describes how she recorded her mother's words. Why does she give us her technique in paragraph 5 before presenting her mother's exact words in paragraph 6?
6. What do we know about Tan's mother when we learn she reads the *Forbes* report and various books? Why is it important for

Tan to understand the way her mother sees the world? What connection does Tan make between the way we use language and the way we see the world?

7. In paragraph 8, Tan tries to find a suitable label for her mother's language. Why is she unwilling to use a description like "broken" or "limited" English? What does her mother's English sound like to you?
8. In what ways did outsiders (like bankers and waiters) make judgments of Tan's mother because of her language? Were the judgments deliberate or unconscious on their part?
9. How does Tan use humor as she contrasts the two Englishes in the telephone conversations she records? How does the tone change when Tan shifts to the hospital scene? Why do the authorities provide different service and different information when the daughter speaks than they do when the mother speaks?
10. How does Tan connect her math test scores with her mother's language? Why does she think she never did well on language tests? Why does she think the tests do not measure a student's language use very well? Why does Tan ultimately become an English major (par. 19)?
11. In paragraph 20, why does Tan show us the sentence: "That was my mental quandary in its nascent state"? How does it compare with the other sentences in her essay? What is wrong with this "terrible" sentence? What does it mean?
12. In her two final paragraphs, Tan returns to her mother. Why does selecting her mother as her reader help Tan learn to become a better writer? What are the elements of good writing her mother recognizes, even if she herself cannot write standard English?

Understanding the Writer's Techniques

1. What is the thesis statement in Tan's essay? Where does it appear?
2. Throughout her essay, Tan uses *dialogue,* the written reproduction of speech or conversation. Why does she do this? What is the effect of dialogue? Which sentences of dialogue do you find especially effective, and why?
3. In paragraph 3, Tan writes fairly long sentences until she writes, "My mother was in the room." Why is this sentence shorter? What is the effect of the short sentence on the reader?

4. How does identifying her mother as her intended audience help Tan make her own language more effective? Does Tan suggest that all writing should be "simple"? Is her writing always "simple"? Why does her mother find it "easy" to read?
5. Why does Tan put quotation marks around "broken" and "limited"? What other words can describe this different English?

✶ MIXING PATTERNS

Narration (see Chapter 4) is the telling of a story or series of events. *Anecdotes* are very short narrations, usually of an amusing or autobiographical nature. Point out uses of narration and anecdote in Tan's essay. Why does she use narration in this essay? How does the technique of narration interact with description here?

Exploring the Writer's Ideas

1. Why is an awareness of different kinds of English necessary for a writer? Why are writers so interested in "different Englishes"? Should all Americans speak and write the same English?
2. What is the role of parents in setting language standards for their children? How did your parents or other relatives influence your language use?
3. Reread Tan's essay, and look more carefully at her *point of view* (see Glossary) about other Englishes. How do we know what her point of view is? Does she state it directly or indirectly? Where?
4. Listen to someone who speaks a "different" English. Try to record a full paragraph of the speech, as Tan does in paragraph 6. Use a tape recorder and (or) a video camera so that you can replay the speech several times. Explain what the difficulties are in capturing the sound of the speech exactly. Write a "translation" of the paragraph into standard English.
5. Tan explores the special relation between mothers and daughters. How would you describe the author's relation with her mother?

IDEAS FOR WRITING

Prewriting

Free-associate on a sheet of paper about the language you use in daily communication, its delights, difficulties, problems, confusions, humor—in short, anything that comes to mind about the language you use in your daily life.

Guided Writing

Write a narrative essay using first-person point of view in which you contrast your language with the language of someone who speaks differently from you.

1. Begin by making some notes on your own language and by deciding whom you will choose as your other subject. It should be someone you can spend time with so that you can record his or her speech.
2. Following Tan's model, create a narrative to frame your subject's language. Tell who you are and why you speak the way you do. Introduce the other speaker, and tell why his or her speech is different.
3. Use dialogue to provide examples of both Englishes.
4. Analyze how listeners other than yourself respond to both types of speech. What are the social implications of speech differences?
5. Show how listening to the other speaker and to yourself has helped you shape your own language and write your essay. What can you learn about good writing from this project?
6. Be sure the essay has a clear thesis in the introduction. Add a strong conclusion that returns to the idea of the thesis.

Thinking and Writing Collaboratively

Exchange a draft version of your Guided Writing essay with another writer in the class. As you read each other's work, make suggestions to help the writer produce the next draft. Is the thesis clear? Is the introduction focused? Is the conclusion linked to the thesis idea? Is the dialogue realistic?

Writing About the Text

Write a critique of the language and style of this selection as though you were Tan's mother. Before writing, look carefully at what the selection tells us about Tan's mother—about what sort of person she is, about her likes and dislikes, about her reading. Write the essay in standard English.

More Writing Projects

1. In your journal, record examples of new words you have heard recently. Divide the list into columns according to whether the words are standard English or a different English. How many different Englishes can you find in your community and in college?
2. Reread question 1 in Exploring the Writer's Ideas, and write a one-paragraph response to it.
3. Tan's experience as a daughter of recent immigrants has clearly shaped her life in fundamental ways. She writes about the "shame" she once felt for her mother's speech. Write about a personal experience in which you were once embarrassed by someone close to you who was "different." Tell how you would feel about the same encounter if it happened today.

SUMMING UP: CHAPTER 1

1. It sounds simple enough. Many writers, famous and unknown, have tried it at one time or another. Now, it's your turn. Write an essay simply titled "On Writing." Develop the essay in any way you please: you may deal with abstract or concrete ideas, philosophical or practical issues, emotional or intellectual processes, and so forth. Just use this essay to focus your own thoughts and to give your reader a clear idea of what writing means to you.
2. William Zinsser ("Simplicity") tells writers to simplify their writing. Select any writer from this section, and write an essay about whether you think the writer achieved (or did not achieve) simplicity. How did the writer achieve it? Where in the selection would you have preferred even more simplicity? You might look at the pieces by John Grisham and Jennifer Lee, for example. Make specific references to the text.
3. Think of how, in their essays, Amy Tan implies that her mother is her ideal audience and Jennifer Lee suggests that today's online generation of young people have their own unique audience. Find your own ideal listener. Then write a letter to that person in which you discuss your reactions to becoming a writer. Include observations you think your listener or reader will enjoy, such as your everyday life as a student, daydreams, descriptions of teachers, or cafeteria food, or of interesting people you have met.
4. Many writers (including many represented in this book) feel that writing entails a certain social responsibility. For example, when French writer Albert Camus received the 1957 Nobel Prize for Literature, the Nobel Committee cited his efforts in "illuminating the problems of the human conscience of our time." And, in his acceptance speech, he stated, "[T]he writer's function is not without arduous duties. By definition, he cannot serve today those who make history; he must serve those who are subject to it."

   What do you believe are writers' responsibilities to themselves and to others? Do you agree with Camus? Do you prefer writing that deals primarily with an individual's experience or with more general social issues? Write an essay concerning the social responsibility of writers. As you consider the issue, refer to points made by writers in this section.

5. William Zinsser says that good writing comes from the head, but many writers would say that good writing comes from the heart. Write an essay based on your experience that explores how each of these approaches is useful to the student of writing.
6. In what ways do intense personal experience affect writing? Choose any two writers in this chapter and explain how their experiences influenced them.
7. The writers in this chapter urge clarity and simplicity of style. Simplicity can be deceiving, however; usually an artist (a writer, a dancer, a painter) achieves simplicity only after spending a career working in his or her discipline and honing his or her craft. Is simplicity too ambitious a goal for students, then? Explain.

✷ FROM SEEING TO WRITING

Examine the cartoon and consider what it says about writing. What does Calvin say about creativity? What role does creativity play in writing? Why does Calvin say that he has to wait for his mood to be "last-minute panic" before he can write? What role does last-minute panic play in your writing? What are the advantages of last-minute panic? The disadvantages? What advice would you offer Calvin to help prevent this mood? Write an essay in which you analyze the cartoon by addressing some of these questions.

Calvin and Hobbes by Bill Watterson

CHAPTER 2

On Reading

WHAT IS READING?

"Reading had changed forever the course of my life," writes Malcolm X in one of the essays in this chapter. For many of us, the acquisition of reading skills may not have been quite as dramatic as it was for the author of "Prison Studies," but if we are to understand the value of literacy in today's society, Malcolm X's analysis of the power of the written word is vital. Reading allows us to engage actively with the minds of many writers who have much to tell us and to hear a variety of viewpoints not always available on television, radio, and other forms of media that vie for our attention. Even the ever-present computer and its brainchild, the Internet, demand active reading for maximum benefit. Learning to read well opens new universes, challenges your opinions, enhances your understanding of yourself and others as well as of your past, present, and future. Knowledge of books is the mark of a literate person.

But how do we learn this complex skill? Eudora Welty's essay on reading as a child may remind you of your own early experiences with printed words. Or, if you are a parent, you may be reading stories to your own children to help them learn to read. As we become mature readers, we read not just as we once did, for the story and its magical pleasures, but also for information and for pleasure in the *style* of writing. We learn not to be passive readers but active ones.

That early love of stories, and the self-esteem that came with mastery of a once impossible task, is, however, only the first step in understanding the power of reading. Malcolm X's "Prison Studies" extends our understanding of what reading is beyond the personal into the cultural sphere. He explores not only the power of reading to excite and inspire, but also the ways in which language connects to social identity. Malcolm X uses reading, and later writing, to challenge existing assumptions and find a place as an alert and engaged member of society. He argues that his reading outside of school made him better educated than most formally educated citizens in America.

Reading gives us access to many printed stories and documents, old and new. It lets us see beyond the highly edited sound bites and trendy video images that tempt us. With print, we can read what we want when we want to read it. We can reread difficult passages to be sure we understand them. We have time to question the author's point—and we have time to absorb and analyze ideas not only from contemporary life but also from ancient cultures and distant places. The diverse materials in libraries allow us to select what we read rather than be channeled into one point of view. On the Web we can access stories, poems, essays, even books, and can create a home library for use on a computer monitor.

Reading lets us share ideas. Reading can teach us practical skills that we need for survival in our complex world, such as how to repair a computer or how to become a biology teacher or a certified public accountant. Good reading can inspire us or entertain us. It can enrich our fantasy lives. Reading critically also helps us analyze how society operates, how power is distributed, how we can improve our local community or the global environment. And reading can lead us to discoveries about the world; it can make us "educated." But more than this, reading can show us the beauty of the written word; it can stir the imagination and create in us a vision of what is and what should be. That is what reading can produce; that is reading.

HOW DO WE READ?

To become a good reader, we need to think about what we read just as we think about what and how we write. In other words, we need to read *self-consciously* and *critically.* Reading, like writing, is a *process*. If we break this process down, we can say that reading involves three large steps or stages. To begin with, we want to grasp the writer's main point and the general outline of what he or she says. Then second, we reflect on what's being said: we probe, analyze, look more deeply, think things through. Finally, we make a judgment—"Wow!" or "Yes, I agree," or "What a lot of rubbish!"

We can focus these three stages of the reading process and enhance our understanding by pursuing certain strategies as we read. It's useful, for example, after reading a chapter to go back through it and then to *summarize* the main idea. A summary is a drastically condensed version of a piece of writing that aims to state the writer's main points by retaining only essential arguments, facts, and statements. A summary is usually brief, a sentence or two. Composing a summary, then, is one good way to help us get a clearer picture of the writer's main idea.

No essay contains just one idea, of course. In addition to the main idea, the writer usually includes a variety of supporting points in her essay. And most writers will support big ideas with facts, arguments, observations, quotations—the writer, in other words, tries to *substantiate* her major points in order to persuade you to see things her way.

Throughout the reading process, we can make sure that we are reading critically by asking ourselves a series of questions about the material in order to arrive at a fair assessment of its significance. The word *critically* here does not mean negatively, in the sense of criticizing what we read for what it's doing wrong. Rather, *critically* is intended to suggest a curious but questioning attitude, an alertness to what is being said and how it is being said, and a certain self-awareness about our responses to what is being said and how it is being said. Here are some questions we might ask ourselves as we start to read:

- What is it that we're reading? (In other words, what *genre,* or type of writing, does it belong to?)

We should first examine what we are about to read to determine what it is: Is it a romance? a history book? a religious tract? Why was it written? How do the answers to these questions shape our attitude toward the material? As readers of novels, for instance, we soon learn that a book with a cover featuring a heroine snatched from a fiery castle belongs to a particular genre of literature: the gothic romance. As potential readers, we might prepare ourselves to be skeptical about the happy ending we know awaits us, but at the same time we are prepared for a romantic tale. In contrast, if we face a hard-covered glossy textbook entitled *Economics,* we prepare ourselves to read with far more concentration. We might enjoy the gothic romance, but if we skip whole chapters it may not matter much. If, however, we skip chapters of the textbook, we may find ourselves confused. The first book *entertains* us, while the second *informs* us. In other words, our initial clue to what we might find as we read further is provided by the *kind* of book, essay, or article that we are reading. Our expectations of a romance novel are different from our expectations of a textbook.

- Who is the writer? For whom is he or she writing? When did he or she write it?

Clues to a writer's identity can often help us establish whether the material we are reading is reliable. Would we read a slave owner's account of life in slave quarters the same way we would read a slave's diary, for instance? If a Sioux writes about the effects of a treaty on Native American family life, we might read the essay one way; if the writer were General Custer we surely would read it another way. The *audience* is also important. If we are reading a handbook on immigration policies in the United States, we might read it differently if we knew it was written for officials at Ellis Island in 1890 from the way we would read it if it were written for Chinese men arriving to work on the railroads in the nineteenth century.

Sometimes we may not know more about a writer than when he wrote. This knowledge can itself be crucial. An essay written in the sixteenth century will be different in important ways from an essay written yesterday. Not only will the sixteenth-century author use a vocabulary that is likely to diverge from ours, but he also will make allusions to people, places, and books that may be unfamiliar to us. Moreover, he will certainly have ideas and beliefs that reflect this unfamiliar world. Today, for example, we wonder only how much interest a bank will charge us on our loan; in the sixteenth century people looked on charging interest as a doubtful if not an outright wicked practice. One of the challenges in reading work from the past, then, is to read it on its own terms, remembering that what we think and what we know are different from—rather than necessarily better than—what people thought and knew in the past. The date of writing also matters with writing published closer to our own day. A writer assessing Bill Clinton before he was impeached, for example, might well have written something significantly different had she put pen to paper after Clinton was impeached. In these ways the date of writing provides important information about what to expect.

- What is the precise issue or problem that the writer treats?

During the first and second stages of the reading process, we seek to identify the writer's *exact* topic. A writer's general topic might be the Battle of Gettysburg, for instance, but if she is writing about the women at Gettysburg, then her precise topic is narrower. What is she saying, we next ask, about these women?

- What information, conclusions, and recommendations does the writer present?

The reader may find that note taking is helpful in improving understanding of a text. Creating an outline of materials after reading can help identify the writer's aims. Both note taking and outlining will help us when we want to make a summary or when we want to pinpoint the subtopics and supporting evidence of an essay.

- How does the writer substantiate, or "prove," his case?

The reader must learn the difference between a writer who merely *asserts* an idea and one who effectively *substantiates* an idea. The writer who only asserts that the Holocaust never happened will be read differently from the writer who substantiates claims that the Holocaust did exist with photographs of Germany in the 1940s, interviews with concentration camp survivors, military records of medical experiments, and eyewitness accounts of gas chambers.

As in the example of the Holocaust, most essays aim to persuade you to see things in a certain way. Most essays, in other words, make what is formally known as an *argument*. An *argument* is not a quarrel but rather a more-or-less formal way of making a point. Often a writer begins an essay by introducing the topic or problem in the opening paragraph or paragraphs—*the introduction*—and then offers a *thesis statement*. The *thesis statement* presents the writer's position; that is, it tells what the writer has to say about the topic or problem. It usually comes early in an essay, at the close of the introduction, frequently at the close of the first paragraph.

After stating a *thesis,* the writer will try to *prove* or *substantiate* it through use of supporting *details* and *facts,* or *reasons.* In the case of the Holocaust, a writer may use a photograph or an eyewitness account to support the position that the Holocaust did in fact occur. It is not enough, though, to see that support has been provided. We also need to assess whether this support is accurate, credible, and relevant.

Usually a writer combines generalities and specifics, facts and reasons. The writer uses reasoning. You'll find a more detailed look at reasoning in Chapter 11, Argumentation and Persuasion. Here it will be enough to say that we want to be sure that the reasoning the writer uses is sound. If the writer says that event A caused event B, we want to be sure that A and B really are related as cause and effect—that they're not two separate events. In a more general way, we want to be comfortable that a writer's conclusions are valid. Does the essay really add up to the conclusions claimed?

- Is the total message successful, objective, valid, or persuasive?

Once you have answered all of the above questions, you are ready to *assess* the work you have read. As you make your evaluation, find specific evidence in the text to back up your position.

Assessment or *evaluation* is not an exact science—assessments and evaluations are ultimately opinions. But this does not mean that we can make them recklessly—"Don't bother me with the facts!" An opinion should not be prejudice in another form. Rather, an opinion should itself be a kind of *argument,* based on fact or reason. Sometimes our deeply held beliefs are refuted by new evidence or by reasons we have not before encountered. In such cases we as educated thinkers cannot say, "Well, that may be so, but I still stick to my opinion." If the facts or reasons contradict our opinions, we have no choice but to reexamine our beliefs. That's what education is all about.

By reading critically—by reading to understand, analyze, and evaluate—you respond to an author's ideas, opinions, and arguments in an informed way. In a sense you enter into a conversation with the author. You agree or disagree with the author, "talk back," and try to understand the author's perspective on the subject. To become a critical reader, you may wish to employ a strategy, called annotation, in which you literally mark up the essay.

Here are the basic elements of this method:

- Underline important ideas in an essay. You can also, for example, use an asterisk, star, or vertical lines in the margins next to the most important information or statements.
- Pose questions in the margins. Place question marks next to the points that you find confusing.
- Take notes in the margins.
- Use numbers in the margins to highlight the sequence of major ideas that the author presents.
- Circle key words and phrases.

Examine the annotations made by one student as she read an essay by Leonid Fridman titled "America Needs Its Nerds."

America Needs Its Nerds

nice title! Is he serious or being funny?

Leonid Fridman

1 * There is something very wrong with the system of values in a society that has only derogatory terms like nerd and geek for the intellectually curious and academically serious.

Intro/Thesis?

2 A geek, according to "Webster's New World Dictionary," is a street performer who shocks the public by biting off heads of live chickens. It is a telling fact about our language and our culture that someone dedicated to pursuit of knowledge is compared to a freak biting the head off a live chicken.

Key definition

3 Even at a prestigious academic institution like Harvard, anti-intellectualism is rampant: Many ?? students are ashamed to admit, even to their friends, how much they study. Although most students try to keep up their grades, there is but a minority of undergraduates for whom pursuing knowledge is the top priority during their years at Harvard. Nerds are ostracized while athletes are idolized.

Is this true? Where is the evidence?

Meaning?

4 The same thing happens in U.S. elementary and high schools. Children who prefer to read books rather than play football, prefer to build model airplanes rather than get wasted at parties with their

He mentions athletes several times. Must they be separated from intellectuals?

Note comparison and contrast throughout essay

classmates, become social outcasts. Ostracized for their intelligence and refusal to conform to society's anti-intellectual values, many are deprived of a chance to learn adequate social skills and acquire good communication tools.

**Call to action?*
Why this fragment?

* Enough is enough. 5

Nerds and geeks must stop being ashamed of who they are. It is high time to face the persecutors who haunt the bright kid with thick glasses from kindergarten to the grave. For America's sake, the anti-intellectual values that pervade our society must be fought. 6

Geeks must rebel?

U.S. vs. rest of world

There are very few countries in the world where anti-intellectualism runs as high in popular culture as it does in the U.S. In most industrialized nations, not least of all our economic rivals in East Asia, a kid who studies hard is lauded and held up as an example to other students. 7

In many parts of the world, university professorships are the most prestigious and materially rewarding positions. But not in America, where average professional ballplayers are much more respected and better paid than faculty members of the best universities. 8

look up

How can a country where typical parents are ashamed of their daughter studying mathematics instead of going dancing, or of their son reading Weber while his friends play baseball, be expected to compete in the technology race with Japan or remain a leading political and cultural force in Europe? How long can America remain a world-class power if we constantly emphasize social skills and physical prowess over academic achievement and intellectual ability? 9

Anti-intellectualism has negative impact on America's political and economic future. Does he prove his point?

Do we really expect to stay afloat largely by importing our scientists and intellectuals from abroad, as we have done for a major portion of this century, without making an effort to also cultivate a pro-intellectual culture at home? Even if we have the political will to spend substantially more money on education than we do now, do we think we can improve our schools if we deride our studious pupils and debase their impoverished teachers? 10

Note series of questions. Are answers self-evident?

11 Our fault lies not so much with our economy or with our politics as within ourselves, our values and our image of a good life. America's culture has not adapted to the demands of our times, to the economic realities that demand a highly educated workforce and innovative intelligent leadership.

12 If we are to succeed as a society in the 21st century, we had better shed our anti-intellectualism and imbue in our children the vision that a good life is impossible without stretching one's mind and pursuing knowledge to the full extent of one's abilities.

Essay comes full circle—reread intro

13 And until the words "nerd" and "geek" become terms of approbation and not derision, we do not stand a chance.

**Idea for essay: "My Favorite Nerd"*

The process that this student follows reflects the sort of active, critical reading expected of you in college courses. Through annotation, you actually bring the acts of reading and writing together in a mutually advantageous way. Reading critically and responding to texts through annotation prepares you for the more sustained writing assignments presented in this anthology.

These steps will help you engage in an active conversation, or dialogue, with the writer, sharing ideas and debating issues. At the same time, becoming a better reader will help you become a better writer. Judith Ortiz Cofer, a well-known writer, tells how reading comic books as a child liberated her imagination. Malcolm X tells us how reading was so powerful for him that it allowed him to break down prison walls. He became a reader as part of his apprenticeship to becoming a writer. For Eudora Welty, reading remains, as it does for most of us, a personal achievement. Welty reminds us that parents can assure a comfortable reading environment for children. And Anna Quindlen reminds us that traditional ways of reading can enhance our appreciation of online texts.

"READING" VISUALS

Living in this era of information technology, we are immersed in a world in which we are constantly confronted by images. To swim through this world successfully, we must learn to think critically about all the images we encounter. From advertising to film to the Internet, we must understand the purpose of the minds behind these works, and we must understand the methods used to move us and to persuade us visually. Even in college textbooks, we are required to come to grips, not only with the words on the page, but also with the photographs, tables, and graphics (like charts and graphs) the authors use to reinforce their message.

Frequently, textbooks for courses in psychology, biology, political science, and other disciplines use tables, charts, and graphs to show relationships discussed in words in the text. When you encounter such graphics, look at them carefully. Just as you often have to reread a verbal text, you also might have to return to charts, graphs, and tables, perhaps from a fresh perspective, to comprehend them fully.

For example, consider the graph below:

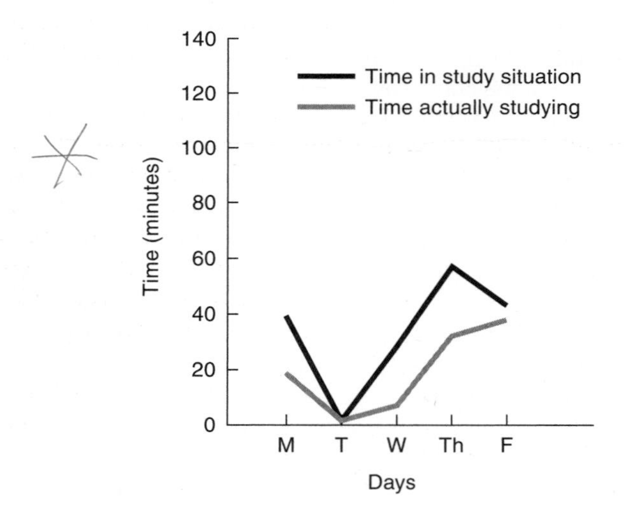

This graph shows the relationship between the amount of time a student spent in a "study situation" (sitting at a desk or in a study carrel in the library, for example) and the amount of time the student actually spent studying, by day of the week. It appeared in an introductory psychology textbook, in a section discussing how to represent data graphically. Consider this graphic. What can you infer about this student's study habits based on this graph? Do you see a change over the course of the week?

When studying a table, chart, or graph in context, ask yourself the following questions:

- What is the purpose of the graphic? What thesis or point of view does it suggest?
- How does the design or structure of the graphic help the author achieve this purpose?
- What information is provided? Is the information appropriate and verifiable? Does the information support the point the visual is trying to make?
- How does the visual support or reinforce the verbal text surrounding it?

When responding to visuals like charts, tables, and graphs that reinforce the message of a verbal text, you must take nothing for granted; you must sift through the evidence and the images with a critical eye in order to understand the strategies the author or graphic artist has used to reinforce the message conveyed by the verbal text.

When visual elements stand alone, as in a painting or a photograph, they often make profound statements about human experience and frequently reflect a persuasive purpose as skillfully composed as an argumentative essay. Consider, for example, the photograph on the next page of three children sleeping, taken by the photographer and social reformer Jacob Riis. Riis, a late-nineteenth-century photojournalist, was determined to alert well-to-do New Yorkers to the conditions in which the poor were living. He took artfully composed photographs, like this one, to show "as no mere description could, the misery and vice that [Riis] had noticed in [his] ten years of experience . . . and suggest[ed] the direction in which good might be done."

Look at the photograph and consider Riis's purpose, focusing your attention on the following features:

- The color, light, and shadow in the item depicted.
- The number and arrangement of objects or people and the relationships among them.
- The foregrounding and backgrounding of images within the frame.
- The inferences and values that you draw from the overall composition.

Jacob Riis, Children Sleeping in Mulberry Street *(1890)*

Although the primary purpose of a work of visual art may not always be persuasive, that is not the case with advertisements. In most cases, advertisements are designed to persuade you to spend money; in the case of public service announcements or political campaign ads, the purpose is to influence your behavior or even change your mind.

How do they achieve their purpose? Frequently, advertisers take advantage of our innate capacity to be affected by symbols. The president framed by American flags, a bottle of Coca-Cola beneath the word "America"—such visual emblems represent ideals and have enormous emotional power that is being drawn on to promote products, personalities, and ideas. Consider, for example, the public service advertisement on the following page.

This advertisement uses a potent emotional appeal to "sell" viewers on the idea that gun manufacturers should be required to include safety locks on all weapons.

When confronted by an ad, whether it is selling a product or an idea, consider the following:

- What is the advertisement designed to get me to do, think, or buy?
- How is the advertisement designed to achieve this goal?
- Does the advertisement work by appealing to my ideals or my emotions?

At the end of each chapter, throughout this text, you will find From Seeing to Writing exercises that will prompt you to look critically at a visual—a photograph, an advertisement, a cartoon—and interpret its meaning and purpose. The skills you will develop by analyzing these images will help you as you confront images not only in your textbooks but in your day-to-day lives as well.

Volar

Judith Ortiz Cofer

A poet, novelist, and essayist, Judith Ortiz Cofer has explored the triumphs, discoveries, and costs of hyphenated Americanism in an impressive variety of highly regarded publications. Born in Puerto Rico and reared in Paterson, New Jersey, Ortiz Cofer identifies herself as "a daughter of the Puerto Rican diaspora," or dispersion, for whose writing nevertheless "a sense of place has been very important." Her collection of autobiographical essays, *Silent Dancing,* was awarded the 1990 Pushcart Prize for Non-Fiction, and her story "Nada" won the prestigious O'Henry Prize for the Short Story in 1994. Her books of poetry include *Peregrina* (1986) and *A Love Story Beginning in Spanish* (2005). Other of her publications are *The Latin Deli: Prose and Poetry* (1993), *Woman in Front of the Sun: On Becoming a Writer* (2000), and *Call Me Maria* (2006), a young adult novel. Ortiz Cofer received her BA from Augusta College, Georgia, in 1974 and is the Franklin Professor of English and the Director of the Creative Writing Program at the University of Georgia. In this selection, she recounts how reading—in this case, reading *Supergirl* comics—can feed a young person's hunger to live. This deftly structured essay also shows how art and life mysteriously—and often, ironically—flow into one another.

To learn more about Ortiz Cofer, click on **More Resources > Chapter 2 > Judith Ortiz Cofer**

PREREADING: THINKING ABOUT THE ESSAY IN ADVANCE

What is *volar*? What expectations are raised by a title in Spanish? What sort of flying are we talking about?

Words to Watch

volar Spanish for "to fly"
aerodynamic (par. 1) relating to bodies in motion
supersonic (par. 1) speed greater than sound
ermine (par. 1) fur of a weasel, sometimes used to trim judge's robes as a symbol of honor and purity

incongruous (par. 1) not in harmony, unsuitable
dismal (par. 2) gloomy, depressing

1 At twelve I was an avid consumer of comic books—*Supergirl* being my favorite. I spent my allowance of a quarter a day on two twelve-cent comic books or a double issue for twenty-five. I had a stack of *Legion of Super Heroes* and *Supergirl* comic books in my bedroom closet that was as tall as I. I had a recurring dream in those days: that I had long blond hair and could fly. In my dream I climbed the stairs to the top of our apartment building as myself, but as I went up each flight, changes would be taking place. Step by step I would fill out: my legs would grow long, my arms harden into steel, and my hair would magically go straight and turn a golden color. Of course I would add the bonus of breasts, but not too large; Supergirl had to be aerodynamic. Sleek and hard as a supersonic missile. Once on the roof, my parents safely asleep in their beds, I would get on tip-toe, arms outstretched in the position for flight and jump out my fifty-story-high window into the black lake of the sky. From up there, over the rooftops, I could see everything, even beyond the few blocks of our barrio; with my X-ray vision I could look inside the homes of people who interested me. Once I saw our landlord, whom I knew my parents feared, sitting in a treasure-room dressed in an ermine coat and a large gold crown. He sat on the floor counting his dollar bills. I played a trick on him. Going up to his building's chimney, I blew a little puff of my super-breath into his fireplace, scattering his stacks of money so that he had to start counting all over again. I could more or less program my Supergirl dreams in those days by focusing on the object of my current obsession. This way I "saw" into the private lives of my neighbors, my teachers, and in the last days of my childish fantasy and the beginning of adolescence, into the secret room of the boys I liked. In the mornings I'd wake up in my tiny bedroom with the incongruous—at least in our tiny apartment—white "princess" furniture my mother had chosen for me, and find myself back in my body; my tight curls still clinging to my head, skinny arms and legs and flat chest unchanged.

2 In the kitchen my mother and father would be talking softy over a café con leche. She would come "wake me" exactly forty-five minutes after they had gotten up. It was their time together at the beginning of each day and even at an early age I could feel

their disappointment if I interrupted them by getting up too early. So I would stay in my bed recalling my dreams of flight, perhaps planning my next flight. In the kitchen they would be discussing events in the barrio. Actually, he would be carrying that part of the conversation; when it was her turn to speak she would, more often than not, try shifting the topic toward her desire to see her *familia* on the Island: *How about a vacation in Puerto Rico together this year, Querido? We could rent a car, go to the beach. We could. . . .* And he would answer patiently, gently. *Mi amor, do you know how much it would cost for all of us to fly there? It is not possible for me to take the time off. . . . Mi vida, please understand. . . .* And I knew that soon she would rise from the table. Not abruptly. She would light a cigarette and look out the kitchen window. The view was of a dismal alley that was littered with refuse thrown from windows. The space was too narrow for anyone larger than a skinny child to enter safely, so it was never cleaned. My mother would check the time on the clock over her sink, the one with a prayer for patience and grace written in Spanish. A birthday gift. She would see that it was time to wake me. She'd sigh deeply and say the same thing the view from her kitchen window always inspired her to say: *Ay, si yo pudiera volar.*

BUILDING VOCABULARY

Writing American English often involves using words from other languages, or words that originated in other languages but have been adopted (sometimes also adapted) into English. If you watch a Woody Allen movie, for example, you will hear characters use Yiddish words or expressions that have become commonplace in New York. This essay includes some words in Spanish. Translate these words into English. Which, if any, do you think have become commonplace, part of contemporary American usage?

a. barrio (par. 1)
b. café con leche (par. 2)
c. Querido (par. 2)
d. Mi amor (par. 2)
e. Mi vida (par. 2)
f. Ay, si yo pudiera volar. (par. 2)

THINKING CRITICALLY ABOUT THE ESSAY

Understanding the Writer's Ideas

1. How old was Cofer at the time of the essay? What clues suggest roughly the calendar year in question?
2. What kinds of stories are found in the comics the writer "consumes"? How do the main characters in these stories differ from the writer?
3. In what kind of community does the writer live?
4. How does the writer use her fantastic powers to affect her everyday world?
5. Why does Cofer describe her bedroom furniture as "incongruous" (par. 1)?
6. Why were the writer's parents "disappointed" if she woke too early (par. 2)?
7. What did the writer's father discuss over breakfast? the writer's mother?
8. Why does Cofer say that when her mother rises from the breakfast table it is "Not abruptly" (par. 2)?
9. What did the writer's mother see outside the kitchen window?
10. What is the connection between the writer's dreams and what the view from the kitchen window "always inspired" her mother to say?

Understanding the Writer's Techniques

1. Does this essay have a thesis statement? If so, what is it? If not, express the essay's main idea in one or two sentences.
2. Compare and contrast the essay's two paragraphs—look, for example, at the similarities and differences in *setting, point of view,* and *theme.*
3. How does Cofer achieve unity in a two-paragraph essay?
4. Show how *incongruity* serves as an organizing principle for each paragraph.
5. What is the role of *irony* in the essay? (See Glossary.)

Exploring the Writer's Ideas

1. The writer, at age twelve, seems attracted to reading as a way of escaping the harsh reality of her barrio existence. What do

you think is the adult writer's attitude toward her youthful habits? And what is your view: is reading or, say, watching television as an "escape" a good thing? a bad thing? neither?

2. Do you think the essay aims to contrast two kinds of "flying"—that of daughter and mother; or does the essay want to suggest *analogies* between the outlook of daughter and mother? Explain.
3. Is this an essay about a certain reaction to poverty, or does the essay have implications beyond the barrio? Explain.

IDEAS FOR WRITING

Prewriting

Think about what you read at age twelve or thirteen that fed your fantasies. List a few book or magazine or comic book titles. Or, if you prefer, list movies or television shows that played this role.

Guided Writing

Write a two-paragraph essay that illustrates the differences between your reality at twelve or thirteen and the fantasy life you led then, as stimulated by your reading or television or movie watching or the Internet.

1. In the first paragraph identify the source of your fantasies.
2. In the same paragraph, describe how the fantasy imitates your reading or viewing and how you apply it to your life.
3. End the paragraph as you come back to reality and discover the incongruity between your fantasy and your true situation.
4. In the second paragraph, identify in a narrative fashion a situation that triggers your mother's or father's (or some other relative's) desire for escape, or that person's refusal to resort to escapism.
5. Conclude with a clinching last sentence that serves as a kind of punch line, linking your fantasizing and that of your relative or your fantasizing and your relative's lack of fantasizing.

Thinking and Writing Collaboratively

In a small group of three or four, explore the ways childhood reading and childhood fantasies work together. List some of the group members' favorite things to read as children that triggered childhood fantasies. On the basis of your discussion, write a paragraph or two about the kinds of things children like to read, and why.

Writing About the Text

Write an essay that shows how Ortiz Cofer achieves the essay's delicate and economical character portrayals—of herself, of her father, of her mother, of the family.

More Writing Projects

1. Are all fantasies of power benign? Pick up an assortment of comics that a young teenager might read and in your journal explore the kinds of fantasies these comics might induce.
2. Children's reading strongly tends toward imaginary worlds. Some of these imaginary worlds, as Ortiz Cofer shows, offer an escape from severe limits into unlimited power. But others are less directly escapist. In an extended paragraph, contrast the imaginary world invoked by *Supergirl* and the world invoked by a children's classic, such as *Winnie the Pooh* or *Alice in Wonderland* or *Little Women* or *The Little House on the Prairie*.
3. By doing some research into children's literature, expand into an essay the topic that is given in an extended paragraph in Thinking and Writing Collaboratively.

Prison Studies

Malcolm X

Born Malcolm Little in Omaha, Nebraska, Malcolm X (1925–1965) was a charismatic leader of the black power movement and founded the Organization of Afro-American Unity. In prison, he became a Black Muslim. (He split with this faith in 1963 to convert to orthodox Islam.) "Prison Studies" is excerpted from the popular and fascinating *Autobiography of Malcolm X,* which he co-wrote with *Roots* author Alex Haley. The selection describes the writer's struggle to learn to read as well as the joy and power he felt when he won that struggle.

PREREADING: THINKING ABOUT THE ESSAY IN ADVANCE

Reflect on what you know about prison life. Could someone interested in reading and learning find a way to pursue these interests in such a setting? Why or why not?

Words to Watch

emulate (par. 2) imitate, especially from respect
motivation (par. 2) reason to do something
tablets (par. 3) writing notebooks
bunk (par. 9) small bed
rehabilitation (par. 10) the process of restoring to a state of usefulness or constructiveness
inmate (par. 10) prisoner
corridor (par. 13) hallway; walkway
vistas (par. 15) mental overviews
confers (par. 15) bestows; gives ceremoniously
alma mater (par. 15) the college that one has attended

Many who today hear me somewhere in person, or on television, or those who read something I've said, will think I went to school far beyond the eighth grade. This impression is due entirely to my prison studies. 1

It had really begun back in the Charlestown Prison, when Bimbi first made me feel envy of his stock of knowledge. Bimbi had always taken charge of any conversation he was in, and I had 2 tried to emulate him. But every book I picked up had few sentences which didn't contain anywhere from one to nearly all of the words that might as well have been in Chinese. When I just skipped those words, of course, I really ended up with little idea of what the book said. So I had come to the Norfolk Prison Colony still going through only book-reading motions. Pretty soon, I would have quit even these motions, unless I had received the motivation that I did.

3 I saw that the best thing I could do was get hold of a dictionary—to study, to learn some words. I was lucky enough to reason also that I should try to improve my penmanship. It was sad. I couldn't even write in a straight line. It was both ideas together that moved me to request a dictionary along with some tablets and pencils from the Norfolk Prison Colony school.

4 I spent two days just riffling uncertainly through the dictionary's pages. I'd never realized so many words existed! I didn't know which words I needed to learn. Finally, to start some kind of action, I began copying.

5 In my slow, painstaking, ragged handwriting, I copied into my tablet everything printed on that first page, down to the punctuation marks.

6 I believe it took me a day. Then, aloud, I read back, to myself, everything I'd written on the tablet. Over and over, aloud, to myself, I read my own handwriting.

7 I woke up the next morning, thinking about those words—immensely proud to realize that not only had I written so much at one time, but I'd written words that I never knew were in the world. Moreover, with a little effort, I also could remember what many of these words meant. I reviewed the words whose meanings I didn't remember. Funny thing, from the dictionary first page right now, that "aardvark" springs to my mind. The dictionary had a picture of it, a long-tailed, long-eared, burrowing African mammal, which lives off termites caught by sticking out its tongue as an anteater does for ants.

8 I was so fascinated that I went on—I copied the dictionary's next page. And the same experience came when I studied that. With every succeeding page, I also learned of people and places and events from history. Actually the dictionary is like a miniature encyclopedia. Finally the dictionary's A section had filled a whole tablet—and I went on into the B's. That was the way I started copying what eventually became the entire dictionary. It went a

lot faster after so much practice helped me to pick up handwriting speed. Between what I wrote in my tablet, and writing letters, during the rest of my time in prison I would guess I wrote a million words.

9 I suppose it was inevitable that as my word-base broadened, I could for the first time pick up a book and read and now begin to understand what the book was saying. Anyone who has read a great deal can imagine the new world that opened. Let me tell you something; from then until I left that prison, in every free moment I had, if I was not reading in the library, I was reading on my bunk. You couldn't have gotten me out of books with a wedge. Between Mr. Muhammad's teachings, my correspondence, my visitors—usually Ella and Reginald—and my reading of books, months passed without my even thinking about being imprisoned. In fact, up to then, I never had been so truly free in my life. . . .

10 As you can imagine, especially in a prison where there was heavy emphasis on rehabilitation, an inmate was smiled upon if he demonstrated an unusually intense interest in books. There was a sizable number of well-read inmates, especially the popular debaters. Some were said by many to be practically walking encyclopedias. They were almost celebrities. No university would ask any student to devour literature as I did when this new world opened to me, of being able to read and *understand.*

11 I read more in my room than in the library itself. An inmate who was known to read a lot could check out more than the permitted maximum number of books. I preferred reading in the total isolation of my own room.

12 When I had progressed to really serious reading, every night at about ten P.M. I would be outraged with the "lights out." It always seemed to catch me right in the middle of something engrossing.

13 Fortunately, right outside my door was a corridor light that cast a glow into my room. The glow was enough to read by, once my eyes adjusted to it. So when "lights out" came, I would sit on the floor where I could continue reading in that glow.

14 At one-hour intervals the night guards paced past every room. Each time I heard the approaching footsteps, I jumped into bed and feigned sleep. And as soon as the guard passed, I got back out of bed onto the floor area of that light-glow, where I would read for another fifty-eight minutes—until the guard approached

again. That went on until three or four every morning. Three or four hours of sleep a night was enough for me. Often in the years in the streets I had slept less than that.

15 I have often reflected upon the new vistas that reading opened to me. I knew right there in prison that reading had changed forever the course of my life. As I see it today, the ability to read awoke inside me some long dormant craving to be mentally alive. I certainly wasn't seeking any degree, the way a college confers a status symbol upon its students. My homemade education gave me, with every additional book that I read, a little bit more sensitivity to the deafness, dumbness, and blindness that was afflicting the black race in America. Not long ago, an English writer telephoned me from London, asking questions. One was, "What's your alma mater?" I told him, "Books." You will never catch me with a free fifteen minutes in which I'm not studying something I feel might be able to help the black man. . . .

16 Every time I catch a plane, I have with me a book that I want to read—and that's a lot of books these days. If I weren't out here every day battling the white man, I could spend the rest of my life reading, just satisfying my curiosity—because you can hardly mention anything I'm not curious about. I don't think anybody ever got more out of going to prison than I did. In fact, prison enabled me to study far more intensively than I would have if my life had gone differently and I had attended some college. I imagine that one of the biggest troubles with colleges is there are too many distractions, too much panty-raiding, fraternities, and boola-boola and all of that. Where else but in prison could I have attacked my ignorance by being able to study intensely sometimes as much as fifteen hours a day?

BUILDING VOCABULARY

1. Throughout the selection, the writer uses *figurative* and *colloquial language* (see Glossary). As you know, figurative language involves imaginative comparisons, which go beyond plain or ordinary statements. Colloquial language involves informal or conversational phrases and expressions.

   The following are examples of some of the figurative and colloquial usages in this essay. Explain each italicized word group in your own words.

a. *going through only book-reading motions* (par. 2)
b. I *was lucky enough* (par. 3)
c. *Funny thing* (par. 7)
d. can imagine *the new world that opened* (par. 9)
e. *You couldn't have gotten me out of books with a wedge* (par. 9)
f. an inmate was *smiled upon* (par. 10)
g. to be practically *walking encyclopedias* (par. 10)
h. ask any student *to devour literature* (par. 10)
i. changed forever *the course of my life* (par. 15)
j. *some long dormant craving to be mentally alive* (par. 15)
k. *the deafness, dumbness, and blindness that was afflicting* the black race in America (par. 15)
l. Every time I *catch a plane* (par. 16)
m. every day *battling the white man* (par. 16)
n. just *satisfying my curiosity* (par. 16)
o. *boola-boola and all of that* (par. 16)
p. I have *attacked my ignorance* (par. 16)

2. Find the following words in the essay. Write brief definitions for them without using a dictionary. If they are unfamiliar to you, try to determine their meaning based on the context in which they appear.
   a. riffling (par. 4)
   b. painstaking (par. 5)
   c. ragged (par. 5)
   d. burrowing (par. 7)
   e. inevitable (par. 9)
   f. emphasis (par. 10)
   g. distractions (par. 16)

THINKING CRITICALLY ABOUT THE ESSAY

Understanding the Writer's Ideas

1. What was the highest level of formal education that the writer achieved? How is this different from the impression most people got from him? Why?
2. Who was Bimbi? Where did Malcolm X meet him? How was Bimbi important to the writer?
3. What does the writer mean by stating that when he tried to read, most of the words "might as well have been in Chinese"?

What happened when he skipped over such words? What motivated him to change his way of reading?

4. Why did Malcolm X start trying to improve his handwriting? How was it connected to his desire to improve his reading ability? Briefly describe how he went about this dual process. How did he feel after the first day of this process? Why?
5. How is the dictionary "like a miniature encyclopedia"?
6. Judging from this essay and his description of his "homemade education," how much time did Malcolm X spend in prison? Does the fact that he was in prison affect your appreciation of his learning process? How?
7. What is a "word-base" (par. 9)? What happened once the author's word-base expanded? How did this give him a sense of freedom?
8. Who is "Mr. Muhammad"?
9. Why did the prison officials like Malcolm X? What special privileges came to him as a result of this favorable opinion?
10. Why was Malcolm X angered with the "lights out" procedure? How did he overcome it?
11. What does the following sentence tell you about Malcolm X's life: "Often in the years in the streets I had slept less than that" (par. 14)?
12. Characterize the writer's opinion of a college education. How does he compare his education to a college degree? How did his education influence his understanding of his place and role in American society?
13. In your own words, describe the writer's attitude toward American blacks. Toward the relation between blacks and whites?
14. To what main purpose in life does the writer refer? What was the relation between this purpose and his feelings about reading? Use one word to describe Malcolm X's attitude toward reading.
15. What does the conclusion mean?

Understanding the Writer's Techniques

1. What is the thesis? Where does the writer place it?
2. In Chapters 5 and 8, you will learn about the techniques of *process analysis* and *cause-and-effect analysis.* Briefly, process analysis tells the reader *how* something is done;

cause-and-effect analysis explains *why* one thing leads to or affects another.

For this essay, outline step-by-step the process whereby Malcolm X developed his ability to read and enthusiasm for reading. Next, for each step in your outline, explain why one step led to the next.

3. *Narration* (see Chapter 4) is the telling of a story or the orderly relating of a series of events. How does Malcolm X use narration in this essay? How does he order the events of his narration?
4. What is the effect of the words "Let me tell you something" in paragraph 9?
5. How is the writer's memory of the first page of the dictionary like a dictionary entry itself? What does this say about the importance of this memory to the author?
6. *Tone* (see Glossary) is a writer's attitude toward his or her subject. Characterize the tone of this essay. What elements of the writing contribute to that tone? Be specific.
7. Which paragraphs make up the conclusion of this essay? How does the writer develop his conclusion? How does he relate it to the main body of the essay? Do you feel that there is a change in tone (see question 6) in the conclusion? Explain, using specific examples.
8. What is Malcolm X's main purpose in writing this essay? For whom is it intended? How do you know?

Exploring the Writer's Ideas

1. Malcolm X writes about his newly found love of reading and ability to read: "In fact, up to then, I never had been so truly free in my life." Has learning any particular skill or activity ever given you such a feeling of freedom or joy? Explain.
2. What do you feel was the source of Malcolm X's attitude toward a college education? Do you think any of his points here are valid? Why? What are your opinions about the quality of the college education you are receiving?
3. The writer also implies that, in some ways, the educational opportunities of prison were superior to those he would have had at college. What is his basis for this attitude? Have you ever experienced a circumstance in which being restricted actually benefited you? Explain.

4. Malcolm X held very strong opinions about the relations between blacks and whites in America. Do some library research on him to try to understand his opinions. You might begin by reading *The Autobiography of Malcolm X,* from which this essay was excerpted. Do you agree or disagree with his feelings? Why?
5. Following Malcolm X's example, handwrite a page from a dictionary (a pocket dictionary will be fine), copying everything—including punctuation—exactly!

   How long did it take you? How did it make you feel? Did you learn anything from the experience?

IDEAS FOR WRITING

Prewriting

Brainstorm on a difficult activity that you learned how to perform. What problems did the activity present? Why did you want to learn how to do it?

Guided Writing

Write an essay in which you tell about an activity that you can now perform but that once seemed impossible to you.

1. Open your essay with an example in which you compare what most people assume about your skill or background in the activity to what the reality is.
2. Mention someone who especially influenced you in your desire to master this activity.
3. Tell what kept you from giving up on learning this activity.
4. Explain, step by step, the *process* by which you learned more and more about the activity. Explain how and why one step led to the next.
5. Use *figurative* and *colloquial* language where you think it appropriate in your essay.
6. Describe in some detail how you overcame an obstacle, imposed by others, which could have impeded your learning process.
7. Use your conclusion to express a deeply felt personal opinion and to generalize your learning of this skill to the population at large.

Thinking and Writing Collaboratively

Exchange a draft version of your Guided Writing essay with another writer in the class. After you read your partner's essay, make recommendations for helping the writer produce the next draft. Use the items numbered 1–7 above to guide your discussion.

Writing About the Text

In this essay, Malcolm X directly connects literacy and power, words and politics. Do you think that if Malcolm were alive today—in the era of the image, of TV and video—he would have been just as likely to have needed and have valued literacy? Write an essay that explores this question, drawing as much as seems appropriate on the selection.

More Writing Projects

1. Select any page of a standard dictionary and copy in your journal at least ten words, with definitions, that are new or somewhat unfamiliar to you. Then jot down some thoughts on the process.
2. Ask yourself formal, journalistic questions about Malcolm X's essay: *What* happened? *Who* was involved? *How* was it done? *Where* did it occur? *When* did it occur? *Why* did it happen? Write out answers to these questions, and then assemble them in a unified, coherent paragraph.
3. Form a group with three other classmates. Focus on the context of Malcolm X's essay and on his comment on "the deafness, dumbness, and blindness that was afflicting the black race in America" (par. 15). Discuss this issue and its connection to education. Then prepare a collaborative essay on the topic.

Mixing Patterns

One Writer's Beginnings

Eudora Welty

Eudora Welty, one of America's most revered twentieth-century writers, was born in 1909 on North Congress Street in Jackson, Mississippi, in the house that she would live in almost all her long life. Although she attended the University of Wisconsin at Madison, studied business for a year at Columbia University, and traveled widely, Welty always returned to the family home in Jackson. She never married. Her brief autobiography, *One Writer's Beginnings* (1980), from which this selection is drawn, ends with these words: "I am a writer who came of a sheltered life. A sheltered life can be a daring life as well. For all serious daring starts from within." The sheltered life to which Welty alludes is the life of a white woman in the Deep South in the first decades of the twentieth century. The ways of life in rural Mississippi are the subject of most of her acclaimed writing. Her novel *The Optimist's Daughter* won the 1972 Pulitzer Prize, and her total work has been collected in two volumes for the authoritative Library of America series. But as this selection shows, her sheltered life was not limited or narrow. Rather, it was rich in sensations and emotions, and through reading she reached out to the ends of the earth and the depths of the heart. Eudora Welty died in 2001.

PREREADING: THINKING ABOUT THE ESSAY IN ADVANCE

What attitudes did your family have toward reading when you were a child? Did books surround you? Which books did your parents or other relatives read to you or suggest that you read? How did you feel about books as a child growing up?

Words to Watch

disposed (par. 4) inclined; receptive
vignettes (par. 5) charming literary sketches
roué (par. 7) lecherous, wasted man
interlocutor (par. 9) partner in a dialogue
quoth (par. 9) archaic form of word *quoted*
wizardry (par. 15) magic
sensory (par. 18) pertaining to the senses

reel (par. 19) fast dance
constellations (par. 20) positions of star groups in sky, considered to look like (and named for) mythological characters

I learned from the age of two or three that any room in our house, at any time of day, was there to read in, or to be read to. My mother read to me. She'd read to me in the big bedroom in the mornings, when we were in her rocker together, which ticked in rhythm as we rocked, as though we had a cricket accompanying the story. She'd read to me in the diningroom on winter afternoons in front of the coal fire, with our cuckoo clock ending the story with "Cuckoo," and at night when I'd got in my own bed. I must have given her no peace. Sometimes she read to me in the kitchen while she sat churning, and the churning sobbed along with *any* story. It was my ambition to have her read to me while *I* churned; once she granted my wish, but she read off my story before I brought her butter. She was an expressive reader. When she was reading "Puss in Boots," for instance, it was impossible not to know that she distrusted *all* cats. 1

It had been startling and disappointing to me to find out that story books had been written by *people,* that books were not natural wonders, coming up of themselves like grass. Yet regardless of where they came from, I cannot remember a time when I was not in love with them—with the books themselves, cover and binding and the paper they were printed on, with their smell and their weight and with their possession in my arms, captured and carried off to myself. Still illiterate, I was ready for them, committed to all the reading I could give them. 2

Neither of my parents had come from homes that could afford to buy many books, but though it must have been something of a strain on his salary, as the youngest officer in a young insurance company, my father was all the while carefully selecting and ordering away for what he and Mother thought we children should grow up with. They bought first for the future. 3

Besides the bookcase in the livingroom, which was always called "the library," there were the encyclopedia tables and dictionary stand under windows in our diningroom. Here to help us grow up arguing around the diningroom table were the Unabridged Webster, the Columbia Encyclopedia, Compton's Pictured Encyclopedia, the Lincoln Library of Information, and later the Book of Knowledge. And the year we moved into our new house, there was room to 4 celebrate it with the new 1925 edition of the Britannica, which my father, his face always deliberately turned toward the future, was of course disposed to think better than any previous edition.

5 In "the library," inside the mission-style bookcase with its three diamond-latticed glass doors, with my father's Morris chair and the glass-shaded lamp on its table beside it, were books I could soon begin on—and I did, reading them all alike and as they came, straight down their rows, top shelf to bottom. There was the set of Stoddard's Lectures, in all its late nineteenth-century vocabulary and vignettes of peasant life and quaint beliefs and customs, with matching halftone illustrations: Vesuvius erupting, Venice by moonlight, gypsies glimpsed by their campfires. I didn't know then the clue they were to my father's longing to see the rest of the world. I read straight through his other love-from-afar: the Victrola Book of the Opera, with opera after opera in synopsis, with portraits in costume of Melba, Caruso, Galli-Curci, and Geraldine Farrar, some of whose voices we could listen to on our Red Seal records.

6 My mother read secondarily for information; she sank as a hedonist into novels. She read Dickens in the spirit in which she would have eloped with him. The novels of her girlhood that had stayed on in her imagination, besides those of Dickens and Scott and Robert Louis Stevenson, were *Jane Eyre, Trilby, The Woman in White, Green Mansions, King Solomon's Mines.* Marie Corelli's name would crop up but I understood she had gone out of favor with my mother, who had only kept *Ardath* out of loyalty. In time she absorbed herself in Galsworthy, Edith Wharton, above all in Thomas Mann of the *Joseph* volumes.

7 *St. Elmo* was not in our house; I saw it often in other houses. This wildly popular Southern novel is where all the Edna Earles in our population started coming from. They're all named for the heroine, who succeeded in bringing a dissolute, sinning roué and atheist of a lover (St. Elmo) to his knees. My mother was able to forgo it. But she remembered the classic advice given to rose growers on how to water their bushes long enough: "Take a chair and *St. Elmo.*"

8 To both my parents I owe my early acquaintance with a beloved Mark Twain. There was a full set of Mark Twain and a short set of Ring Lardner in our bookcase, and those were the volumes that in time united us all, parents and children.

9 Reading everything that stood before me was how I came upon a worn old book without a back that had belonged to my

father as a child. It was called *Sanford and Merton.* Is there anyone left who recognizes it, I wonder? It is the famous moral tale written by Thomas Day in the 1780s, but of him no mention is made on the title page of *this* book; here it is *Sanford and Merton in Words of One Syllable* by Mary Godolphin. Here are the rich boy and the poor boy and Mr. Barlow, their teacher and interlocutor, in long discourses alternating with dramatic scenes—anger and rescue allotted to the rich and the poor respectively. It may have only words of one syllable, but one of them is "quoth." It ends with not one but two morals, both engraved on rings: "Do what you ought, come what may," and "If we would be great, we must first learn to be good."

This book was lacking its front cover, the back held on by strips of pasted paper, now turned golden, in several layers, and the pages stained, flecked, and tattered around the edges; its garish illustrations had come unattached but were preserved, laid in. I had the feeling even in my heedless childhood that this was the only book my father as a little boy had had of his own. He had held onto it, and might have gone to sleep on its coverless face: he had lost his mother when he was seven. My father had never made any mention to his own children of the book, but he had brought it along with him from Ohio to our house and shelved it in our bookcase. **10**

My mother had brought from West Virginia that set of Dickens; those books looked sad, too—they had been through fire and water before I was born, she told me, and there they were, lined up—as I later realized, waiting for *me*. **11**

I was presented, from as early as I can remember, with books of my own, which appeared on my birthday and Christmas morning. Indeed, my parents could not give me books enough. They must have sacrificed to give me on my sixth or seventh birthday—it was after I became a reader for myself—the ten-volume set of Our Wonder World. These were beautifully made, heavy books I would lie down with on the floor in front of the diningroom hearth, and more often than the rest volume 5, *Every Child's Story Book,* was under my eyes. There were the fairy tales—Grimm, Andersen, the English, the French, "Ali Baba and the Forty Thieves"; and there was Aesop and Reynard the Fox; there were the myths and legends, Robin Hood, King Arthur, and St. George and the Dragon, even the history of Joan of Arc; a whack of *Pilgrim's Progress* and a long piece of *Gulliver*. They all carried their classic illustrations. **12**

I located myself in these pages and could go straight to the stories and pictures I loved; very often "The Yellow Dwarf" was first choice, with Walter Crane's Yellow Dwarf in full color making his terrifying appearance flanked by turkeys. Now that volume is as worn and backless and hanging apart as my father's poor *Sanford and Merton.* The precious page with Edward Lear's "Jumblies" on it has been in danger of slipping out for all these years. One measure of my love for Our Wonder World was that for a long time I wondered if I would go through fire and water for it as my mother had done for Charles Dickens; and the only comfort was to think I could ask my mother to do it for me.

13 I believe I'm the only child I know of who grew up with this treasure in the house. I used to ask others, "Did you have Our Wonder World?" I'd have to tell them The Book of Knowledge could not hold a candle to it.

14 I live in gratitude to my parents for initiating me—as early as I begged for it, without keeping me waiting—into knowledge of the word, into reading and spelling, by way of the alphabet. They taught it to me at home in time for me to begin to read before starting to school. I believe the alphabet is no longer considered an essential piece of equipment for traveling through life. In my day it was the keystone to knowledge. You learned the alphabet as you learned to count to ten, as you learned "Now I lay me" and the Lord's Prayer and your father's and mother's name and address and telephone number, all in case you were lost.

15 My love for the alphabet, which endures, grew out of reciting it but, before that, out of seeing the letters on the page. In my own story books, before I could read them for myself, I fell in love with various winding, enchanted-looking initials drawn by Walter Crane at the heads of fairy tales. In "Once upon a time," an "O" had a rabbit running it as a treadmill, his feet upon flowers. When the day came, years later, for me to see the Book of Kells, all the wizardry of letter, initial, and word swept over me a thousand times over, and the illumination, the gold, seemed a part of the word's beauty and holiness that had been there from the start.

16 Learning stamps you with its moments. Childhood's learning is made up of moments. It isn't steady. It's a pulse.

17 In a children's art class, we sat in a ring on kindergarten chairs and drew three daffodils that had just been picked out of the yard; and while I was drawing, my sharpened yellow pencil and the cup

of the yellow daffodil gave off whiffs just alike. That the pencil doing the drawing should give off the same smell as the flower it drew seemed part of the art lesson—as shouldn't it be? Children, like animals, use all their senses to discover the world. Then artists come along and discover it the same way, all over again. Here and there, it's the same world. Or now and then we'll hear from an artist who's never lost it.

In my sensory education I include my physical awareness of the *word*. Of a certain word, that is; the connection it has with what it stands for. At around age six, perhaps, I was standing by myself in our front yard waiting for supper, just at that hour in a late summer day when the sun is already below the horizon and the risen full moon in the visible sky stops being chalky and begins to take on light. There comes the moment, and I saw it then, when the moon goes from flat to round. For the first time it met my eyes as a globe. The word "moon" came into my mouth as though fed to me out of a silver spoon. Held in my mouth the moon became a word. It had the roundness of a Concord grape Grandpa took off his vine and gave me to suck out of its skin and swallow whole, in Ohio. **18**

This love did not prevent me from living for years in foolish error about the moon. The new moon just appearing in the west was the rising moon to me. The new should be rising. And in early childhood the sun and moon, those opposite reigning powers, I just as easily assumed rose in east and west respectively in their opposite sides of the sky, and like partners in a reel they advanced, sun from the east, moon from the west, crossed over (when I wasn't looking) and went down on the other side. My father couldn't have known I believed that when, bending behind me and guiding my shoulder, he positioned me at our telescope in the front yard and, with careful adjustment of the focus, brought the moon close to me. **19**

The night sky over my childhood Jackson was velvety black. I could see the full constellations in it and call their names; when I could read, I knew their myths. Though I was always waked for eclipses, and indeed carried to the window as an infant in arms and shown Halley's Comet in my sleep, and though I'd been taught at our diningroom table about the solar system and knew the earth revolved around the sun, and our moon around us, I never found out the moon didn't come up in the west until I was a writer and Herschel Brickell, the literary critic, told me after I misplaced it in a story. He said valuable words to me about my new profession: "Always be sure you get your moon in the right part of the sky." **20**

BUILDING VOCABULARY

1. Identify the following references to authors, books, and stories from Welty's essay:
   a. Charles Dickens
   b. Robert Louis Stevenson
   c. *Jane Eyre*
   d. *The Woman in White*
   e. Edith Wharton
   f. Thomas Mann
   g. Mark Twain
   h. Ring Lardner
   i. *Pilgrim's Progress*
   j. *Gulliver*
2. Write definitions and your own sentences for the following words:
   a. quaint (par. 5)
   b. hedonist (par. 6)
   c. dissolute (par. 7)
   d. allotted (par. 9)
   e. garish (par. 10)
   f. heedless (par. 10)
   g. gratitude (par. 14)
   h. essential (par. 14)
   i. keystone (par. 14)
   j. reigning (par. 19)

THINKING CRITICALLY ABOUT THE ESSAY

Understanding the Writer's Ideas

1. Why does the writer say of her mother, "I must have given her no peace" (par. 1)?
2. Why was it "startling and disappointing" for Welty to find out that storybooks were written by *people*? Where did she think they came from? Aside from the stories themselves, what is it that the author loves so much about books?
3. How did the way Welty's mother felt toward books affect her child's attitude toward reading? In what ways did the conditions in Welty's home contribute to her attitude toward books?
4. What is it, exactly, that Welty loved about books as a child?

5. Why did Welty's parents make sacrifices to buy books for the household? What were their hopes for their children? What kinds of books did the parents choose to buy and to read? What, if anything, do these choices tell us about the parents' characters?
6. For what reasons does the writer feel that learning the alphabet is so important? To what other learning processes does she compare it? Before she learned to recite her alphabet, why was it so important to her?
7. Explain in your own words what the writer considers to be the relation between physical sensations and learning words. According to the author why is it important for parents to read to their children?
8. What does Welty mean when she says a child's learning "isn't steady. It's a pulse"?
9. Explain the significance of Welty's description of her experience of the moon at age six.
10. What, if anything, do we learn from Herschel Brickell's advice?

Understanding the Writer's Techniques

1. What is the main idea of Welty's essay? Is there any point at which she directly states that main idea? Explain.
2. A *reminiscence* is a narrative account of a special memory. How does the writer use reminiscence in this essay?
3. The *tone* (see Glossary) of an essay is the expression of the writer's attitude toward the topic. State the tone of this essay. What specifically about the writing contributes to that tone?
4. Placing words in italics emphasizes them. Where does the author use italics in this essay? Why does she use them?
5. What does the writer mean by stating that the set of Dickens books "had been *through fire and water* before I was born" (par. 11)? How does the image contribute to the point she's making?
6. In paragraph 1, Welty employs a technique called *personification* (see Glossary) in stating that "the churning sobbed along with any story." Consider the effect of this technique, along with her description of her mother's reading style ("it was impossible not to know that she distrusted all cats") in the same paragraph. What does Welty seem to suggest about the connection between emotion (or expressiveness) and reading?
7. Why does Welty make a point of vividly describing books' physical characteristics, as in paragraphs 2, 10, and 15? What

do her descriptions contribute to our understanding of her relationship to reading?

8. *Similes* (see Glossary) are imaginative comparisons using the word *like* or *as*. Use of similes often enlivens the writing and makes it memorable.

In your own words, explain what is being compared in the following similes (in italics) drawn from Welty's essay, and tell how they contribute to the essay:

a. . . . we were in her rocker together, which ticked in rhythm as we rocked, *as though we had a cricket accompanying the story.* (par. 1)

b. . . . books were not natural wonders, coming up of themselves like grass. (par. 2)

c. The word "moon" came into my mouth *as though fed to me out of a silver spoon.* (par. 18)

9. Welty makes a number of references to other writers, artists, and books, in addition to those listed in the "Building Vocabulary" section: for example, Nellie Melba, Enrico Caruso, Amelita Galli-Curci, and Geraldine Farrar; Sir Walter Scott, *Green Mansions,* and John Galsworthy; Walter Crane and Edward Lear—there are many others too.

a. See if you can find some information on each of these references. When did the writers and artists live? When were the books written?

b. Why do you think Welty makes these references? Do you think she expects her readers to recognize them? (Keep in mind that *One Writer's Beginnings* was first published in book form in 1984.) Do the references in any way contribute to your understanding of her piece, even if they were unfamiliar to you?

✷ MIXING PATTERNS

Description helps the reader to "see" objects and scenes and to feel their importance through the author's eyes. *Narration*—the telling of a story—helps the reader follow a sequence of events. (See Chapters 3 and 4.) Both techniques rely on the writer's skill in choosing and presenting details. In what way does Welty make use of description and narration in this essay? How would you evaluate her use of details?

Exploring the Writer's Ideas

1. The writer believes that it is very important for parents to read to their children. Some specialists in child development even advocate reading to infants still in the womb and to babies before they've spoken their first words. For what reasons might such activities be important? Do you personally feel they are important or useful? Would you read to an unborn infant? Why or why not? If you would, *what* would you read?
2. Welty was born in 1909 and obviously belongs to a different generation from the vast majority of college students today. Do you feel that her type of love and advocacy of reading are as valid for the current generation, raised on television, video, CDs, cable, MTV, and the Internet? Explain.
3. Welty describes her love of books as going beyond the words and stories they contain to their physical and visual attributes. What objects—not other people—do you love or respect with that intensity? Tell a little about why and how you have developed this feeling.

IDEAS FOR WRITING

Prewriting

In the visual and auditory age in which we live—we watch and listen to television, tune in the radio, see movies regularly—what is the proper role for reading? Talk to friends, teachers, and fellow students about the matter. Record their observations and try to classify their responses.

Guided Writing

Write an essay that indicates your own attitude toward reading.

1. In order to set the stage for the discussion of your attitude, begin by recalling details about a moment with a parent or other adult.
2. Use dialogue as part of this scene.
3. Go as far back in your childhood as you can possibly remember, and narrate two or three incidents that help explain the formation of your current attitude toward reading.

4. Use sensory language (color, sound, smell, touch, and taste) to show how the environment of the home where you grew up helped shape your attitude.
5. Tell about a particular, special childhood fascination with something you *saw*—not read—in a book.
6. Try to describe the first time you were conscious of the *meaning* of a particular word.
7. Use at least one *simile* in your essay.
8. Create and keep a consistent *tone* throughout the essay.
9. End your essay with an explanation of how a particular book has been continually influential to you as well as to others of your generation.
10. Give your essay an unusual title that derives from some description in your essay.

Thinking and Writing Collaboratively

Form groups of three to five students and read the essays you each prepared for the Guided Writing assignment. Together, make a list of the various attitudes expressed about reading by group members. Report to the class as a whole on the reading attitudes of your group.

Writing About the Text

This selection is written by someone whom many critics consider to be a great writer, a notch above the group of excellent, admirable, or fine writers. What qualities in Welty's writing support this high praise? How do these qualities square with the prescriptions for good writing offered in Chapter 1?

More Writing Projects

1. Enter in your journal early memories of people who read to you or of books that you read on your own. Try to capture the sensation and importance of these early reading experiences.
2. Return to question 2 in Exploring the Writer's Ideas, and write a one-paragraph response to it.
3. Write an essay on the person who most influenced your childhood education. Did this person read to you, give you books, make you do your homework? Assess the impact of this person on your life.

Mixing Patterns

Turning the Page

Anna Quindlen

Anna Marie Quindlen was born in Philadelphia on July 8, 1952. She graduated from South Brunswick High School in New Jersey in 1970, and completed a bachelor's degree at Barnard College in New York City. From 2000 to 2009, Quindlen wrote the "Last Word" column for *Newsweek* while also establishing herself as a major writer of fiction and nonfiction. Quindlen's nonfiction books include *How Reading Changed My Life* (1998), *Being Perfect* (2005), and *Good Dog, Stay* (2007). Three of her best-selling novels were adapted to film: *One True Thing* (1997) was a popular feature film for which Meryl Streep received an Academy Award nomination as best actress; *Black and Blue* (1998) and *Blessings* (2002) became television movies. Her most recent novel is *Every Last One* (2010). In this column for *Newsweek,* which appeared in 2010, Quindlen explores the future of reading in the digital age.

PREREADING: THINKING ABOUT THE ESSAY IN ADVANCE

It is a truism that in this digital era, e-reading will expand. But do you think that reading from hard copy will actually become obsolete? Or might traditional modes of reading coexist with "reading off-paper" as Quindlen puts it? Could reading actually benefit from new media forms? Why or why not? Finally, what is *your* favorite form of reading?

Words to Watch

byline (par. 1) the name of the author of an article in a newspaper or magazine
siblings (par. 2) brothers or sisters
antediluvian (par. 2) in or from the time before the biblical Flood; extremely old-fashioned or out-of-date
lamentations (par. 3) sad, mournful, or pitiful statements
affluent (par. 5) wealthy
disconcerting (par. 7) making someone feel uneasy or confused
eulogy (par. 7) a tribute to somebody who has recently died

1 The stages of a writer's professional life are marked not by a name on an office door, but by a name in ink. There was the morning when my father came home carrying a stack of Sunday papers because my byline was on page one, and the evening that I persuaded a security guard to hand over an early edition, still warm from the presses, with my first column. But there's nothing to compare to the day when someone—in my case, the FedEx guy—hands over a hardcover book with your name on the cover. And with apologies to all the techies out there, I'm just not sure the moment would have had the same grandeur had my work been downloaded instead into an e-reader.

2 The book is dead, I keep hearing as I sit writing yet another in a room lined with them. Technology has killed it. The libraries of the world are doomed to become museums, storage facilities for a form as antediluvian as cave paintings. Americans, however, tend to bring an either-or mentality to most things, from politics to prose. The invention of television led to predictions about the demise of radio. The making of movies was to be the death knell of live theater; recorded music, the end of concerts. All these forms still exist—sometimes overshadowed by their siblings, but not smothered by them. And despite the direct predictions, reading continues to be part of the life of the mind, even as computers replace pencils, and books fly into handhelds as well as onto store shelves. Anton Chekhov, meet Steve Jobs.

3 There's no question that reading off-paper, as I think of it, will increase in the years to come. The nurse-midwives of literacy, public librarians, are already loaning e-readers; a library that got 10 as gifts reported that within a half hour they had all been checked out. And there's no question that once again we will be treated to lamentations suggesting that true literacy has become a lost art. The difference this time is that we will confront elitism from both sides. Not only do literary purists now complain of the evanescent nature of letters onscreen, the tech aficionados have become equally disdainful of the old form. "This book stinks," read an online review of the bestseller *Game Change* before the release of the digital version. "The thing reeks of paper and ink."

4 Perhaps those of us who merely want to hunker down and be transported should look past both sides to concern ourselves with function instead of form. I am cheered by the Gallup poll that asks a simple question: do you happen to be reading any books or novels at present? In 1952 a mere 18 percent of respondents said

yes. The last time the survey was done, in 2005, that number was 47 percent. So much for the good old days.

5 But not so fast: the National Endowment for the Arts released a report in 2007 that said reading fiction was declining sharply, especially among younger people. Market research done for booksellers has found that the number of so-called avid readers, those who buy more than 10 books a year, skews older and overwhelmingly female. One of the most surprising studies indicates that the biggest users of e-readers are not the YouTube young but affluent middle-aged men. (Some analysts suggest that this may be about adaptable font size; oh, our failing eyes!) The baby boomers are saving publishing; after them, the deluge?

6 The most provocative account of the effect of technology on literacy is now 16 years old, and while it remains a good read—in ink on paper but not, alas, digitally—the passage of time shows that its dark view of the future is overstated. Sven Birkerts's *The Gutenberg Elegies* notes, correctly, that "our entire collective subjective history—the soul of our societal body—is encoded in print." But the author rejects the notion that words can appear on a computer screen in a satisfactory fashion: "The assumptions that underlie their significance are entirely different depending on whether we are staring at a book or a circuit-generated text," he says.

7 Is that true? Is Jane Austen somehow less perceptive or entertaining when the words "It is a truth universally acknowledged" appear onscreen? It's disconcerting to read that many of the best-selling novels in Japan in recent years have been cell-phone books. But it's also cheering to hear from e-book owners who say they find themselves reading more because the books come to them rather than the other way around. I remember an impassioned eulogy for the typewriter delivered years ago by one of my newspaper colleagues: how, he asked, could we write on a keyboard that *made no sound*? Just fine, it turned out.

8 There is and has always been more than a whiff of snobbery about lamentations that reading is doomed to extinction. That's because they're really judgments on human nature. If you've convinced yourself that America is a deeply anti-intellectual country, it must follow that we don't read, or we read the wrong things, or we read them in the wrong fashion. And now we have gleeful e-elitism as well, the notion that the conventional product, printed and bound, is a hopeless dinosaur. Tech snobbery is every bit as silly as the literary variety. Both ignore the tremendous power of

book love. As Kafka once said, "A book must be the ax for the frozen sea within us."

9 Reading is not simply as intellectual pursuit but an emotional and spiritual one. It lights the candle in the hurricane lamp of self; that's why it survives. There are book clubs and book Websites and books on tape and books online. There are still millions of people who like the paper version, at least for now. And if that changes—well, what is a book, really? Is it its body, or its soul? Would Dickens have recognized a paperback of *A Christmas Carol,* or, for that matter, a Braille version? Even on a cell-phone screen, Tiny Tim can God-bless us, every one.

BUILDING VOCABULARY

1. Use the words in Words to Watch in sentences of your own.
2. Identify and explain at least three hyphenated words in Quindlen's essay. What is the function of a hyphen in writing?

THINKING CRITICALLY ABOUT THE ESSAY

Understanding the Writer's Ideas

1. Quindlen is an established writer. What do you learn about her? How do you respond to her ideas and opinions? Refer to specific lines and passages to support your response.
2. What impresses Quindlen about reading today? Does she think that technology will "kill" traditional modes of reading? Why or why not?
3. What facts and data does Quindlen present, and where?
4. What does Quindlen mean when she writes, "Anton Chekhov, meet Steve Jobs" (par. 2)?
5. According to Quindlen, reading "lights the candle in the hurricane lamp of self"(par. 9). Explain what she means.

Understanding the Writer's Techniques

1. What is Quindlen's main idea and what is her purpose? Does she state or infer this main idea? Explain.
2. How does Quindlen's title resonate in the essay?
3. Quindlen wrote this essay for a popular weekly newsmagazine. What elements of content, style, and organization would appeal to a general audience?

4. Why does Quindlen begin her essay on a personal note? Is this strategy appropriate in the context of the essay? Whv or why not?
5. What types of evidence does Quindlen present? How does this evidence support her thesis or claim?
6. Identify and explain at least five allusions in this essay. What does Quindlen assume about her audience when she uses these references?
7. How would you describe the style and tone of Quindlen's concluding paragraph? Do you find the conclusion effective? Justify your response.

✷ MIXING PATTERNS

Quindlen draws on several patterns to build her essay. Where and for what purpose does she use comparison and contrast (Chapter 7), classification (Chapter 9), and argumentation and persuasion (Chapter 11)?

Exploring the Writer's Ideas

1. Do you think that Quindlen is basically optimistic about the future of reading? Why or why not?
2. Quindlen writes: "Americans tend to bring an either-or mentality to most things, from politics to prose" (par. 2). Do you agree or disagree with this statement? Why does she make this generalization, and what is its relevance to the essay?
3. Do you think that Quindlen captures the essence of reading today? Justify your response.

IDEAS FOR WRITING

Prewriting

For five to ten minutes, jot down as many ideas about e-reading as possible.

Guided Writing

Write an essay titled "The Future of Reading."

1. Imagine that you are writing for *Newsweek* or *Time*, in other words, for a general audience interested in current issues and events.
2. Begin with a personal statement about your reading habits, both traditional and online.
3. Develop a clear point of view, presented as a claim or main idea that you plan to argue.
4. Conduct basic online research to support your key points about the changing nature of reading today.
5. Compare and contrast traditional ways of reading with "reading off-paper."
6. Develop a conclusion that reinforces the essential point that you want to make about the future of reading.

Thinking and Writing Collaboratively

Share with another class member the ideas and details that you senerated for the Prewriting exercise.

Writing about the Text

Various "literary" or stylistic features enhance Quindlen's article. Write an essay that analyzes and evaluates these stylistic techniques—for example, Quindlen's use of allusion and figurative language.

More Writing Projects

1. In your journal, write an entry about your own e-reading.
2. In a 100-word paragraph, explain the advantages of using e-textbooks rather than hardcopy ones.
3. Develop the previous paragraph into a 750- to 1,000-word essay.

SUMMING UP: CHAPTER 2

1. In one way or another, most of the writers in this chapter explain how reading has provided them with emotional ease or intellectual stimulation at some point in their lives. Which of these writers, alone or in combination, best reflects your own view of reading? Write an essay in which you address this question.
2. On the average, Americans are said to read less than one book per person annually. Take a survey of several people who are not students to find out how often and what kinds of books they read. In an essay, analyze the results. Indicate the types of people you interviewed, and explain why your results either conformed to or differed from the norm. Indicate the types of books each person read.
3. List all the books you have read in the past six months. For each, write a brief two- or three-sentence reaction. Compare your list with those of your classmates. What reading trends do you notice? Do you find patterns in the reactions to reading? What generalizations can you draw about the reading habits of students at your school?
4. The United States ranks forty-ninth among nations in literacy. People often ask, "Why is there such a low rate of literacy in such an advanced country?" What is your answer to this question? Write an essay that explains your response. Refer to the opinions on reading of Ortiz Cofer, Malcolm X, Welty, and Quindlen. Suggest some ways to reverse this trend in American reading.
5. Using Ortiz Cofer as an example, write an essay in which you reflect on your early memories of reading. Describe when you learned to read, when you experienced pleasure at being read to, or when you started appreciating a particular kind of reading. Call your essay, "Reading When I Was Young."
6. Several writers represented in this chapter speak about reading in a distinctly personal way. In each case reading is vital to their sense of personal identity. But it is through the discovery of the world beyond the self, the great world found in books, that the writers find themselves. Write an essay that explores this paradox of reading.
7. Compare and contrast the essays by Ortiz Cofer and Quindlen on the subject of reading. Predict at least one disagreement that they might likely have about reading and popular media.

8. Malcolm X goes through the dictionary learning words because he sees vocabulary as power. How does ambition in reading relate to ambition in life? Explain your response in an essay.

✷ FROM SEEING TO WRITING

Examine the photograph below and write an essay in which you analyze the reasons that the Read Across America program chose to present such an image in the national media. Why did the organization use a photograph of Michelle Obama reading from the book *The Cat in the Hat* by Dr. Seuss? Why and how does the photo link celebrity and reading? Is this a good idea? Why or why not? Try to address these questions in your analysis.

CHAPTER 3

Description

WHAT IS DESCRIPTION?

Description is a technique for showing readers what the writer sees: objects, scenes, characters, ideas, and even emotions and moods. Good description relies on the use of *sensory language*—that is, language that evokes our five senses of sight, touch, taste, smell, and sound. In writing, description uses specific *nouns* and *adjectives* to create carefully selected vivid details. The word *vehicle* is neutral, but a "rusty, green 1959 Pontiac convertible" creates a picture. Description is frequently used to make abstract ideas more *concrete*. While the abstract word *liberty* may have a definition for each reader, a description of the Statue of Liberty gleaming in New York's harbor at twilight creates an emotional description of liberty. Writers who want their readers to *see* what they are writing about, then, use description to great advantage. A writer like Barry Lopez uses description in order to capture the morbid memory of animals killed on the road by speeding cars. Annie Dillard uses description of the natural world to reflect on our life on earth. Maxine Hong Kingston uses description of her mother's collection of turtles, catfish, pigeons, skunks, and other unexpected food sources to re-create for her readers a culture different from their own. Suzanne Berne describes the former site of the World Trade Center to sort out her feelings about 9/11. Each writer, then, uses description to help us, as readers, *see* the material about which he or she is writing. As writers, we can study their techniques to improve our own essays.

HOW DO WE READ DESCRIPTION?

Reading a descriptive essay requires us to

- Identify what the writer is describing, and ask why he or she is describing it.
- Look for the concrete nouns, supportive adjectives, or other sensory words that the writer uses to create vivid pictures.
- Find the perspective or angle from which the writer describes: Is it top to bottom, left to right, front to back? Or is it a mood description that relies on feelings? How has the writer *selected* details to create the mood?
- Determine how the writer has organized the description. Here we must look for a "dominant impression." This arises from the writer's focus on a single subject and the feelings that the writer brings to that subject. Each one should be identified.
- Identify the purpose of the description. What is the *thesis* of the writing?
- Determine what audience the writer is aiming toward. How do we know?

HOW DO WE WRITE DESCRIPTION?

After reading some of the selections of descriptive writing in this chapter, you should be ready to write your own description. Don't just read about Kingston's animals, though, or Dillard's Napo River jungle. Think critically about how you can adapt their methods to your needs.

Select a topic and begin to write a thesis statement, keeping in mind that you will want to give the reader information about what you are describing and what angle you are taking on the topic. Your descriptive paper must have a thesis; otherwise, you'll be simply cataloguing details with no unifying point.

Look at this sample thesis sentence:

> For a first-time tourist in New York City, the subway trains can seem confusing and threatening, but the long-time resident finds the train system a clever, speedy network for traveling around the city.

Here, we see the thesis statement sets out a purpose and an audience. The purpose is to demonstrate the virtues of the New York transit system, and the audience is not the well-traveled New Yorker, but a visitor. All details in the paper would support the assertions in the thesis.

Collect a list of sensory words.

New York City's subway trains are noisy and crowded, labeled with brightly colored letters, made of shiny corrugated stainless steel, travel at 90 miles per hour, display colorful graffiti and advertising signs, run on electricity.

Use the five senses:

What are subway sounds? Music by street musicians, the screech of brakes, conductors giving directions over scratchy loudspeakers, people talking in different languages.
What are subway smells? Pretzels roasting, the sweaty odor of human bodies crowded together on a hot summer day.
What are subway textures? Colored metal straps and poles for balance, the crisp corner of a newspaper you're reading.
What are subway tastes? A candy bar or chewing gum you buy at the newsstand.
What are subway sights? Crowds of people rushing to work; the colorful pillars freshly painted in each station; the drunk asleep on a bench; the police officer in a blue uniform; the litter on the ground; the subway system maps near each token booth; the advertising posters on the walls and trains.

Plan a dominant impression and an order for arranging details. You might look at the subway from a passenger's point of view and describe the travel process from getting onto the train to arriving at the destination. Your impression might be that to the uninitiated, the subway system seems confusing, but to the experienced New Yorker, trains are the fastest and safest way to get around town.

Express a *purpose* for the description. The purpose might be to prepare a visitor from out of town for her first subway ride by writing a letter to her before she arrives in New York.

Identify the audience: Who will read the essay?

If you were writing to the Commissioner of Transportation in New York, or to a cousin from Iowa whom you know well, you would write differently in each case. Awareness of audience can help you choose a level of diction and formality. Knowing your audience can also help you decide which details to include and which your readers might know. It is always best to assume that the audience knows less than you do and to include details even if they seem obvious to you.

For example, even if you, as a native New Yorker, know that subway trains run twenty-four hours a day, your cousin from Iowa would not be expected to know this, so you should include it as part of your description of how efficient the system is.

Writing the Draft

Use the thesis statement to set up an introductory paragraph. Then plan the body paragraphs so that they follow the order you decided on—from beginning the journey to arriving, from the top of a subway car to the bottom, or from the outside of the train to the inside. Include as many details in the first draft as possible; it is easier to take them out in a second or third draft than to add them later. Then plan the conclusion to help the reader understand what the purpose of the description has been.

Reading and Revising the Draft

Read your first draft, circling each description word. Then go back and add *another* description word after the ones already in the essay. If you can't think of any more words, use a *thesaurus* to find new words.

If possible, read your essay aloud to a classmate. Ask him or her to tell you if the details are vivid. Have your classmate suggest where more details are needed. Check to see that you have included some description in each sensory category: sight, sound, taste, touch, and smell.

Proofread your essay for correctness.
Make a clean, neat final copy.

A STUDENT PARAGRAPH: DESCRIPTION

Read the student paragraph below about the New York City subway. Look for descriptive elements that can help you write your own paper on description. Comments in the margin highlight important features of descriptive writing.

A first-time visitor to the New York City subway system will probably find the noise overwhelming, at least at first. The variety of sounds, and their sheer volume, can send most unprepared tourists running for the exit; those who remain tend to slip into a state of deep shock. As I wait for the Number 4 train at the Lexington

Topic sentence announces purpose

Supporting detail

Avenue station, the passing express cars explode from the tunnel in a blur of red and gray. Sometimes as many as three trains roar by at the same time. A high-pitched squeal of brakes adds powerfully to the din. A few passengers heave sighs or mutter under their breath as the crackle and hiss of an unintelligible announcement coming over the public address system adds to the uproar. As I continue to wait for the local, I can hear fragments of the shouted exchanges between weary booth attendants and impatient customers trying to communicate through the bulletproof glass. Irritably, I watch one of the many subway musicians, an old bald man who sings "O Solo Mio" off-key as a battered tape recorder behind him plays warped-sounding violin music. Once in a while some goodhearted passenger tosses a crumpled dollar bill into an old straw hat at the singer's feet. Why are they encouraging these horrible sounds, I wonder to myself? I obviously haven't been here long enough to tune them out.

Supporting detail

Supporting detail

Supporting detail

Concluding sentence returns to topic; providing *coherence*

Apologia

Barry Lopez

Barry Lopez often fixes his writer's eye on the natural environment. He writes nonfiction: his book *Arctic Dreams* (1986) won the National Book Award and *Of Wolves and Men* (1978) was a National Book Award finalist. He has nine works of fiction to his credit, including *Resistance* (2004), which won the Oregon Book Award. His latest work of nonfiction is *Home Ground: Language for an American Landscape* (2010). His writing has appeared in *Harper's, Orion, The New York Times Magazine, Granta, The Sun, Manoa,* and *Best American Essays*. Born in Port Chester, New York, Lopez grew up in Southern California and New York City and attended college in the Midwest before moving to Oregon. An archive of Lopez's manuscripts and other work has been established at Texas Tech University, where he is the university's Visiting Distinguished Scholar. This selection appeared in *Literary Cavalcade* and bears the same name as his 1998 book, *Apologia,* which explores the tragedy of animals killed by automobiles along a stretch of America's roads from Oregon to Indiana.

PREREADING: THINKING ABOUT THE ESSAY IN ADVANCE

What are your thoughts when you come across a dead animal on the road, probably killed by a speeding automobile?

Words to Watch

barrow pit (par. 1) large hole dug in a sandy area
maniacally (par. 1) so uncontrolled as to appear to be affected by obsession
muslin (par. 2) thin cotton fabric
semblance (par. 4) appearance; impression
acrid (par. 7) harsh and unpleasant
proprietary (par. 8) relating to ownership
ramulose (par. 14) having many small branches
splayed (par. 16) spread wide and outward
limpid (par. 21) clear and transparent

A few miles east of home in the Cascades I slow down and pull over for two raccoons, sprawled still as stones in the road. I carry them to the side and lay them in sun-shot windblown grass in the barrow pit. In eastern Oregon, along U.S. 20, black-tailed jackrabbits lie like welts of sod—three, four, then a fifth. By the bridge over Jordan Creek, just shy of the Idaho border in the drainage of the Owyhee River, a crumpled adolescent porcupine leers up almost maniacally over its blood-flecked teeth. I carry each one away from the pavement into a cover of grass or brush out of decency. I think. And worry. Who are these animals, their lights gone out? What journeys have fallen apart here? 1

I do not stop to remove each dark blister from the road. I wince before the recently dead, feel my lips tighten, see something else, a fence post, in the spontaneous aversion of my eyes, and pull over. I imagine white silk threads of life still vibrating inside them, even if the body's husk is stretched out for yards, stuck like oiled muslin to the road. The energy that once held them erect leaves like a bullet, but the memory of that energy fades slowly from the wrinkled cornea, the bloodless fur. 2

The raccoons and, later, a red fox carry like sacks of wet gravel and sand. Each animal is like a solitary, child's shoe in the road. 3

Once a man asked, Why do you bother? 4

You never know, I said. The ones you give some semblance of burial, to whom you offer an apology, may have been like seers in a parallel culture. It is an act of respect, a technique of awareness. 5

In Idaho I hit a young sage sparrow—*thwack* against the right fender in the very split second I see it. Its companion rises from the same spot but a foot higher, slow as smoke, and sails off clean into the desert. I rest the walloped bird in my left hand, my right thumb pressed to its chest. I feel for the wail of the heart. Its eyes glisten like rain on crystal. Nothing but warmth. I shut the tiny eyelids and lay it beside a clump of bunchgrass. Beyond a barbed-wire fence thc over-grazed range is littered with cow flops. The road curves away to the south. I nod before I go, a ridiculous gesture, out of simple grief. 6

I pass four spotted skunks. The swirling air is acrid with the rupture of each life. 7

Darkness rises in the valleys of Idaho. East of Grand view, south of the Snake River, nighthawks swoop the roads for gnats, silent on the wing as owls. On a descending curve I see two of them lying soft as clouds in the road. I turn around and come back. 8

The sudden slowing down and my K-turn at the bottom of the hill draw the attention of a man who steps away from a tractor, a dozen yards from where the birds lie. I can tell by his step, the suspicious tilt of his head, that he is wary, vaguely proprietary. Offended, or irritated, he may throw the birds back into the road when I leave. So I wait, subdued like a penitent, a body in each hand.

9 He speaks first, a low voice, a deep murmur weighted with awe. He has been watching these flocks feeding just above the road for several evenings. He calls them whippoorwills. He gestures for a carcass. How odd, yes, the way they concentrate their hunting right on the road, I say. He runs a finger down the smooth arc of the belly and remarks on the small whiskered bill. He pulls one long wing out straight, but not roughly. He marvels. He glances at my car, baffled by this out-of-state courtesy. Two dozen nighthawks careen past, back and forth at arm's length, feeding at our height and lower. He asks if I would mind—as though I owned it—if he took the bird up to the house to show his wife. "She's never seen anything like this." He's fascinated. "Not close."

10 I trust, later, he will put it in the fields, not throw the body in the trash, a whirligig.

11 North of Pinedale in western Wyoming on U.S. 189, below the Gros Ventre Range, I see a big doe from a great distance, the low rays of first light gleaming in her tawny reddish hair. She rests askew, like a crushed tree. I drag her to the shoulder, then down a long slope by the petals of her ears. A gunnysack of plaster mud, ears cold as rain gutters. All of her doesn't come. I climb back up for the missing leg. The stain of her is darker than the black asphalt. The stains go north and off to the south as far as I can see.

12 On an afternoon trafficless, quiet as a cloister, headed across South Pass in the Wind River Range, I swerve violently but hit a bird, and then try to wrestle the gravel-spewing skid in a straight line along the lip of an embankment. I know even as I struggle for control the irony of this: I could easily pitch off here to my own death. The bird is dead somewhere in the road behind me. Only a few seconds and I am safely back on the road, nauseated, light-headed.

13 It is hard to distinguish among younger gulls. I turn this one around slowly in my hands. It could be a western gull, a mew gull, a California gull. I do not remember well enough the bill markings, the color of the legs. I have no doubt about the vertebrae shattered beneath the seamless white of its ropy neck.

East of Lusk, Wyoming, in Nebraska, I stop for a badger. I squat on the macadam to admire the long claws, the perfect set of its teeth in the broken jaw, the ramulose shading of its fur—how it differs slightly, as does every badger's, from the drawings and pictures in the field guides. A car drifts toward us over the prairie, coming on in the other lane, a white 1962 Chevrolet station wagon. The driver slows to pass. In the bright sunlight I can't see his face, only an arm and the gesture of his thick left hand. It opens in a kind of shrug, hangs briefly in limp sadness, then extends itself in supplication. Gone past, it curls into itself against the car door and is still. **14**

Farther on in western Nebraska I pick up the small bodies of mice and birds. While I wait to retrieve these creatures I do not meet the eyes of passing drivers. Whoever they are, I feel anger toward them, in spite of the sparrow and the gull I myself have killed. We treat the attrition of lives on the road like the attrition of lives in war: horrifying, unavoidable, justified. Accepting the slaughter leaves people momentarily fractious, embarrassed. South of Broken Bow, at dawn, I cannot avoid an immature barn swallow. It hangs by its head, motionless in the slats of the grille . **15**

I stop for a rabbit on Nebraska 806 and find, only a few feet away, a garter snake. What else have I missed, too small, too narrow? What has gone under or past me while I stared at mountains, hay meadows, fencerows, the beryl surface of rivers? In Wyoming I could not help but see pronghorn antelope swollen big as barrels by the side of the road, their legs splayed rigidly aloft. For animals so large, people will stop. But how many have this habit of clearing the road of smaller creatures, people who would remove the ones I miss? I do not imagine I am alone. As much sorrow as the man's hand conveyed in Nebraska, it meant gratitude too for burying the dead. **16**

Still, I do not wish to meet anyone's eyes. **17**

In Southwestern Iowa, outside Clarinda, I haul a deer into high grass out of sight of the road and begin to examine it. It is still whole, but the destruction is breathtaking. The skull, I soon discover, is fractured in four places; the jaw, hanging by shreds of mandibular muscle, is broken at the symphysis, beneath the incisors. The pelvis is crushed, the left hind leg unsocketed. All but two ribs are dislocated along the vertebral column, which is **18** complexly fractured. The intestines have been driven forward into the chest. The heart and lungs have ruptured the chest wall at the base of the neck. The signature of a tractor-trailer truck: 80,000 pounds at 65 mph.

19 In front of a motel room in Ottumwa I finger-scrape the dry, stiff carcasses of bumblebees, wasps, and butterflies from the grille and headlight mountings, and I scrub with a wet cloth to soften and wipe away the nap of crumbles, the insects, the aerial plankton of spiders and mites. I am uneasy carrying so many of the dead. The carnage is so obvious.

20 In Illinois, west of Kankakee, two raccoons as young as the ones in Oregon. In Indiana another raccoon, a gray squirrel. When I make the left turn into the driveway at the house of a friend outside South Bend, it is evening, hot and muggy. I can hear cicadas in a lone elm. I'm glad to be here.

21 From the driveway entrance I look back down Indiana 23, toward Indiana 8, remembering the farm roads of Illinois and Iowa. I remember how beautiful it was in the limpid air to drive Nebraska 2 through the sand hills, to see how far at dusk the land was etched east and west of Wyoming 28. I remember the imposition of the Wind River Range in a hard, blue sky beneath white ranks of buttonhook clouds, windy hay fields on the Snake River plain, the welcome of Russian olive trees and willows in western creek bottoms. The transformations of the heart such beauty engenders is not enough tonight to let me shed the heavier memory, a catalog too morbid to write out, too vivid to ignore.

22 I stand in the driveway now, listening to the cicadas whirring in the dark tree. My hands grip the sill of the open window at the driver's side, and I lean down as if to speak to someone still sitting there. The weight I wish to fall I cannot fathom, a sorrow over the world's dark hunger.

23 A light comes on over the porch. I hear a dead bolt thrown, the shiver of a door pulled free. The words of atonement I pronounce are too inept to offer me release. Or forgiveness. My friend is floating across the tree-shadowed lawn. What is to be done with the desire for exculpation?

24 "Later than we thought you'd be," he says.

25 I do not want the lavabo. I wish to make amends.

26 "I made more stops than I thought I would," I answer.

27 "Well, bring in your things. And whatever I can take," he offers.

I anticipate, in the powerful antidote of our conversation, the reassurance of a human enterprise, the forgiving embrace of the rational. It waits within, beyond the slow tail-wagging of two dogs standing at the screen door. 28

BUILDING VOCABULARY

Denotation refers to the dictionary definition of a word; *connotation* refers to the various shades of meaning and feelings readers bring to a word or phrase (see Glossary). Look up and write dictionary definitions for each of the words in italics. Then explain in your own words the connotative meaning of each word. An effective strategy for weighing the connotation of a word is to think about why the writer chose it over a synonym. For example, why did Lopez use *aversion* (in item *a* below from paragraph 2) instead of *dislike*, *hatred*, or *loathing*?

a. spontaneous *aversion* (par. 2)
b. *subdued* like a *penitent* (par. 8)
c. quiet as a *cloister* (par. 12)
d. extends itself in *supplication* (par. 14)
e. *attrition* of lives (par. 15)
f. momentarily *fractious* (par. 15)
g. *transformations* of the heart (par. 21)
h. desire for *exculpation* (par. 23)
i. do not want the *lavabo* (par. 25)
j. *antidote* of our conversation (par. 28)

THINKING CRITICALLY ABOUT THE ESSAY

Understanding the Writer's Ideas

1. What does Lopez see "a few miles east of home in the Cascades"? What does he do as a result of what he sees?
2. What does he answer to the man who asked "Why bother?"
3. What happens with a sage sparrow in Idaho?
4. How does a man near a tractor react when he sees the writer slow his automobile down suddenly and make a K-turn? What does Lopez fear the man might do? Why does he suspect what he does?

5. What, in fact, does the man do when he sees the nighthawks in Lopez's hands?
6. What happens in Wyoming when Lopez tries to avoid hitting a bird? Why is he "nauseated, light-headed"?
7. What does he admire about the dead badger in Nebraska? the deer in Southwestern Iowa?
8. What does the writer's friend say to him at the end of the journey? What does he reply?

Understanding the Writer's Techniques

1. What is Lopez's thesis? What does the title *Apologia* mean, and how does it support the thesis?
2. What descriptive details do you find most original or engaging? Identify two or three of the best images, in your opinion.
3. Right from details in the first sentence—"two raccoons sprawled *still as stones*"—the writer provides a number of *similes and metaphors* (see Glossary) to help the reader see the scene more clearly. Identify several of them. Which do you find most vivid and original?
4. The writer uses a number of words that have a religious significance, for example *penitent* (par. 8), *cloister* (par. 12), and *supplication* (par. 14). What other words with religious significance do you find? Why has Lopez chosen these kinds of words? How do they contribute to the purpose of the essay?
5. Lopez is careful to identify very specifically the places that he drives through when he spots animal carcasses on the road. Why does he name the places so painstakingly? What do they contribute to the description?
6. Why does Lopez describe with such precision the animal carcasses that he finds? Why is it important for him to try to identify the kind of gull that he hits with his car (see par. 13)?

Exploring the Writer's Ideas

1. Lopez bemoans the loss of animal life along the roads, mostly through automobile accidents, yet he himself is responsible for some of these deaths. How do you explain the obvious contradiction here?
2. How do you feel about Lopez's actions, the removal of dead animals to a quiet place off the roads? Do you find them

generous, ridiculous, respectful, incomprehensible, or something else? Explain your answer. Would you ever stop to do what Lopez does when he sees an animal carcass? Why or why not?

3. Which do you think compels Lopez's actions more, the violent death of the animals or the role that humans play in that death? Explain your response.
4. In this essay we see a prime example of humans coming into conflict with nature. Can we as humans behave more responsibly in facing the natural environment, particularly in the unwitting slaughter of forest animals that come too close to roads and highways? What other instances can you identify of human needs and wants coming up against the natural world?

IDEAS FOR WRITING

Prewriting

Try to recall an animal that you have seen that was killed by an automobile. Make a list of details that you remember and your impressions of the moment.

Guided Writing

Write an essay about an automobile, train, bus, or bicycle trip that you took on city streets or country roads and highways in which you noticed some recurrent object or event produced by humans in the natural world. Like Lopez, you can write about animal carcasses that you saw; but you also might have noticed trash along the roads, or billboards, gasoline stations, roadways themselves—anything that catches your eye as evidence of humans coming up against nature.

1. Write a thesis that identifies your subject and your attitude toward it. You can decide after you draft your essay where you want to place the thesis, at the beginning, middle, or near the end of your essay.
2. Identify the first point in your journey where you first noticed the object.
3. Describe the object carefully.

4. Show the object in relation to the natural environment in which you found it.
5. Then show the object in other places along your route.
6. Be sure to name places and objects as specifically as possible.
7. Use similes and metaphors to enhance your description.
8. Choose words carefully for their connotation as well as their denotation.
9. Write a closing paragraph that ties together your reactions to the human-produced object or event that you are describing.
10. Give your essay a title.

Thinking and Writing Collaboratively

Form groups of three or four students and read aloud your descriptive essays about a road trip. Discuss the relative success of each classmate's effort to show the effects of human activity on the natural world.

Writing About the Text

Lopez writes often about the relationship between the physical landscape and human culture. In what ways does this essay reflect his interests? Write an essay in which you analyze the ideas in this piece for the way it addresses the interaction between humanity and nature.

More Writing Projects

1. Write a journal entry about how you think we could cut down on animal traffic deaths.
2. Write a paragraph or two about the effects of the automobile on nature.
3. Write an essay in which you explore ways that humans can interact positively with the natural environment.

In the Jungle

Annie Dillard

Essayist, novelist, and poet Annie Dillard, best known for her reflective, critically acclaimed writing about nature, was born in Pittsburgh, Pennsylvania, in 1945. She attended Hollins College in Virginia. Her book *Pilgrim at Tinker Creek* (1974), a collection of lyrical observations and meditations on the natural world of Virginia's Blue Ridge Mountains, was awarded the Pulitzer Prize for general nonfiction. Among Dillard's many books are *Teaching a Stone to Talk* (1982), a collection of essays; *An American Childhood* (1987), an autobiography; and *The Living* (1992), a novel. Her most recent book is *The Maytrees* (2007). This selection, from *Teaching a Stone to Talk,* illustrates Dillard's gift for evocative description that at the same time is a form of meditation on our residence on earth.

To learn more about description, click on **More Resources > Chapter 3 > Annie Dillard**

PREREADING: THINKING ABOUT THE ESSAY IN ADVANCE

What do you associate with the word *jungle*? What is nature like in the jungle? Do you expect to meet people in the jungle? If so, what sort of people? How do they live? Why might someone from the postmodern world of video and cities travel to a jungle?

Words to Watch

headwaters (par. 1) sources of a river
tributaries (par. 9) streams that feed larger streams
fronds (par. 14) large, fernlike leaves
boles (par. 14) trunks of trees
flanges (par. 14) supporting rims or ribs
iridescent (par. 14) shimmering with colors (as in a soap bubble)
dinghies (par. 14) small boats
reciprocate (par. 19) repay

1 Like any out-of-the-way place, the Napo River in the Ecuadorian jungle seems real enough when you are there, even central. Out of the way of *what?* I was sitting on a stump at the edge of a bankside palm-thatch village, in the middle of the night, on the headwaters of the Amazon. Out of the way of human life, tenderness, or the glance of heaven?

2 A nightjar in a deep-leaved shadow called three long notes, and hushed. The men with me talked softly in clumps: three North Americans, four Ecuadorians who were showing us the jungle. We were holding cool drinks and idly watching a hand-sized tarantula seize moths that came to the lone bulb on the generator shed beside us.

3 It was February, the middle of summer. Green fireflies spattered lights across the air and illumined for seconds, now here, now there, the pale trunks of enormous, solitary trees. Beneath us the brown Napo River was rising, all in silence; it coiled up the sandy bank and tangled its foam in vines that trailed from the forest and roots that looped the shore.

4 Each breath of night smelled sweet, more moistened and sweet than any kitchen, or garden, or cradle. Each star in Orion seemed to tremble and stir with my breath. All at once, in the thatch house across the clearing behind us, one of the village's Jesuit priests began playing an alto recorder, playing a wordless song, lyric, in a minor key, that twined over the village clearing, that caught in the big trees' canopies, muted our talk on the bankside, and wandered over the river, dissolving downstream.

5 This will do, I thought. This will do, for a weekend, or a season, or a home.

6 Later that night I loosed my hair from its braids and combed it smooth—not for myself, but so the village girls could play with it in the morning.

7 We had disembarked at the village that afternoon, and I had slumped on some shaded steps, wishing I knew some Spanish or some Quechua so I could speak with the ring of little girls who were alternately staring at me and smiling at their toes. I spoke anyway, and fooled with my hair, which they were obviously dying to get their hands on, and laughed, and soon they were all braiding my hair, all five of them, all fifty fingers, all my hair, even my bangs. And then they took it apart and did it again, laughing, and teaching me Spanish nouns, and meeting my eyes and each other's with open delight, while their small brothers in blue jeans climbed

down from the trees and began kicking a volleyball around with one of the North American men.

8 Now, as I combed my hair in the little tent, another of the men, a free-lance writer from Manhattan, was talking quietly. He was telling us the tale of his life, describing his work in Hollywood, his apartment in Manhattan, his house in Paris. . . ."It makes me wonder," he said, "what I'm doing in a tent under a tree in the village of Pompeya, on the Napo River, in the jungle of Ecuador." After a pause he added, "It makes me wonder why I'm going *back*."

9 The point of going somewhere like the Napo River in Ecuador is not to see the most spectacular anything. It is simply to see what is there. We are here on the planet only once, and might as well get a feel for the place. We might as well get a feel for the fringes and hollows in which life is lived, for the Amazon basin, which covers half a continent, and for the life that—there, like anywhere else—is always and necessarily lived in detail: on the tributaries, in the riverside villages, sucking this particular white-fleshed guava in this particular pattern of shade.

10 What is there is interesting. The Napo River itself is wide (I mean wider than the Mississippi at Davenport) and brown, opaque, and smeared with floating foam and logs and branches from the jungle. White egrets hunch on shoreline deadfalls and parrots in flocks dart in and out of the light. Under the water in the river, unseen, are anacondas—which are reputed to take a few village toddlers every year—and water boas, stingrays, crocodiles, manatees, and sweet-meated fish.

11 Low water bares gray strips of sandbar on which the natives build tiny palm-thatch shelters, arched, the size of pup tents, for overnight fishing trips. You see these extraordinarily clean people (who bathe twice a day in the river, and whose straight black hair is always freshly washed) paddling down the river in dugout canoes, hugging the banks.

12 Some of the Indians of this region, earlier in the century, used to sleep naked in hammocks. The nights are cold. Gordon MacCreach, an American explorer in these Amazon tributaries, reported that he was startled to hear the Indians get up at three in the morning. He was even more startled, night after night, to hear them walk down to the river slowly, half asleep, and bathe in the water. Only later did he learn what they were doing: they were getting warm. The cold woke them; they warmed their skins in the

river, which was always ninety degrees; then they returned to their hammocks and slept through the rest of the night.

13 The riverbanks are low, and from the river you see an unbroken wall of dark forest in every direction, from the Andes to the Atlantic. You get a taste for looking at trees: trees hung with the swinging nests of yellow troupials, trees from which ant nests the size of grain sacks hang like black goiters, trees from which seven-colored tanagers flutter, coral trees, teak, balsa and breadfruit, enormous emergent silk-cotton trees, and the pale-barked *samona* palms.

14 When you are inside the jungle, away from the river, the trees vault out of sight. It is hard to remember to look up the long trunks and see the fans, strips, fronds, and sprays of glossy leaves. Inside the jungle you are more likely to notice the snarl of climbers and creepers round the trees' boles, the flowering bromeliads and epiphytes in every bough's crook, and the fantastic silk-cotton tree trunks thirty or forty feet across, trunks buttressed in flanges of wood whose curves can make three high walls of a room—a shady, loamy-aired room where you would gladly live, or die. Butterflies, iridescent blue, striped, or clear-winged, thread the jungle paths at eye level. And at your feet is a swath of ants bearing triangular bits of green leaf. The ants with their leaves look like a wide fleet of sailing dinghies—but they don't quit. In either direction they wobble over the jungle floor as far as the eye can see. I followed them off the path as far as I dared, and never saw an end to ants or to those luffing chips of green they bore.

15 Unseen in the jungle, but present, are tapirs, jaguars, many species of snake and lizard, ocelots, armadillos, marmosets, howler monkeys, toucans and macaws and a hundred other birds, deer, bats, peccaries, capybaras, agoutis, and sloths. Also present in this jungle, but variously distant, are Texaco derricks and pipelines, and some of the wildest Indians in the world, blowgun-using Indians, who killed missionaries in 1956 and ate them.

16 Long lakes shine in the jungle. We traveled one of these in dugout canoes, canoes with two inches of freeboard, canoes paddled with machete-hewn oars chopped from buttresses of silk-cotton trees, or poled in the shallows with peeled cane or bamboo. Our part-Indian guide had cleared the path to the lake the day before; when we walked the path we saw where he had impaled the lopped head of a boa, open-mouthed, on a pointed stick by the canoes, for decoration.

The lake was wonderful. Herons, egrets, and ibises plodded the sawgrass shores, kingfishers and cuckoos clattered from sunlight to shade, great turkeylike birds fussed in dead branches, and hawks lolled overhead. There was all the time in the world. A turtle slid into the water. The boy in the bow of my canoe slapped stones at birds with a simple sling, a rubber thong and leather pad. He aimed brilliantly at moving targets, always, and always missed; the birds were out of range. He stuffed his sling back in his shirt. I looked around. 17

The lake and river waters are as opaque as rain-forest leaves; they are veils, blinds, painted screens. You see things only by their effects. I saw the shoreline water roil and the sawgrass heave above a thrashing *paichi,* an enormous black fish of these waters; one had been caught the previous week weighing 430 pounds. Piranha fish live in the lakes, and electric eels. I dangled my fingers in the water, figuring it would be worth it. 18

We would eat chicken that night in the village, and rice, yucca, onions, beets, and heaps of fruit. The sun would ring down, pulling darkness after it like a curtain. Twilight is short, and the unseen birds of twilight wistful, uncanny, catching the heart. The two nuns in their dazzling white habits—the beautiful-boned young nun and the warm-faced old—would glide to the open cane-and-thatch schoolroom in darkness, and start the children singing. The children would sing in piping Spanish, high-pitched and pure; they would sing "Nearer My God to Thee" in Quechua, very fast. (To reciprocate, we sang for them "Old MacDonald Had a Farm"; I thought they might recognize the animal sounds. Of course they thought we were out of our minds.) As the children became excited by their own singing, they left their log benches and swarmed around the nuns, hopping, smiling at us, everyone smiling, the nuns' faces bursting in their cowls, and the clear-voiced children still singing, and the palm-leafed roofing stirred. 19

The Napo River: it is not out of the way. It is *in* the way, catching sunlight the way a cup catches poured water; it is a bowl of sweet air, a basin of greenness, and of grace, and, it would seem, of peace. 20

BUILDING VOCABULARY

1. An important tool of description is *diction,* the word choices a writer makes. In the sentences below, substitute your own words for those in italics:

a. Beneath us the brown Napo River was rising . . . it *coiled* up the *sandy* bank and *tangled* its *foam* in vines that *trailed* from the forest and roots that *looped* the shore (par. 3).

b. [O]ne of the village's Jesuit priests began playing . . . a wordless song, lyric, in a minor key, that *twined* over the village clearing, that *caught* in the big trees' *canopies, muted* our talk on the *bankside,* and *wandered* over the river, *dissolving* downstream (par. 4).

2. One way the writer suggests the jungle is out of the way is to name its inhabitants. Look up the animal or plant names you don't know that appear in pars. 13, 14, 15, and 17.

THINKING CRITICALLY ABOUT THE ESSAY

Understanding the Writer's Ideas

1. The writer begins by saying that the jungle is out of the way. Out of the way of what? She ends, however, by saying that the jungle river is "*in* the way." Of what? What is the implication of these apparently opposite points of view?
2. Why does the writer go to the jungle?
3. Where is the jungle that Dillard writes about?
4. At what time of year, and in what season, does she visit the jungle?
5. Who inhabits the village where Dillard disembarks?
6. What does the writer mean when she says, "This will do" (par. 5)? Who else that is there evidently agrees with her?
7. The writer says that what she finds in the jungle is "interesting." How is it interesting for her?
8. What does Dillard mean by saying "it would be worth it" when she dangles her fingers in water that is supposed to contain piranha—flesh-eating jungle fish?
9. Are the writer and her companions at home in the jungle? How are they viewed by the natives?
10. Dillard concludes by saying that Napo River is a place "of grace, and, it would seem, of peace." What evidence can you find in the essay to support this conclusion? What evidence is there that seems to support a different conclusion? Does the writer simply ignore this contrary evidence, or does she incorporate it into her view of the jungle? Explain.

Understanding the Writer's Techniques

1. What is the main idea of this essay? Where is it stated?
2. What is the effect of the opening paragraph of the essay? What is the relation of the opening paragraph to the thesis of the essay?
3. How does Dillard establish that the jungle is "out of the way"?
4. The essay's introduction takes up five paragraphs. In what ways does the rest of the essay amplify the introduction?
5. How does the writer convey her attitude toward the natives?
6. What is the connection between the concluding sentence of par. 17—"I looked around"—and the theme of the essay? Why do you think this sentence appears at this point of the essay?
7. What aspects of the final two paragraphs contribute to an effective conclusion for the essay?

Exploring the Writer's Ideas

1. The writer ends her introduction with this sentence: "This will do, for a weekend, for a season, for a home." Do you find this progression of commitments believable—that is, are you persuaded that the writer is actually considering making the Napo River her home? If so, what evidence in the essay supports such a reading? If not, what evidence do you find to the contrary?
2. The writer says that, since we are "on the planet only once," we "might as well get a feel for the place." Does the writer persuade you that going to the jungle offers a significantly different "feel for the place" than staying at home (wherever home may be)? The nineteenth-century poet Emily Dickinson, who is considered one of the greatest American poets, is said almost never to have left her home village—Amherst, Massachusetts. What do you think she might have said to the writer about the pointlessness of traveling to the jungle? What might Dillard have said to persuade Emily Dickinson to come along to the Napo River?
3. The natives of this region, the writer reports, have eaten people in the past. One native boy in her party aims at birds with stones, and the part-native guide puts a snake's head on a pole

for decoration. What is Dillard's attitude toward these "out-of-the-way" behaviors? Do you share her attitude? If so, why? If not, why not?

IDEAS FOR WRITING

Prewriting

Think about an experience of yours that was "out-of-the-way" and whose "strangeness" seemed full of lessons or richness of experience. Write down some of the things you particularly remember about that experience.

Guided Writing

Write an essay describing a place or experience that is as "out-of-the-way" of your usual lifestyle as possible, but which you can show as "interesting" in itself and instructive about what to value in your usual everyday life. (You might think of a neighborhood completely different from your own, or, say, a meal—Thanksgiving dinner at the soup kitchen—completely different from what to you is "usual.")

1. Begin, as Dillard does, by identifying where you are, and catching yourself thinking what an out-of-the-way place or experience this is.
2. Give a graphic description of the place—but not yet of the people who inhabit it.
3. Suggest, through more description, how this place has features deeper, richer, more intense than the places where you usually spend your days.
4. Now pause to reflect: hmm, is this a place where I might want to live?
5. Describe the people in this place through your interaction with them.
6. Write about what you notice in the place upon better acquaintance, maybe later in the day or just before leaving.
7. End by thinking back, now that you have returned to your routine, about how the out-of-the-way place is *in* the way of . . .

Thinking and Writing Collaboratively

In small groups discuss your impressions of places you have been that are different from those you are used to and people you have known who are completely different from you. What qualities of these other places and other people most impress you? What do other places and people make you miss most about your usual life? What do they make you want most to add to your usual life?

Writing About the Text

Dillard tells us, through many details, about the jungle. She contrasts the jungle with an implicit picture of the nonjungle where she lives. Write an essay that looks at those implicit contrasts and that explores her essay not in terms of *description* but rather in terms of *argument* or *persuasion.* Is the jungle a place rich in things and values that are absent from the nonjungle? Does Dillard "romanticize" the jungle? Does Dillard make you want to go to the jungle? If yes, why? If not, why not?

More Writing Projects

1. In your journal write about traveling as a nuisance, a bore, a rip-off . . .
2. Spend a day in a place that is as close to being wild as you can find near where you live. For at least an hour of that day, sit still in one spot. Write a descriptive paragraph about your day.
3. Who are the nuns and priests in the jungle? Why do the boys wear blue jeans? On the basis of some outside reading, or online research, write an essay that discusses some aspect of the encounter, in the Amazon, between the old and new worlds and between the "first world" and the "third."

Catfish in the Bathtub

Maxine Hong Kingston

Born in 1940 in Stockton, California, Maxine Hong Kingston is the daughter of Chinese immigrants. Her first language was Say Yup, a dialect of Cantonese. She was named "Maxine" after a lucky blonde gambler who frequented the gambling house where her scholarly father was forced to find work. She received a BA from the University of California at Berkeley, where she taught for many years. Her first book, *The Woman Warrior* (1976), vividly depicts her experience growing up as a girl and young woman in the United States but within an intensely Chinese American home and culture. *China Men* (1980) is a sequel to *The Woman Warrior,* exploring the experience of being Chinese American males. Kingston has also published a collection of prose writing about her residence in Hawaii—*Hawaii One Summer* (1987)—and the novel *Tripmaster Monkey: His Fake Book* (1989). Her more recent work includes *To Be the Poet* (2002) and *The Fifth Book of Peace* (2006). This selection from *The Woman Warrior* is one of many vignettes in that book about Kingston's mother, a larger-than-life figure. Through a colorful evocation of the strange food her mother served up, Kingston portrays a world of difference that is at once rich and weird, powerful and repelling. She brings that world to life by means of a style that is characteristically fierce, poetic, and tender all at the same time.

To learn more about Kingston, click on **More Resources > Chapter 3 > Maxine Hong Kingston**

PREREADING: THINKING ABOUT THE ESSAY IN ADVANCE

What unusual foods have you eaten? What unusual dish can you remember one of your relatives preparing when you were a child? How did you feel about eating this food?

Words to Watch

dromedaries (par. 1)   one-humped camels
sensibility (par. 1)   ability to receive sensations
perched (par. 1)   resting on a bird's roost

scowls (par. 1) expressions of displeasure
dismembering (par. 1) taking apart bodily limbs and innards
sprains (par. 2) sudden twists of joints such as ankles or wrists
unsettle (par. 3) make uneasy or uncomfortable
tufts (par. 4) forms into small patches of hair
awobble (par. 6) unsteady; teetering
toadstools (par. 7) mushrooms
revulsion (par. 8) a strong reaction away from something

My mother has cooked for us: raccoons, skunks, hawks, city pigeons, wild ducks, wild geese, black-skinned bantams, snakes, garden snails, turtles that crawled about the pantry floor and sometimes escaped under refrigerator or stove, catfish that swam in the bathtub. "The emperors used to eat the peaked hump of purple dromedaries," she would say. "They used chopsticks made from rhinoceros horn, and they ate ducks' tongues and monkeys' lips." She boiled the weeds we pulled up in the yard. There was a tender plant with flowers like white stars hiding under the leaves, which were like the flower petals but green. I've not been able to find it since growing up. It had no taste. When I was as tall as the washing machine, I stepped out on the back porch one night, and some heavy, ruffling, windy, clawed thing dived at me. Even after getting chanted back to sensibility, I shook when I recalled that perched everywhere there were owls with great hunched shoulders and yellow scowls. They were a surprise for my mother from my father. We children used to hide under the beds with our fingers in our ears to shut out the bird screams and the thud, thud of the turtles swimming in the boiling water, their shells hitting the sides of the pot. Once the third aunt who worked at the laundry ran out and bought us bags of candy to hold over our noses; my mother was dismembering skunk on the chopping block. I could smell the rubbery odor through the candy. 1

In a glass jar on a shelf my mother kept a big brown hand with pointed claws stewing in alcohol and herbs. She must have brought it from China because I do not remember a time when I did not have the hand to look at. She said it was a bear's claw, and for many years I thought bears were hairless. My mother used the tobacco, leeks, and grasses swimming about the hand to rub our sprains and bruises. 2

Just as I would climb up to the shelf to take one look after another at the hand, I would hear my mother's monkey story. I'd take my fingers out of my ears and let her monkey words enter my 3 brain. I did not always listen voluntarily, though. She would begin telling the story, perhaps repeating it to a homesick villager, and I'd overhear before I had a chance to protect myself. Then the monkey words would unsettle me; a curtain flapped loose inside my brain. I have wanted to say, "Stop it. Stop it," but not once did I say, "Stop it."

4 "Do you know what people in China eat when they have the money?" my mother began. "They buy into a monkey feast. The eaters sit around a thick wood table with a hole in the middle. Boys bring in the monkey at the end of a pole. Its neck is in a collar at the end of the pole, and it is screaming. Its hands are tied behind it. They clamp the monkey into the table; the whole table fits like another collar around its neck. Using a surgeon's saw, the cooks cut a clean line in a circle at the top of its head. To loosen the bone, they tap with a tiny hammer and wedge here and there with a silver pick. Then an old woman reaches out her hand to the monkey's face and up to its scalp, where she tufts some hairs and lifts off the lid of the skull. The eaters spoon out the brains."

5 Did she say, "You should have seen the faces the monkey made"? Did she say, "The people laughed at the monkey screaming"? It was alive? The curtain flaps closed like merciful black wings.

6 "Eat! Eat!" my mother would shout at our heads bent over bowls, the blood pudding awobble in the middle of the table.

7 She had one rule to keep us safe from toadstools and such: "If it tastes good, it's bad for you," she said. "If it tastes bad, it's good for you."

8 We'd have to face four- and five-day-old leftovers until we ate it all. The squid eye would keep appearing at breakfast and dinner until eaten. Sometimes brown masses sat on every dish. I have seen revulsion on the faces of visitors who've caught us at meals.

9 "Have you eaten yet?" the Chinese greet one another.

10 "Yes, I have," they answer whether they have or not. "And you?"

11 I would live on plastic.

BUILDING VOCABULARY

1. Go through this essay again and list every animal mentioned. Then, write a short description of each, using the dictionary or encyclopedia if necessary.
2. Use any five of the Words to Watch in sentences of your own.

THINKING CRITICALLY ABOUT THE ESSAY

Understanding the Writer's Ideas

1. What is Kingston saying about her childhood? How does her opening catalog of foods that her mother prepared, combined with further descriptions of foods, support this point? What are some of the "strange" foods that she ate but that are not mentioned in this first paragraph?
2. Who are "the emperors" mentioned in paragraph 1? What were some of their more unusual dishes?
3. What attacks and frightens the young Kingston on her back porch? Where did they come from? How do we know that she was a young girl at the time? Explain the meaning of "even after getting chanted back to sensibility."
4. At the end of the first paragraph, the writer mentions methods that she and her siblings used to shut out unpleasant sensory input. What were they?
5. For what purpose did her mother keep a bear's claw in a glass jar? Where did Kingston think it came from? Why?
6. What are the "monkey words"? Summarize the "monkey words" in your own language. Kingston says that she wanted to say "Stop it" to the monkey words, but didn't. Why didn't she?
7. What was Kingston's mother's attitude toward the taste of things in relation to their healthfulness?
8. Why would there sometimes be "revulsion on the faces of visitors" who watched the author's family eating?
9. What is the traditional Chinese greeting?
10. What is the writer's overall attitude toward her mother? Explain.

Understanding the Writer's Techniques

1. Does Kingston ever make a direct *thesis statement?* Why or why not?
2. In this essay, Kingston seems to shift in and out of various tenses deliberately. For example, in paragraph 3, she writes: ". . . a curtain *flapped* loose inside my brain. I *have wanted* to say . . ." Why do you think that Kingston uses such a technique? List three other examples of such tense shifts.

3. Comment on Kingston's use of transitions. How do they contribute to the overall *coherence* (see Glossary) of the essay?
4. How does Kingston use the five senses to create descriptive imagery? Give examples of her use of sounds, tastes, smells, sights, and feelings. Which are the most effective?
5. Eliminating the specific references to China, how do we know that the writer is of Chinese background? Which details or references contribute to this understanding?
6. Evaluate the use of *dialogue* (records of spoken words or conversations) in this essay. What effect does it have on the flow of the writing? on our understanding of Kingston's main point?
7. In paragraph 1, why does the writer give so much attention to the white flower stars with no taste? Is she merely describing yet another thing she ate, or does she have some other purpose? Explain.
8. Although other incidents or ideas are described rather briefly, Kingston devotes a full, detailed paragraph to a description of the monkey feast. Why?
9. Throughout the essay, Kingston combines very realistic description (the bear's claw, the turtles thudding against the cook pot, the monkey feast) with various *similes* and *metaphors* (see Glossary). Explain the meaning of the following uses of *figurative language* (see Glossary):
   a. a curtain flapped loose inside my brain (par. 3)
   b. The curtain flaps closed like merciful black wings. (par. 5)
   c. Sometimes brown masses sat on every dish. (par. 8)
10. What is the effect of the series of questions in paragraph 5? Why are some in quotations and others not?
11. Explain the meaning of the last sentence. How does it relate to Kingston's *purpose* (see Glossary) in this essay?

Exploring the Writer's Ideas

1. Kingston certainly describes some "strange" foods and eating habits in this essay. But what makes particular foods "strange"? What are some of the strangest foods you have ever eaten? Where did they come from? Why did you eat them? How did you react to them? What foods or eating habits that are common to your everyday life might be considered strange by people from other cultures?

2. In this essay, Kingston concentrates on her mother, mentioning her father only once. Speculate on why she excludes her father in this way, but base your speculation on the material of the essay.
3. As we all know, different cultures have very different customs. In this essay, for example, the writer describes the Chinese way of greeting one another as well as the monkey feast, both of which are quite foreign to American culture. Describe different cultural customs that you have observed in your school, among your friends, in places around your city or town. How do you feel when you observe customs different from the ones you are familiar with? Do you believe that any particular custom is "right" or "wrong"? Why? Which custom among your own culture's would you most like to see changed? Why?
4. Describe your reaction to the monkey feast description.
5. For what reason do you think the Chinese greet each other with the words "Have you eaten yet?" Attempt to do further research on this custom. List as many different ways as you know of people greeting one another.

IDEAS FOR WRITING

Prewriting

Write the words "Family Food" on top of a sheet of paper and write everything that comes to mind about the topic. Give yourself about five minutes or so. Do not edit your writing: put as many of your ideas as you can on paper.

Guided Writing

Write an essay entitled "Food" in which you describe its importance to you, your family, and your cultural background.

1. Begin with a list of important foods related to your family's lifestyle.
2. Show the role of your parents or other relatives in relation to these foods.
3. Briefly tell about an incident involving food that affected you deeply.

4. Create strong sensory imagery. Attempt to use at least one image for each of the five senses.
5. If possible, relate food customs to your family's ethnic or cultural background.
6. Use dialogue in your essay, including some of the dialogue of your "inner voice."
7. Use transitions to make the parts of your essay cohere.
8. Mention how outsiders experienced this custom.
9. End your essay with a direct statement to summarize your current attitude toward the food you have described and those times in your life.

Thinking and Writing Collaboratively

Read a draft of the Guided Writing essay by one of your classmates. Then, write a paragraph to indicate what you learned about the importance of food to the writer and to his or her family and cultural background. What parts of the essay stand out most in your mind? Where do you think the writer might have included further details?

Writing About the Text

The power of Kingston's writing derives in part from the power of her descriptions. These are often startling, even bizarre. Write an essay that takes a close, careful look at some of her descriptions. Aim to weigh the question of whether she has painted an exaggerated picture in order to shock, or whether her pictures reflect a complex reality, one aspect of which is indeed shocking.

More Writing Projects

1. In your journal, write a description of an interesting custom or activity that you witnessed, a custom coming from outside your own cultural or social background. Include vivid sensory details.
2. Write a paragraph describing in detail the most wonderful meal you have ever eaten.
3. Research and write a short report about the food and eating customs of a culture other than your own.

Mixing Patterns

My Ticket to the Disaster

Suzanne Berne

Suzanne Berne is the author of *A Crime in the Neighborhood* (1997) and *A Perfect Arrangement* (2002), popular novels in both the United States and Great Britain. She has published fiction and essays in many publications, including the *New York Times*. In this essay, she describes an emotional trip to the site of the World Trade Center in early 2002.

PREREADING: THINKING ABOUT THE ESSAY IN ADVANCE

People from all over the world come to see the sixteen acres where the World Trade Center used to stand before 9/11. Why do people come to peer at a location that has been cleared of the rubble from the attacks? Should the place be a tourist spot? Why or why not?

Words to Watch

shearling (par. 2) skin of a lamb with short wool attached
periphery (par. 8) the area around the edge
welter (par. 9) messy pile
swags (par. 9) hung-up ornaments
kiosk (par. 15) a stand where items are sold
reverence (par. 20) feeling of profound respect

1 On a cold, damp March morning, I visited Manhattan's financial district, a place I'd never been, to pay my respects at what used to be the World Trade Center. Many other people had chosen to do the same that day, despite the raw wind and spits of rain, and so the first thing I noticed when I arrived on the corner of Vesey and Church Streets was a crowd.

2 Standing on the sidewalk, pressed against aluminum police barricades, wearing scarves that flapped into their faces and woolen hats pulled over their ears, were people apparently from everywhere. Germans, Italians, Japanese. An elegant-looking Norwegian family

in matching shearling coats. People from Ohio and California and Maine. Children, middle-age couples, older people. Many of them were clutching cameras and video recorders, and they were all craning to see across the street, where there was nothing to see.

3 At least, nothing is what it first looked like, the space that is now ground zero. But once your eyes adjust to what you are looking at, "nothing" becomes something much more potent, which is absence.

4 But to the out-of-towner, ground zero looks at first simply like a construction site. All the familiar details are there: the wooden scaffolding; the cranes, the bulldozers and forklifts; the trailers and construction workers in hard hats; even the dust. There is the pound of jackhammers, the steady beep-beep-beep of trucks backing up, the roar of heavy machinery.

5 So much busyness is reassuring, and it is possible to stand looking at the cranes and trucks and feel that mild curiosity and hopefulness so often inspired by construction sites.

6 Then gradually your eyes do adjust, exactly as if you have stepped from a dark theater into a bright afternoon, because what becomes most striking about this scene is the light itself.

7 Ground zero is a great bowl of light, an emptiness that seems weirdly spacious and grand, like a vast plaza amid the dense tangle of streets in lower Manhattan. Light reflecting off the Hudson River vaults into the site, soaking everything—especially on an overcast morning—with a watery glow. This is the moment when absence begins to assume a material form, when what is not there becomes visible.

8 Suddenly you notice the periphery, the skyscraper shrouded in black plastic, the boarded windows, the steel skeleton of the shattered Winter Garden. Suddenly there are the broken steps and cracked masonry in front of Brooks Brothers. Suddenly there are the firefighters, the waiting ambulance on the other side of the pit, the police on every corner. Suddenly there is the enormous cross made of two rusted girders.

9 And suddenly, very suddenly, there is the little cemetery attached to St. Paul's Chapel, with tulips coming up, the chapel and grounds miraculously undamaged except for a few plastic-sheathed gravestones. The iron fence is almost invisible beneath a welter of dried pine wreaths, banners, ribbons, laminated poems and prayers and photographs, swags of paper cranes, withered flowers, baseball hats, rosary beads, teddy bears. And flags, flags everywhere, little American flags fluttering in the breeze, flags

on posters drawn by Brownie troops, flags on T-shirts, flags on hats, flags streaming by, tied to the handles of baby strollers.

It takes quite a while to see all of this; it takes even longer to come up with something to say about it. **10**

An elderly man standing next to me had been staring fixedly across the street for some time. Finally he touched his son's elbow and said: "I watched those towers being built. I saw this place when they weren't there." Then he stopped, clearly struggling with, what for him, was a double negative, recalling an absence before there was an absence. His son, waiting patiently, took a few photographs. "Let's get out of here," the man said at last. **11**

Again and again I heard people say, "It's unbelievable." And then they would turn to each other, dissatisfied. They wanted to say something more expressive, more meaningful. But it is unbelievable, to stare at so much devastation, and know it for devastation, and yet recognize that it does not look like the devastation one has imagined. **12**

Like me, perhaps, the people around me had in mind images from television and newspaper pictures: the collapsing buildings, the running office workers, the black plume of smoke against a bright blue sky. Like me, they were probably trying to superimpose those terrible images onto the industrious emptiness right in front of them. The difficulty of this kind of mental revision is measured, I believe, by the brisk trade in World Trade Center photograph booklets at tables set up on street corners. **13**

Determined to understand better what I was looking at, I decided to get a ticket for the viewing platform beside St. Paul's. This proved no easy task, as no one seemed to be able to direct me to South Street Seaport, where the tickets are distributed. Various police officers whom I asked for directions, waved me vaguely toward the East River, differing degrees of boredom and resignation on their faces. Or perhaps it was a kind of incredulousness. Somewhere around the American Stock Exchange, I asked a security guard for help and he frowned at me, saying, "You want tickets to the disaster?" **14**

Finally, I found myself in line at a cheerfully painted kiosk, watching a young juggler try to entertain the crowd. He kept dropping the four red balls he was attempting to juggle, and having to chase after them. It was noon; the next available viewing was at 4 p.m. **15**

Back I walked, up Fulton Street, the smell of fish in the air, to wander again around St. Paul's. A deli on Vesey Street advertised a view of the World Trade Center from its second-floor dining area. **16**

I went in and ordered a pastrami sandwich, uncomfortably aware that many people before me had come to that same deli for pastrami sandwiches who would never come there again. But I was here to see what I could, so I carried my sandwich upstairs and sat down beside one of the big plate-glass windows.

17 And there, at last, I got my ticket to the disaster.

18 I could see not just into the pit now, but also its access ramp, which trucks had been traveling up and down since I had arrived that morning. Gathered along the ramp were firefighters in their black helmets and black coats. Slowly they lined up, and it became clear that this was an honor guard, and that someone's remains were being carried up the ramp toward the open door of an ambulance.

19 Everyone in the dining room stopped eating. Several people stood up; whether out of respect or to see better, I don't know. For a moment, everything paused.

20 Then the day flowed back into itself. Soon I was outside once more, joining the tide of people washing around the site. Later, as I huddled with a little crowd on the viewing platform, watching people scrawl their names or write "God Bless America" on the plywood walls, it occurred to me that a form of repopulation was taking effect, with so many visitors to this place, thousands of visitors, all of us coming to see the wide emptiness where so many were lost. And by the act of our visiting—whether we are motivated by curiosity or horror or reverence or grief, or by something confusing that combines them all—that space fills up again.

BUILDING VOCABULARY

In her descriptive essay, Berne chooses words carefully to bring the World Trade Center (WTC) site to life and to further her argument. Define each of the following, using the context of the essay to develop your definition. Explain for each what makes the use of the word effective.

a. raw (par. 1)
b. craning (par. 2)
c. shrouded (par. 8)
d. cracked (par. 8)
e. plume (par. 13)
f. superimpose (par. 13)

THINKING CRITICALLY ABOUT THE ESSAY

Understanding the Writer's Ideas

1. Why does Berne go to the site of the WTC?
2. From where are most of the people at the site visiting?
3. What is special to Berne about the light at the WTC site?
4. What does Berne mean in paragraphs 8 and 9 when she says that she noticed the area surrounding the site, including the cemetery "suddenly"?
5. Why does Berne find the sight of the WTC "unbelievable" (par. 12)?
6. Why in paragraph 14 does the security guard frown at Berne and answer her rudely?
7. Why does Berne want to visit the viewing platform?
8. What does Berne see when she views the site from the deli's dining room?
9. Berne ends her essay by saying that by visiting the WTC, the "space fills up again." What does she mean by this?

Understanding the Writer's Techniques

1. What is the main idea of this essay? Where does the writer best express it?
2. Is the description of the crowd in paragraph 2 effective? Why or why not?
3. How does Berne create the feeling of the financial district in New York City?
4. How does she create the geography for readers who might never have been to New York?
5. In what way does Berne describe the weather? Why does she describe it?
6. In paragraphs 6 through 8, Berne uses the second person, writing that "your eyes adjust" and "you notice the periphery." Why does she make this switch? Is this effective? At what point does she switch back to first person, and why?
7. What is effective about the scene in the deli?
8. What does Berne mean when she writes that "the day flowed back into itself"?
9. Do you think the last paragraph is effective? Why or why not?

✷ MIXING PATTERNS

Description is the basic mode of development in this essay, but Berne also uses narrative. In what ways does narrative help advance her point?

Exploring the Writer's Ideas

1. In this essay, Berne shows the frustration some New Yorkers feel about tourism around the 9/11 site. Why does she focus on this frustration, in your opinion? What are your feelings about tourism at a place of such terrible destruction? Explain your answer fully.
2. There is a certain spiritual, almost religious, aspect to Berne's pilgrimage to the WTC site. How is this spiritualism conveyed by the text? Why do you think Berne develops this aspect of the essay? How did you react to it, and why?
3. Berne implies that in part, the disbelief people feel in looking at the WTC site is that it conflicts with their memories of the site on 9/11. How does Berne deal with the disbelief? How have you dealt with the same feelings? In what other ways might people deal with this disbelief?

IDEAS FOR WRITING

Prewriting

Think about a historical event, such as a Civil War battle or a civil rights march, that occurred in your community and that is commemorated by a monument or plaque. Something momentous happened there, something that people wanted to remember and wanted others to remember. Jot down your experience of the site. If you have no particular memories, visit the site, think about its historical and emotional significance to you and others, and make a note of your reactions.

Guided Writing

Write an essay describing a historical site. If the site of the 9/11 attack seemed to Berne to be disconnected from the event itself while rescue workers were still pulling bodies out of the rubble, very likely your chosen place has a different atmosphere from the original event's importance. Write about your attempt to connect with the feelings you *should* be feeling.

1. Begin by identifying the location you will describe.
2. Next, describe the people you see at the site.
3. Describe in clear, vivid terms the site itself.
4. Explain next how the feelings attached to the site as it exists now do not match the importance of the original event.
5. End with your attempt to reconcile the current state of the site with the event.

Thinking and Writing Collaboratively

In groups of three, exchange your Guided Writing paper so that you end up reading at least two papers other than your own. Write a short report in an extended paragraph for each author, explaining what is effective or ineffective in each paper. Collect the reports on your paper, and rewrite your essay in light of the suggestions you receive.

Writing About the Text

Berne uses the concepts of absence and emptiness and their opposite to make several points. Write an essay that explains how Berne uses these concepts to be argumentative and persuasive. What meaning, finally, does she associate with those concepts, and how effective is she in using them?

More Writing Projects

1. Do some research on the origins of the phrase "ground zero," and write a journal entry explaining why the phrase is used to describe the World Trade Center site.
2. Spend an hour in a public place near your home sitting in one spot. In an extended paragraph, describe the relation between the location and the people you see.
3. The city of New York is in the process of rebuilding the World Trade Center site. Do some research on the arguments over what should be built there, and write an essay on your findings. Focus on either the 9/11 memorial, the tower, the fight over arts organizations relocating there, or transportation.

SUMMING UP: CHAPTER 3

1. As you have discovered in this chapter, one of the keys to writing effective description is the selection and creation of vivid and relevant images. How do the writers in this chapter use imagery? Which writer's images do you find most concrete, original, vivid, and creative? For each of the four descriptive essays in this chapter, write a paragraph in which you evaluate the writer's use of imagery. Save the last paragraph for the writer you think has used imagery most effectively.
2. All the writers in this chapter provide vivid descriptions of people, places, and objects. What general guidelines for such descriptions do you derive from reading these writers? Write a short essay called "How to Write Description," basing your observations on at least two of the writer's techniques.
3. The essays by Lopez and Berne focus on the meaning of life in the face of death or the passing of a season. How does each writer approach the issue? Which essay do you find most effective and why?
4. Both Dillard and Lopez write about the relation between the human and nonhuman worlds. Compare and contrast their observations and discoveries. How do you think their outlook on nature affects the way they write?
5. A common complaint about fiction is that it contains too much description, which readers sometimes find boring. Write a note to such a complainer. Encourage that person to reconsider her view of description, making your case on the basis of the essays in this chapter.
6. As these essays show, description is rarely an end in itself. The writer usually uses description to make an abstract point concrete, to advance an argument by using vivid imagery, or to offer an example that can help the reader understand something better. But one thing is clear: description works best when it is enjoyable; a dull description is worse than no description at all. Find examples in these essays where you sense that the writer enjoys writing and thus is writing lively descriptions. Discuss what qualities these lively passages share.
7. Compare and contrast how Amy Tan and Maxine Hong Kingston describe their mothers.

✷ FROM SEEING TO WRITING

Examine the photograph below of the busy marketplace and write a descriptive essay about it, drawing on sensory impressions implied by the scene. Remember to avoid description for its own sake. Develop a thesis about what you see in the photograph, and present descriptive details to support that thesis.

CHAPTER 4

Narration

WHAT IS NARRATION?

Narration is the telling of a story. As a technique in essay writing, it normally involves a discussion of events that are "true" or real, events that take place over a period of time. Narration helps a writer explain things and, as such, it is an important skill for the kind of writing often required of you.

Narration often includes the use of *description* in order to make the *purpose* of the story clear. A good narrative, then, must have a *thesis*. The thesis tells the reader that the narrative goes beyond just telling a story for entertainment. Like description, the narrative has a purpose, and an audience. The writer puts forth a main idea through the events and details of the story. For example, a writer might decide to *narrate* the events that led her to leave her native country and come to the United States as an immigrant. She would establish her thesis—her main point—quickly, and then use the body of the essay to tell about the event itself. She would use narration as the means to an end—to make a significant statement about the important decision that changed her life.

Writer Elizabeth Wong uses narrative to explore the pitfalls of divorcing herself from her cultural heritage as she discusses events in her youth to point out the dangers of becoming "All-American." In his comic narrative "Salvation," Langston Hughes reveals the disillusionment he feels when he cannot find Jesus as his family expects him to. Essayist Andrew Lam tells about a visit to Waterloo, a famous European battlefield. The renowned writer George Orwell narrates events at a hanging he witnessed in Burma to call attention to how, all too often, we take the value of life for granted. Each writer, then, whose work you will read in this chapter uses narrative to tell a story of events that take place over a period of time, but also to put forward a thesis or main idea that comes directly out of events in the story.

HOW DO WE READ NARRATIVE?

Reading narrative requires us to look for more than the story, but not to overlook the story. So, as we read, we should ask ourselves:

- What are the main events in the narrative or story?
- What is the writer's purpose in telling us about these events, as stated in the thesis?
- How is the story organized? Is it chronological? Does the writer use *flashback* (see Glossary)? How much time is covered in the narrative?
- Does the author use description to make the narrative more vivid for a reader?
- What point of view does the author use? Are events told through his or her own eyes, or from a detached and objective point of view? Why did the writer make this choice about point of view? How would altering the point of view alter the purpose of the narrative?
- What transitions of time does the writer use to connect events? Look for expressions that link events: *next, soon after, a day later, suddenly, after two years*. These expressions act like bridges to connect the various moments in the narrative pattern.
- Does the writer use dialogue? What is the effect of dialogue in the narrative?
- What audience is the author aiming at? How do we know?

HOW DO WE WRITE NARRATIVE?

After reading the selections of narrative writing in this chapter, you should be ready to try narrative writing on your own. Fortunately, most individuals have a basic storytelling ability and know how to develop stories that make a point. Once you master narration as a writing pattern, you will be able to use it in a variety of situations.

Select the event you want to tell a story about. Begin with a thesis statement that gives the reader the purpose of the narrative.

Sample thesis statement:

> My year studying abroad in Paris was an adventure that taught me not only skills in a foreign language but also a new respect for people with cultural values different from my own.

Decide which point of view you will use: first person? third person? Think about who your audience is, and choose the point of view best suited for that audience. If you are writing to a friend, first person may be more informal. If you are writing to address a wider public audience, as Orwell is, third person might be more effective.

First person: I saw a man hanged, and the experience changed my views on capital punishment.

Third person: Spending a day at a Planned Parenthood clinic would help opponents of abortion understand the other side's fervent commitment to choice.

Determine the purpose of the narrative in relation to your audience. If you were writing for a Roman Catholic newspaper, for instance, your audience would be different from the audience you'd address in a feminist magazine like *Ms.:* the purpose would be different as well. In one case, you might be trying to get readers to change their views through your description. In another case, you might be showing how weak the opposition was by the way you described them.

Plan the scope of the piece: How much time will events cover? Can you describe all the events within the required length of the essay?

Plan to include dialogue. For example, you might include a few fragments of conversation between lost or confused freshmen to give a "first day at school" story real-life flavor:

"Did you buy your books yet?"

"No, I couldn't find the bookstore!"

"Well, I already spent $125, and that was only for two courses. I'm going to have to ask my mom for more money."

"Yeah, I'm thinking maybe I'm going to need a part-time job."

"Yeah, maybe we can work in the bookstore and get a discount."

Make a list of *transitions* that show the passage of time and use (without overusing) as many as you need to help your reader follow the narrative sequence. Check that there are transitions between events: *after that, a few hours later, by the time the day ended.*

State your *thesis*. Write out the thesis statement so that you know the *subject* and the *purpose* of the essay. Then make a list of the major events in the story. You might begin with why you chose the college you did, and how you felt when you got accepted. Or you might begin with your arrival on the first day of classes, and go through the main events of the day—going to class, buying books, meeting other new students, evaluating teachers, having lunch, and so forth.

Plan an arrangement of events. Most narratives benefit from a clear chronological sequence. All the writers here pay careful attention to the march of events over time, and you should follow their lead. As in Orwell's focused narrative, integrate commentary, analysis, or assessment, but keep your eye on the order of events.

Writing the Draft

Once you have structured your essay, build your ideas by including descriptive details. Insert as many descriptive words as possible to help a reader *see* the campus, the students, the cafeteria, and so on:

the bright-colored sofas in the student lounge, filled with cigarette burns
the smells of French fries from the cafeteria, with its long rows of orange tables
the conversations of the biology majors at the next table, who were talking about cutting up frogs
the large, imposing library, with its rows of blue computer terminals and its hushed whispered sounds

Discuss how these events made you feel about your decision. Did you choose the right college?

Write a conclusion that reinforces the purpose of the essay. Make a direct statement of the way the events in the narrative changed you, or how your expectations for the day compare with what really happened.

Reading and Revising the Draft

Read the essay aloud to a classmate who is also a new freshman. Ask your listener if his or her day was the same as yours. Did you put the events in a logical sequence? Can your listener suggest more ideas to add? Have you included enough details so that a reader who was not a member of the college community could see the events as you saw them?

Proofread carefully for correctness and make a neat final copy.

A STUDENT PARAGRAPH: NARRATION

In preparation for the essay on narration, one student wrote a narrative paragraph to tell part of the story of his first day on campus. Look at the selection and the annotations, which highlight important elements of narrative writing.

It was my first official day as a student here at State; the September morning had hardly begun, and I was already in a sweat. The crisp, colorful map I'd picked up shortly after passing through the iron gates had collapsed into a moist crumpled ball in my fist. Now I was flushed, panting, and miserable, as I tried to decide which seemingly endless line of students I needed to join next in order to fix the financial mess the university's computers had put me in. Standing in the middle of the quad, hemmed in on all sides by towering brick and marble buildings, I gazed helplessly around me. Suddenly, I caught a glimpse of a familiar face: Dan Merritt, a tall, skinny kid with bright red hair who had quit the Westmont High football team in his sophomore year, a few weeks before I did. Springing into action, I virtually tackled the poor guy, frantic lest he should escape and leave me alone with my rapidly disappearing self-confidence. I felt a real jolt of pleasure, though, when I saw relief flood his face. "Boy, am I glad to see you," Dan said. "I was beginning to think I wouldn't get out of here alive."

- Topic sentence
- Statement of time and place helps set narrative scene.
- "I" sets narrative point of view (first person).
- Supporting detail
- Transitions ("now," "next") promote chronological sequence.
- Supporting detail
- Supporting detail
- Dialogue adds real-life flavor.

The Struggle to Be an All-American Girl

Elizabeth Wong

Elizabeth Wong is an award-winning Chinese American playwright. *Letters to a Student Revolutionary* (1991), her best-known work to date, has been produced around the world. Her other plays include *Kimchee and Chitlins* (1990), about relations between Korean Americans and African Americans, and *The Happy Prince* (1997). A new play, *China Doll,* debuted in Los Angeles in 2004 and came to New York City in 2005. Wong was a staff writer for the ABC sitcom *All-American Girl,* the first network series to feature an Asian American woman as its central character. In this selection, which originally appeared in the *Los Angeles Times,* Wong effectively blends concrete description and imaginative comparisons. She uses her storytelling gifts to give the reader a vivid look into the life of a child who felt that she had a Chinese exterior but an American interior.

PREREADING: THINKING ABOUT THE ESSAY IN ADVANCE

America prides itself on its ability to assimilate cultures, yet the process of assimilation is not without difficulties, particularly for children. What problems do you foresee for a child of one cultural background growing up in the midst of another culture?

Words to Watch

stoically (par. 1) without showing emotion
dissuade (par. 2) to talk out of doing something
ideographs (par. 7) Chinese picture symbols used to form words
disassociate (par. 8) to detach from association
vendors (par. 8) sellers of goods
gibberish (par. 9) confused, unintelligible speech or language
pidgin (par. 10) simplified speech that is usually a mixture of two or more languages

1 It's still there, the Chinese school on Yale Street where my brother and I used to go. Despite the new coat of paint and the high wire fence, the school I knew 10 years ago remains remarkably, stoically the same.

2 Every day at 5 P.M., instead of playing with our fourth- and fifth-grade friends or sneaking out to the empty lot to hunt ghosts and animal bones, my brother and I had to go to Chinese school. No amount of kicking, screaming, or pleading could dissuade my mother, who was solidly determined to have us learn the language of our heritage.

3 Forcibly, she walked us the seven long, hilly blocks from our home to school, depositing our defiant tearful faces before the stern principal. My only memory of him is that he swayed on his heels like a palm tree, and he always clasped his impatient twitching hands behind his back. I recognized him as a repressed maniacal child killer, and knew that if we ever saw his hands we'd be in big trouble.

4 We all sat in little chairs in an empty auditorium. The room smelled like Chinese medicine, an imported faraway mustiness. Like ancient mothballs or dirty closets. I hated that smell. I favored crisp new scents. Like the soft French perfume that my American teacher wore in public school.

5 There was a stage far to the right, flanked by an American flag and the flag of the Nationalist Republic of China, which was also red, white and blue but not as pretty.

6 Although the emphasis at the school was mainly language—speaking, reading, writing—the lessons always began with an exercise in politeness. With the entrance of the teacher, the best student would tap a bell and everyone would get up, kowtow, and chant, "Sing san ho," the phonetic for "How are you, teacher?"

7 Being ten years old, I had better things to learn than ideographs copied painstakingly in lines that ran right to left from the tip of a *moc but,* a real ink pen that had to be held in an awkward way if blotches were to be avoided. After all, I could do the multiplication tables, name the satellites of Mars, and write reports on "Little Women" and "Black Beauty." Nancy Drew, my favorite book heroine, never spoke Chinese.

8 The language was a source of embarrassment. More times than not, I had tried to disassociate myself from the nagging loud voice that followed me wherever I wandered in the nearby American supermarket outside Chinatown. The voice belonged to my grandmother, a fragile woman in her seventies who could outshout the best of the street vendors. Her humor was raunchy, her Chinese rhythmless, patternless. It was quick, it was loud, it was unbeautiful. It was not like the quiet, lilting romance of French or the gentle

refinement of the American South. Chinese sounded pedestrian. Public.

9 In Chinatown, the comings and goings of hundreds of Chinese on their daily tasks sounded chaotic and frenzied. I did not want to be thought of as mad, as talking gibberish. When I spoke English, people nodded at me, smiled sweetly, said encouraging words. Even the people in my culture would cluck and say that I'd do well in life. "My, doesn't she move her lips fast," they would say, meaning that I'd be able to keep up with the world outside Chinatown.

10 My brother was even more fanatical than I about speaking English. He was especially hard on my mother, criticizing her, often cruelly, for her pidgin speech—smatterings of Chinese scattered like chop suey in her conversation. "It's not 'What it is,' Mom," he'd say in exasperation. "It's 'What *is* it, what *is* it, what *is* it!' Sometimes Mom might leave out an occasional "the" or "a," or perhaps a verb of being. He would stop her in mid-sentence: "Say it again, Mom. Say it right." When he tripped over his own tongue, he'd blame it on her: "See, Mom, it's all your fault. You set a bad example."

11 What infuriated my mother most was when my brother cornered her on her consonants, especially "r." My father had played a cruel joke on Mom by assigning her an American name that her tongue wouldn't allow her to say. No matter how hard she tried, "Ruth" always ended up "Luth" or "Roof."

12 After two years of writing with a *moc but* and reciting words with multiples of meanings, I finally was granted a cultural divorce. I was permitted to stop Chinese school.

13 I thought of myself as multicultural. I preferred tacos to egg rolls; I enjoyed Cinco de Mayo more than Chinese New Year.

14 At last, I was one of you; I wasn't one of them.

15 Sadly, I still am.

BUILDING VOCABULARY

For each of the words in italics, choose the letter of the word or expression that most closely matches its meaning.

1. the *stern* principal (par. 3)
 a. military
 b. very old
 c. immoral
 d. strict

2. *repressed* maniacal child killer (par. 3)
  a. quiet
  b. ugly
  c. held back
  d. retired

3. an imported faraway *mustiness* (par. 4)
  a. country
  b. mothballs
  c. chair
  d. staleness

4. a *fragile* woman (par. 8)
  a. elderly
  b. frail
  c. tall
  d. inconsistent

5. her humor was *raunchy* (par. 8)
  a. obscene
  b. unclear
  c. childish
  d. very funny

6. quiet, *lilting* romance of French (par. 8)
  a. musical
  b. tilting
  c. loving
  d. complicated

7. thought of as *mad* (par. 9)
  a. foreign
  b. angry
  c. stupid
  d. crazy

8. what *infuriated* my mother most (par. 11)
  a. angered
  b. humiliated
  c. made laugh
  d. typified

THINKING CRITICALLY ABOUT THE ESSAY

Understanding the Writer's Ideas

1. What did Elizabeth Wong and her brother do every day after school? How did that make them different from their friends?

What was their attitude toward what they did? How do you know?
2. What does Wong mean when she says of the principal "I recognized him as a repressed maniacal child killer"? Why were she and her brother afraid to see his hands?
3. What was the main purpose of going to Chinese school? What did Wong feel she had learned at "regular" American school? Which did she feel was more important? What are *Little Women, Black Beauty,* and Nancy Drew?
4. In the first sentence of paragraph 8, what language is "the language"?
5. What was Wong's grandmother like? What was Wong's attitude toward her? Why?
6. When Wong spoke English in Chinatown, why did the others think it was good that she moved her lips quickly?
7. What was her brother's attitude toward speaking English? How did he treat their mother when she tried to speak English? Why was it unfortunate that the mother had the American name *Ruth?* Who gave her that name? Why?
8. Explain the expression "he tripped over his own tongue" (par. 10).
9. In paragraph 13, Wong states, "I thought of myself as multicultural." What does that mean? What are tacos, egg rolls, and Cinco de Mayo? Why is it surprising that Wong includes those items as examples of her multiculturalism?
10. Who are the "you" and "them" of paragraph 14? Explain the significance of the last sentence. What does it indicate about Wong's attitude toward Chinese school from the vantage point of being an adult?

Understanding the Writer's Techniques

1. Wong does not state a thesis directly in a thesis sentence. How does her title imply a thesis? If you were writing a thesis sentence of your own for this essay, what would it be?
2. What is Wong's purpose in writing this narrative? Is the technique of narration an appropriate one to her purpose? Why or why not?
3. This narrative contains several stories. The first one ends after paragraph 7 and tells about Wong's routine after 5 P.M. on school days. Paragraphs 8 and 9, 10 and 11, and 12 and 13 offer other related narratives. Summarize each of these

briefly. How does Wong help the reader shift from story to story?

4. The writer of narration will present *time* in a way that best fulfills the purpose of the narration. This presentation may take many forms: a single, personal event; a series of related events; a historical occurrence; an aging process. Obviously Wong chose a series of related events. Why does she use such a narrative structure to make her point? Could she have chosen an alternative plan, do you think? Why or why not?

5. Writers of narration often rely upon descriptive details to flesh out their stories. Find examples of sensory language here that make the scene come alive for the reader.

6. Writers often use figurative comparisons to enliven their writing and to make it more distinctive. A *simile* is an imaginative form of figurative comparison using *like* or *as* to connect two items. One thing is similar to another in this figure. A *metaphor* is a figure of speech in which the writer compares two items not normally thought of as similar, but unlike in a simile, the comparison is direct—that is, it does not use *like* or *as*. (See Glossary for *simile* and *metaphor*.) In other words, one thing is said to be the other thing, not merely to be like it. For example, if you wanted to compare love to a rose, you might use these two comparisons:

Simile:
　　My love is *like* a red, red rose.
Metaphor:
　　My love *is* a red, red rose.

In Wong's essay, find the similes and metaphors in paragraphs 2, 3, 4, 10, and 12. For each, name the two items compared and explain the comparison in your own words.

7. Narratives often include lines of spoken language—that is, one person in the narrative talking alone or to another. Wong uses quoted detail sparsely here. Why did she choose to limit the dialogue? How effective is the dialogue that appears here? Where do you think she might have used more dialogue to advance the narrative?

8. The last two paragraphs are only one sentence each. Why do you think the author chose this technique?

9. What is the *irony* (see Glossary) in the last sentence of the essay? How would the meaning of the last sentence change if

you eliminated the word "sadly"? What is the irony in the title of the essay?
10. What is the *tone* (see Glossary) of this essay? How does Wong create that tone?

Exploring the Writer's Ideas

1. Wong and her brother deeply resented being forced to attend Chinese school. When children very clearly express displeasure or unhappiness, should parents force them to do things anyway? Why or why not?
2. On one level this essay is about a clash of cultures, here the ancient Chinese culture of Wong's ancestry and the culture of twentieth-century United States. Is it possible for someone to maintain connections to his or her ethnic or cultural background and at the same time to become an All-American girl or boy? What do people of foreign backgrounds gain when they become completely Americanized? What do they lose?
3. Because of their foreign ways, the mother and grandmother clearly embarrassed the Wong children. Under what other conditions that you can think of do parents embarrass children? Children, parents?

IDEAS FOR WRITING

Prewriting

Do timed writing—that is, write nonstop for fifteen or twenty minutes without editing or correcting your work—on the topic of your grade school or high school. What experience stands out most in your mind? What moment taught you most about yourself?

Guided Writing

Write a narration in which you tell about some difficult moment that took place in grade school or high school, a moment that taught you something about yourself, your needs, or your cultural background.

1. Provide a concrete description of the school.
2. Tell in correct sequence about the event.

3. Identify people who play a part in this moment.
4. Use concrete, sensory description throughout your essay.
5. Use original similes and metaphors to make your narrative clearer and more dramatic.
6. Use dialogue (or spoken conversation) appropriately in order to advance the narrative.
7. In your conclusion, indicate what your attitude toward this moment is now that you are an adult.
8. Write a title that implies your thesis.

Thinking and Writing Collaboratively

In groups of two or three, read aloud drafts of each other's essays, looking particularly at the use of concrete sensory detail and figures of speech—metaphors and similes. Which images strike you as most clear, original, and easy to visualize?

Writing About the Text

Write an essay that explores the ambivalence of the concluding two sentences. Why is Wong sad? Is the mixed emphasis of these final sentences, for example, felt throughout the essay? Is the ending a surprise?

More Writing Projects

1. Did you have any problems in grade school or high school because of your background or ancestry? Did you know someone who had such problems? Record a specific incident in your journal.
2. Write a narrative paragraph explaining some basic insights about your heritage or culture.
3. Get together with other classmates in a small group and brainstorm or bounce ideas off one another on troubling ethnic, racial, or cultural issues on campus. Write down all the incidents. Then write a narrative essay tracing one episode or connecting a series of them.

Salvation

Langston Hughes

One of the great American writers of the twentieth century, Langston Hughes was born in 1902 in Joplin, Missouri. His parents divorced while he was still an infant, and he was reared by his maternal grandmother, Mary Langston. His grandmother, whose first husband died in the raid on Harpers Ferry as a follower of John Brown, was an abiding influence on Hughes. Nonetheless, he suffered from parental absence; he later said that it was childhood loneliness that led him to books "and the wonderful world in books." Hughes studied for a year at Columbia University and later completed his college education at the historically black Lincoln University in Pennsylvania.

In 1926 Hughes published "The Negro Artist and the Racial Mountain," an essay that served as a manifesto for the Harlem Renaissance, of which he was a leading figure—as a poet, an essayist, a novelist, and a playwright. His poetry brilliantly employed the sounds of African American speech and of jazz, as suggested by the titles of two of his books of poems, *The Weary Blues* (1926) and *Montage of a Dream Deferred* (1951). In 1942 Hughes began to write a weekly column for the *Chicago Defender.* For two decades the column featured an offbeat Harlem character, Jesse B. Simple, Hughes's best-known and most-loved creation. Simple appears in five collections that Hughes edited, beginning with *Simple Speaks His Mind* (1950). This selection, from Hughes's autobiography, *The Big Sea* (1940), tells the story of his "conversion" to Christ. Salvation was a key event in the life of his community, but Hughes tells comically, and poignantly, of how he bowed to pressure by permitting himself to be "saved from sin." Hughes died in 1967.

To learn more about Hughes, click on **More Resources > Chapter 4 > Langston Hughes**

PREREADING: THINKING ABOUT THE ESSAY IN ADVANCE

What is the role of religion today in the lives of most Americans? What role does religion play in your life? In what ways do the religious values of your family compare and contrast with your own?

Words to Watch

dire (par. 3) terrible; disastrous
gnarled (par. 4) knotty; twisted
rounder (par. 6) watchman; policeman
deacons (par. 6) members of the clergy or laypersons who are appointed to help the minister
serenely (par. 7) calmly; tranquilly
knickerbockered (par. 11) dressed in short, loose trousers that are gathered below the knees

1 I was saved from sin when I was going on thirteen. But not really saved. It happened like this. There was a big revival at my Auntie Reed's church. Every night for weeks there had been much preaching, singing, praying, and shouting, and some very hardened sinners had been brought to Christ, and the membership of the church had grown by leaps and bounds. Then just before the revival ended, they held a special meeting for children, "to bring the young lambs to the fold." My aunt spoke of it for days ahead. That night I was escorted to the front row and placed on the mourners' bench with all the other young sinners, who had not yet been brought to Jesus.

2 My aunt told me that when you were saved you saw a light, and something happened to you inside! And Jesus came into your life! And God was with you from then on! She said you could see and hear and feel Jesus in your soul. I believed her. I had heard a great many old people say the same thing and it seemed to me they ought to know. So I sat there calmly in the hot, crowded church, waiting for Jesus to come to me.

3 The preacher preached a wonderful rhythmical sermon, all moans and shouts and lonely cries and dire pictures of hell, and then he sang a song about the ninety and nine safe in the fold, but one little lamb was left out in the cold. Then he said: "Won't you come? Won't you come to Jesus? Young lambs, won't you come?" And he held out his arms to all us young sinners there on the mourners' bench. And the little girls cried. And some of them jumped up and went to Jesus right away. But most of us just sat there.

4 A great many old people came and knelt around us and prayed, old women with jet-black faces and braided hair, old men with work-gnarled hands. And the church sang a song about the lower

lights are burning, some poor sinners to be saved. And the whole building rocked with prayer and song.

Still I kept waiting to *see* Jesus. 5

Finally all the young people had gone to the altar and were saved, but one boy and me. He was a rounder's son named Westley. Westley and I were surrounded by sisters and deacons praying. It was very hot in the church, and getting late now. Finally Westley said to me in a whisper: "God damn! I'm tired o' sitting here. Let's get up and be saved." So he got up and was saved. 6

Then I was left all alone on the mourners' bench. My aunt came and knelt at my knees and cried, while prayers and songs swirled all around me in the little church. The whole congregation prayed for me alone, in a mighty wail of moans and voices. And I kept waiting serenely for Jesus, waiting, waiting—but he didn't come. I wanted to see him, but nothing happened to me. Nothing! I wanted something to happen to me, but nothing happened. 7

I heard the songs and the minister saying: "Why don't you come? My dear child, why don't you come to Jesus? Jesus is waiting for you. He wants you. Why don't you come? Sister Reed, what is this child's name?" 8

"Langston," my aunt sobbed. 9

"Langston, why don't you come? Why don't you come and be saved? Oh, Lamb of God! Why don't you come?" 10

Now it was really getting late. I began to be ashamed of myself, holding everything up so long. I began to wonder what God thought about Westley, who certainly hadn't seen Jesus either, but who was now sitting proudly on the platform, swinging his knickerbockered legs and grinning down at me, surrounded by deacons and old women on their knees praying. God had not struck Westley dead for taking his name in vain or for lying in the temple. So I decided that maybe to save further trouble, I'd better lie, too, and say that Jesus had come, and get up and be saved. 11

So I got up. 12

Suddenly the whole room broke into a sea of shouting, as they saw me rise. Waves of rejoicing swept the place. Women leaped in the air. My aunt threw her arms around me. The minister took me by the hand and led me to the platform. 13

When things quieted down, in a hushed silence, punctuated by a few ecstatic "Amens," all the new young lambs were blessed in the name of God. Then joyous singing filled the room. 14

15 That night, for the last time in my life but one—for I was a big boy twelve years old—I cried. I cried, in bed alone, and couldn't stop. I buried my head under the quilts, but my aunt heard me. She woke up and told my uncle I was crying because the Holy Ghost had come into my life, and because I had seen Jesus. But I was really crying because I couldn't bear to tell her that I had lied, that I had deceived everybody in the church, that I hadn't seen Jesus, and that now I didn't believe there was a Jesus any more, since he didn't come to help me.

BUILDING VOCABULARY

1. Throughout this essay, Hughes selects words dealing with religion to emphasize his ideas. Look up the following words in a dictionary. Then tell what *connotations* (see Glossary) the words have for you.
   a. sin (par. 1)
   b. mourner (par. 1)
   c. lamb (par. 3)
   d. salvation (title)
2. Locate additional words that deal with religion.
3. When Hughes talks about lambs in the fold—and lambs in general—he is using a figure of speech, a comparison (see Chapter 7). What is being compared? How does religion enter into the comparison? Why is it useful as a figure of speech?

THINKING CRITICALLY ABOUT THE ESSAY

Understanding the Writer's Ideas

1. According to Hughes's description, what is a revival meeting like? What is the effect of the "preaching, singing, praying, and shouting" on the "sinners" and the "young lambs"?
2. Why does Westley "see" Jesus? Why does Langston Hughes come to Jesus?
3. How does the author feel after his salvation? Does Hughes finally believe in Christ after his experience? How do you know?

Understanding the Writer's Techniques

1. Is there a thesis statement in the essay? Where is it located?
2. How does the first paragraph serve as an introduction to the narrative?
3. What is the value of description in this essay? List several instances of vivid description that contribute to the narrative.
4. Where does the main narration begin? How much time passes in the course of the action?
5. In narration, it is especially important to have effective *transitions*—or word bridges—from stage to stage in the action. Transitions help the reader shift easily from idea to idea, event to event. List several transition words that Hughes uses.
6. A piece of writing has *coherence* (see Glossary) if all its parts relate clearly and logically to one another. Each sentence grows naturally from the sentence before it; each paragraph grows naturally from the paragraph before it. Is Hughes's essay coherent? Which transitions help advance the action and relate the parts of a single paragraph to one another? Which transitions help connect paragraphs together? How does the way Hughes organized this essay help establish coherence?
7. A story (whether it is true or fiction) has to be told from the first-person ("I, we"), second-person ("you"), or third-person ("he, she, it, they") *point of view.* Point of view in narration sets up the author's position in regard to the action, making the author either a part of the action or an observer of it.
   a. What is the point of view in "Salvation"—is it first, second, or third person?
   b. Why has Hughes chosen this point of view instead of any other? Can you think of any advantages to this point of view?
8. What is your opinion about the last paragraph, the conclusion of this selection? What does it suggest about the mind of a twelve-year-old boy? What does it say about adults' misunderstanding of the activities of children?
9. What does the word *conversion* mean? What conversion really takes place in this piece? How does that compare with what people usually mean when they use *conversion* in a religious sense?

Exploring the Writer's Ideas

1. Hughes seems to suggest that we are forced to do things because of social pressures. Do you agree with his suggestion? Do people do things because their friends or families expect them to? To what extent are we part of the "herd"? Is it possible for a person to retain individuality under pressure from a group? When did you bow to group pressures? When did you resist?
2. Do you find the religious experience in Hughes's essay unusual or extreme? Why or why not? How do *you* define religion?
3. Under what circumstances might a person lie in order to satisfy others? Try to recall a specific episode in which you or someone you know was forced to lie in order to please others.

IDEAS FOR WRITING

Prewriting

Write a few sentences to define *group pressure*. Then give an example or two of a time when you gave in to group pressure or were forced to lie in order to impress others.

Guided Writing

Narrate an event in your life where you (or someone you know) gave in to group pressure or were forced to lie in order to please those around you.

1. Start with a thesis statement.
2. Set the stage for your narrative in the opening paragraph by telling where and when the incident took place. Use specific names for places.
3. Try to keep the action within as brief a time period as possible. If you can write about an event that took no more than a few minutes, so much the better.
4. Use description to sketch in the characters around you. Use colors, actions, sounds, smells, sensations of touch to fill in details of the scene.
5. Use effective transitions of time to link sentences and paragraphs.

6. Use the last paragraph to explain how you felt immediately after the incident.

Thinking and Writing Collaboratively

Exchange drafts of your Guided Writing essay with one other person in the class. Then, write out a brief outline of the events the writer has presented in the narrative. Is the sequence clear? Do the introduction and thesis set the stage appropriately for the sequence of events? Do the transitions link paragraphs and sentences effectively? Return the paper with your written response.

Writing About the Text

Write an essay that speculates about whether, as an adult, Hughes did—or didn't—discover a meaning in his life through religion. Use evidence from this essay, written, after all, when Hughes was an adult.

More Writing Projects

1. Explain in a journal entry an abstract word like *salvation, sin, love,* or *hatred* by narrating an event that reveals the meaning of the word to you.
2. Write an extended paragraph on an important event that affected your relationship with family, friends, or your community during your childhood.
3. Make a list of all the important details that you associate with some religious occasion in your life. Then write a narrative essay on the experience.

Waterloo

Andrew Lam

Andrew Lam was born in Vietnam in 1964, and lives today in San Francisco. In Vietnam, he led a privileged life as the son of General Lam Quang Thi of the Army of the Republic. Lam left Vietnam with his family during the fall of Saigon in April 1975. He attended the University of California, Berkeley, majoring in biochemistry, but gave up plans to attend medical school in favor of embarking on a creative writing degree at San Francisco State University. While still in graduate school, Lam began writing for Pacific News Service and in 1993 won the Outstanding Young Journalist Award from the Society of Professional Journalists. He is the editor of the Pacific News Service, a regular commentator on National Public Radio's "All Things Considered," and a frequent contributor to major magazines and newspapers. Lam is also the author of two collections of essays, *Perfume Dreams* (2005) and *East Meets West* (2010). In this selection from the latter collection, the author weaves an intricate narrative about his father and his own life across cultures.

PREREADING: THINKING ABOUT THE ESSAY IN ADVANCE

Go online and find out about Waterloo. Keep this basic knowledge in mind as you read Lam's essay.

Words to Watch

indelible (par. 1) not capable of being erased, removed, or blotted out
subordinate (par. 5) one who occupies a lower class or rank
knoll (par. 6) a small, round hill; a mound
suave (par. 12) smoothly polite
brocades (par. 13) heavy fabrics with raised interwoven patterns
inextricably (par. 18) not capable of being freed from or disentangled
contemplative (par. 21) deeply thoughtful

There's a moment from many years ago that remains indelible on my mind. I don't remember much on our way there to Waterloo, except that the countryside was streaked and blurred, light green over darker green, all under a persistent gray sky. 1

Father drove. My older sister sat next to him and navigated, a map on her lap. A pouting teenager, I sat behind with Mother, who complained of a mild headache and wondered out loud why we needed to find this distant battlefield, and why we couldn't go freshen up at our hotel after having just arrived in Belgium. 2

"It would be dark by the time we got to Waterloo had we gone to the hotel!" Father snapped. I didn't have to turn to know Mother was rolling her eyes. If she had a choice she would have been at the hotel and would not have been stuck in the backseat as we searched for some pasture where long ago Napoleon was defeated. 3

I thought I saw a sign in French. I said so to Father. Except it took me five minutes to get around to doing this. He cursed, calling me names in French. I responded in French, rather rudely, which surprised him since I rarely spoke the language after we came to America. 4

I felt terrible afterward, and the air in the car was tense. I remember thinking, were we still in the war and I his subordinate, Father, as a three-star general in the South Vietnamese army, no doubt would have me confined to the brig for whatever it was that I said. But it was half a dozen years since the Vietnam War ended and we'd already turned into an American family on a European vacation, complete with a sulky teenager stuck in the backseat and his responsible but equally sullen sister stuck in front, while their quarreling parents kept at it. 5

We finally stopped and asked for directions. Father drove frantically after that. We arrived at Waterloo at last—and it was still bright out when he, my sister, and I rushed up the windswept knoll that overlooked the battlefield. Mother declined the climb and went to the shop to buy souvenirs instead. 6

As we climbed, Father could barely hide his excitement. When we finally stood on top, almost out of breath, he began to narrate the story of the old battle. He pointed wildly: where Napoleon's army stood, which direction the Prussian soldiers came from, and how the Duke of Wellington arrived with his Anglo-Allied forces to turn the tide, defeating Father's favorite military tactician and ultimately exiling him to St. Helena, where he died a few years later. 7

8 "It rained before the battle," he was saying. "It delayed Napoleon, you see, he wanted the ground to dry out a little before the attack. Wellington's army was positioned on Mont-Saint-Jean, but they withstood repeated attacks. By nightfall they counterattacked and drove the French from the field. Then the Prussians broke through Napoleon's right flank as his army was pulling back. There were heavy losses on all sides."

9 I already knew the story. I also knew that Father was, in part, trying to make up for cursing at me by telling the old story. It occurred to me that my older brother would have enjoyed this trip far more than me, had he come, and it also occurred to me later that never once had Father told any of his children a fairy tale, and that most likely he remembered none. But this story of a long-ago battle he had told many times, turning our dining room table into the battlefield, our spoons and chopsticks into battalions, bowls into hills. The Duke of Wellington was drunk. Napoleon was not. But there was nothing he could do, was there, against fate?

10 My father was second in command at I Corps near the end of the war. He was fighting at the DMZ and nearly lost his life but managed to escape back to Saigon. He boarded a naval ship on the day Saigon fell and headed for Guam. After four years in America, in a remarkable feat, he had remade himself at age forty-six into a bank executive. Yet Father's passion remains extraterritorial. Life in America turned out to be, for him and for my mother, a big letdown, a reality defined by disappointment and a deep sense of loss. They would never have in America what had been taken from them in Vietnam.

11 For years their biography of sorts was on display on the mantel in the living room: framed black-and-white photos that my brother managed to take with him, as a foreign student in the United States, before the war ended. In one photo, Father is emerging from his helicopter, silver baton in his left hand, his right reaching out to a young army officer who stands with hunched shoulders under the whirling rotor blades that send wind to press down on the elephant grass. In the distance are the silhouettes of bent-backed farmers in conical hats. Father's face is dark and somber.

12 In another: Mother and Father. "A beautiful couple" would be understating it. She wears her multistranded gold bead necklace outside her lavender brocade. She looks stunning and regal. Father, on the thin side, is dignified and suave in a gray silk suit, a cigarette in his hand. The picture is most definitely posed. It is the

first day of Tet. Behind them, two Chinese brush paintings hang on the wall, one showing a gathering of Chinese fairies on clouds, the other a ferocious dragon descending from a misty mountain.

I don't know why, but sometimes when I think of that picture I have a flashback to being a little boy, hiding inside Mother's walk-in closet, the size of a small room, with windows opened and the breeze swaying the hundred or so painted and embroidered ao dai dresses and brocades. I can still smell the camphor and Mother's perfume, Guerlain. I am lost amid the fabric. From far away I hear my brother's voice calling out: "Father's home! Father's home!" 13

None of the pictures shows how it all ended. There are plenty of those online, under "Fall of Saigon" or "April 30, 1975," "Vietnam evacuation," "Evacuation+Saigon." Tens of thousands of them. Tanks rolling into Saigon; helicopters flying out to awaiting American ships; fear-stricken Vietnamese climbing over the barbed-wire walls of the U.S. embassy. There are many pictures of refugees in crowded cargo planes landing in the Philippines, and I suppose somewhere there are pictures of me and my mother and sister and two grandmothers emerging from one of those planes with small bags in our hands, looking very, very lost. 14

I remember much of the day we left: the wails of a woman, the smell of vomit, night turning into day then back into night, the humming of the plane's engines, then we landed in Subic Bay. Then there's another flight to Guam. Then green tents flapping in the wind, a scorching sun, a very long line for food, adults weeping and screaming as the BBC announces the fall of Saigon. 15

Father left after us, on a warship with hundreds of well-placed others, for the U.S. Navy base at Subic Bay and asylum. He folded away his army uniform, changed into a pair of jeans and a T-shirt, and tossed his gun into the sea. 16

After that, Vietnam, his defeat, his raison d'être, his crucible, was never far from his consciousness. The war, his role in it, have become for him the touchstone of his life. He knows wars, studies wars, has read countless books on battle strategies and warfare. And Napoleon is his hero. 17

After so many years of hearing about Napoleon, it should have been exciting seeing the place finally, yet that late summer afternoon I was no longer intrigued. I was homesick for California. I missed my lover terribly, my first love—our tender kisses, the smell of our sweat. I kept replaying our visit to the ocean, with the breeze carrying the smell of the ocean, how shy we both were, 18 yet how inextricably drawn we were to each other, the orange-red sunset and an unfinished sand castle between us. All I could think of, the entire trip, was getting back to California to possess, to love.

19 This was why it had taken me a long time to process that we were going in the wrong direction. It was also why, while Father talked on, I was miles away. It was only when he himself stopped talking and looked out to the far-off distance, to where I supposed Napoleon fled, that I turned to look too.

20 But I didn't see anything resembling a battlefield. What I saw was a thin gray mist drifting lazily over a green pasture below, and in the cold air I smelled a musky odor of newly upturned earth. The pastoral scene at twilight stirred in me no martial passion, but instead poetry, and an unspeakable yearning.

21 Father talked on. His hair was tousled by the wind, his face contemplative. As I watched him, the image of him on that naval ship near the Philippines came to me suddenly. The government of the Philippines wouldn't let the South Vietnamese ship dock unless all personnel turned in their arms. I imagined him, his face creased with contemplation as he stared at his gun for some time before tossing it into the churning sea below.

22 Something, a welling, a sharp pain, rose suddenly within me then, and it surprised me that I hadn't felt anything like it before, and it felt close to pity. It lodged in my throat and it took some effort not to cry out loud. There on the wind-blown hill, with the statue of a lion on a pedestal above us as a memorial for all fallen soldiers, Father seemed so utterly alone. But then, suddenly, so was I. Frightened and full of my own inarticulate longings, I had to look away for fear that Father might see tears brim in my eyes and think that I, too, was mourning for Napoleon's defeat.

23 Was it not then that my life turned? Was it not then that I, still owned by a collective sense of loss, nevertheless took some profound step out from under his shadow?

24 I went on to college in the fall, in any case, and then, after bouts of bickering with my parents, on to my own writing life, following my own passion. I've been to Europe a few times since then, to Amsterdam and even to Brussels, and though I'd think about it, even entertain the idea, not once did I feel compelled to visit that old battlefield again.

BUILDING VOCABULARY

In this essay, Lam alludes to historical events and figures. Explain the following references:

a. Waterloo (par. 1)
b. Vietnam War (par. 5)
c. Napoleon (par. 7)
d. Prussian soldiers (par. 7)
e. Duke of Wellington (par. 7)
f. DMZ (par. 10)
g. Tet (par. 12)
h. Fall of Saigon (par. 14)

THINKING CRITICALLY ABOUT THE ESSAY

Understanding the Writer's Ideas

1. Where did Lam grow up?
2. Who is Lam's father? What is his background? What is Lam's attitude toward his father? How do you know?
3. Why does Lam's father drag the family to Waterloo?
4. What connection does Lam draw between Waterloo and the Vietnam War?
5. Explain the significance of the flashback that Lam experiences in paragraph 13.
6. Why does Lam yearn for California?
7. What, if anything, does Lam learn from his trip to Waterloo?

Understanding the Writer's Techniques

1. Does this essay have a conventional thesis statement? Why or why not? State the thesis in your own words.
2. How many stories does Lam tell in this essay? List them and explain how these multiple stories converge.
3. Lam organizes his narrative around a series of comparisons. What are these comparative episodes, and precisely how does the author present them?
4. Where and why does Lam use description in this story? What is the effect?

5. Why does Lam pause frequently in his narrative in order to explain the action? Do you find this strategy to be effective or not? Cite examples to justify your response.
6. There are several shifts in tone in this essay. Identify these shifts and their effect.
7. What varieties of conflict does Lam use to highlight the narrative?
8. How do the questions that Lam asks in paragraph 23 prepare you for his conclusion in the final paragraph?

Exploring the Writer's Ideas

1. Lam seems to suggest that we are influenced by history. Do you agree or disagree with his opinion, and why? Might Lam's case be special rather than universal? Explain.
2. We are a nation of immigrants, some older and others more recent. Where do you think Lam stands in relation to this continuum? Where do *you* stand?
3. Lam presents his father as the dominant figure in his family. Is this a conventional aspect of traditional families or immigrant families? How do you both honor family tradition and break away from it—or at least create your own identity not wholly dependent on family mores?

IDEAS FOR WRITING

Prewriting

Freewrite for ten or fifteen minutes about the conflicts in your family, especially as they relate to older and younger family members.

Guided Writing

Write a narrative essay in which you relate an incident or series of related incidents in which you came into conflict with an older family member.

1. Begin with a brief paragraph in which you identify the incident and explain its significance for you.
2. Present and describe the main and secondary characters at appropriate stages in the action.

3. Incorporate more than one type of conflict to propel the action.
4. Compare and contrast the behavior of the principal characters in your story.
5. Pay attention to the tone and mood that you want to convey in the narrative.
6. End on a serious note explaining what you learned from the episode.

Thinking and Writing Collaboratively

In a small group of three or four, exchange the first draft of your Guided Writing essay. After each paper has been read once by each student, discuss each essay as a group, offering support for the best features and suggestions for revision. Pay special attention to the effectiveness of the description and the use the writer makes of various types of conflict.

Writing about the Text

One motif running through Lam's narrative essay is the ambiguous nature of *memory*. How does the author use this motif to both reveal the essence of his family's identity and the problems that memory presents as he tries to construct his own sense of self? Write an essay on this topic.

More Writing Projects

1. Write a journal entry about your personal response to Lam's essay.
2. Summarize what you learned about Waterloo and the Vietnam War from your work on the essay and discussion of it in class.
3. Write a narrative essay of about 1,000 words on the Tet offensive during the Vietnam War.

Mixing Patterns

A Hanging

George Orwell

George Orwell (the pen name of Eric Blair) was born in Bengal, India, in 1903. His parents were members of the British Civil Service in India, and Orwell followed in their footsteps when as a young man he joined the Imperial Police in Burma. But ironically Orwell's experience as a policeman in Burma turned him against British colonialism, as he recounts in a famous essay, "Shooting an Elephant." Indeed, he became a committed socialist but a fiercely antiautocratic one. In the mid-1930s, like many left-wing intellectuals and writers, he went to Spain to fight with the International Brigade in support of the recently elected Popular Front government, then under military attack by Fascist forces led by the ultimately victorious General Franco. Orwell was seriously wounded in the Spanish Civil War, and when the Spanish Communists, under orders from Moscow, attempted to wipe out their allies on the left, he fought against them, finally fleeing for his life.

Orwell became famous in the early years of the Cold War for two prophetic, satirical books fed by his experiences with Communism, books that brilliantly attack totalitarian forms of government. The first, *Animal Farm* (1945), tells the story of the terror tactics and deception that pigs use to take over a farm—but it is an allegorical fable aimed against Stalinism. The second, *Nineteen Eighty-Four* (1949), is a "dystopian" novel, a futuristic novel that portrays the future as dreadful rather than an amazing improvement on life as we have known it (as "utopian" works do). It is to *Nineteen Eighty-Four* that we owe the idea and the expression, "Big Brother is watching you." This selection is one of a group of enormously influential essays by Orwell that employ personal narrative to explore issues of broad concern, in particular social and political issues. In "Politics and the English Language," Orwell maintained that muddy writing, obscurity, inaccuracy, pretentiousness are closely related to a flawed political outlook, and that democracy and equality are strengthened by clear, honest, and direct writing. Saying things clearly, writing to be understood, were, for Orwell, *political* virtues. Orwell died of tuberculosis in 1950.

www.mhhe.com/
shortprose13e

To learn more about Orwell, click on
More Resources > Chapter 4 > George Orwell

PREREADING: THINKING ABOUT THE ESSAY IN ADVANCE

The number of people executed through the system of justice in the United States has increased dramatically over the past few years. How do you explain this increase in the number of executions by lethal injection or the electric chair? Why does U.S. society continue to use capital punishment? Under what circumstances is a person sentenced to capital punishment?

Words to Watch

sodden (par. 1) heavy with water
absurdly (par. 2) ridiculously
desolately (par. 3) gloomily; lifelessly; cheerlessly
prodding (par. 3) poking or thrusting at something
Dravidian (par. 4) any member of a group of intermixed races of southern India and Burma
pariah (par. 6) outcast; a member of a low caste of southern India and Burma
servile (par. 11) slavelike; lacking spirit or independence
reiterated (par. 12) repeated
abominable (par. 13) hateful; disagreeable; unpleasant
timorously (par. 15) fearfully
oscillated (par. 16) moved back and forth between two points
garrulously (par. 20) in a talkative manner
refractory (par. 22) stubborn
amicably (par. 24) in a friendly way; peaceably

It was in Burma, a sodden morning of the rains. A sickly light, like yellow tinfoil, was slanting over the high walls into the jail yard. We were waiting outside the condemned cells, a row of sheds fronted with double bars, like small animal cages. Each cell measured about ten feet by ten and was quite bare within except for a plank bed and a pot of drinking water. In some of them brown silent men were squatting at the inner bars, with their blankets draped round them. These were the condemned men, due to be hanged within the next week or two. 1

One prisoner had been brought out of his cell. He was a Hindu, a puny wisp of a man, with a shaven head and vague liquid eyes. He had a thick, sprouting moustache, absurdly too big for his body, rather like the moustache of a comic man on the films. 2

Six tall Indian warders were guarding him and getting him ready for the gallows. Two of them stood by with rifles with fixed bayonets, while the others handcuffed him, passed a chain through his handcuffs and fixed it to their belts, and lashed his arms tight to his sides. They crowded very close about him, with their hands always on him in a careful, caressing grip, as though all the while feeling him to make sure he was there. It was like men handling a fish which is still alive and may jump back into the water. But he stood quite unresisting, yielding his arms limply to the ropes, as though he hardly noticed what was happening.

3 Eight o'clock struck and a bugle call, desolately thin in the wet air, floated from the distant barracks. The superintendent of the jail, who was standing apart from the rest of us, moodily prodding the gravel with his stick, raised his head at the sound. He was an army doctor, with a grey toothbrush moustache and a gruff voice. "For God's sake hurry up, Francis," he said irritably. "The man ought to have been dead by this time. Aren't you ready yet?"

4 Francis, the head jailer, a fat Dravidian in a white drill suit and gold spectacles, waved his black hand. "Yes sir, yes sir," he bubbled. "All iss satisfactorily prepared. The hangman iss waiting. We shall proceed."

5 "Well, quick march, then. The prisoners can't get their breakfast till this job's over."

6 We set out for the gallows. Two warders marched on either side of the prisoner, with their files at the slope; two others marched close against him, gripping him by arm and shoulder, as though at once pushing and supporting him. The rest of us, magistrates and the like, followed behind. Suddenly, when we had gone ten yards, the procession stopped short without any order or warning. A dreadful thing had happened—a dog, come goodness knows whence, had appeared in the yard. It came bounding among us with a loud volley of barks, and leapt round us wagging its whole body, wild with glee at finding so many human beings together. It was a large woolly dog, half Airedale, half pariah. For a moment it pranced round us, and then, before anyone could stop it, it had made a dash for the prisoner, and jumping up tried to lick his face. Everyone stood aghast, too taken aback even to grab at the dog.

7 "Who let that bloody brute in here?" said the superintendent angrily. "Catch it, someone!"

8 A warder, detached from the escort, charged clumsily after the dog, but it danced and gambolled just out of his reach, taking

everything as part of the game. A young Eurasian jailer picked up a handful of gravel and tried to stone the dog away, but it dodged the stones and came after us again. Its yaps echoed from the jail walls. The prisoner, in the grasp of the two warders, looked on incuriously, as though this was another formality of the hanging. It was several minutes before someone managed to catch the dog. Then we put my handkerchief through its collar and moved off once more, with the dog still straining and whimpering.

It was about forty yards to the gallows. I watched the bare brown back of the prisoner marching in front of me. He walked clumsily with his bound arms, but quite steadily, with that bobbing gait of the Indian who never straightens his knees. At each step his muscles slid neatly into place, the lock of hair on his scalp danced up and down, his feet printed themselves on the wet gravel. And once, in spite of the men who gripped him by each shoulder, he stepped slightly aside to avoid a puddle on the path. 9

It is curious, but till that moment I had never realised what it means to destroy a healthy, conscious man. When I saw the prisoner step aside to avoid the puddle, I saw the mystery, the unspeakable wrongness, of cutting a life short when it is in full tide. This man was not dying, he was alive just as we were alive. All the organs of his body were working—bowels digesting food, skin renewing itself, nails growing, tissues forming—all toiling away in solemn foolery. His nails would still be growing when he stood on the drop, when he was falling through the air with a tenth of a second to live. His eyes saw the yellow gravel and the grey walls, and his brain still remembered, foresaw, reasoned—reasoned even about puddles. He and we were a party of men walking together, seeing, hearing, feeling, understanding the same world; and in two minutes, with a sudden snap, one of us would be gone—one mind less, one world less. 10

The gallows stood in a small yard, separate from the main grounds of the prison, and overgrown with tall prickly weeds. It was a brick erection like three sides of a shed, with planking on top, and above that two beams and a crossbar with the rope dangling. The hangman, a grey-haired convict in the white uniform of the prison, was waiting beside his machine. He greeted us with a servile crouch as we entered. At a word from Francis the two warders, gripping the prisoner more closely than ever, half led, half pushed him to the gallows and helped him clumsily up the 11 ladder. Then the hangman climbed up and fixed the rope round the prisoner's neck.

12 We stood waiting, five yards away. The warders had formed in a rough circle round the gallows. And then, when the noose was fixed, the prisoner began crying out on his god. It was a high, reiterated cry of "Ram! Ram! Ram! Ram!", not urgent and fearful like a prayer or a cry for help, but steady, rhythmical, almost like the tolling of a bell. The dog answered the sound with a whine. The hangman, still standing on the gallows, produced a small cotton bag like a flour bag and drew it down over the prisoner's face. But the sound, muffled by the cloth, still persisted, over and over again: "Ram! Ram! Ram! Ram! Ram!"

13 The hangman climbed down and stood ready, holding the lever. Minutes seemed to pass. The steady, muffled crying from the prisoner went on and on, "Ram! Ram! Ram!" never faltering for an instant. The superintendent, his head on his chest, was slowly poking the ground with his stick; perhaps he was counting the cries, allowing the prisoner a fixed number—fifty, perhaps, or a hundred. Everyone had changed colour. The Indians had gone grey like bad coffee, and one or two of the bayonets were wavering. We looked at the lashed, hooded man on the drop, and listened to his cries—each cry another second of life; the same thought was in all our minds: oh, kill him quickly, get it over, stop that abominable noise!

14 Suddenly the superintendent made up his mind. Throwing up his head he made a swift motion with his stick. "Chalo!" he shouted almost fiercely.

15 There was a clanking noise, and then dead silence. The prisoner had vanished, and the rope was twisting on itself. I let go of the dog, and it galloped immediately to the back of the gallows; but when it got there it stopped short, barked, and then retreated into a corner of the yard, where it stood among the weeds, looking timorously out at us. We went round the gallows to inspect the prisoner's body. He was dangling with his toes pointed straight downwards, very slowly revolving, as dead as a stone.

16 The superintendent reached out with his stick and poked the bare body; it oscillated, slightly. "*He's* all right," said the superintendent. He backed out from under the gallows, and blew out a deep breath. The moody look had gone out of his face quite suddenly. He glanced at his wristwatch. "Eight minutes past eight. Well, that's all for this morning, thank God."

The warders unfixed bayonets and marched away. The dog, sobered and conscious of having misbehaved itself, slipped after them. We walked out of the gallows yard, past the condemned cells with their waiting prisoners, into the big central yard of the prison. The convicts, under the command of warders armed with lathis, were already receiving their breakfast. They squatted in long rows, each man holding a tin pannikin, while two warders with buckets marched round ladling out rice; it seemed quite a homely, jolly scene, after the hanging. An enormous relief had come upon us now that the job was done. One felt an impulse to sing, to break into a run, to snigger. All at once everyone began chattering gaily. 17

The Eurasian boy walking beside me nodded towards the way we had come, with a knowing smile: "Do you know, sir, our friend (he meant the dead man), when he heard his appeal had been dismissed, he pissed on the floor of his cell. From fright—Kindly take one of my cigarettes, sir. Do you not admire my new silver case, sir? From the boxwallah, two rupees eight annas. Classy European style." 18

Several people laughed—at what, nobody seemed certain. 19

Francis was walking by the superintendent, talking garrulously: "Well, sir, all hass passed off with the utmost satisfactoriness. It wass all finished—flick! like that. It iss not always so—oah, no! I have known cases where the doctor wass obliged to go beneath the gallows and pull the prisoner's legs to ensure decease. Most disagreeable!" 20

"Wriggling about, eh? That's bad," said the superintendent. 21

"Ach, sir, it iss worse when they become refractory! One man, I recall, clung to the bars of hiss cage when we went to take him out. You will scarcely credit, sir, that it took six warders to dislodge him, three pulling at each leg. We reasoned with him. My dear fellow, we said, think of all the pain and trouble you are causing to us! But no, he would not listen! Ach, he wass very troublesome!" 22

I found that I was laughing quite loudly. Everyone was laughing. Even the superintendent grinned in a tolerant way. "You'd better all come out and have a drink," he said quite genially. "I've got a bottle of whisky in the car. We could do with it." 23

We went through the big double gates of the prison, into the road. "Pulling at his legs!" exclaimed a Burmese magistrate suddenly, and burst into a loud chuckling. We all began laughing again. At that moment Francis's anecdote seemed extraordinarily funny. We all had a drink together, native and European alike, quite amicably. The dead man was a hundred yards away. 24

BUILDING VOCABULARY

1. Use *context clues* (see Glossary) to make an "educated guess" about the definitions of the following words in italics. Before you guess, look back to the paragraph for clues. Afterward, check your guess in a dictionary.
   - **a.** *condemned* men (par. 1)
   - **b.** puny *wisp* of a man (par. 2)
   - **c.** Indian *warders* (par. 2)
   - **d.** careful, *caressing* grip (par. 2)
   - **e.** stood *aghast* (par. 6)
   - **f.** it danced and *gambolled* (par. 8)
   - **g.** *solemn* foolery (par. 10)
   - **h.** armed with *lathis* (par. 17)
   - **i.** a tin *pannikin* (par. 17)
   - **j.** quite *genially* (par. 23)
2. What are definitions for the words below? Look at words within them, which you may be able to recognize.
   - **a.** moodily
   - **b.** dreadful
   - **c.** Eurasian
   - **d.** incuriously
   - **e.** formality

THINKING CRITICALLY ABOUT THE ESSAY

Understanding the Writer's Ideas

1. The events in the essay occur in a country in Asia, Burma (also called Myanmar, since 1989). Describe in your own words the specific details of the action.
2. Who are the major characters in this essay? Why might you include the dog as a major character?
3. In a narrative essay the writer often tells the events in chronological order. Examine the following events from "A Hanging." Arrange them in the order in which they occurred.
   - **a.** A large woolly dog tries to lick the prisoner's face.
   - **b.** A Eurasian boy talks about his silver case.
   - **c.** The superintendent signals "Chalo!" to the hangman.
   - **d.** One prisoner, a Hindu, is brought from his cell.

  - **e.** Francis discusses with the superintendent a prisoner who had to be pulled off the bars of his cage.
  - **f.** The prisoner steps aside to avoid a puddle as he marches to the gallows.

4. What is the author's opinion of *capital punishment* (legally killing someone who has disobeyed the laws of society)? How does the incident with the puddle suggest that opinion, even indirectly?

Understanding the Writer's Techniques

1. What is the main point that the writer wishes to make in this essay? Which paragraph tells the author's thesis most clearly? Which sentence in that paragraph best states the main idea of the essay?

2. In the first paragraph of the essay, we see clear images such as "brown silent men were squatting at the inner bars, with their blankets draped around them." The use of color and action makes an instant appeal to our sense of sight.

  - **a.** What images in the rest of the essay do you find most vivid?
  - **b.** Which sentence gives the best details of sound?
  - **c.** What word pictures suggest action and color?
  - **d.** Where do you find words that describe a sensation of touch?

3. In order to make their images clearer, writers use *figurative language* (see Glossary). "A Hanging" is especially rich in *similes,* which are comparisons using the word *like* or *as.*

  - **a.** What simile does Orwell use in the first paragraph in order to let us see how the light slants over the jail yard walls? How does the simile make the scene clearer?
  - **b.** What other simile does Orwell use in the first paragraph?
  - **c.** Discuss the similes in the paragraphs listed below. What are the things being compared? Are the similes, in your opinion, original? How do they contribute to the image the author intends to create?
    - **(1)** It was like men handling a fish (par. 2)
    - **(2)** a thick sprouting moustache . . . rather like the moustache of a comic man on the films (par. 2)
    - **(3)** It was a high, reiterated cry . . . like the tolling of a bell. (par. 12)

(4) The Indians had gone grey like bad coffee (par. 13)
(5) He was dangling with his toes pointed straight downwards, very slowly revolving, as dead as a stone. (par. 15)

4. You know that an important feature of narration is the writer's ability to look at a brief span of time and to expand that moment with specific language.
   a. How has Orwell limited the events in "A Hanging" to a specific moment in time and place?
   b. How does the image "a sodden morning of the rains" in paragraph 1 set the mood for the main event portrayed in the essay? What is the effect of the image "brown silent men"? Why does Orwell describe the prisoner as "a puny wisp of a man, with a shaven head and vague liquid eyes" (par. 2)? Why does the author present him in almost a comic way?
   c. What is the effect of the image about the bugle call in paragraph 3? Why does Orwell create the image of the dog trying to lick the prisoner's face (par. 6)? How does it contribute to his main point? In paragraph 12, Orwell tells us that the dog whines. Why does he give that detail? Discuss the value of the images about the dog in paragraphs 15 and 17.
   d. Why does Orwell offer the image of the prisoner stepping aside "to avoid a puddle on the path"? How does it advance the point of the essay? What is the effect of the image of the superintendent poking the ground with his stick (par. 13)?
   e. What is the importance of the superintendent's words in paragraph 3? What is the value of the Eurasian boy's conversation in paragraph 18? How does the dialogue in paragraphs 20 to 24 contribute to Orwell's main point?
   f. Why has Orwell left out information about the crime the prisoner committed? How would you feel about the prisoner if you knew he were, say, a rapist, a murderer, a molester of children, or a heroin supplier?
5. Analyze the point of view in the essay. Is the "I" narrator an observer, a participant, or both? Is he neutral or involved? Support your opinion.

6. In "A Hanging," Orwell skillfully uses several forms of *irony* to support his main ideas. Irony, in general, is the use of language to suggest the opposite of what is said. First, there is *verbal irony,* which involves a contrast between what is said and what is actually meant. Second, there is *irony of situation,* where there is a contrast between what is expected or thought appropriate and what actually happens. Then, there is *dramatic irony,* in which there is a contrast between what a character says and what the reader (or the audience) actually knows or understands.

- **a.** In paragraph 2, why does Orwell describe the prisoner as a *comic* type? Why does he emphasize the prisoner's *smallness?* Why does Orwell write that the prisoner "hardly noticed what was happening"? Why might this be called ironic?
- **b.** When the dog appears in paragraph 6, how is its behavior described? How do the dog's actions contrast with the situation?
- **c.** What is the major irony that Orwell analyzes in paragraph 10?
- **d.** In paragraph 11, how does the fact that one prisoner is being used to execute another prisoner strike you?
- **e.** Why is the superintendent's remark in paragraph 16—"*He's* all right"—a good example of verbal irony?
- **f.** After the hanging, the men engage in seemingly normal actions. However, Orwell undercuts these actions through the use of irony. Find at least two examples of irony in paragraphs 17 to 24.

✷ MIXING PATTERNS

"Description," we say in the introduction to Chapter 3, "is frequently used to make abstract ideas more *concrete.*" In this essay, basically a narrative, how does Orwell use description to make an abstract idea—capital punishment is wrong—concrete? Identify three or four examples.

Exploring the Writer's Ideas

1. Orwell is clearly against capital punishment. Why might you agree or disagree with him? Are there any crimes for which capital punishment is acceptable to you? If not, what should society do with those convicted of serious crimes?
2. Do you think the method used to perform capital punishment has anything to do with the way we view it? Is death by hanging or firing squad worse than death by gas or by the electric chair? Or are they all the same? Socrates—a Greek philosopher convicted of conspiracy—was forced to drink *hemlock,* a fast-acting poison. Can you accept that?
3. Orwell shows a variety of reactions people have to an act of execution. Can you believe the way the people behave here? Why? How do you explain the large crowds that gathered to watch public executions in Europe in the sixteenth and seventeenth centuries?

IDEAS FOR WRITING

Prewriting

Make two columns on a sheet of paper that you have headed "Capital Punishment." In one column, jot down all the reasons you can think of in favor of capital punishment. In the other column, indicate all the reasons you can think of against it.

Guided Writing

Write a narrative essay in which you tell about a punishment you either saw or received. Use sensory language, selecting your details carefully. At one point in your paper—as Orwell does in paragraph 10—state your opinion or interpretation of the punishment clearly.

1. Use a number of images that name colors, sounds, smells, and actions.
2. Try to write at least three original similes. Think through your comparisons carefully. Make sure they are logical. Avoid overused comparisons like "He was white as a ghost."

3. Set your narrative in time and place. Tell the season of the year and the place in which the event occurred.
4. Fill in details of the setting. Show what the surroundings look like.
5. Name people by name. Show details of their actions. Quote some of their spoken dialogue.
6. Use the first-person point of view.

Thinking and Writing Collaboratively

In small groups, read drafts of each other's essays for the Guided Writing activity. Look especially at the point at which the writer states an opinion about or interprets the punishment received. Does the writer adequately explain the event? What insights has the writer brought to the moment by analyzing it? How could either the narrative itself or the interpretation be made clearer or more powerful?

Writing About the Text

Write an essay in which you consider why Orwell chose to include the dog in this essay. How would the essay be different without the dog? Do you think the dog was *actually* present at the scene of the hanging, or do you suspect that Orwell made him up?

More Writing Projects

1. Narrate in your journal an event that turned out differently from what you expected—a blind date, a picnic, a holiday. Try to stress the irony of the situation.
2. Write a narrative paragraph that describes a vivid event in which you hid your true feelings about the event, such as a postelection party, the wedding of someone you disliked, a job interview, a visit to the doctor.
3. Write an editorial for your college newspaper supporting or attacking the idea of capital punishment. Communicate your position through the use of real or hypothetical narration of a relevant event.

SUMMING UP: CHAPTER 4

1. Orwell's essay has remained one of the outstanding essays of our age. It is widely anthologized and often read in English composition classes. How do you account for its popularity? Would you consider it the best essay in this chapter or in the four chapters you have read in this book so far? Why or why not? Write an essay in which you analyze and evaluate "A Hanging."
2. Both Langston Hughes and Andrew Lam make serious points about their childhoods. Using their essays as a starting point, write an essay about your childhood view of an adult decision.
3. What have you learned about writing strong narratives from the writers in this chapter? What generalizations can you draw? What "rules" can you derive? Write an essay called "How to Write Narratives" based on what you have learned from Wong, Hughes, Lam, and (or) Orwell. Make specific references to the writer(s) of your choice.
4. Hughes's essay highlights the role of religion in life. Write an essay in which you narrate an important religious experience that you remember.
5. Writers often use narrative to re-create a memory, as with the essays in this chapter. But our memories, especially of emotional moments from long ago, are notoriously unreliable. How do the writers in this chapter deal—or not deal—with the problem of the possible unreliability of memory? How much would it matter if some of the incidents narrated here were *in*-accurately recalled by the writer, or even altered to make a better essay?
6. Compare and contrast the attitudes toward language as reflected in the essays of Amy Tan (pp. 39–45) and Elizabeth Wong (pp. 144–146).
7. Hughes and Orwell explore the ambiguities involved in thinking or feeling things that distinguish them from most people around them—such as being a skeptic in an evangelical church or a colonial policeman opposed to colonialism. Compare and contrast how these writers treat the situation of a person who does not conform to society's values and beliefs.

✷ FROM SEEING TO WRITING

Write a narrative essay in which you tell what you think is the story of the photograph reprinted here. Develop your thesis, present lively details to hold your reader's attention, and introduce your details in a sequence that is easy to follow.

CHAPTER 5

Process Analysis

WHAT IS PROCESS ANALYSIS?

Process analysis explains to a reader how to do something, how something works, or how something occurs. Like narration, it is a form of sequencing or presentation of events in order, or taking apart a process in order better to understand how it functions. This kind of writing is often called *expository* because it *exposes* or shows us information. If you use cookbooks, you are encountering process analysis each time you read a recipe. If you are setting up a new DVD, you may wish the writer of the manual were more adept at writing process analysis when you find the steps hard to follow. "How to" writing can therefore give the reader steps for carrying out a process. The writer might also analyze the steps someone took already in completing a process, such as explaining how Harriet Tubman organized the Underground Railroad or how women won the right to vote.

Planning a good process analysis requires the writer to include all the essential steps. Be sure you have all the tools or ingredients needed. Arrange the steps in the correct sequence. Like all good writing, a good process essay requires a thesis to tell the reader the *significance* of the process. The writer can tell the reader how to do something, but also should inform the reader about the usefulness or importance of the endeavor.

In this chapter, Mark Shiffrin and Avi Silberschatz explain how to stop people from using cellphones while driving. Nora Ephron injects humor into her essay on how to foil a terrorist plot. From Ernest Hemingway, we learn how to make our next experience of camping a success. And Henry Louis Gates Jr. explains how to "de-kink" hair. As you read about these processes, watch how each writer uses the same technique to achieve a different result.

HOW DO WE READ PROCESS ANALYSIS?

Identify what process the writer is going to analyze. As you read, make a quick outline of the steps the writer introduces.

Watch the use of transitions as the writer moves from one step to the next.

Assess the audience that the writer has aimed at. Is the writer addressing innocents or experts? If the writer's purpose was to explain how to prepare beef stew, he would give different directions to a college freshman who has never cooked before than he would give to a cooking class at the Culinary Institute of America, where everyone was familiar with the fundamentals of cooking. Ask yourself, then: Is there enough information in the analysis? too much?

How does the writer try to make the piece lively? Does it sound as dry as a technical manual, or is there an engaging tone?

HOW DO WE WRITE PROCESS ANALYSIS?

Decide to analyze a process with which you are very familiar. Unless you can do it well yourself, you won't be able to instruct or inform your readers.

Process begins with a good shopping list. Once you have your topic, make lists of ingredients or tools.

Arrange the essential steps in logical order. Don't assume your reader already knows how to do the process. As you know from those often incomprehensible instructions for putting together a child's toy, the reader should be given *every* step.

List the steps to *avoid* when carrying out the procedure.

If possible, actually try out the process, using your list as a guide, if you are presenting a method for a tangible product, like making an omelet. Or imagine that you are explaining the procedure over the telephone.

If your topic is abstract, like telling someone how to become an American citizen, read it aloud to a willing listener to see if he or she can follow the steps clearly.

Use *definition* to explain terms the reader may not know, especially if you are presenting a technical process. At the same time, avoid jargon. Make the language as plain as possible.

Describe the appearance of the product or *compare* an unfamiliar item with a familiar one.

Be sure to think about your audience. Link the audience to the purpose of the process.

Formulate a thesis statement that tells what the process is, and why it is a good process to know.

Sample thesis statement:

> Buying and renovating an old car is a time-consuming process, but the results are worthwhile.

Writing the Draft

Write a rough draft. Turn your list into an essay by developing the steps into sentences, using your thesis to add significance and coherence to the process you are presenting. Don't just list; analyze the procedure as you go along. Keep in mind the techniques of writers like Ernest Hemingway, who doesn't just cook a trout but uses the process to represent the whole morality of "doing things right," raising his process analysis beyond the ordinary.

Add transitions when necessary to alert the reader that a new step is coming. The most common transition words help a reader to follow steps: *first, second, third; first, next, after, last.*

Proofread, revise, and create a final draft.

A STUDENT PARAGRAPH: PROCESS ANALYSIS

Process analysis lends itself to a variety of approaches, ranging from a methodical step-by-step explanation of a task such as how to prepare a pie, to assessment of a series of related historical events. As you read the following one-paragraph composition, consider the student's success in providing the reader with a flexible approach to a typical problem.

Finding the right used car can be a real challenge. Unless you are totally open to possibilities, the first step in the process is to focus on one make and model that interests you. Next, you should consult the Blue Book, which lists car makes and models by

Topic sentence

Phrase "the first step" starts the process.

"Next" signals the second step.

year, and provides a rough guide to fair prices based on condition. It's a good idea to have the book handy before moving to the next stage in your search; you can probably disqualify a number of cars based on asking price alone. (If the asking price is significantly higher than the Blue Book suggests, the seller is not always trying to hoodwink you. There might be a good reason for the price—exceptionally good condition, or an unusual number of "add-ons," for example. Still, it makes sense to use caution in these cases.) At this point, you are ready to start the actual search, beginning with a scanning of these resources. Don't limit your search to these resources, however; continue your hunt by consulting more local venues, such as campus bulletin-board postings. There are several other promising routes to finding the wheels of your dreams: car rental companies usually sell off their rentals after they've reached a ripe old age—sometimes a venerable 3 to 5 years! Police auctions are another possibility, though the successful bidder is usually required to plunk down cash for the car right away, and the cars come with no warranty—you can find a real bargain here, but it's only really a safe bet if you can take along a mechanic. In fact, consulting a good mechanic should *always* be the last step in the process: after you have located the car of your dreams, get an inspection before you write that check, just to make sure that your dream machine doesn't explode.

Parenthetical remark qualifies earlier statement.

"At this point" moves reader to third step.

"Continue your hunt by consulting" advances the process.

"Several other promising routes" adds to process.

Concluding step cautions, adds humor.

Thumbs on the Wheel

Mark A. Shiffrin and Avi Silberschatz

Mark A. Shiffrin is a lawyer who lives in New Haven, Connecticut, and writes on technology and policy issues. During the administration of President George H. W. Bush he served as Deputy General Counsel of the U.S. Department of Education. In state government he served as Connecticut's Commissioner of Consumer Protection. His writings have appeared in publications including the *New York Times, Boston Globe, Washington Post, Hartford Courant,* and *Industry Standard.* **Avi Silberschatz** is a professor of computer science and the Chair of the Computer Science Department at Yale University. He is a member of the Connecticut Academy of Science and Engineering. Silberschatz writes about the need to regulate the Internet so that we can use it in a free manner. In this editorial opinion piece for the *New York Times*, written in 2009, the two writers look at ways to prevent cellphone use by drivers of automobiles, a major cause of highway accidents.

PREREADING: THINKING ABOUT THE ESSAY IN ADVANCE

When do you find it most convenient to use a cellphone? Do you send and receive text messages at will, or do you impose any restrictions for yourself, like no texting in class or while driving? Why or why not?

Words to Watch

distractions (par. 1) interruptions
tweak (par. 2) adjust; fine-tune
equivalent (par. 4) equal
arguably (par. 5) possibly; perhaps
tether (par. 5) joining; tying
distracting (par. 6) disturbing; attention-drawing
impeded (par. 6) obstructed; hindered
innovations (par. 7) novelties; new ideas

1 President Obama has forbidden federal employees from texting while driving. The federal Transportation Department plans to do the same for commercial-truck and Interstate-bus drivers. And

support is building in Congress for legislation that would require states to outlaw texting or e-mailing while driving. Such distractions cause tens of thousands of deaths each year.

2 But the way to stop people from using cellphones while driving is not to make it a crime. Too many drivers value convenience more than safety and would assume they wouldn't get caught. A more effective approach is to get telecommunications companies to tweak technology to make it difficult or impossible to text and drive.

3 When a cellphone is used in a moving car, its signal must be handed off from one cell tower to the next along the route. This process tells the service provider that the phone is in motion. Cellphone towers could be engineered to not transmit while a phone is traveling. After a phone had stopped moving for a certain amount of time—three minutes, maybe—it would be able to transmit again.

4 Another solution would be to install hardware in cars and software in cellphones that would disable some phone functions when cars are moving. It would be the electronics equivalent of putting a guard on a knife handle or a grill over the blades of a fan.

5 This would, of course, affect passengers in moving cars as well as drivers. The inconvenience would arguably be worth it. But it is also easy to imagine technology that would allow only passengers to use their phones—by tethering them to devices, placed on the passenger side of the car, that would override the system.

6 Just as the text function could be disabled from a moving vehicle, so could the talk function be limited—at least when used without hands-free operating technology like Bluetooth. Given the evidence suggesting that even hands-free operation is dangerously distracting to drivers, we may need to ask whether all cellphone use should be technologically impeded in moving cars. There is nothing unreasonable in expecting drivers to park before making calls.

7 While texting behind the wheel is a problem today, innovations may give rise to other risky behaviors within a few years, if not months. The best solutions will come not from lawmakers plugging holes in the dike, but from the engineers finding ways to make products safer.

BUILDING VOCABULARY

The writers employ a number of words that apply to the technology of cellphones and their use. Look up the following words and terms and write clear definitions.

a. texting (par. 1)
b. telecommunications (par. 2)
c. cell tower (par. 3)
d. service provider (par. 3)
e. transmit (par. 3)
f. install (par. 4)
g. disable (par. 4)
h. hardware (par. 4)
i. software (par. 4)
j. override (par. 5)

THINKING CRITICALLY ABOUT THE ESSAY

Understanding the Writers' Ideas

1. What do Shiffrin and Silberschatz say about the use of cellphones while driving?
2. How do they feel about laws passed to prevent cellphone use by a driver in an automobile?
3. What do the writers believe that we should program cell towers to do?
4. What kinds of modifications would they propose for automobiles in order to prevent drivers from using cellphones?
5. Why do the writers believe that we might consider preventing all cellphone use in moving cars?

Understanding the Writers' Techniques

1. In what ways is this a process essay? What process do the writers analyze?
2. What is the thesis in this selection? Who is the audience? Clearly, the writers don't expect a general reader of a daily newspaper to carry out their recommended steps to curtail telephone use. So for whom are Shiffrin and Silberschatz writing? What is their purpose?
3. How would you characterize the style of this essay? Examine word choice, sentence length, and paragraph length. Why have the writers chosen the style that they use?
4. What does the title mean? We rarely think of thumbs as essential for steering an automobile. What situation does the title aim to counteract?

5. Which transitions have the writers used to connect the paragraphs in this selection? Are they effective? Why or why not?
6. What does the phrase "plugging holes in the dike" mean? Why have the writers used it to refer to lawmakers?
7. How do the introductory and concluding paragraphs compare? What ideas do they both convey? How effective is the strategy of repeating important ideas at the beginning and end of this essay?

Exploring the Writers' Ideas

1. What is your view on cellphone use in automobiles? Should we somehow prevent drivers of automobiles from using phones in their cars while driving? Should we prevent all cellphone use in cars unless the cars are completely stopped? Why or why not?
2. The writers believe that making it a crime to use a cellphone while driving will not prevent people from using it. Why might you agree or disagree? Should we be pursuing legislation to outlaw the use of cellphones in cars? Why or why not?
3. The writers say that only making products safer will prevent dangerous use of equipment. Why might you agree or disagree? Why might manufacturers of cellphones support proper use? Why, on the other hand, might they oppose efforts to curtail texting and e-mailing while a person is driving?

IDEAS FOR WRITING

Prewriting

Freewrite for about fifteen minutes on why you think many people choose to send and receive text messages as opposed to speaking on the telephone.

Guided Writing

Write a process essay in which you identify how to prevent some other destructive behavior among humans: how to stop teenagers from smoking, for example, or how to prevent child abuse or drug use or obesity.

1. Start your essay by identifying steps that others may have taken or recommended and explain why they might not work. Or, if

you think that they are working, explain why your plan will supplement and improve on steps already being implemented.
2. Propose a thesis that identifies your subject and states your attitude toward or opinion about it.
3. Like the writers of "Thumbs on the Wheel," be sure to suggest more than one step in the process of preventing the behavior you have chosen to write about.
4. Provide any technical information as needed and define any terms with which your readers may not be familiar.
5. Use transitions to connect your paragraphs smoothly.
6. In your conclusion, return to the ideas that you expressed in your introduction. Remind your reader of the other (failed or only partially successful) efforts that your suggestions will improve upon.
7. Give your essay an effective title.

Thinking and Writing Collaboratively

Working in small groups, take a survey of people on your campus about how, when, and where they use cellphones for text messaging and other available technological functions on the telephone. How do most people feel about texting while driving an automobile? in a movie theater? at a social setting like a restaurant?

Writing About the Text

Write an essay about the style and word choice that Shiffrin and Silberschatz use in this piece. Why have they chosen a simple and direct style? Why have they written very short paragraphs?

More Writing Projects

1. In your journal, write about your own cellphone use and whether or not you believe you use it dangerously at times.
2. Try to imagine the technologies that you think you or your children will face in the next decades and the potentially "risky behaviors" that the technologies might bring about. Write a paragraph or two to address the issue.
3. Write a process essay about how to purchase and (or) use appropriately some modern technology—3D television, for example, or Bluetooth, Blackberry, iTouch, iPad, or some similar product—so that it doesn't become a danger.

How to Foil a Terrorist Plot in Seven Simple Steps

Nora Ephron

Nora Ephron has enjoyed a varied and successful career as a reporter, columnist, essayist, novelist, screenwriter, movie director, and producer. Born in New York City in 1941 but raised in Beverly Hills, where her parents were famous screenwriters, Ephron returned to the East Coast to attend Wellesley College (BA, 1962). Subsequently she was hired as a reporter for the *New York Post*, then did freelance work before joining the staff at *New York* and *Esquire*. She achieved notoriety with the publication of *Heartburn* (1983), a comic novel recounting Ephron's highly publicized breakup with her second husband, Watergate journalist Carl Bernstein. Ephron wrote the screenplay for *Heartburn* (1986), and wrote and/or produced the films *Silkwood* (1983), *When Harry Met Sally* (1989), *Sleepless in Seattle* (1993), *You've Got Mail* (1998), and *Bewitched* (2005). Known as one of the most powerful women in Hollywood, Ephron is also an acclaimed essayist whose collections include *Wallflower at the Orgy* (1970), *Crazy Salad* (1975), and *I Feel Bad About My Neck* (2006). The following selection, which appeared in the online *Huffington Post* on June 4, 2007, is typical of Ephron's witty, often quirky style.

PREREADING: THINKING ABOUT THE ESSAY IN ADVANCE

Writers tend to view terrorists (and terrorism) as a serious subject. What is the value or appropriateness of treating serious subjects in comic fashion?

Words to Watch

foil (par. 1) to keep from being successful; frustrate
deter (par. 2) to keep a person from doing something; prevent
impending (par. 4) about to happen
remuneration (par. 6) reward; pay; compensation
feasible (par. 7) capable of being done or carried out; possible

1. In order to foil a terrorist plot, you must first find a terrorist plot. This is not easy. 1

2. Not just anyone can find and then foil a terrorist plot. You must have an incentive. The best incentive is to be an accused 2

felon, looking at a long prison term. Under such circumstances, your lawyer will explain to you, you may be able to reduce your sentence by acting as an informant in a criminal case, preferably one involving terrorists.

3 3. The fact that you do not know any actual terrorists should not in any way deter you. Necessity is the mother of invention: if you can find the right raw material—a sad, sick, lonely, drunk, deranged, disgruntled or just plain anti-American Muslim somewhere in the United States—you can make your very own terrorist.

4 4. Now the good part begins. Money! The FBI will give you lots of money to take your very own terrorist out to lots of dinners where you, wearing a wire, can record yourself making recommendations to him about possible targets and weapons that might be used in the impending terrorist attack that your very own terrorist is going to mastermind, with your help. It will even buy you a computer so you can go to Google Earth in order to show your very own terrorist a "top secret" aerial image of the target you have suggested.

5 5. More money!! The FBI will give you even more money to travel to foreign countries with your very own terrorist, and it will make suggestions about terrorist groups you can meet while in said foreign countries.

6 6. Months and even years will pass in this fashion, while you essentially get the FBI to pay for everything you do. (Incidentally, be sure your lawyer negotiates your expense account well in advance, or you may be forced—as the informant was in the Buffalo terrorist case—to protest your inadequate remuneration by setting yourself on fire in front of the White House.)

7 7. At a certain point, something will go wrong. You may have trouble recruiting other people to collaborate with your very own terrorist, who is, as you yourself know, just an ordinary guy in a really bad mood. Or, alternatively, the terrorist cell you have carefully cobbled together may malfunction and fail to move forward—probably as a result of sheer incompetence or of simply not having been genuinely serious about the acts of terrorism you were urging it to commit. At this point, you may worry that the FBI is going to realize that there isn't much of a terrorist plot going on here at all, just a case of entrapment. Do not despair: the FBI is way ahead of you. The FBI knows perfectly well what's going on. The FBI has as much at stake as you do. So before it can be obvious to the world that there's no case, the FBI will arrest your very own terrorist,

hold a press conference and announce that a huge terrorist plot has been foiled. It will of course be forced to admit that this plot did not proceed beyond the pre-planning stage, that no actual weapons or money were involved, and that the plot itself was "not technically feasible," but that will not stop the story from becoming a front-page episode all over America and, within hours, boilerplate for all the Republican politicians who believe that you need to arrest a "homegrown" terrorist now and then to justify the continuing war in Iraq. Everyone will be happy, except for the schmuck you shmikeled into becoming a terrorist, and no one really cares about him anyway.

So congratulations. You have foiled a terrorist plot. Way to go. 8

BUILDING VOCABULARY

1. Examine the words and definitions in the Words to Watch section, and write an original sentence that uses each word correctly.
2. Consult a specialized dictionary of slang terms in order to explain the expression "the schmuck you shmikeled" (par. 7).

THINKING CRITICALLY ABOUT THE ESSAY

Understanding the Writer's Ideas

1. Briefly summarize Ephron's strategy for foiling a terrorist plot.
2. Why, according to Ephron, is a convicted felon the ideal informant?
3. What does Ephron mean when she writes "Necessity is the mother of invention" (par. 3)? Explain this expression in the context of the paragraph and essay.
4. Why should the informant have a lawyer?
5. What is Ephron's attitude toward the FBI? How do you know?
6. In the final analysis, according to Ephron, is it important that a terrorist or terrorist plot might not exist, despite what authorities and the media claim? Justify your response.

Understanding the Writer's Techniques

1. Why doesn't Ephron ever state a thesis directly in this essay? What *is* her main idea? How does she present and develop this idea?
2. For whom is Ephron writing this essay? How does her *tone* (see Glossary) reflect her audience?
3. What is Ephron's level of *diction?* (See Glossary.) Is her language formal or informal, and why? Cite specific examples to support your response.
4. Why do you suppose Ephron numbers all her paragraphs (except the last one)? In what way is this strategy part of her process analysis?
5. What are the steps in the process that Ephron presents? Are these steps mutually exclusive or do they overlap? Explain.
6. Many of Ephron's paragraphs are brief, no more than a sentence or two, including the introductory and concluding paragraphs. What is Ephron's purpose in designing such short paragraphs?
7. Would you say that Ephron is ironic in this essay? Is she ever *sarcastic* or *satiric?* (See Glossary.) Point to places in the essay that demonstrate these varieties of humor.

Exploring the Writer's Ideas

1. Although this essay is written in a humorous vein, there are certainly many serious implications to the subject and content. Discuss your position on such issues as terrorism, informants, the FBI, "anti-American Muslims," the media, and the war in Iraq.
2. Is it possible for anyone reading this essay to take it seriously? Is it possible for someone to be offended? Why or why not?
3. Has Ephron presented a balanced picture of the issues or is her claim or main argument one-sided? Support your opinion with specific references to the essay.

IDEAS FOR WRITING

Prewriting

Write a preliminary outline for a process essay dealing with some aspect of current events.

Guided Writing

Write a humorous essay on a serious subject drawn from politics, economics, or popular culture. As preparation for your essay of process analysis, provide a title beginning "How to___________," and fill in the blank.

1. In imitation of Ephron, begin with a numbered paragraph and continue this strategy throughout the essay.
2. In a brief introductory paragraph, explain your thesis and the basic purpose in presenting the process.
3. Introduce a new step or procedure for each successive paragraph. Provide at least five steps, procedures, or rules that will lead readers through the process.
4. Employ a colloquial style of writing.
5. Try using irony and satire to make your point. (Avoid any sarcasm, which generally is inappropriate in college writing.)
6. Conclude on a note that suggests you are highly critical of the process you have just analyzed.

Thinking and Writing Collaboratively

With one or two other classmates, log onto the *Huffington Post* to find out more about the site and its contributors (including Ephron). Take notes, and share your findings with the class.

Writing About the Text

Satire is one of the more difficult forms to master. Write an analysis of Ephron's satiric method in "How to Foil a Terrorist Plot in Seven Simple Steps," and evaluate her relative effectiveness in using this strategy.

More Writing Projects

1. In your journal, write an entry exploring your feelings about the issue of terrorism.
2. Compose a humorous paragraph in which you list the steps involved in managing an important activity—for instance, getting along with a roommate, doing the laundry, getting to class on time.
3. Write an essay giving directions and providing steps that should be taken in the event of a natural or "homegrown" disaster.

Camping Out

Ernest Hemingway

Through his life and his work, Ernest Hemingway influenced world culture more than any other American writer of his time. Born in Oak Park, Illinois, in 1899, Hemingway began his writing career as a reporter, and throughout his life he worked for newspapers, often on the front lines of armed conflicts such as the Spanish Civil War (1936–1939) and the Second World War (1939–1945). His adventures brought him close to death several times—in the Spanish Civil War when shells landed in his hotel room, in the Second World War when he was struck by a taxi during a blackout, and in 1954 when his plane crashed in Africa.

Writing in an unadorned, unemotional but taut style, Hemingway placed at the heart of his fiction the search for meaning in a world disenchanted with old ideals. In his life as in his writing he was drawn to individuals committed to the art of doing things well regardless of the larger world's lack of direction or faith; he especially admired those who achieved grace or beauty in the face of death, such as bullfighters, hunters, and soldiers. His best-known books are *The Sun Also Rises* (1926), the novel that established his reputation; *A Farewell to Arms* (1929); *For Whom the Bell Tolls* (1940); and *The Old Man and the Sea* (1953). For the last he was awarded a Pulitzer Prize, and in the following year he received the Nobel Prize in Literature. Hemingway committed suicide in Ketchum, Idaho, in 1961.

In this essay, Hemingway uses the pattern of process analysis to order his materials on the art of camping. He wrote this piece for the *Toronto Star* in the early 1920s, before he gained worldwide recognition as a major American writer. In it, we see his lifelong interest in the outdoors and his desire to do things well.

PREREADING: THINKING ABOUT THE ESSAY IN ADVANCE

As you prepare to read Hemingway's essay, take a minute or two to think about your own experiences in nature or any unknown place you once visited. If you have ever camped out or attended summer camp, for example, how did you prepare for, enter into, and survive the experience? What problems did you encounter, and how did you overcome them?

Words to Watch

relief map (par. 2) a map that shows by lines and colors the various heights and forms of the land
Caucasus (par. 2) a mountain range in southeastern Europe
proprietary (par. 7) held under patent or trademark
rhapsodize (par. 9) to speak enthusiastically
browse bed (par. 9) a portable cot
tyro (par. 11) an amateur; a beginner in learning something
dyspepsia (par. 13) indigestion
mulligan (par. 18) a stew made from odds and ends of meats and vegetables

Thousands of people will go into the bush this summer to cut the high cost of living. A man who gets his two weeks' salary while he is on vacation should be able to put those two weeks in fishing and camping and be able to save one week's salary clear. He ought to be able to sleep comfortably every night, to eat well every day and to return to the city rested and in good condition. 1

But if he goes into the woods with a frying pan, an ignorance of black flies and mosquitoes, and a great and abiding lack of knowledge about cookery the chances are that his return will be very different. He will come back with enough mosquito bites to make the back of his neck look like a relief map of the Caucasus. His digestion will be wrecked after a valiant battle to assimilate half-cooked or charred grub. And he won't have had a decent night's sleep while he has been gone. 2

He will solemnly raise his right hand and inform you that he has joined the grand army of never-agains. The call of the wild may be all right, but it's a dog's life. He's heard the call of the tame with both ears. Waiter, bring him an order of milk toast. 3

In the first place he overlooked the insects. Black flies, no-see-ums, deer flies, gnats and mosquitoes were instituted by the devil to force people to live in cities where he could get at them better. If it weren't for them everybody would live in the bush and he would be out of work. It was a rather successful invention. 4

But there are lots of dopes that will counteract the pests. The simplest perhaps is oil of citronella. Two bits' worth of this purchased at any pharmacist's will be enough to last for two weeks in the worst fly and mosquito-ridden country. 5

Rub a little on the back of your neck, your forehead and your wrists before you start fishing, and the blacks and skeeters will 6 shun you. The odor of citronella is not offensive to people. It smells like gun oil. But the bugs do hate it.

7 Oil of pennyroyal and eucalyptol are also much hated by mosquitoes, and with citronella they form the basis for many proprietary preparations. But it is cheaper and better to buy the straight citronella. Put a little on the mosquito netting that covers the front of your pup tent or canoe tent at night, and you won't be bothered.

8 To be really rested and get any benefit out of a vacation a man must get a good night's sleep every night. The first requisite for this is to have plenty of cover. It is twice as cold as you expect it will be in the bush four nights out of five, and a good plan is to take just double the bedding that you think you will need. An old quilt that you can wrap up in is as warm as two blankets.

9 Nearly all outdoor writers rhapsodize over the browse bed. It is all right for the man who knows how to make one and has plenty of time. But in a succession of one-night camps on a canoe trip all you need is level ground for your tent floor and you will sleep all right if you have plenty of covers under you. Take twice as much cover as you think that you will need, and then put two-thirds of it under you. You will sleep warm and get your rest.

10 When it is clear weather you don't need to pitch your tent if you are only stopping for the night. Drive four stakes at the head of your made-up bed and drape your mosquito bar over that, then you can sleep like a log and laugh at the mosquitoes.

11 Outside of insects and bum sleeping the rock that wrecks most camping trips is cooking. The average tyro's idea of cooking is to fry everything and fry it good and plenty. Now, a frying pan is a most necessary thing to any trip, but you also need the old stew kettle and the folding reflector baker.

12 A pan of fried trout can't be bettered and they don't cost any more than ever. But there is a good and bad way of frying them.

13 The beginner puts his trout and his bacon in and over a brightly burning fire; the bacon curls up and dries into a dry tasteless cinder and the trout is burned outside while it is still raw inside. He eats them and it is all right if he is only out for the day and going home to a good meal at night. But if he is going to face more trout and bacon the next morning and other equally well-cooked dishes for the remainder of two weeks he is on the pathway to nervous dyspepsia.

14 The proper way is to cook over coals. Have several cans of Crisco or Cotosuet or one of the vegetable shortenings along that are as good as lard and excellent for all kinds of shortening. Put

the bacon in and when it is about half cooked lay the trout in the hot grease, dipping them in corn meal first. Then put the bacon on top of the trout and it will baste them as it slowly cooks.

15 The coffee can be boiling at the same time and in a smaller skillet pancakes being made that are satisfying the other campers while they are waiting for the trout.

16 With the prepared pancake flours you take a cupful of pancake flour and add a cup of water. Mix the water and flour and as soon as the lumps are out it is ready for cooking. Have the skillet hot and keep it well greased. Drop the batter in and as soon as it is done on one side loosen it in the skillet and flip it over. Apple butter, syrup or cinnamon and sugar go well with the cakes.

17 While the crowd have taken the edge from their appetites with flapjacks the trout have been cooked and they and the bacon are ready to serve. The trout are crisp outside and firm and pink inside and the bacon is well done—but not too done. If there is anything better than that combination the writer has yet to taste it in a lifetime devoted largely and studiously to eating.

18 The stew kettle will cook you dried apricots when they have resumed their predried plumpness after a night of soaking, it will serve to concoct a mulligan in, and it will cook macaroni. When you are not using it, it should be boiling water for the dishes.

19 In the baker, mere man comes into his own, for he can make a pie that to his bush appetite will have it all over the product that mother used to make, like a tent. Men have always believed that there was something mysterious and difficult about making a pie. Here is a great secret. There is nothing to it. We've been kidded for years. Any man of average office intelligence can make at least as good a pie as his wife.

20 All there is to a pie is a cup and a half of flour, one-half teaspoonful of salt, one-half cup of lard and cold water. That will make pie crust that will bring tears of joy into your camping partner's eyes.

21 Mix the salt with the flour, work the lard into the flour, make it up into a good workmanlike dough with cold water. Spread some flour on the back of a box or something flat, and pat the dough around a while. Then roll it out with whatever kind of round bottle you prefer. Put a little more lard on the surface of the sheet of dough and then slosh a little flour on and roll it up and then roll it out again with the bottle.

22 Cut out a piece of the rolled out dough big enough to line a pie tin. I like the kind with holes in the bottom. Then put in your dried apples that have soaked all night and been sweetened, or

your apricots, or your blueberries, and then take another sheet of the dough and drape it gracefully over the top, soldering it down at the edges with your fingers. Cut a couple of slits in the top dough sheet and prick it a few times with a fork in an artistic manner.

23 Put it in the baker with a good slow fire for forty-five minutes and then take it out and if your pals are Frenchmen they will kiss you. The penalty for knowing how to cook is that the others will make you do all the cooking.

24 It is all right to talk about roughing it in the woods. But the real woodsman is the man who can be really comfortable in the bush.

BUILDING VOCABULARY

For each word below write your own definition, based on how the word is used in the selection. Check back to the appropriate paragraph in the essay for more help, if necessary.

a. abiding (par. 2)
b. valiant (par. 2)
c. assimilate (par. 2)
d. charred (par. 2)
e. solemnly (par. 3)
f. requisite (par. 8)
g. succession (par. 9)
h. studiously (par. 17)
i. concoct (par. 18)
j. soldering (par. 22)

THINKING CRITICALLY ABOUT THE ESSAY

Understanding the Writer's Ideas

1. What is Hemingway's main purpose in this essay? Does he simply want to explain how to set up camp and how to cook outdoors?
2. What, according to the writer, are the two possible results of camping out on your vacation?
3. Why is oil of citronella the one insecticide that Hemingway recommends over all others?
4. Is it always necessary to pitch a tent when camping out? What are alternatives to it? How can you sleep warmly and comfortably?

5. Explain the writer's process for cooking trout. Also explain his process for baking a pie.
6. Is it enough for Hemingway simply to enjoy "roughing it" while camping out?

Understanding the Writer's Techniques

1. Does Hemingway have a stated thesis? Explain.
2. Identify those paragraphs in the essay that involve process analysis, and explain how Hemingway develops his subject in each.
3. What is the main writing pattern in paragraphs 1 and 2? How does this method serve as an organizing principle throughout the essay?
4. How would you characterize Hemingway's style of writing? Is it appropriate to a newspaper audience? Is it more apt for professional fishermen?
5. In what way does Hemingway employ classification (see Chapter 9) in this essay?
6. Analyze the tone of the essay.
7. The concluding paragraph is short. Is it effective, nevertheless, and why? How does it reinforce the opening paragraph?

Exploring the Writer's Ideas

1. Camping out was popular in the 1920s, as it is today. What are some of the reasons that it remains so attractive today?
2. Hemingway's essay describes many basic strategies for successful camping. He does not rely on "gadgets" or modern inventions to make camping easier. Do such gadgets make camping more fun today than it might have been in the 1920s?
3. The writer suggests that there is a right way and a wrong way to do things. Does it matter if you perform a recreational activity correctly as long as you enjoy doing it? Why?

IDEAS FOR WRITING

Prewriting

Freewrite for fifteen minutes about your favorite pastime, activity, or hobby. How do you approach this activity? What steps must be observed in order to be successful at it? How might other people fail at it whereas you are successful?

Guided Writing

Write an essay on how to do something wrong, and how to do it right—going on vacation, looking for a job, fishing, or whatever.

1. Reexamine the author's first three paragraphs and imitate his method of introducing the right and wrong ways about the subject, and the possible results.
2. Adopt a simple, informal, "chatty" style. Feel free to use a few well-placed clichés and other forms of spoken English. Use several similes.
3. Divide your subject into useful categories. Just as Hemingway treated insects, sleeping, and cooking, try to cover the main aspects of your subject.
4. Explain the process involved for each aspect of your subject. Make certain that you compare and contrast the right and wrong ways of your activity.
5. Write a short, crisp conclusion that reinforces your longer introduction.

Thinking and Writing Collaboratively

As a class, choose a process—for example, applying to college—which clearly involves a "right way" and "wrong way" of accomplishing the activity. Then divide the class into two groups, with one group outlining the correct steps and the other the incorrect or incomplete steps to completing the process. List both approaches on the chalkboard for comparative discussion.

Writing About the Text

Write an essay discussing Hemingway's view of doing things "the proper way" (par. 14), looking at how his personal views are translated into authoritative instructions. Is Hemingway being overly judgmental? Or does "the proper way" mean everything in life?

More Writing Projects

1. How do you explain the fascination that camping out holds for many people? Reflect on this question in your journal.
2. In a paragraph, describe how to get to your favorite vacation spot, and what to do when you get there.
3. If you have ever camped out, write a process paper explaining one important feature of setting up camp.

In the Kitchen

Henry Louis Gates Jr.

Mixing Patterns

One of the nation's leading literary scholars, Henry Louis Gates Jr., was born in 1950 in Piedmont, West Virginia. Educated in the newly desegregated local public schools, Gates went on to receive his BA from Yale and his PhD from Clare College at the University of Cambridge (England). Having begun his career writing for *Time* magazine in London, Gates established his reputation as a major literary critic with his book *The Signifying Monkey: Toward a Theory of Afro-American Literary Criticism* (1989), which received the National Book Award. He is editor of the authoritative *Norton Anthology of African American Literature* and co-editor of *Transition* magazine. He is the author of *Wonders of the African World* (1999), the book companion to the public television series of the same name. Gates's many awards include the prestigious MacArthur Foundation "Genius Award." Gates is W. E. B. Du Bois Professor of Humanities and Chair of Afro-American Studies at Harvard University. In this selection, which first appeared in the *New Yorker* in 1994, Gates examines the politics of the hairdo by recalling his experiences as a child in his mother's home beauty parlor.

To learn more about Gates, click on
More Resources > Chapter 5 > Henry Louis Gates Jr.

PREREADING: THINKING ABOUT THE ESSAY IN ADVANCE

Michael Jackson, America's pop icon, was criticized by some in the African American community for altering his appearance to conform to Anglo features (such as straight hair). Do you think you should have the right to change your looks even if it means trying to conform to the standards of beauty of an ethnic or cultural group other than your own?

Words to Watch

transform (par. 4) to change the appearance or form of
southpaw (par. 4) a left-handed person, especially a left-handed baseball pitcher

refrain (par. 7) repeated phrase or utterance
preposterous (par. 7) absurd
tiara (par. 24) a crown or fine headdress

We always had a gas stove in the kitchen, in our house in Piedmont, West Virginia, where I grew up. Never electric, though using electric became fashionable in Piedmont in the sixties, like using Crest toothpaste rather than Colgate, or watching Huntley and Brinkley rather than Walter Cronkite. But not us: gas, Colgate, and good ole Walter Cronkite, come what may. We used gas partly out of loyalty to Big Mom, Mama's Mama, because she was mostly blind and still loved to cook, and could feel her way more easily with gas than with electric. But the most important thing about our gas-equipped kitchen was that Mama used to do hair there. The "hot comb" was a fine-toothed iron instrument with a long wooden handle and a pair of iron curlers that opened and closed like scissors. Mama would put it in the gas fire until it glowed. You could smell those prongs heating up. 1

I liked that smell. Not the smell so much, I guess, as what the smell meant for the shape of my day. There was an intimate warmth in the women's tones as they talked with my Mama, doing their hair. I knew what the women had been through to get their hair ready to be "done," because I would watch Mama do it to herself. How that kink could be transformed through grease and fire into that magnificent head of wavy hair was a miracle to me, and still is. 2

Mama would wash her hair over the sink, a towel wrapped around her shoulders, wearing just her slip and her white bra. (We had no shower—just a galvanized tub that we stored in the kitchen—until we moved down Rat Tail Road into Doc Wolverton's house, in 1954.) After she dried it, she would grease her scalp thoroughly with blue Bergamot hair grease, which came in a short, fat jar with a picture of a beautiful colored lady on it. It's important to grease your scalp real good, my Mama would explain, to keep from burning yourself. Of course, her hair would return to its natural kink almost as soon as the hot water and shampoo hit it. To me, it was another miracle how hair so "straight" would so quickly become kinky again the second it even approached some water. 3

My Mama had only a few "clients" whose heads she "did"—did, I think, because she enjoyed it, rather than for the few pennies it brought in. They would sit on one of our red plastic kitchen chairs, the kind with the shiny metal legs, and brace themselves 4 for the process. Mama would stroke that red-hot iron—which by this time had been in the gas fire for half an hour or more—slowly but firmly through their hair, from scalp to strand's end. It made a scorching, crinkly sound, the hot iron did, as it burned its way through kink, leaving in its wake straight strands of hair, standing long and tall but drooping over at the ends, their shape like the top of a heavy willow tree. Slowly, steadily, Mama's hands would transform a round mound of Odetta kink into a darkened swamp of everglades. The Bergamot made the hair shiny; the heat of the hot iron gave it a brownish-red cast. Once all the hair was as straight as God allows kink to get, Mama would take the well-heated curling iron and twirl the straightened strands into more or less loosely wrapped curls. She claimed that she owed her skill as a hairdresser to the strength in her wrists, and as she worked her little finger would poke out, the way it did when she sipped tea. Mama was a southpaw, and wrote upside down and backward to produce the cleanest, roundest letters you've ever seen.

5 The "kitchen" she would all but remove from sight with a hand-held pair of shears, bought just for this purpose. Now, the kitchen was the room in which we were sitting—the room where Mama did hair and washed clothes, and where we all took a bath in that galvanized tub. But the word has another meaning, and the kitchen that I'm speaking of is the very kinky bit of hair at the back of your head, where your neck meets your shirt collar. If there was ever a part of our African past that resisted assimilation, it was the kitchen. No matter how hot the iron, no matter how powerful the chemical, no matter how stringent the mashed-potatoes-and-lye formula of a man's "process," neither God nor woman nor Sammy Davis, Jr., could straighten the kitchen. The kitchen was permanent, irredeemable, irresistible kink. Unassimilably African. No matter what you did, no matter how hard you tried, you couldn't de-kink a person's kitchen. So you trimmed it off as best you could.

6 When hair had begun to "turn," as they'd say—to return to its natural kinky glory—it was the kitchen that turned first (the kitchen around the back, and nappy edges at the temples). When the kitchen started creeping up the back of the neck, it was time to get your hair done again.

7 Sometimes, after dark, a man would come to have his hair done. It was Mr. Charlie Carroll. He was very light-complected and had a ruddy nose—it made me think of Edmund Gwenn, who played Kris

Kringle in "Miracle on 34th Street." At first, Mama did him after my brother, Rocky, and I had gone to sleep. It was only later that we found out that he had come to our house so Mama could iron his hair—not with a hot comb or a curling iron but with our very own Proctor-Silex steam iron. For some reason I never understood, Mr. Charlie would conceal his Frederick Douglass-like mane under a big white Stetson hat. I never saw him take it off except when he came to our house, at night, to have his hair pressed. (Later, Daddy would tell us about Mr. Charlie's most prized piece of knowledge, something that the man would only confide after his hair had been pressed, as a token of intimacy. "Not many people know this," he'd say, in a tone of circumspection, "but George Washington was Abraham Lincoln's daddy." Nodding solemnly, he'd add the clincher: "A white man told me." Though he was in dead earnest, this became a humorous refrain around our house—"a white man told me"—which we used to punctuate especially preposterous assertions.)

My mother examined my daughters' kitchens whenever we went home to visit, in the early eighties. It became a game between us. I had told her not to do it, because I didn't like the politics it suggested—the notion of "good" and "bad" hair. "Good" hair was "straight," "bad" hair kinky. Even in the late sixties, at the height of Black Power, almost nobody could bring themselves to say "bad" for good and "good" for bad. People still said that hair like white people's hair was "good," even if they encapsulated it in a disclaimer, like "what we used to call 'good.'" **8**

Maggie would be seated in her high chair, throwing food this way and that, and Mama would be cooing about how cute it all was, how I used to do just like Maggie was doing, and wondering whether her flinging her food with her left hand meant that she was going to be left-handed like Mama. When my daughter was just about covered with Chef Boyardee Spaghetti-O's, Mama would seize the opportunity: wiping her clean, she would tilt Maggie's head to one side and reach down the back of her neck. Sometimes Mama would even rub a curl between her fingers, just to make sure that her bifocals had not deceived her. Then she'd sigh with satisfaction and relief: No kink . . . yet. Mama! I'd shout, pretending to be angry. Every once in a while, if no one was looking, I'd peek, too. **9**

I say "yet" because most black babies are born with soft, silken hair. But after a few months it begins to turn, as inevitably as do the seasons or the leaves on a tree. People once thought baby oil would stop it. They were wrong. **10**

11 Everybody I knew as a child wanted to have good hair. You could be as ugly as homemade sin dipped in misery and still be thought attractive if you had good hair. “Jesus moss,” the girls at Camp Lee, Virginia, had called Daddy’s naturally “good” hair during the war. I know that he played that thick head of hair for all it was worth, too.

12 My own hair was “not a bad grade,” as barbers would tell me when they cut it for the first time. It was like a doctor reporting the results of the first full physical he has given you. Like “You’re in good shape” or “Blood pressure’s kind of high—better cut down on salt.”

13 I spent most of my childhood and adolescence messing with my hair. I definitely wanted straight hair. Like Pop’s. When I was about three, I tried to stick a wad of Bazooka bubble gum to that straight hair of his. I suppose what fixed that memory for me is the spanking I got for doing so: he turned me upside down, holding me by my feet, the better to paddle my behind. Little *nigger,* he had shouted, walloping away. I started to laugh about it two days later, when my behind stopped hurting.

14 When black people say “straight,” of course, they don’t usually mean literally straight—they’re not describing hair like, say, Peggy Lipton’s (she was the white girl on “The Mod Squad”), or like Mary’s of Peter, Paul & Mary fame; black people call that “stringy” hair. No, “straight” just means not kinky, no matter what contours the curl may take. I would have done *anything* to have straight hair—and I used to try everything, short of getting a process.

15 Of the wide variety of techniques and methods I came to master in the challenging prestidigitation of the follicle, almost all had two things in common: a heavy grease and the application of pressure. It’s not an accident that some of the biggest black-owned companies in the fifties and sixties made hair products. And I tried them all, in search of that certain silken touch, the one that would leave neither the hand nor the pillow sullied by grease.

16 I always wondered what Frederick Douglass put on *his* hair, or what Phillis Wheatley put on hers. Or why Wheatley has that rag on her head in the little engraving in the frontispiece of her book. One thing is for sure: you can bet that when Phillis Wheatley went to England and saw the Countess of Huntingdon she did not stop by the Queen’s coiffeur on her way there. So many black people still get their hair straightened that it’s a wonder we don’t have a national holiday for Madame C. J. Walker, the woman who invented the process of straightening kinky hair. Call it Jheri-Kurled or call it “relaxed,” it’s still fried hair.

I used all the greases, from sea-blue Bergamot and creamy vanilla Duke (in its clear jar with the orange-white-and-green label) to the godfather of grease, the formidable Murray's. Now, Murray's was some *serious* grease. Whereas Bergamot was like oily jello, and Duke was viscous and sickly sweet, Murray's was light brown and *hard*. Hard as lard and twice as greasy, Daddy used to say. Murray's came in an orange can with a press-on top. It was so hard that some people would put a match to the can, just to soften the stuff and make it more manageable. Then, in the late sixties, when Afros came into style, I used Afro Sheen. From Murray's to Duke to Afro Sheen: that was my progression in black consciousness. 17

We used to put hot towels or washrags over our Murray-coated heads, in order to melt the wax into the scalp and the follicles. Unfortunately, the wax also had the habit of running down your neck, ears, and forehead. Not to mention your pillowcase. Another problem was that if you put two palmfuls of Murray's on your head your hair turned white. (Duke did the same thing.) The challenge was to get rid of that white color. Because if you got rid of the white stuff you had a magnificent head of wavy hair. That was the beauty of it: Murray's was so hard that it froze your hair into the wavy style you brushed it into. It looked really good if you wore a part. A lot of guys had parts *cut* into their hair by a barber, either with the clippers or with a straightedge razor. Especially if you had kinky hair—then you'd generally wear a short razor cut, or what we called a Quo Vadis. 18

We tried to be as innovative as possible. Everyone knew about using a stocking cap, because your father or your uncle wore one whenever something really big was about to happen, whether sacred or secular: a funeral or a dance, a wedding or a trip in which you confronted official white people. Any time you were trying to look really sharp, you wore a stocking cap in preparation. And if the event was really a big one, you made a new cap. You asked your mother for a pair of her hose, and cut it with scissors about six inches or so from the open end—the end with the elastic that goes up to the top of the thigh. Then you knotted the cut end, and it became a beehive-shaped hat, with an elastic band that you pulled down low on your forehead and down around your neck in the back. To work well, the cap had to fit tightly and snugly, like a press. And it had to fit that tightly because it *was* a press: it pressed your hair with the force of the hose's elastic. If you greased your hair down real good, and left the stocking cap on 19 long enough, voilá: you got a head of pressed-against-the-scalp waves. (You also got a ring around your forehead when you woke up, but it went away.) And then you could enjoy your concrete do. Swore we were bad, too, with all that grease and those flat heads. My brother and I would brush it out a bit in the mornings, so that it looked—well, "natural." Grown men still wear stocking caps—especially older men, who generally keep their stocking caps in their top drawers, along with their cufflinks and their see-through silk socks, their "Maverick" ties, their silk handkerchiefs, and whatever else they prize the most.

20 A Murrayed-down stocking cap was the respectable version of the process, which, by contrast, was most definitely not a cool thing to have unless you were an entertainer by trade. Zeke and Keith and Poochie and a few other stars of the high-school basketball team all used to get a process once or twice a year. It was expensive, and you had to go somewhere like Pittsburgh or D.C. or Uniontown—somewhere where there were enough colored people to support a trade. The guys would disappear, then reappear a day or two later, strutting like peacocks, their hair burned slightly red from the lye base. They'd also wear "rags"—cloths or handkerchiefs—around their heads when they slept or played basketball. Do-rags, they were called. But the result was straight hair, with just a hint of wave. No curl. Do-it-yourselfers took their chances at home with a concoction of mashed potatoes and lye.

21 The most famous process of all, however, outside of the process Malcolm X describes in his "Autobiography," and maybe the process of Sammy Davis, Jr., was Nat King Cole's process. Nat King Cole had patent-leather hair. That man's got the finest process money can buy, or so Daddy said the night we saw Cole's TV show on NBC. It was November 5, 1956. I remember the date because everyone came to our house to watch it and to celebrate one of Daddy's buddies' birthdays. Yeah, Uncle Joe chimed in, they can do shit to his hair that the average Negro can't even *think* about—secret shit.

22 Nat King Cole was *clean.* I've had an ongoing argument with a Nigerian friend about Nat King Cole for twenty years now. Not about whether he could sing—any fool knows that he could—but about whether or not he was a handkerchief head for wearing that patent-leather process.

23 Sammy Davis, Jr.'s process was the one I detested. It didn't look good on him. Worse still, he liked to have a fried strand

dangling down the middle of his forehead, so he could shake it out from the crown when he sang. But Nat King Cole's hair was a thing unto itself, a beautifully sculpted work of art that he and he alone had the right to wear. The only difference between a process and a stocking cap, really, was taste; but Nat King Cole, unlike, say, Michael Jackson, looked *good* in his. His head looked like Valentino's head in the twenties, and some say it was Valentino the process was imitating. But Nat King Cole wore a process because it suited his face, his demeanor, his name, his style. He was as clean as he wanted to be.

24 I had forgotten all about that patent-leather look until one day in 1971, when I was sitting in an Arab restaurant on the island of Zanzibar surrounded by men in fezzes and white caftans, trying to learn how to eat curried goat and rice with the fingers of my right hand and feeling two million miles from home. All of a sudden, an old transistor radio sitting on top of a china cupboard stopped blaring out its Swahili music and started playing "Fly Me to the Moon," by Nat King Cole. The restaurant's din was not affected at all, but in my mind's eye I saw it: the King's magnificent sleek black tiara. I managed, barely, to blink back the tears.

BUILDING VOCABULARY

For each word below write your own definition based on how the word is used in the selection. Check back to the appropriate paragraph in the essay for more help, if necessary.

a. galvanized (par. 5)
b. assertions (par. 7)
c. prestidigitation (par. 15)
d. follicle (par. 15)
e. din (par. 24)

THINKING CRITICALLY ABOUT THE ESSAY

Understanding the Writer's Ideas

1. The word *kitchen* in the title takes on two meanings in the essay. What are they?
2. Gas was used in Gates's kitchen even though people had turned to electricity in the 1960s. Why?

3. What does the writer mean when he states that his mother "did hair"?
4. What does the word *turn* (par. 6) describe?
5. What is the history behind "good" and "bad" hair?
6. As a child, how did Gates worry about his hair? Explain.
7. Describe the two things all hair-straightening techniques have in common.
8. What was it about Nat King Cole's hair that impressed this writer so much?
9. How were the hot irons used to straighten hair?
10. Hearing a Nat King Cole song while in Zanzibar, the writer says he had to "blink back the tears." Why?

Understanding the Writer's Techniques

1. Find the thesis and paraphrase it.
2. What process does Gates describe in paragraph 3? Give examples of the process he describes there.
3. Given the detailed descriptions of de-kinking hair, what audience does this writer have in mind in employing this strategy?
4. Where in the essay does the writer make a transition to describe two of the most common processes of hair straightening? How are these processes detailed?
5. Though the other de-kinking processes mentioned in the essay are detailed, the most famous one (Nat King Cole's) is not described at all. What might this suggest about the writer's attitude toward this subject?
6. What makes Gates's concluding paragraph different from others more common in essays?

✷ MIXING PATTERNS

The essay's structure is not focused entirely on process. What other rhetorical pattern does the writer use? Identify the places where this pattern occurs.

Exploring the Writer's Ideas

1. Gates claims the "kitchen," those hairs on the back of the neck, are "unassimilably" African. Yet, his mother specialized

in getting rid of the kitchen. Do you think this writer approves or disapproves of his mother's activity? Explain.

2. Gates tells of jokes about the "white man." Gates says he found the jokes funny even though he also admits he wanted good hair, like that of whites. How would you explain this writer's contradictory feelings about white people?
3. How do you feel about this writer's claims that most everyone he knew thought kinky hair was "bad"? Do you think this is an exaggeration? Why or why not?
4. What examples exist today of people who remake themselves to look "white" or like those who are held up as role models, like Eminem or other rock stars? Is this impulse positive or negative? Why?
5. The author suggests that the de-kinking was physically painful. Does anything in the essay suggest all the pain was worth it? Explain.
6. By calling Nat King Cole's straightened hair a "black tiara" is this author concluding that straight hair (looking white) is indeed admirable? How do you feel?

IDEAS FOR WRITING

Prewriting

Use your journal to recall times when you felt good or bad about the way you look.

Guided Writing

Write an essay on how you once may have tried to make yourself look the "right" or "wrong" way. Remember the time you dressed for a date or to go to church or to get a job.

1. Examine Gates's first paragraph and imitate his method of introducing the thesis.
2. Divide your process into its important parts, like Gates who divides de-kinking into its steps: hot comb, the kitchen, the clients, the grease, and the pressure.
3. Make sure that your process is detailed in a way that keeps a general audience in mind (or people who don't know your process).

4. Try to use definition paragraphs to explain terms that describe your process which are unknown to your general audience.
5. Write a conclusion that tells a story, like Gates on Nat King Cole. Remember that this story should reflect an overall feeling you have about your topic.

Thinking and Writing Collaboratively

Your group is responsible for creating a behavior code pamphlet for your school. Use process technique to make clear how students should act in different situations. Explain what happens (the process) if someone's behavior challenges the guidelines.

Writing About the Text

This essay is a reminiscence, an essay about a dear memory. Yet the writer seems ambivalent about his mother's hairdressing. Write an essay that explores the relation between Gates's *tone* and his attitude toward his mother's activity.

More Writing Projects

1. In your journal, make notes on the ways that you have seen people change their looks to please others.
2. In a paragraph, describe the process by which people learn who looks the right way or the wrong way.
3. Write a process essay on something your parents or caregiver taught you as a child. Tell of learning to swim or to ride a bike.

SUMMING UP: CHAPTER 5

1. Write an essay about the one piece in this chapter that you feel most clearly and logically presents an understandable process.
2. Write a recipe for your favorite dish to include in a class cookbook. In addition to describing the step-by-step process for preparing the food, you should also tell something about the tradition behind the food, special occasions for eating it, the first time you ate it, and so forth. The goal should be to make the process clear and reassuring, to emphasize how following these simple steps will yield a delicious meal.
3. Interview a classmate about something that he or she does very well. Make sure the questions you ask don't omit any important steps or materials used in the process. Take careful notes during the interview, then try to replicate the process on your own. If you have difficulties in accomplishing the process, reinterview your classmate. After you are satisfied that no steps or materials have been left out, write up the procedure in such a way that someone else could easily follow it.
4. Both Ernest Hemingway and Henry Louis Gates Jr. show how to perform a process with great rigor and devotion, not to say enthusiasm; they also show how to perform a process less carefully and even, according to Hemingway, indifferently. Choose a process that you care about—playing an instrument, cooking a dish, playing a sport—and discuss how to do it either well or poorly, and what it means to you to see it done well or poorly.
5. Many essays in this book look back to the writer's childhood; frequently the writers remember vividly the process of doing something, or of watching something being done, that symbolizes or epitomizes childhood. Write an essay about your childhood that focuses on a process—either something that you did or that you watched being done—that stands out as especially evocative of your childhood in particular and childhood in general.

✷ FROM SEEING TO WRITING

Consider the standard legal process the judge in this cartoon ignored in arriving at his sentencing decision. Explain the precise steps he should have followed, the order of those steps, and the relation of the steps to the final decision. In your essay, help the reader understand the situation or circumstances under which a judge normally performs any legal process.

"In the interest of streamlining the judicial process, we'll skip the evidence and go directly to sentencing."

CHAPTER 6

Illustration

WHAT IS ILLUSTRATION?

One convenient way for writers to present and to support a point is through *illustration*—that is, by means of several examples to back up an idea. Illustration (or *exemplification*) helps a writer put general or abstract thoughts into specific examples. As readers, we often find that we are able to understand a writer's point more effectively because we respond to the concrete examples. We are familiar with illustration in everyday life. If a police officer is called a racist, the review board will want *illustrations* of the racist behavior. The accuser will have to provide concrete examples of racist language, or present arrest statistics that show the officer was more likely to arrest Korean Americans, for instance, than white Americans.

Writing that uses illustration is most effective if it uses *several* examples to support the thesis. A single, isolated example might not convince anyone easily, but a series of examples builds up a stronger case. Writers can also use an *extended example,* which is one example that is developed at length.

For instance, you might want to illustrate your thesis that American patchwork quilts are an important record of women's history. Since your reader might not be familiar with quilts, you would have to illustrate your argument with examples such as these:

- Baltimore album quilts were given to Eastern women heading West in the nineteenth century and contain signatures and dates stitched in the squares to mark the event.
- Women used blue and white in quilt patterns to show their support for the temperance movement that opposed the sale of alcohol.

- Women named patterns after geographic and historical events, creating such quilts as Rocky Road to Kansas and Abe Lincoln's Platform.
- African American quilters adapted techniques from West Africa to make blankets for slave quarters.
- One quilter from Kentucky recorded all the deaths in her family in her work. The unusual quilt contains a pattern of a cemetery and coffins with names for each family member!

If you visited a museum and there was only one painting on the wall, you would probably feel that you hadn't gotten your money's worth. You expect a museum to be a *collection* of paintings, so that you can study a variety of types of art or several paintings by the same painter. In the same way, through the accumulation of illustrations, the writer builds a case for the thesis.

In this chapter, writers use illustration forcefully to make their points. Brent Staples, an African American journalist, shows how some people perceive his mere presence on a street at night as a threat. Barbara Ehrenreich uses irony to illustrate, from a feminist perspective, what women can learn from men. Eleanor Bader offers profiles of homelessness on campus. Finally, Jared Diamond uses examples from history to demonstrate that globalization is nothing new. Each writer knows that one example is insufficient to create a case, but that multiple examples make a convincing case.

HOW DO WE READ ILLUSTRATION?

Reading illustration requires us to ask ourselves these questions:

- What is the writer's thesis? What is the *purpose* of the examples?
- What audience is the writer addressing? How do we know?
- What other techniques is the writer using? Is there narration? description? How are these used to help the illustration?
- In what order has the writer arranged the examples? Where is the most important example placed?
- How does the writer use *transitions*? Often, transitions in illustration essays enumerate: *first, second, third; one, another.*

HOW DO WE WRITE WITH ILLUSTRATIONS?

Read the selections critically to see the many ways in which writers can use illustrations to support an idea.

Select your topic and write a thesis that tells the reader what you are going to illustrate and what your main idea is about the subject.

Sample thesis statement:

> Many people have long cherished quilts for their beautiful colors and patterns, but few collectors recognize the history stitched into the squares.

Make a list of *examples* to support the thesis.

Examples by quilt types: Baltimore album quilts, political quilts, suffrage quilts, slave quilts, graveyard quilts

Examples by quilt pattern names: Radical Rose; Drunkard's Path; Memory Blocks; Old Maid's Puzzle; Wheel of Mystery; Log Cabin; Rocky Road to Kansas; Slave Chain; Underground Railroad; Delectable Mountains; Union Star; Jackson Star; Old Indian Trail; Trip around the World

Determine who the audience will be: a group of experienced quilters? museum curators? a PTA group? Each is a different audience with different interests and needs.

Plan an arrangement of the examples. Begin with the least important and build up to the most important. Or arrange the examples in chronological order.

Plan to use other techniques (such as description), especially if your audience is unfamiliar with your subject. If you are writing the quilt paper and using the example of the Baltimore album quilt, you would then have to *describe* it for readers who do not know what such a quilt looks like.

Be sure that the *purpose* of the illustrations is clearly stated, especially in the conclusion. In the quilt essay, for instance, different quilt patterns might be illustrated in order to encourage readers to preserve and study quilts.

Writing and Revising the Draft

Use the first paragraph to introduce the subject and to set up a clear thesis. You might introduce an *abstract* idea, such as forgotten history, that will be *illustrated* in the examples.

Plan the body to give the reader lots of examples, and to develop the examples if necessary. Use narration, description, and dialogue to enhance the illustrations. Write a conclusion that returns to the abstract idea you began with in the introduction.

Write a second draft for reading aloud.

Revise, based on your listener's comments. Proofread the essay carefully. Check spelling and grammar. Make a final copy.

A STUDENT PARAGRAPH: ILLUSTRATION

This paragraph from a student's illustration paper on quiltmaking shows how the use of examples advances the thesis of the essay. The thesis, which you examined on page 218, asserts that, the colors and patterns of quilts aside, "few collectors recognize the history stitched into the squares."

We can find a significant example of the historical, record-keeping function of quiltmaking in Mary Kinsale's needlework. Kinsale lived in Kentucky in the mid-nineteenth century. Unlike the political quilts discussed earlier, and the various quilts that document "official" history, Kinsale's quilts deal only with the history of her family. Specifically, Kinsale set out to document the precise dates of death of all her family members, illustrating the squares with coffins, open graves, and other symbols of death. What we might call morbid or tasteless today probably struck members of Kinsale's community as natural and proper; the American culture had not yet restricted images of gaunt, grinning skulls, mossy tombstones, and other symbols of death to horror movies. In fact, Kinsale's images served an important religious and social purpose by reminding family and friends to reform their lives while there was still time. Kinsale decided to record the vital dates of her dearly departed, and remind the living of their duty in life, by stitching a quilt, rather than simply writing an entry in the family Bible, or leaving the task to the government. Her quiltmaking illustrates nineteenth-century society's old-fashioned attitude towards death, as well as their understanding of the role ordinary individuals could play in recording history.

Reference to essay thesis, "history stitched into squares"

Transition ("a significant example") asserts order according to significance

Reference to other points in essay provides *unity*

Kinsale's work is main *illustration* developed in the paragraph

Supporting detail

Supporting detail

Closing sentence connects to essay's thesis

Night Walker

Brent Staples

Born in Chester, Pennsylvania, Brent Staples is an editorial writer for the *New York Times* who holds a PhD in psychology from the University of Chicago. He is the author of *Parallel Time: Growing Up in Black and White* (1994). Yet, since his youth, he has instilled fear and suspicion in many just by taking nighttime walks to combat his insomnia. In this essay, which appeared in the *Los Angeles Times* in 1986, Staples explains how others perceive themselves as his potential victims simply because he is a black man in "urban America."

To learn more about Staples, click on **More Resources > Chapter 6 > Brent Staples**

PREREADING: THINKING ABOUT THE ESSAY IN ADVANCE

Imagine this scene: you are walking alone at night in your own neighborhood and you hear footsteps behind you that you believe are the footsteps of someone of a different race from yours. How do you feel? What do you do? Why?

Words to Watch

affluent (par. 1) wealthy
discreet (par. 1) showing good judgment; careful
quarry (par. 2) prey; object of a hunt
dismayed (par. 2) discouraged
taut (par. 4) tight; tense
warrenlike (par. 5) like a crowded tenement district
bandolier (par. 5) gun belt worn across the chest
solace (par. 5) relief; consolation; comfort
retrospect (par. 6) review of past event
ad hoc (par. 7) unplanned; for the particular case at hand
labyrinthine (par. 7) like a maze
skittish (par. 9) nervous; jumpy
constitutionals (par. 10) regular walks

1 My first victim was a woman—white, well dressed, probably in her early 20s. I came upon her late one evening on a deserted street in Hyde Park, a relatively affluent neighborhood in an otherwise mean, impoverished section of Chicago. As I swung onto the avenue behind her, there seemed to be a discreet, uninflammatory distance between us. Not so. She cast back a worried glance. To her, the youngish black man—a broad six feet two inches with a beard and billowing hair, both hands shoved into the pockets of a bulky military jacket—seemed menacingly close. She picked up her pace and was soon running in earnest. Within seconds she disappeared into a cross street.

2 That was more than a decade ago. I was 22 years old, a graduate student newly arrived at the University of Chicago. It was in the echo of that terrified woman's footfalls that I first began to know the unwieldy inheritance I'd come into—the ability to alter public space in ugly ways. It was clear that she thought herself the quarry of a mugger, a rapist, or worse. Suffering a bout of insomnia, however, I was stalking sleep, not defenseless wayfarers. As a softy who is scarcely able to take a knife to a raw chicken—let alone hold one to a person's throat—I was surprised, embarrassed, and dismayed all at once. Her flight made me feel like an accomplice in tyranny. It also made it clear that I was indistinguishable from the muggers who occasionally seeped into the area from the surrounding ghetto. I soon gathered that being perceived as dangerous is a hazard in itself: Where fear and weapons meet—and they often do in urban America—there is always the possibility of death.

3 In that first year, my first away from my hometown, I was to become thoroughly familiar with the language of fear. At dark, shadowy intersections, I could cross in front of a car stopped at a traffic light and elicit the *thunk, thunk, thunk, thunk* of the driver—black, white, male, female—hammering down the door locks. On less traveled streets after dark, I grew accustomed to but never comfortable with people crossing to the other side of the street rather than pass me. Then there were the standard unpleasantries with policemen, doormen, bouncers, cabdrivers, and others whose business it is to screen out troublesome individuals *before* there is any nastiness.

4 I moved to New York nearly two years ago and I have remained an avid night walker. In central Manhattan, the near-constant crowd covers the tense one-on-one street encounters. Elsewhere, things can get very taut indeed.

After dark, on the warrenlike streets of Brooklyn where I live, I often see women who fear the worst from me. They seem to have set their faces on neutral, and with their purse straps strung across their chests bandolier-style, they forge ahead as though bracing themselves against being tackled. I understand, of course, that the danger they perceive is not a hallucination. Women are particularly vulnerable to street violence, and young black males are drastically overrepresented among the perpetrators of that violence. Yet these truths are no solace against the alienation that comes of being ever the suspect, an entity with whom pedestrians avoid making eye contact. 5

It is not altogether clear to me how I reached the ripe old age of 22 without being conscious of the lethality nighttime pedestrians attributed to me. Perhaps it was because in Chester, Pa., the small, angry industrial town where I came of age in the 1960s, I was scarcely noticeable against a backdrop of gang warfare, street knifings, and murders. I grew up one of the good boys, had perhaps a half-dozen fistfights. In retrospect, my shyness of combat has clear sources. As a boy, I saw countless tough guys locked away; I have since buried several, too. They were babies, really—a teen-age cousin, a brother of 22, a childhood friend in his mid-20s—all gone down in episodes of bravado played out in the streets. I chose, perhaps unconsciously, to remain a shadow—timid, but a survivor. 6

The fearsomeness mistakenly attributed to me in public places often has a perilous flavor. The most frightening of these confusions occurred in the late 1970s and early 1980s, when I worked as a journalist in Chicago. One day, rushing into the office of a magazine I was writing for with a deadline story in hand, I was mistaken for a burglar. The office manager called security and, with an ad hoc posse, pursued me through the labyrinthine halls, nearly to my editor's door. I had no way of proving who I was. I could only move briskly toward the company of someone who knew me. 7

Relatively speaking, however, I never fared as badly as another black male journalist. He went to nearby Waukegan, Ill., a couple of summers ago to work on a story about a murderer who was born there. Mistaking the reporter for the killer, police officers hauled him from his car at gunpoint and but for his press credentials would probably have tried to book him. Such episodes are not uncommon. Black men trade tales like this all the time. 8

9 Over the years, I learned to smother the rage I felt at so often being mistaken for a criminal. Not to do so would surely have led to madness. I now take precautions to make myself less threatening. I move about with care, particularly late in the evening. I give a wide berth to nervous people on subway platforms during the wee hours. If I happen to be entering a building behind some people who appear skittish, I may walk by, letting them clear the lobby before I return, so as not to seem to be following them. I have been calm and extremely congenial on those rare occasions when I've been pulled over by the police.

10 And on late-evening constitutionals I employ what has proved to be an excellent tension-reducing measure: I whistle melodies from Beethoven and Vivaldi and the more popular classical composers. Even steely New Yorkers hunching toward nighttime destinations seem to relax, and occasionally they even join in the tune. Virtually everybody seems to sense that a mugger wouldn't be warbling bright, sunny selections from Vivaldi's *Four Seasons*. It is my equivalent of the cowbell that hikers wear when they are in bear country.

BUILDING VOCABULARY

1. Use context clues to determine the meaning of each word in italics. Return to the appropriate paragraph in the essay for more clues. Then, if necessary, check your definitions in a dictionary and compare the dictionary meaning with the meaning you derived from the context.

- **a.** seemed *menacingly* close (par. 1)
- **b.** I was *indistinguishable* from the muggers who occasionally *seeped* into the area (par. 2)
- **c.** I have remained an *avid* night walker (par. 4)
- **d.** they *forge* ahead (par. 5)
- **e.** Women are particularly *vulnerable* to street violence (par. 5)
- **f.** the *lethality* nighttime pedestrians attributed to me (par. 6)
- **g.** episodes of *bravado* played out in the streets (par. 6)
- **h.** I learned to *smother* the rage I felt . . . so often (par. 9)
- **i.** I now take *precautions* to make myself less threatening (par. 9)

j. Even *steely* New Yorkers *hunching* toward nighttime destinations (par. 10)

2. Reread paragraph 1. List all the words suggesting action and all the words involving emotion. What is the cumulative effect?

THINKING CRITICALLY ABOUT THE ESSAY

Understanding the Writer's Ideas

1. How does Staples describe himself in paragraph 1? What point is he making by such a description?
2. Explain in your own words the incident Staples narrates in paragraph 1. Where does it take place? when? How old was the author at the time? What was he doing? During the incident, why did the woman "cast back a worried glance"? Was she really his "victim"? Explain. What was Staples's reaction to the incident?
3. What is the "unwieldy inheritance" mentioned in paragraph 2? What is Staples's definition of it? What is the implied meaning?
4. How would you describe Staples's personality? What does he mean when he describes himself as "a softy"? How does he illustrate the fact that he is "a softy"? Why did he develop this personality?
5. Explain the meaning of the statement, "I soon gathered that being perceived as dangerous is a hazard in itself" (par. 2).
6. What is "the language of fear" (par. 3)? What examples does Staples provide to illustrate this "language"?
7. Why did car drivers lock their doors when the author walked in front of their cars? How did Staples feel about that?
8. Where did Staples grow up? Did he experience the same reactions there to his nighttime walks as he did in Chicago? Why? How was Manhattan different from Chicago for the author? How was Brooklyn different from Manhattan?
9. What has been Staples's reaction to the numerous incidents of mistaken identity? How has he dealt with that reaction? What "precautions" does he take to make himself "less threatening"?
10. Summarize the example Staples narrates about the black journalist in Waukegan.
11. What have been the author's experiences with the police? Explain.

12. Does the author feel that all the danger people attribute to him when he takes night walks is unfair or unwarranted? Explain.
13. Why does his whistling selections from Beethoven and Vivaldi seem to make people less afraid of the author?

Understanding the Writer's Techniques

1. What is Staples's thesis in this essay?
2. How do the title and opening statement of this essay grasp and hold the reader's interest?
3. Reread the first paragraph. What *mood* or *tone* does Staples establish here? How? Does he sustain that mood? Is there a shift in tone? Explain.
4. How does the author use *narration* in paragraph 1 as a way to illustrate a point? What point is illustrated? Where else does he use narration?
5. What is the effect of the two-word sentence "Not so" in paragraph 1?
6. Staples uses *description* in this essay. Which descriptions serve as illustrations? Explain what ideas they support.
7. *Onomatopoeia* is the use of words whose sounds suggest their sense or action. Where in the essay does Staples use this technique? What action does the sound represent? Why does the author use this technique instead of simply describing the action?
8. What examples from Staples's childhood illustrate why he developed his particular adult personality?
9. Explain the meaning of the final sentence in the essay.
10. *Stereotypes* are oversimplified, uncritical judgments about people, races, issues, events, and so forth. Where in this essay does the author present stereotypes? For what purpose?
11. For whom was this article intended? Why do you think so? Is it written primarily for a white or black audience? Explain.

Exploring the Writer's Ideas

1. In this essay, Staples gives not only examples of his own experiences but also those of other black men. It is interesting, however, that he does not include examples of the experiences of black women. Why do you think he omitted these references? How do you feel about the omission? Are there any

recent news stories, either in your city or in others, that might be included as such illustrations?
2. What prejudices and stereotypes about different racial and cultural groups do people in your community hold? Where do these prejudices and stereotypes come from? Do you think any are justified?
3. What everyday situations do you perceive as most dangerous? Why do you perceive them as such? How do you react to protect yourself? Do you feel your perceptions and reactions are realistic? Explain.

IDEAS FOR WRITING

Prewriting

Write down a few of your personality traits, and then jot down ways in which people identify those traits. Also, indicate how people misperceive you—that is, how they reach wrong conclusions about your personality.

Guided Writing

Write an essay that illustrates how something about your personality has been incorrectly perceived at some time or over a period of time.

1. Begin your essay by narrating a single incident that vividly illustrates the misperception. Begin this illustration with a statement.
2. Explain the time context of this incident as it fits into your life or into a continuing misperception.
3. Describe and illustrate "who you really are" in relation to this misperception.
4. Explain how this misperception fits into a larger context outside your immediate, personal experience of it.
5. Write a series of descriptive illustrations to explain how this misperception has continued to affect you over time.
6. Explain how you first became aware of the misperception.
7. If possible, offer illustrations of others who have suffered the same or similar misperceptions of themselves.
8. Write about your emotional reaction to this overall situation.

9. Illustrate how you have learned to cope with the situation.
10. Give your essay a "catchy" title.

Thinking and Writing Collaboratively

Form groups of four or five, and recommend productive ways to solve the key problems raised by Staples in his essay. Take notes, and then as a group write down the problems and their possible solutions. Share the group's writing with the rest of the class.

Writing About the Text

To advance his thesis, Staples relies on language that suggests anger, fear, and violence. Write an essay in which you examine this language in "Night Walker." Which words seem to express those elements? How do they relate to Staples's thesis? In what ways, if at all, is Staples angry, fearful, or violent? the people around him?

More Writing Projects

1. Usually stereotypes are thought of as negative. Illustrate at least three *positive* stereotypes in your latest journal entry.
2. Write a paragraph in which you illustrate your family's or friends' misconceptions about your girlfriend/boyfriend, wife/husband, or best friend.
3. What tension-reducing measures do you use in situations that might frighten you or in which you might frighten others? Write an essay to address the issue.

What I've Learned from Men

Barbara Ehrenreich

In this essay from *Ms.* magazine, the feminist author and historian Barbara Ehrenreich illustrates the qualities that have made her one of our most-read voices of dissent. Among these qualities is a sense of humor—though she can use her humor to deadly effect, as readers of her regular contributions to *The Nation* magazine, a weekly devoted to left-liberal commentary, can attest. Her work has been characterized by the *New York Times* as "elegant, trenchant, savagely angry, morally outraged and outrageously funny." Ehrenreich is the author of numerous essays and books, including *Fear of Falling: The Inner Life of the Middle Class* (1989), *The Snarling Citizen* (1995), and *Nickel and Dimed: On (Not) Getting By in America* (2001). *Nickel and Dimed* recounts three month-long stints in different American cities where Ehrenreich lived entirely on earnings from jobs paying \$7 or \$8 per hour. A recent essay for *The Nation,* "The Faith Factor" (2004), takes on politicians who use faith to obscure important social and political issues. Ehrenreich is the recipient of a National Magazine Award for Excellence in Reporting and of a Guggenheim Fellowship. In this selection, Ehrenreich shows that sometimes you can learn the most important things from your enemies, in this case, men. Aside from being able to catch the eye of a waiter, a not inconsiderable attribute, men have one wrongly maligned quality that women would do well to learn, Ehrenreich argues: how to be tough.

To learn more about Ehrenreich, click on **More Resources > Chapter 6 > Barbara Ehrenreich**

PREREADING: THINKING ABOUT THE ESSAY IN ADVANCE

What have you learned from the opposite sex? What expectations are raised by a woman saying she has learned something from men?

Words to Watch

euthanasia (par. 1) mercy killing
lecherous (par. 3) lewd

unconscionable (par. 3) beyond reasonable bounds
servility (par. 4) attitude appropriate to servants
AWOL (par. 4) used in military for Absent Without Leave
veneer (par. 4) mere outside show
rueful (par. 4) regretful
aura (par. 6) distinctive air
self-deprecation (par. 6) putting oneself down
brazenly (par. 6) shamelessly
taciturn (par. 9) silent
purveyors (par. 10) providers
emulating (par. 11) imitating
basso profundo (par. 11) deep bass voice
blandishments (par. 12) allurements

1 For many years I believed that women had only one thing to learn from men: how to get the attention of a waiter by some means short of kicking over the table and shrieking. Never in my life have I gotten the attention of a waiter, unless it was an off-duty waiter whose car I'd accidentally scraped in a parking lot somewhere. Men, however, can summon a maître d' just by thinking the word "coffee," and this is a power women would be well advised to study. What else would we possibly want to learn from them? How to interrupt someone in mid-sentence as if you were performing an act of conversational euthanasia? How to drop a pair of socks three feet from an open hamper and keep right on walking? How to make those weird guttural gargling sounds in the bathroom?

2 But now, at mid-life, I am willing to admit that there are some real and useful things to learn from men. Not from all men—in fact, we may have the most to learn from some of the men we like the least. This realization does not mean that my feminist principles have gone soft with age: what I think women could learn from men is how to get *tough*. After more than a decade of consciousness-raising, assertiveness training, and hand-to-hand combat in the battle of the sexes, we're still too ladylike. Let me try that again—we're just too *damn* ladylike.

3 Here is an example from my own experience, a story that I blush to recount. A few years ago, at an international conference held in an exotic and luxurious setting, a prestigious professor invited me to his room for what he said would be an intellectual discussion on matters of theoretical importance. So far, so good.

I showed up promptly. But only minutes into the conversation—held in all-too-adjacent chairs—it emerged that he was interested in something more substantial than a meeting of minds. I was disgusted, but not enough to overcome 30-odd years of programming in ladylikeness. Every time his comments took a lecherous turn, I chattered distractingly; every time his hand found its way to my knee, I returned it as if it were something he had misplaced. This went on for an unconscionable period (as much as 20 minutes); then there was a minor scuffle, a dash for the door, and I was out—with nothing violated but my self-esteem. I, a full-grown feminist, conversant with such matters as rape crisis counseling and sexual harassment at the workplace, had behaved like a ninny—or, as I now understand it, like a lady.

4 The essence of ladylikeness is a persistent servility masked as "niceness." For example, we (women) tend to assume that it is our responsibility to keep everything "nice" even when the person we are with is rude, aggressive, or emotionally AWOL. (In the above example, I was so busy taking responsibility for preserving the veneer of "niceness" that I almost forgot to take responsibility for myself.) In conversations with men, we do almost all the work: sociologists have observed that in male-female social interactions it's the woman who throws out leading questions and verbal encouragements ("So how did you *feel* about that?" and so on) while the man, typically, says "Hmmmm." Wherever we go, we're perpetually smiling—the on-cue smile, like the now-outmoded curtsy, being one of our culture's little rituals of submission. We're trained to feel embarrassed if we're praised, but if we see a criticism coming at us from miles down the road, we rush to acknowledge it. And when we're feeling aggressive or angry or resentful, we just tighten up our smiles or turn them into rueful little moues. In short, we spend a great deal of time acting like wimps.

5 For contrast, think of the macho stars we love to watch. Think, for example, of Mel Gibson facing down punk marauders in "The Road Warrior" . . . John Travolta swaggering his way through the early scenes of "Saturday Night Fever" . . . or Marlon Brando shrugging off the local law in "The Wild One." Would they simper their way through tight spots? Chatter aimlessly to keep the conversation going? Get all clutched up whenever they think they might—just might—have hurt someone's feelings? No, of course not, and therein, I think, lies their fascination for us.

6 The attraction of the "tough guy" is that he has—or at least seems to have—what most of us lack, and that is an aura of power and control. In an article, feminist psychiatrist Jean Baker Miller writes that "a Woman's using self-determined power for herself is equivalent to selfishness [and] destructiveness"—an equation that makes us want to avoid even the appearance of power. Miller cites cases of women who get depressed just when they're on the verge of success—and of women who do succeed and then bury their achievement in self-deprecation. As an example, she describes one company's periodic meetings to recognize outstanding salespeople: when a woman is asked to say a few words about her achievement, she tends to say something like, "Well, I really don't know how it happened. I guess I was just lucky this time." In contrast, the men will cheerfully own up to the hard work, intelligence, and so on, to which they owe their success. By putting herself down, a woman avoids feeling brazenly powerful and potentially "selfish"; she also does the traditional lady's work of trying to make everyone else feel better ("She's not really so smart, after all, just lucky").

7 So we might as well get a little tougher. And a good place to start is by cutting back on the small acts of deference that we've been programmed to perform since girlhood. Like unnecessary smiling. For many women—waitresses, flight attendants, receptionists—smiling is an occupational requirement, but there's no reason for anyone to go around grinning when she's not being paid for it. I'd suggest that we save our off-duty smiles for when we truly feel like sharing them, and if you're not sure what to do with your face in the meantime, study Clint Eastwood's expressions—both of them.

8 Along the same lines, I think women should stop taking responsibility for every human interaction we engage in. In a social encounter with a woman, the average man can go 25 minutes saying nothing more than "You don't say?" "Izzat so?" and, of course, "Hmmmm." Why should we do all the work? By taking so much responsibility for making conversations go well, we act as if we had much more at stake in the encounter than the other party—and that gives him (or her) the power advantage. Every now and then, we deserve to get more out of a conversation than we put into it: I'd suggest not offering information you'd rather not share ("I'm really terrified that my sales plan won't work") and not, out of sheer politeness, soliciting information you don't

really want ("Wherever did you get that lovely tie?"). There will be pauses, but they don't have to be awkward for *you*.

It is true that some, perhaps most, men will interpret any decrease in female deference as a deliberate act of hostility. Omit the free smiles and perky conversation-boosters and someone is bound to ask, "Well, what's come over *you* today?" For most of us, the first impulse is to stare at our feet and make vague references to a terminally ill aunt in Atlanta, but we should have as much right to be taciturn as the average (male) taxi driver. If you're taking a vacation from smiles and small talk and some fellow is moved to inquire about what's "bothering" you, just stare back levelly and say, the international debt crisis, the arms race, or the death of God. 9

There are all kinds of ways to toughen up—and potentially move up—at work, and I leave the details to the purveyors of assertiveness training. But Jean Baker Miller's study underscores a fundamental principle that anyone can master on her own. We can stop acting less capable than we actually are. For example, in the matter of taking credit when credit is due, there's a key difference between saying "I was just lucky" and saying "I had a plan and it worked." If you take the credit you deserve, you're letting people know that you were confident you'd succeed all along, and that you fully intend to do so again. 10

Finally, we may be able to learn something from men about what to do with anger. As a general rule, women get irritated: men get *mad*. We make tight little smiles of ladylike exasperation; they pound on desks and roar. I wouldn't recommend emulating the full basso profundo male tantrum, but women do need ways of expressing justified anger clearly, colorfully, and, when necessary, crudely. If you're not just irritated, but *pissed off*, it might help to say so. 11

I, for example, have rerun the scene with the prestigious professor many times in my mind. And in my mind, I play it like Bogart. I start by moving my chair over to where I can look the professor full in the face. I let him do the chattering, and when it becomes evident that he has nothing serious to say, I lean back and cross my arms, just to let him know that he's wasting my time. I do not smile, neither do I nod encouragement. Nor, of course, do I respond to his blandishments with apologetic shrugs and blushes. Then, at the first flicker of lechery, I stand up and announce coolly, "All right, I've had enough of this crap." Then I walk out—slowly, deliberately, confidently. Just like a man. 12

Or—now that I think of it—just like a woman. 13

BUILDING VOCABULARY

1. The writer uses a number of words ascribed to "ladies" for ironic effect. Try the same in sentences of your own that use the following:
   a. curtsy
   b. simper
   c. chatter
2. The writer is comfortable using a mixture of formal and informal words, as the essay requires. Use the following combinations of words in sentences or paragraphs of your own:
   a. prestigious (par. 3) *and* hand-to-hand combat (par. 2)
   b. theoretical (par. 3) *and* clutched up (par. 5)
   c. deliberate (par. 9) *and* perky (par. 9)

THINKING CRITICALLY ABOUT THE ESSAY

Understanding the Writer's Ideas

1. What does Ehrenreich's opening paragraph tell us about her attitude toward men?
2. The writer contrasts "being tough" and "being ladylike." What are the attitudes and behaviors that she associates with these opposing ways of being?
3. Why does the writer risk embarrassing herself by telling the story of her encounter with the "prestigious professor" of paragraph 3?
4. According to Ehrenreich, why are women reluctant to exert power?
5. The writer advocates two alternative strategies women should pursue "to get tough." The first is to stop doing things that are subservient; the second is to begin to act differently. What does she recommend women should stop doing, and why? What does she recommend women should start doing, and why?

Understanding the Writer's Techniques

1. *Tone* (see Glossary) expresses a writer's attitude toward his or her subject. What is the tone of the opening paragraph? What

does the tone of this paragraph suggest we can expect in the rest of the essay?
2. Why does Ehrenreich delay her thesis statement until close to the end of the second paragraph?
3. One key to a smooth, graceful essay is effective use of transitions. Explain how the writer establishes effective transitions between paragraphs 3 and 4, 4 and 5, and 6 and 7.
4. Writers sometimes seek to strengthen their arguments by quoting supporting views from authorities. For what reasons does the writer quote Jean Baker Miller?
5. Why does Ehrenreich mix informal and formal diction in this essay? What does this choice of diction suggest about her intended audience?
6. Why does the writer "rerun" the scene with the "prestigious professor" to conclude her essay?

Exploring the Writer's Ideas

1. Perhaps it is in the nature of waiters—who are often busy and pestered by customers—to make it hard for you to catch their attention, regardless of your gender. In that case, was Ehrenreich's envy of "men's" sway over waiters another case of a feminine inferiority complex, or is Ehrenreich simply using a rhetorical ploy to grab your attention at the start of her essay? Explain.
2. Ehrenreich seems to want us to distinguish between the servile characteristics of what is ladylike and the more robust qualities of women. Do you believe her portrait of a lady is fair and accurate? Why?
3. Is it a moral failing of the essay that the writer acknowledges only one possible character for all men, and that is the unattractive character of the "macho" male? Ought the essay to have provided us with a positive example of male character too? Does the absence of positive male role models weaken the essay's argument about women? Why or why not?
4. Ehrenreich's argument proceeds by building one generalization on another. She quotes Jean Baker Miller, for example, to make the point that *for all women* the exercise of power is associated with selfishness and destructiveness. If you can think of exceptions to her main general statements, does this undermine her argument for you, or do you remain persuaded

of her generalizations despite the exceptions? Discuss this in relation to one or two examples.

5. You are likely to have heard someone described as "one tough lady." How are the attributes of such a person the same as or different from those that Ehrenreich advocates for all women?

IDEAS FOR WRITING

Prewriting

Make a list of character traits generally associated with men, and another of traits generally associated with women. Then make a second list of those traits men might wish to adapt from women, and women from men.

Guided Writing

Write an essay titled "What I've Learned from ______." Fill in the blank with a word of your choice. Your essay should illustrate how you came to realize you could learn something positive from those you had long ago given up on as sources of wisdom. Some possible titles might be "What I've Learned from Parents," "What I've Learned from Professional Wrestlers," or "What I've Learned from the Boss."

1. Begin your essay by indicating why you long ago abandoned the idea that you could learn anything from "______."
2. But then explain why you have realized that the very thing that made "______" so unattractive might be instructive after all.
3. Provide an example from your own behavior where having a little more of that something undesirable you always disliked in "______" might have been a good thing.
4. Now explain how that nice quality of your own character that is just the opposite of the undesirable "______" might actually reflect a weakness or flaw in your character.
5. If possible, quote an authoritative source to underscore how your apparently good quality masks a serious weakness (as in the flaws of being a lady).
6. Now illustrate how adopting some of "______" behaviors would be a good thing.

7. Conclude by showing how this quality in "________," when adopted by you and those like you, actually better brings out what you are truly like.

Thinking and Writing Collaboratively

In small groups, discuss the lists of attributes of men and women you drew up in your Prewriting exercise. Do the qualities listed compose stereotypes, or do they reflect abiding truths about the differences between the sexes? Compare the lists made up by the students in your group—what can you conclude from the similarities and differences among these lists?

Writing About the Text

Many words in this essay are "man" words, that is, words that our culture often uses to describe and identify males. Similarly, many "woman" words appear here too. How does Ehrenreich use "man" and "woman" language to advantage here? Identify several words that she uses in each gender category and explore their effect on the essay.

More Writing Projects

1. For a journal entry, write about a quality, usually associated with the opposite sex, that you secretly admire, or wish you could say was a quality of your own.
2. In an essay, explore a quality in yourself or in people more generally that is commonly viewed as good—such as kindness—for its possibly "weak" or self-defeating underside (in the case of kindness, for example, always doing for others and never thinking of yourself).
3. Write an essay on the dangers of stereotyping, that is, of thinking of individuals as necessarily having the characteristics of a group.

Homeless on Campus

Eleanor J. Bader

Eleanor J. Bader is a social worker, freelance writer, and adjunct college instructor who has reviewed books for *Library Journal*. She is the coauthor of *Targets of Hatred: Anti-Abortion Terrorism* (2001), a study analyzing attitudes toward abortion and tracing crimes against family-planning clinics and personnel from the time of *Roe v. Wade* through the 1990s. Bader begins the following essay, published in *The Progressive* in July 2004, by profiling a young college student named Aesha, whom she taught at a New York City community college in the fall 2003 semester.

PREREADING: THINKING ABOUT THE ESSAY IN ADVANCE

Imagine that you discover a student who, unknown to others, is homeless on campus. What could you do to help this individual?

Words to Watch

respite (par. 2) an interval of temporary rest or relief
confide (par. 4) share secrets or discuss private affairs
rendered (par. 7) caused to be or become
temperate (par. 11) mild

1 Aesha is a twenty-year-old at Kingsborough Community College in Brooklyn, New York. Until the fall of 2003, she lived with five people—her one-year-old son, her son's father, her sister, her mother, and her mother's boyfriend—in a three-bedroom South Bronx apartment. Things at home were fine until her child's father became physically abusive. Shortly thereafter, Aesha realized that she and her son had to leave the unit.

2 After spending thirty days in a temporary shelter, they landed at the city's emergency assistance unit (EAU). "It was horrible," Aesha says. "We slept on benches, and it was very crowded. I was so scared I sat on my bag and held onto the stroller day and night, from Friday to Monday." Aesha and her son spent several nights in the EAU before being sent to a hotel. Sadly, this proved to be a temporary respite. After a few days, they were returned to

the EAU, where they remained until they were finally moved to a family shelter in Queens.

3 Although Aesha believes that she will be able to stay in this facility until she completes her associate's degree, the ordeal of being homeless has taken a toll on her and her studies. "I spend almost eight hours a day on the trains," she says. "I have to leave the shelter at 5:00 a.m. for the Bronx where my girlfriend watches my son for me. I get to her house around 7:00. Then I have to travel to school in Brooklyn—the last stop on the train followed by a bus ride—another two hours away."

4 Reluctantly, Aesha felt that she had no choice but to confide in teachers and explain her periodic absences. "They've all said that as long as I keep up with the work I'll be OK," she says. But that is not easy for Aesha or other homeless students.

5 Adriana Broadway lived in ten places, with ten different families, during high school. A native of Sparks, Nevada, Broadway told the LeTendre Education Fund for Homeless Children, a scholarship program administered by the National Association for the Education of Homeless Children and Youth, that she left home when she was thirteen. "For five years, I stayed here and there with friends," she wrote on her funding application. "I'd stay with whoever would take me in and allow me to live under their roof."

6 Johnny Montgomery also became homeless in his early teens. He told LeTendre staffers that his mother threw him out because he did not get along with her boyfriend. "She chose him over me," he wrote. "Hard days and hard nights have shaped me." Much of that time was spent on the streets.

7 Asad Dahir has also spent time on the streets. "I've been homeless more than one time and in more than one country," Dahir wrote on his scholarship application. Originally from Somalia, he and his family fled their homeland due to civil war and ended up in a refugee camp in neighboring Kenya. After more than a year in the camp, he and his thirteen-year-old brother were resettled, first in Atlanta and later in Ohio. There, high housing costs once again rendered the pair homeless.

8 Broadway, Montgomery, and Dahir are three of the forty-four homeless students from across the country who have been awarded LeTendre grants since 1999. Thanks, in part, to these funds, all three have been attending college and doing well.

9 But few homeless students are so lucky. "Each year at our national conference, homeless students come forward to share

their stories," says Jenn Hecker, the organizing director of the National Student Campaign Against Hunger and Homelessness. "What often comes through is shame. Most feel as though they should be able to cover their costs." Such students usually try to blend in and are reluctant to disclose either their poverty or homelessness to others on campus, she says. Hecker blames rising housing costs for the problem and cites a 2003 survey that found the median wage needed to pay for a two-bedroom apartment in the United States to be $15.21, nearly three times the federal minimum.

10 Even when doubled up, students in the most expensive states—Massachusetts, California, New Jersey, New York, and Maryland—are scrambling. "In any given semester, there are four or five families where the head of household is in college," says Beth Kelly, a family service counselor at the Clinton Family Inn, a New York City transitional housing program run by Homes for the Homeless.

11 Advocates for the homeless report countless examples of students sleeping in their cars and sneaking into a school gym to shower and change clothes. They speak of students who couch surf or camp in the woods—bicycling or walking to classes—during temperate weather. Yet, for all the anecdotes, details about homeless college students are hazy.

12 "I wish statistics existed on the number of homeless college students," says Barbara Duffield, executive director of the National Association for the Education of Homeless Children and Youth. "Once state and federal responsibility to homeless kids stops—at the end of high school—it's as if they cease to exist. They fall off the map."

13 Worse, they are neither counted nor attended to.

14 "Nobody has ever thought about this population or collected data on them because nobody thinks they are a priority to study," says Martha Burt, principal research associate at the Urban Institute.

15 Critics say colleges are not doing enough to meet—or even recognize—the needs of this group.

16 "The school should do more," says Aesha. "They have a child care center on my campus, but they only accept children two and up. It would have helped if I could've brought my son to day care at school." She also believes that the college should maintain emergency housing for homeless students.

"As an urban community college, our students are commuters," responds Uda Bradford, interim dean of student affairs at Kingsborough Community College. "Therefore, our student support services are developed within that framework." 17

"As far as I know, no college has ever asked for help in reaching homeless students," says Mary Jean LeTendre, a retired Department of Education administrator and creator of the LeTendre Education Fund. "Individual colleges have come forward to help specific people, but there is nothing systematic like there is for students in elementary and high school." 18

"There is a very low awareness level amongst colleges," Duffield adds. "People have this 'you can pull yourself up by your bootstraps' myth about college. There is a real gap between the myth and the reality for those who are trying to overcome poverty by getting an education." 19

Part of the problem is that the demographics of college attendance have changed. "Most educational institutions were set up to serve fewer, less diverse, more privileged students," says Andrea Leskes, a vice president with the Association of American Colleges and Universities. "As a result, we are not successfully educating all the students who come to college today. This means that nontraditional students—the older, returning ones as well as those from low income or other disenfranchised communities—often receive inadequate support services." 20

"It's not that colleges are not concerned, but attention today is not on serving the poor," says Susan O'Malley, chair of the faculty senate at the City University of New York. "It's not in fashion. During the 1960s, people from all over the country were going to Washington and making a lot of noise. The War on Poverty was influenced by this noise. Now the poor are less visible." 21

Mary Gesing, a counselor at Kirkwood Community College in Cedar Rapids, Iowa, agrees. "Nothing formal exists for this population, and the number of homeless students on campus is not tracked," she says. Because of this statistical gap, programs are not devised to accommodate homeless students or address their needs. 22

Despite these programmatic shortfalls, Gesing encounters two to three homeless students—often single parents—each semester. Some became homeless when they left an abuser. Others lost their housing because they could no longer pay for it due to a lost job, the termination of unemployment benefits, illness, the cessation of child support, or drug or alcohol abuse. 23

24 Kirkwood's approach is a "patchwork system," Gesing explains, and homeless students often drop out or fail classes because no one knows of their plight. "When people don't know who to come to for help they just fade away," she says.

25 "Without housing, access to a work space, or access to a shower, students' lives suffer, their grades suffer, and they are more likely to drop classes, if not withdraw entirely from school. I've seen it happen," says Amit Rai, an English professor at a large, public university in Florida. "If seen from the perspective of students, administrators would place affordable housing and full access to health care at the top of what a university should provide."

26 Yet for all this, individual teachers—as well as administrators and counselors—can sometimes make an enormous difference.

27 B.R., a faculty member who asked that neither her name nor school be disclosed, has allowed several homeless students to sleep in her office during the past decade. "Although there is no institutional interest or involvement in keeping these students enrolled, a few faculty members really care about the whole student and don't shy away from helping," she says.

28 One of the students she sheltered lived in the space for three months, whenever she couldn't stay with friends. Like Aesha, this student was fleeing a partner who beat her. Another student had been kicked out of the dorm because her stepfather never paid the bill. She applied for financial assistance to cover the cost, but processing took months. "This student stayed in my office for an entire semester," B.R. says.

29 A sympathetic cleaning woman knew what was going on and turned a blind eye to the arrangement. "Both students showered in the dorms and kept their toothbrushes and cosmetics in one of the two department bathrooms which I gave them keys to," B.R. adds. "The administration never knew a thing. Both of the students finished school and went on to become social workers. They knew that school would be their saving grace, that knowledge was the only thing that couldn't be snatched."

BUILDING VOCABULARY

1. Bader uses a number of words and phrases connected with the social sciences, including sociology, economics, and public

policy. Consider the following words and phrases in context, and then write definitions for them:
   a. emergency assistance unit (par. 2)
   b. median (par. 9)
   c. federal minimum (par. 9)
   d. transitional housing program (par. 10)
   e. principal research associate (par. 14)
   f. demographics (par. 20)
   g. nontraditional students (par. 20)
2. The key word in this essay is *homeless*. List some of the connotations that you associate with this word.

THINKING CRITICALLY ABOUT THE ESSAY

Understanding the Writer's Ideas

1. Identify the students whom Bader discusses in this essay. Where do they live? What are their backgrounds? How do they cope with their problems?
2. According to Bader, do college administrations acknowledge that they have homeless students on their campus? Explain.
3. What is a LeTendre grant? Do you think that such grants are an answer to the problem of homelessness on campus? Why or why not?
4. What do you think of Bader's observation that "for all the anecdotes, details about homeless college students are hazy"? Does such an admission undercut or compromise her article? Why or why not?
5. Why do you think the faculty member that Bader presents in the last section of the essay doesn't want her name or college disclosed? How does this fact temper your overall response to the problem that Bader presents?

Understanding the Writer's Techniques

1. Bader wrote this essay for a progressive magazine. Why would this magazine's audience be interested in Bader's subject? How do you think the readership would respond? Would readers accept the writer as an authority on the subject? Why or why not?

2. How does the opening paragraph of Bader's essay color the rest of what she writes about students who are homeless on campus? Does this opening paragraph have a thesis? More broadly, what *is* the thesis of the essay?
3. Bader's essay is made up largely of extended examples. What are they, and what do they have in common? What do they contribute to the essay? How successful would the essay be without them?
4. What other types of illustration does Bader use, and where? What is her specific purpose in each instance?
5. Why does Bader divide her essay into four sections? How does she maintain *unity* and *coherence* (see Glossary for these terms) from section to section?

Exploring the Writer's Ideas

1. Colleges and universities confront numerous problems that seem larger and more consequential than the possibility of homelessness. Do you think that colleges should devote time, attention, and money to a small group of students who might lack proper housing?
2. If, as Bader admits, it is hard to quantify the issue that she discusses, is it truly an issue? Why or why not? Can you think of another campus issue that might be hard to quantify completely?
3. According to Bader, certain cultural and demographic differences separate "ordinary" college students from those among their peers who are homeless. Discuss some of these differences, and how they might color campus life.

IDEAS FOR WRITING

Prewriting

Look around your classroom, and jot down several examples that serve to create a demographic profile of the students registered for the course.

Guided Writing

Write an essay titled "__________ on Campus." Fill in the blank with a problem or issue that you consider significant.

1. Begin with a profile, actual or imaginary, of a typical student who exemplifies the problem.
2. Provide a clearly stated thesis rather than an implied one.
3. Write, as Bader does, with an objective or calm tone.
4. Do some research or interview subjects, and incorporate your findings into the essay.
5. Present both extended and specific examples, making sure you have a variety of illustrative facts that illuminate your thesis.
6. End your paper with one final extended example that reinforces the main idea of the essay.

Thinking and Writing Collaboratively

In a group of four or five students, discuss the issue of homelessness on campus. Does anyone know of a homeless student or suspect that someone might be homeless? Are there forms of dress or behavior that might serve to "profile" a homeless student? Alternately, is your student body so homogenous and affluent, and the university so famous, that campus homelessness could never occur or be a problem?

Writing About the Text

Bader, as you already have discovered, makes use of several types of illustration. Write an essay in which you analyze these varieties of exemplification and the ways in which examples provide a center of gravity and unity for Bader's article.

More Writing Projects

1. Imagine that you are suddenly homeless on campus. In your journal, recount a typical day in your life.
2. Write a 150-word paragraph that gives an extended example of one type of student common to your campus.
3. Write an essay illustrating what you consider the inadequacy of your college to address a specific problem—for example, parking facilities, cafeteria cuisine, or campus violence.

Mixing Patterns

Globalization Rocked the Ancient World Too

Jared Diamond

Jared Diamond has published several well-received books and hundreds of articles spanning the fields of geography, ecology, evolutionary biology, physiology, history, and economics. Born in Boston in 1937, Diamond received his BA from Harvard University (1958) and a PhD from Cambridge University (1961). Currently a professor of geography at UCLA, he has conducted notable field research in New Guinea and other Pacific islands, and has served as director of the World Wildlife Fund. He received a Pulitzer Prize for *Guns, Germs, and Steel: The Fates of Human Societies* (1997) and also wrote the best-selling *Collapse: How Societies Choose to Fail or Succeed* (2004). Most recently, he is coauthor with James A. Robinson of *Natural Experiments of History* (2010). Diamond brings his wide-ranging expertise and knowledge to bear in an inquiry into globalization that appeared in the *Los Angeles Times* on September 14, 2003.

PREREADING: THINKING ABOUT THE ESSAY IN ADVANCE

There are few words more controversial or provocative today than *globalization*. What does this term mean to you? Why do people, organizations, and nations argue about it? Do you think that this argument is new—the result of recent trends or phenomena—or has globalization been a feature of political, economic, and social life for a long time?

Words to Watch

dispersal (par. 1) a distribution or scattering in all directions
domesticated (par. 3) tamed; to cause plants or animals to be no longer wild
pods (par. 5) the seedcase of peas, beans, etc.

nomadic (par. 7) characteristic of peoples who move about constantly in search of food, pasture, or conditions favorable to survival
conferred (par. 8) gave; bestowed on
intrinsic (par. 13) essential; inherent; not dependent on external circumstances
paradox (par. 16) a statement that seems contradictory or unbelievable but that may actually be true in fact

We tend to think of globalization as uniquely modern, a product of 20th century advances in transportation, technology, agriculture and communications. But widespread dispersal, from a few centers, of culture, language, political ideas and economic systems—even genetically modified foods—is actually quite an ancient phenomenon. 1

The first wave of globalization began around 8500 BC, driven primarily by genetically modified foods created in the Mideast and China, and to a lesser extent Mexico, the Andes and Nigeria. As those foods spread to the rest of the world, so did the cultures that created them, a process that reshaped the ancient world in much the same way the U.S., Europe and Japan are reshaping today's world. 2

Our ancient ancestors' method of genetically modifying food was of course much different from the way it is done today. When humans lived as hunters and gatherers, they had to make do with whatever wild plants and animals they found. It turned out, though, that some of the wild species upon which humans relied for food could be domesticated. Early farmers soon learned not only how to cultivate the resulting crops and raise livestock but also how to select the traits they valued, thereby genetically modifying foods. 3

In choosing to sow seeds from wild plants with particularly desirable traits—often the result of mutations—early farmers changed genetically, albeit unconsciously, the foods they raised. 4

Take the case of peas. Most wild pea plants carry a gene that makes their pods pop open on the stalk, causing the peas to spill onto the ground. It is no surprise that early farmers sought out mutant plants with a gene for pods that stayed closed, which made for an easier harvest. As a consequence of their preference, by selecting, over many generations, seeds from the plants that best served them, they ended up with a genetically modified variety of peas. 5

6 Would-be farmers in some regions had a huge advantage. It turned out that only a few species of wild plants and animals could be domesticated, most of them native to the Mideast, China, Mexico, the Andes or Nigeria—precisely those places that became ancient centers of power. The crops and livestock of those five restricted homelands of agriculture still dominate our foods today. Many of the lands most productive for modern agriculture—including California, Europe, Japan and Java—contributed no species that were domesticated.

7 Ancient people lucky enough to live in one of the few areas with wild plants that could be domesticated radically altered their societies. Hunters and gatherers traded their nomadic lifestyles for safer, more settled lives in villages near their gardens, orchards and pastures. Agricultural surpluses, like wheat and cheese, could be stored for winter or used to feed inventors and bureaucrats. For the first time in history, societies could support individuals who weren't directly involved in producing food and who therefore had time to govern or to figure out how to smelt iron and steel. As a result of all the extra food and stability, farming societies increased in population density a thousandfold over neighboring hunter-gatherers.

8 Ultimately, ancient genetically modified foods conferred military and economic might on the societies that possessed them. It was easy for armies of 1,000 farmers, brandishing steel swords and led by a general, to kill or drive out small bands of nomads armed only with wooden spears. The result was globalization, as early farmers spread out from those first five homelands, carrying their genes, foods, technologies, cultures, scripts and languages around the world.

9 It is because of this first wave of globalization that almost every literate person alive today uses one of only two writing systems: an alphabet derived from the first Mideastern alphabet or a character-based language that grew out of Chinese. This is also why more than 90% of people alive today speak languages belonging to just a half-dozen language families, derived thousands of years ago from a half-dozen languages of the five ancient homelands. The Indo-European family that includes English, for example, originated in the Mideast. But then as now, there was also a cost: Countless other ancient languages and cultures were eliminated as the early farmers and their languages spread.

The first wave of globalization moved faster along east-west axes than along north-south axes. The explanation is simple: Regions lying due east or west of one another share the same latitude, and therefore the same day length and seasonality. They are also likely to share similar climates, habitats and diseases, all of which means that crops, livestock and humans can spread east and west more easily, since the conditions to which they have adapted are similar. Conversely, crops, animals and technologies adapted to one latitude spread only with difficulty north or south to another latitude with a different seasonality and climate. 10

There are certainly differences between modern globalization and that first ancient wave. Today, crops are deliberately engineered in the laboratory rather than unconsciously in the field. And globalizing influences spread much more quickly by plane, phone and Internet than they did on foot and horseback. But the basic similarity remains: Now, as then, a few centers of innovation and power end up dominating the world. 11

Even in our modern wave of globalization, genetically modified crops tend to spread along an east-west rather than a north-south axis. That's because crops still remain as tied to particular climates as in ancient times. Plant breeders at U.S. firms like Monsanto concentrate on genetically modifying wheat, corn and other temperate-zone crops rather than coconuts, oil palms and other plants that grow in the tropics. That makes good business sense for American plant breeders, because the rich farmers who can afford their products live in the temperate zone, not in the tropics. But it also contributes to the widening gap between rich and poor countries. 12

Does this mean that tropical Paraguay and Zambia are eternally cursed, and that their citizens should accept poverty as fate? Of course not. Europeans and Americans themselves enjoy no intrinsic biological advantages: They just had the good luck to acquire useful technologies and institutions through accidents of geography. Anyone else who now acquires those same things can reap the same benefits. Japan, Malaysia, Singapore, South Korea and Taiwan already have; China and others are trying and will probably succeed. In addition, some poor countries that don't acquire enough technology to become rich can still acquire enough technology (like a few nukes, missiles, chemical weapons, germs or box-cutters) to cause a lot of trouble. 13

14 The biggest problem with today's wave of globalization involves differences between the First and Third worlds. Today, citizens in North America, Europe and Japan consume, on average, 32 times more resources (and produce 32 times more waste) than the billions of citizens of the Third World. Thanks to TV, tourism and other aspects of globalization, though, people in less affluent societies know about our lifestyle, and of course they aspire to it.

15 Vigorous debates are going on today about whether our world could sustain double its present population (along with its consumption and waste), or even whether our world's economy is sustainable at its present level. Yet those aren't the biggest risks. If, through globalization, everyone living on Earth today were to achieve the standard of living of an average American, the effect on the planet would be some 10 times what it is today, and it would certainly be unsustainable.

16 We can't prevent people around the world from aspiring to match our way of life any more than the exporters of culture during the first wave of globalization could expect other cultures not to embrace the farming way of life. But since the world couldn't sustain even its present population if all people lived the way that those in the First World do now, we are left with a paradox. Globalization, most analysts feel, is unstoppable. But its consequences may overtax the Earth's ability to support us. That's a paradox that needs resolving.

BUILDING VOCABULARY

1. Write sentences using the following words. Consult a dictionary if you are uncertain of a word's meaning.
   a. genetically modified foods (par. 2)
   b. species (par. 3)
   c. mutations (par. 4)
   d. Indo-European (par. 9)
   e. temperate zone (par. 12)
2. The word *globalization* appears often in this essay, but Diamond never defines it. Nevertheless, by examining the word in context, you can arrive at an understanding of what the writer means by the term. Write your own definition of globalization based on the evidence that Diamond offers.

THINKING CRITICALLY ABOUT THE ESSAY

Understanding the Writer's Ideas

1. What is the "first wave" of globalization as Diamond presents it? What are some of this first wave's features?
2. Identify the paragraph or paragraphs that focus on genetically modified foods. What effect do they have?
3. Where does Diamond discuss language, and why?
4. According to Diamond, what are the differences between ancient and modern globalization?
5. Explain the "paradox" that Diamond presents in paragraph 16. Does this paradox make him optimistic or pessimistic about the future, in your opinion?

Understanding the Writer's Techniques

1. What paragraphs mark Diamond's introduction and conclusion? How are the two connected?
2. How does Diamond establish his authority in this essay? Does he use his extensive knowledge to convince his audience? Is he objective or subjective in the presentation of facts? How do you know?
3. Which paragraphs constitute the first and second halves of the essay? What paragraph functions as a transitional unit?
4. Diamond supports his thesis with examples drawn from numerous fields of knowledge. What are some of the areas that he taps for facts and information? Which examples are the most effective and why?
5. What types of illustration does Diamond use, and where do they appear in the essay?
6. Explain whether you find Diamond's examples sufficient evidence for his thesis.

✷ MIXING PATTERNS

Illustration is a major rhetorical strategy that Diamond uses here, but comparison and contrast (see Chapter 7) is also a key organizing method. How do these two writing strategies interact? How do illustration and comparison and contrast, working together, help to advance Diamond's thesis?

Exploring the Writer's Ideas

1. Diamond concludes his essay with the statement, "Globalization, most analysts feel, is unstoppable. But its consequences may overtax the Earth's ability to support us. That's a paradox that needs resolving." Do you think that this paradox can be resolved? Why or why not?
2. Why does Diamond focus so much on genetically modified foods? Is his concentration on this subject justified? Justify your response.
3. Does Diamond persuade you to his point of view that globalization seems to be as old as civilization itself? Explain.

IDEAS FOR WRITING

Prewriting

What might history—ancient or more modern—tell us about today's global problems? Can we learn anything from history? For five or ten minutes, brainstorm in response to these questions.

Guided Writing

Write an essay responding to Diamond's claim that globalization contributes to the widening gap between rich and poor nations.

1. Write an introduction that clearly states your thesis or opinion on the subject.
2. Begin the body of your essay by limiting your scope and time frame. Will you focus exclusively on the present, provide historical background (which might require research on your part), concentrate on one country, region, or continent, or what?
3. Offer vivid examples designed to illustrate how globalization affects rich and poor, developed and underdeveloped nations and regions.
4. Draw at least two examples from Diamond's essay, being certain to cite him for this information.
5. Write with an objective tone—as if you are trying to lay out a problem (or paradox) in a calm, balanced way.
6. Offer a conclusion in which you state your opinion as to whether the issues raised by globalization can be resolved.

Thinking and Writing Collaboratively

Exchange your Guided Writing essay with another student and write a one-paragraph response to it in which you focus on the nature and effectiveness of the examples. Does your classmate provide sufficient examples to support the thesis? What types of examples—for instance, facts, statistics, expert testimony—appear in the essay? Which types work best? For those essays where you find insufficient evidence, explain how your fellow student could strengthen the paper with new examples.

Writing About the Text

Diamond makes many references to peoples, nations, and regions in order to make his point. Write an essay in which you identify and analyze the use of these examples. How do they advance Diamond's thesis?

More Writing Projects

1. Write a journal entry about your own experience with the forces of globalization.
2. Compose a paragraph outlining your opinion of genetically modified foods.
3. Assume that you have been asked by the editor of your college newspaper to write an article on globalization and its effect on your campus. Prepare a 750-word response to this request.

SUMMING UP: CHAPTER 6

1. Staples's essay is about problems between ethnic and racial groups. Ehrenreich's essay is about gender problems. How do both selections deal with the way these problems affect society today? Write your own essay about this issue. Draw on examples from both of these essays to help illustrate your argument.
2. From this chapter select the essay that you think best uses the mode of illustration. Write an essay entitled "How to Write an Exemplification Essay" in which you analyze the writer's techniques and strategies and explain how to make use of them. Make sure you use specific references to the text.
3. The world of the night, the environment of Staples's "Night Walker," challenges our senses and our perceptions, simply because it is so different from the typical daytime worlds we usually inhabit. What unusual nighttime experiences have you had? How do you feel about the nighttime? Write an essay of illustration to address these questions.
4. Both Staples and Bader write about how stereotypes can prevent us from seeing a more diverse truth. What ideas and examples from Bader's essay would support Staples's thesis? What ideas and examples from Staples's essay would support Bader's thesis?
5. All the writers in this chapter use illustration to challenge a widely held view. The view, these essays suggest, is held by many people, maybe by most people. For example, many white women feel nervous about black men walking behind them on dark deserted streets; many people don't think about how globalization affects the wider environment; and so forth. How is illustration an effective method for writers to use in order to achieve this purpose? What other rhetorical means could these writers have used? Write an essay that argues for or against the view that illustration is an extremely effective tool for poking holes in a commonly held point of view.
6. You could easily overhear the following comment in a casual conversation: "I don't know about that—give me an example." The comment implies that the speaker has heard something she's skeptical about; she wants an example to support the contention. A social scientist might say skeptically to Diamond, "Globalization isn't new? I don't believe it. Give

me an example." Or one of us might ask Bader, "What do you mean by saying homelessness on campus is a problem? I don't get it. Give me an example." Do the examples provided in "Homelessness on Campus" and "Globalization Rocked the Ancient World Too" persuade you to agree with the thesis of the essays? Explain your answer in an essay.

✷ FROM SEEING TO WRITING

Look at the photograph of the destruction caused by a devastating earthquake and tsunami that hit Japan in March 2011. Develop a thesis about the picture that you can support through the strategies of illustration explored in this chapter. Then, write an essay in which you draw on features of the photographic image to support your thesis. Make specific references to what you see in the picture.

CHAPTER 7

Comparison and Contrast

WHAT IS COMPARISON AND CONTRAST?

When we compare two things, we look for similarities. When we contrast, we look for differences. The comparison-contrast writing strategy, then, is a way of analyzing likenesses and differences between two or more subjects. Usually, the purpose is to evaluate or judge which is superior. Thus we might appreciate soccer if we compare it with football; we understand Roman Catholicism better if we see it in light of Buddhism.

Writers who use the comparison-contrast technique know that careful planning is required to *organize* the likenesses and differences into logical patterns. Some authors might use only *comparison* to look at the similarities between subjects. Others might use only *contrast*. Often, writers combine the two in a carefully structured essay that balances one with the other.

Like many of the writing and reading strategies you have learned, comparison and contrast is familiar from everyday life. If you were about to buy a new car, for instance, you would look at several models before you made a choice. You might consider price, size, horsepower, options, safety features, status, and dependability before you spent such a large amount of money. If you were deciding whether to send your daughter to a public school or a private school, you would compare and contrast the features of each type of institution: cost, teacher quality, class size, location, curriculum, and composition of the student body might all be considered. If you were an art historian, you might compare and contrast an early picture by Matisse with one he completed late in life in order to understand his development as an artist.

Writing a comparison-contrast essay requires more careful planning, however, than the everyday life application technique. Both call for common sense. You wouldn't compare parochial schools with an Oldsmobile, for instance; they simply don't relate. But you would compare The Dalton School with Public School 34, or a Cutlass Supreme with a Volvo, a Matisse with a Cézanne. Clearly, any strong pattern of comparison and contrast treats items that are in the same category or class. Moreover, there always has to be a basis for comparison; in other words, you compare or contrast two items in order to try to deal with all-important aspects of the objects being compared before arriving at a final determination. These commonsense characteristics of comparison and contrast apply to our pattern of thought as well as our pattern of writing.

Author Rachel Carson, for instance, contrasts two visions of the future for planet Earth: a flourishing environment or a devastated landscape. Thus she has a common category: the condition of the global ecology. She can use *contrast* because she has a common ground for her analysis. Dave Barry looks at social behaviors among men and women, Michele Ingrassia discusses the different body images of black girls and white girls. Finally, Deborah Tannen examines the striking ways in which mothers and daughters relate to each other. Each author sets up a formal pattern for contrasting and comparing subjects within a related class. One side of the pattern helps us understand the other. Finally, we may establish a preference for one or the other subject.

HOW DO WE READ COMPARISON AND CONTRAST?

Reading comparison and contrast requires us to ask ourselves these questions:

- What subjects has the author selected? Are they from a similar class or category?
- What is the basis for the comparison or contrast? What is the writer's *thesis*?
- What is the arrangement of topics? How has the writer organized each paragraph? Notice where transitional expressions (*on the one hand, on the other hand, similarly, in contrast*) help the reader follow the writer's train of thought.
- Is the writer fair to each subject, devoting an equal amount of space to each side? Make an outline of one of the reading selections to see how the writer has balanced the two subjects.

- Has the writer used narration, description, or illustration to develop the comparison? What other techniques has the author used?
- Does the conclusion show a preference for one subject over the other? Is the conclusion justified by the evidence in the body?

HOW DO WE WRITE COMPARISON AND CONTRAST?

After reading the professional writers in this chapter, you will be better prepared to organize your own essay. Begin by clearly identifying the subjects of your comparison and by establishing the basis for it. The thesis sentence performs this important function for you.

Sample thesis statement:

> Living in a small town is better than living in a big city because life is safer, friendlier, and cheaper.

Plan a strategy for the comparison and contrast. Writers can use one of three main techniques: block, alternating, or combination. The *block method* requires that the writer put all the points about one side (the small town in this case) in one part of the essay, and all the points about the other side (big-city life) together in another part of the essay. In the *alternating method,* the writer explains one point about small-town life and then immediately gives the contrasting point about big-city life. The *combination* pattern allows the writer to use both alternating and block techniques.

Make a careful outline. For each point about one side, try to find a balancing point about the other. If, for instance, you write about the housing available in a small town, write about housing in the big city. Although it may be impossible to manage exact matches, try to be as fair as possible to each side.

Writing and Revising the Draft

Set up a purpose for the comparison and contrast in the thesis sentence.

Write an outline using paragraph blocks to indicate subject A and subject B. For instance, if you were going to write in the block form, your outline would look like this:

Introduction (with thesis)
Block A: Small Town
1. housing
2. jobs
3. social life
Block B: Big City
1. housing
2. jobs
3. social life
Conclusion

If you were going to use the alternating form, the outline would look as follows:

Introduction (with thesis)
Block A: Housing
1. big city
2. small town
Block B: Jobs
1. big city
2. small town
Block C: Social Life
1. big city
2. small town
Conclusion

Use transitional devices, especially with the alternating form. Each time you shift from one subject to the other, use a transition as needed: *like, unlike, on the one hand, on the other hand, in contrast, similarly.*

In the conclusion, offer your view of the two subjects.

Proofread carefully. Check the draft for clarity and correctness and make a final copy.

A STUDENT PARAGRAPH: COMPARISON AND CONTRAST

Here is a body paragraph from a student essay comparing small-town life and city life. Using the alternating method described above, the student concentrates here on housing, presenting the efforts she made first to find an apartment in her home town and then to find a place to live in Chicago.

Finding an apartment back home in Quincy was easy, but Chicago was a whole different ball game. In Quincy, I found an affordable one-bedroom place with the help of a friendly local real estate agent. The apartment consisted of three huge, sunny, high-ceilinged rooms that looked out over a stretch of velvety green lawn—and it was all just for me, no roommates, since I could easily pay the rent out of my weekly paycheck. When I moved to the big city, however, my luck ran out. The phonebook's long list of realtors looked too intimidating, so I first scoured the classified ads in the Chicago Tribune. After visiting all the places I could afford, I realized that in the language of the classifieds, "cozy" meant the size of a Quincy closet, and "fixer-upper" meant that slamming a door would bring the place tumbling down over my ears. I decided to try an apartment-finding service instead. When I admitted how little I had to spend on rent, a grim-faced woman who worked there offered me a list of apartments to share. The first potential roomie I met this way opened the door flushed, sweating, and dressed in blue Spandex from head to toe. Bad 1980s dance music blared from the living room. She looked put out that I had interrupted her aerobics routine and handed me a list of rules that specified, among other things, that I could bring only fat-free food into the kitchen. Another required an oath to engage only in "healthy thoughts" while on the premises. I excused myself as politely as I could and called home to Quincy to see if I could get my old place back.

Topic statement

Alternating method of contrast: Quincy first

Supporting detail

Transition reminds reader of previous point and flows smoothly into next point to produce *coherence*

Alternating method: Chicago second

Supporting detail

"Quincy closet" connects to previous point

Supporting detail

Supporting detail

Closing sentence clinches paragraph's main point

A Fable for Tomorrow

Rachel Carson

Rachel Carson (1907–1964), "the mother of the modern environmental movement," was raised in a simple farmhouse outside the river town of Springdale in western Pennsylvania. The first woman to take and pass the civil service exam, Carson worked for the Bureau of Fisheries from 1936 to 1952, rising to be the editor-in-chief of publications for the U.S. Fish and Wildlife Service. In 1951 she published *The Sea Around Us,* a groundbreaking book on life under the sea based on her years of work as a marine biologist. Her most famous book, *Silent Spring* (1962), raised the alarm about the use of pesticides and other chemicals in the production of food. The book was one of the earliest popular works alerting Americans to the dangers facing our natural environment. *Silent Spring* impressed President Kennedy, who ordered testing of and research into the substances Carson brought under scrutiny in the book. In this selection from *Silent Spring,* Carson establishes contrasts for an imaginary town as part of a literary strategy to call attention to the implications of today's practices for tomorrow. A concerned citizen and an informed advocate for a clean environment, Carson here makes her argument not through statistics or other facts, but through a *fable*. A fable is a story, usually fictitious, intended to point to a moral. Why does Carson choose to make her argument through a fable?

To learn more about Carson, click on
More Resources > Chapter 7 > Rachel Carson

PREREADING: THINKING ABOUT THE ESSAY IN ADVANCE

What dangers do you see affecting our environment over the next decades? How can we as a society address these environmental problems?

Words to Watch

migrants (par. 2) people, animals, or birds that move from one place to another

blight (par. 3) a disease or condition that kills or checks growth

DESCRIPTION AND NARRATION

1. What story do you think this photograph tells? What sensory elements, such as action and colors, does the photograph present? What sensory images, such as sound, touch, and smell, does the photograph imply?
2. Write a few paragraphs in which you tell the story of this photograph. Use clear sensory images to bring the scene to life. Or, if you prefer, write a lively narrative about an athletic experience in your life.

PROCESS

1. Throughout the days we go through many processes. For example, there is the process of getting ready for work or school, and the steps involved in both those activities. If you cook a meal for yourself or your family, you are following a number of steps that culminate in the finished meal. Building something—as the photo illustrates—is yet another process. What do you think are the steps involved in building (or assembling) something? How are those steps similar or different from other process, such as cooking, exercising, or studying?
2. Write a few paragraphs about a creative process (such as writing or painting) as you see it. Identify the various steps: remember that the steps do not have to be linear, that is, they need not follow each other in an exact sequence.

ILLUSTRATION

1. What point do you think this series of ads is attempting to make? What similarities and differences do you note among them? How do you account for the differences?
2. Write a brief illustrative essay about how these advertisements for Coca-Cola use women to sell the product. Or select a series of advertisements for some other product or products, and write an essay about how they use women to improve sales.

COMPARISON AND CONTRAST

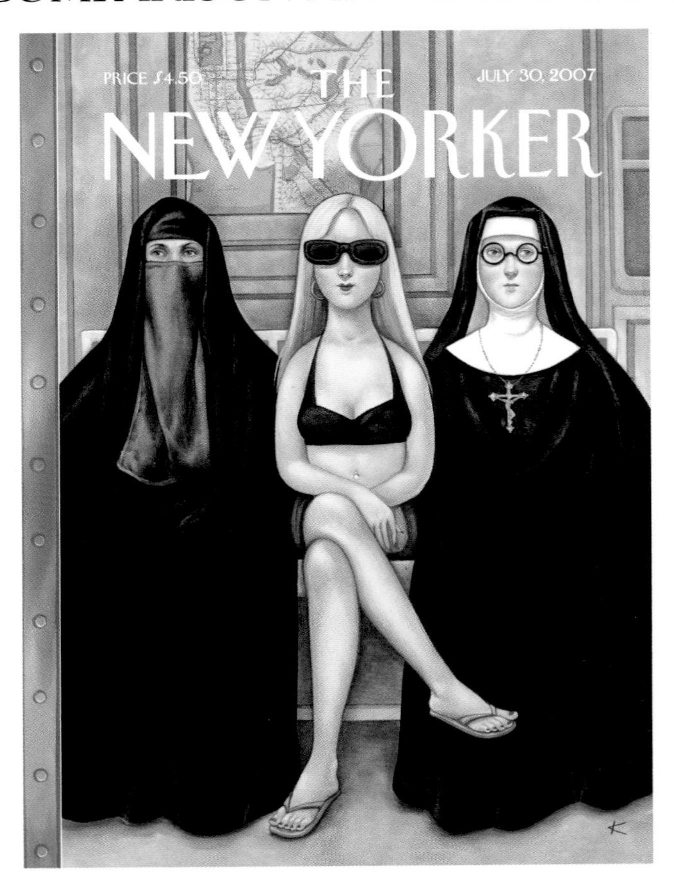

1. Describe the three characters portrayed in this magazine cover. What does their clothing tell you about them? How are they different? In what ways are they similar?
2. Write a brief paper in which you compare and contrast the basic values implied by the three figures in this illustration. What point is the illustrator making about the generations and about systems of belief?

CAUSE AND EFFECT

1. What do you think is happening in the photograph? What emotions does the photograph stir within you?
2. Write a few paragraphs in which you identify the causes that led to the scene portrayed here. Or write about the effects of the scene on the couple seated at the table, and the young woman standing behind them.

CLASSIFICATION

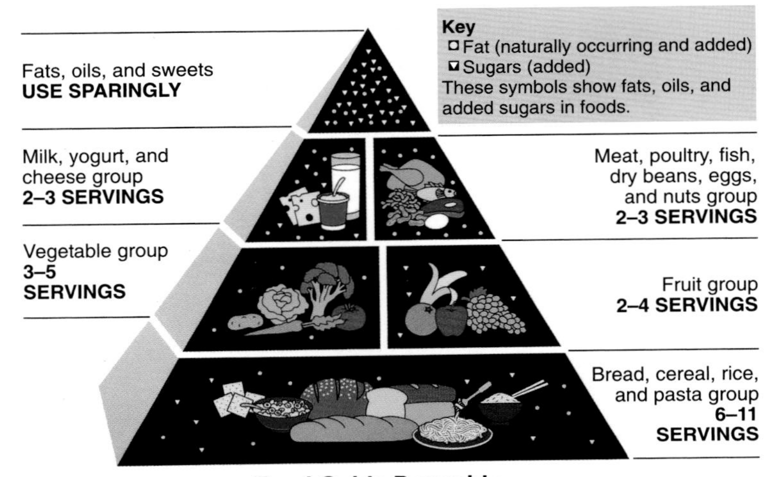

Food Guide Pyramid

1. What is the main point of the classification scheme shown here? What categories appear, and how are they organized? Why was a pyramid selected as the key design element?
2. Write a brief essay in which you classify the types of food that you enjoy and those that you tend to avoid. How well does your diet reflect the recommendations contained in the U.S. Department of Agriculture's Food Guide Pyramid?

DEFINITION

1. What does this ad imply about the nature of work in today's marketplace? What exactly is a workaholic? Do you think the ad is legitimate or just a humorous attempt to make us think about work in a new light?
2. Write a brief paper defining the word *workaholic*. Draw on your own experience or readings, and use the ad above as a springboard for your paper.

ARGUMENT

1. Why did the milk promotion board select race car driver Danica Patrick for this advertisement? What elements in this ad stand out? How does the image of Patrick reinforce the ad.
2. Write an essay on the power of celebrities from the worlds of sports, music, and film to sell a product or promote a cause. Refer to specific stars to support your main idea or claim.

maladies (par. 3) illnesses
moribund (par. 4) dying
pollination (par. 5) the transfer of pollen (male sex cells) from one part of the flower to another
granular (par. 7) consisting of grains
specter (par. 9) a ghost; an object of fear or dread
stark (par. 9) bleak; barren; standing out in sharp outline

1 There was once a town in the heart of America where all life seemed to live in harmony with its surroundings. The town lay in the midst of a checkerboard of prosperous farms, with fields of grain and hillsides of orchards where, in spring, white clouds of bloom drifted above the green fields. In autumn, oak and maple and birch set up a blaze of color that flamed and flickered across a backdrop of pines. Then foxes barked in the hills and deer silently crossed the fields, half-hidden in the mists of the fall mornings.

2 Along the roads, laurel, viburnum and alder, great ferns and wildflowers delighted the traveler's eye through much of the year. Even in winter the roadsides were places of beauty, where countless birds came to feed on the berries and on the seed heads of the dried weeds rising above the snow. The countryside was, in fact, famous for the abundance and variety of its bird life, and when the flood of migrants was pouring through in spring and fall people traveled from great distances to observe them. Others came to fish the streams, which flowed clear and cold out of the hills and contained shady pools where trout lay. So it had been from the days many years ago when the first settlers raised their houses, sank their wells, and built their barns.

3 Then a strange blight crept over the area and everything began to change. Some evil spell had settled on the community: mysterious maladies swept the flocks of chickens; the cattle and sheep sickened and died. Everywhere was a shadow of death. The farmers spoke of much illness among their families. In the town the doctors had become more and more puzzled by new kinds of sickness appearing among their patients. There had been several sudden and unexplained deaths not only among adults but even among children, who would be stricken suddenly while at play and die within a few hours.

4 There was a strange stillness. The birds, for example—where had they gone? Many people spoke of them, puzzled and disturbed. The feeding stations in the backyards were deserted.

The few birds seen anywhere were moribund; they trembled violently and could not fly. It was a spring without voices. On the mornings that had once throbbed with the dawn chorus of robins, catbirds, doves, jays, wrens, and scores of other bird voices there was now no sound; only silence lay over the fields and woods and marsh.

On the farms the hens brooded, but no chicks hatched. The farmers complained that they were unable to raise any pigs—the litters were small and the young survived only a few days. The apple trees were coming into bloom but no bees droned among the blossoms, so there was no pollination and there would be no fruit. 5

The roadsides, once so attractive, were now lined with browned and withered vegetation as though swept by fire. These, too, were silent, deserted by all living things. Even the streams were now lifeless. Anglers no longer visited them, for all the fish had died. 6

In the gutters under the eaves and between the shingles of the roofs, a white granular powder still showed a few patches; some weeks before it had fallen like snow upon the roofs and the lawns, the fields and streams. 7

No witchcraft, no enemy action had silenced the rebirth of new life in this stricken world. The people had done it themselves. 8

This town does not actually exist, but it might easily have a thousand counterparts in America or elsewhere in the world. I know of no community that has experienced all the misfortunes I describe. Yet every one of these disasters has actually happened somewhere, and many real communities have already suffered a substantial number of them. A grim specter has crept upon us almost unnoticed, and this imagined tragedy may easily become a stark reality we all shall know. 9

BUILDING VOCABULARY

1. In the second paragraph, find at least five concrete words that relate to trees, birds, and vegetation. How many of these objects could you identify? Look in a dictionary for the meanings of those words you do not know.
2. Try to identify the italicized words through the *context clues* (see Glossary) provided by the complete sentence.

a. half-hidden in the *mists* (par. 1)
b. when the first settlers *raised* their houses (par. 2)
c. *stricken* suddenly while at play (par. 3)
d. the hens *brooded,* but no chicks hatched (par. 5)
e. *Anglers* no longer visited them, for all the fish had died. (par. 6)

THINKING CRITICALLY ABOUT THE ESSAY

Understanding the Writer's Ideas

1. What is the quality of the world that Carson describes in her opening paragraph? If you had to describe it in just one or two words, which would you use?
2. What are some of the natural objects that Carson describes in her first two paragraphs? Why does she not focus on simply one aspect of nature—like animals, trees, or flowers?
3. How does Carson describe the "evil spell" that settles over the countryside?
4. What does Carson mean when she declares, "It was a spring without voices" (par. 4)? Why does she show that the critical action takes place in the springtime?
5. What do you think is the "white granular powder" that Carson refers to in paragraph 7? Why does she not explain what it is or where it came from?
6. In paragraph 9, the writer states her basic point. What is it? Does she offer a solution to the problem that she poses?

Understanding the Writer's Techniques

1. A *fable* is a story with a moral; in other words, a fable is a form of teaching narrative. How does Carson structure her narrative in this essay? What is the "moral" or thesis?
2. What is the purpose of the description in this essay? Why does the writer use such vivid and precise words?
3. Where in this essay does the writer begin to shift from an essentially positive tone to a negative one?
4. Does Carson rely on comparison or contrast in this essay? Defend your choice with references to the text.

5. In the *block method* of comparison and contrast, the writer presents all information about one subject, and then all information about a second subject, as in the following:

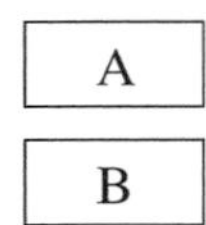

   a. How does Carson use this pattern in her essay?
   b. Are there actually two subjects in this essay, or two different aspects of one subject? How does chronology relate to the block structure?
   c. Are the two major parts of Carson's essay equally weighted? Why or why not?
   d. In the second part of the essay, does Carson ever lose sight of the objects introduced in the first part? What new terms does she introduce?
6. How can you explain paragraphs 8 and 9—which do not involve narration, description, or comparison and contrast—in relation to the rest of the essay? What is the nature of Carson's conclusion?

Exploring the Writer's Ideas

1. Today we use chemicals to destroy crop insects, to color and preserve food, and to purify our water, among other things. Would Carson term this "progress"? Would you? Do you think that there are inadequate safeguards and controls in the use of chemicals? What recent examples of chemical use have made the news?
2. Why would you agree or disagree that factories and corporations should protect the environment that they use? Should a company, for example, be forced to clean up an entire river that it polluted? What about oil spills?
3. What problems with the use of chemicals and the environment can you identify in your own area? How do local citizens feel about these problems?

4. Do you think that it will be possible in the future for Americans to "live in harmony" with their natural surroundings? Why do you believe what you do?

IDEAS FOR WRITING

Prewriting

Define the word *fable*. List the various elements that you think contribute to successful fables.

Guided Writing

Write a fable (an imaginary story with a moral) in which you contrast one aspect of the life of a person, community, or nation with another.

1. Begin with a phrase similar to Carson's "There was once. . . ." so that the reader knows you are writing a narrative fable.
2. Relate your story to an American problem.
3. Use the block method in order to establish your contrast. Write first about one aspect of the topic and then about the other.
4. Use sensory detail in order to make your narrative clear and interesting.
5. Make certain that you establish an effective transition as you move into the contrast.
6. In the second part of your essay, be sure to refer to the same points you raised in the first part.
7. Use the conclusion to establish the "moral" of your fable.

Thinking and Writing Collaboratively

Exchange Guided Writing essays with another member of the class. Has the writer produced a successful fable? Why or why not? Is the moral clear? Is the American problem well defined? Finally, discuss the structure of the essay. Has the writer used the block method of development appropriately? Does an effective transition link the contrast with the stated problem?

Writing About the Text

Write an essay arguing *either* that Carson's fable changed your view of the responsibility of corporations to protect the environment *or* that Carson's fable was too imaginary to influence your thinking one way or another.

More Writing Projects

1. In a journal entry, describe a place you know well, one that has changed for better or worse. Contrast the place as it once was with the way it is now. Use concrete images that appeal to color, action, sound, smell, taste, and touch.
2. Examine in two block paragraphs the two sides of a specific ecological issue today—for instance, acid rain, the global warming trend, or the use of nuclear energy.
3. Using the block method, compare and contrast Carson's fable with the fable you wrote in Guided Writing.

Punch and Judy

Dave Barry

Dave Barry, a syndicated columnist for *The Miami Herald,* has a reputation as one of the funniest writers in the country. He started his career as a reporter but found his great success in writing his regular column, for which he won the Pulitzer Prize for commentary in 1988. Barry is the author of *Dave Barry's Money Secrets* (2006), *Dave Barry's History of the Millennium, So Far* (2007), and *I'll Mature When I'm Dead* (2010), among many others. Network television turned his life into a sitcom called *Dave's World,* which ran from 1993 to 1997. In this selection, Barry explains the difference between how men and women play.

PREREADING: THINKING ABOUT THE ESSAY IN ADVANCE

Think about jobs you've held or classes you've been in. Have you noticed any differences between how men and women approach work? What are some of those differences, and why do you think they exist?

Words to Watch

snag (par. 2) problem
deadlock (par. 2) seemingly unsolvable problem
compromise (par. 2) agreement to resolve a matter
syndrome (par. 5) combinations of symptoms that point to a particular problem
subatomic (par. 7) relating to particles smaller than an atom
puncturing (par. 8) damaging by making a hole

1 Are you a male, or a female? To find out, take this scientific quiz:

2 **1.** Your department is on a tight deadline for developing a big sales proposal, but you've hit a snag on a key point. You want to go one way; a co-worker named Bob strongly disagrees. To break the deadlock, you:

- **a.** Present your position, listen to the other side, then fashion a workable compromise.
- **b.** Punch Bob.

2. Your favorite team is about to win the championship, but at the last second the victory is stolen away by a terrible referee's call. You: 3
   - a. Remind yourself that it's just a game, and that there are far more important things in your life.
   - b. Punch Bob again.

How to score: If you answered "b" to both questions, then you are a male. I base this statement on a recent article in the *New York Times* about the way animals, including humans, respond to stress. According to the article, a group of psychology researchers have made the breakthrough discovery that—prepare to be astounded—males and females are different. 4

The researchers discovered this by studying both humans and rats, which are very similar to humans except that they are not stupid enough to purchase lottery tickets. The studies show that when males are under stress, they respond by either fighting or running away (the so-called "fight or flight" syndrome); whereas females respond by nurturing others and making friends (the so-called "tend and befriend" syndrome). 5

This finding is big news in the psychology community, which apparently is located on a distant planet. Here on Earth, we have been aware for some time that males and females respond differently to stress. We know that if two males bump into each other, they will respond like this: 6

FIRST MALE: Hey, watch it!
SECOND MALE: No, *you* watch it!
FIRST MALE: Oh yeah?
(They deliberately bump into each other again.)

Two females, in the identical situation, will respond like this:

FIRST FEMALE: I'm sorry!
SECOND FEMALE: No, it's my fault!
FIRST FEMALE: Say, those are cute shoes!
(They go shopping.)

If the psychology community needs further proof of the difference between genders, I invite it to attend the party held in my neighborhood each Halloween. This party is attended by several hundred small children, who are experiencing stress because their bloodstreams—as a result of the so-called "trick or treat" 7 syndrome—contain roughly the same sugar content as Cuba. Here's how the various genders respond:

— The females, 97 percent of whom are dressed as either a ballerina or a princess, sit in little social groups and exchange candy.
— The males, 97 percent of whom are dressed as either Batman or a Power Ranger, run around making martial-arts noises and bouncing violently off one another like crazed subatomic particles.

8 Here are some other gender-based syndromes that the psychology community might want to look into:

— The "laundry refolding" syndrome: This has been widely noted by both me and a friend of mine named Jeff. What happens is, the male will attempt to fold a piece of laundry, and when he is done, the female, with a look of disapproval, will immediately pick it up and refold it so that it is much neater and smaller. "My wife can make an entire bed-sheet virtually disappear," reports Jeff.
— The "inflatable pool toy" syndrome: From the dawn of human civilization, the task of inflating the inflatable pool toy has always fallen to the male. It is often the female who comes home with an inflatable pool toy the size of the Hindenburg, causing the youngsters to become very excited. But it is inevitably the male who spends two hours blowing the toy up, after which he keels over with skin the color of a Smurf, while the kids, who have been helping out by whining impatiently, leap joyfully onto the toy, puncturing it immediately.

9 I think psychology researchers should find out if these syndromes exist in other species. They could put some rats into a cage with tiny pool toys and miniature pieces of laundry, then watch to see what happens. My guess is that there would be fighting. Among the male researchers, I mean. It's a shame, this male tendency toward aggression, which has caused so many horrible problems, such as war and ice hockey. It frankly makes me ashamed of my gender. I'm going to punch Bob.

BUILDING VOCABULARY

In this essay, Barry makes several cultural references. It is important for his jokes that you understand the references. Identify the following and explain why Barry uses them in the essay:

a. Punch and Judy (title)
b. "the same sugar content as Cuba" (par. 7)
c. Power Ranger (par. 7)
d. Hindenburg (par. 8)
e. Smurf (par. 8)
f. ice hockey (par. 9)

THINKING CRITICALLY ABOUT THE ESSAY

Understanding the Writer's Ideas

1. What point does Barry make with his "scientific quiz" at the beginning of the essay?
2. Why does Barry write "prepare to be astounded" in paragraph 4?
3. According to Barry, how do males and females respond differently to stress?
4. What purpose do the dialogues serve in paragraph 6?
5. According to Barry, how do boys and girls react differently during Halloween?
6. Barry makes a slightly different point in paragraph 8 than he does in the rest of the essay. What is the point, and why does he make it?
7. What does Barry's friend Jeff mean when he says, "My wife can make an entire bed-sheet virtually disappear" (par. 8)?
8. Why does Barry say that he's going to "punch Bob" at the end? What serious point does he make?

Understanding the Writer's Techniques

1. How is Barry's first sentence an example of *irony* (see Glossary)? Explain the irony.
2. Does Barry have a *thesis* statement in his essay? If so, where is it? If not, where does he best express his main point?
3. Who is Barry's audience for this essay? How can you tell?
4. In what ways is the "scientific quiz" at the beginning of the essay effective?
5. How does Barry transition from the quiz to the point he's trying to make in the essay?
6. Why does Barry keep referring to researchers and psychology in his essay?

7. How would you describe the *tone* of Barry's essay? Cite at least three examples to support your answer.
8. What is the central comparison and contrast that appears in this essay? How does it support the writer's thesis?
9. Does this essay use one of the traditional methods of writing comparison essays—*block* or *alternating*—or does he use a combination? Explain your answer.
10. Where in the essay does Barry use *hyperbole* (see Glossary)?
11. There are four jokes in the last paragraph. What are they, and why are they funny? Does the humor help make Barry's point, or does it weaken it? Explain fully.

Exploring the Writer's Ideas

1. Are Barry's conclusions about male aggression generally true? Explain your answer. Have you seen men or boys act in a different way? When?
2. Why does Barry stick to stereotypes of men and women instead of showing exceptions? How do the stereotypes strengthen or weaken his essay?
3. Where in popular culture do we see stereotypes of men and women?
4. When women are stereotyped, people often get upset, but when men are stereotyped, there usually isn't a problem. Why?

IDEAS FOR WRITING

Prewriting

In two columns, marked "Men" and "Women," list the ways the two sexes react differently to the pressures of college life. Be specific. For each item in one column, write a contrasting item in the other column.

Guided Writing

Write a humorous essay that contrasts the ways in which men and women deal differently with the stresses of college life. Narrow your topic down to one aspect of college life: writing papers, social life, staying in the dorms, commuting, and so on.

1. Begin with a "quiz" that highlights the difference you are going to discuss.
2. Next, phrase your thesis statement in an ironic fashion, as in the last two lines of Barry's essay.
3. Develop your contrast by offering at least three differences.
4. Illustrate your contrast by providing examples in quick succession.
5. Emphasize the differences by using *hyperbole* (see Glossary).
6. Conclude your essay with a paragraph that sums up the major points you have made.
7. End with a sentence that recalls a joke from the beginning of your essay.

Thinking and Writing Collaboratively

Working in groups of three or four, read each other's Guided Writing essays. Focus on the tone of the essay. Which of the ironic, humorous statements is most effective? Which is least effective? Why? Where in the essay is the writer's *tone* clearest?

Writing About the Text

Write an essay in which you discuss at least two strengths and two weaknesses in Barry's use of comparison and contrast. Refer to the opening material of this chapter and the questions that appear in Understanding the Writer's Techniques on pages 270–271.

More Writing Projects

1. Make a journal entry in which you compare how gender differences have changed since you were a child.
2. Write an extended paragraph in which you compare how men and women approach the idea of war differently.
3. Watch some television commercials and then write an essay explaining how the commercials portray men and women differently. Identify specific categories of difference (such as self-confidence, body image, and so forth), and organize your essay according to these categories.

The Body of the Beholder

Michele Ingrassia

Michele Ingrassia has worked as a writer, reporter, and features editor for several publications, including *Newsday*, *Newsweek*, and the *New York Times*. In an essay that originally appeared in *Newsweek*, Ingrassia takes a look at a study that shows why white girls dislike their bodies, but black girls are proud of theirs. Why do some find that being fat can also mean being fit?

PREREADING: THINKING ABOUT THE ESSAY IN ADVANCE

Look in the mirror. What do you see? How do you feel about your body? Why do you feel that way?

Words to Watch

dissect (par. 1) to cut apart or separate (tissue), especially for anatomical study

anthropologist (par. 3) a scientist who studies the origin, behavior, and physical, social, and cultural development of human beings

superwaif (par. 4) a slang phrase meaning a model who makes a lot of money because she looks gaunt, like an orphaned child (waif)

magnetism (par. 5) unusual power to attract, fascinate, or influence

1 When you're a teenage girl, there's no place to hide. Certainly not in gym class, where the shorts are short, the T shirts revealing and the adolescent critics eager to dissect every flaw. Yet out on the hardwood gym floors at Morgan Park High, a largely African-American school on Chicago's Southwest Side, the girls aren't talking about how bad their bodies are, but how good. Sure, all of them compete to see how many sit-ups they can do—Janet Jackson's washboard stomach is their model. But ask Diane Howard about weight, and the African-American senior, who carries 133 pounds on her 5-foot 7½-inch frame, says she'd happily add 15 pounds—if she could ensure they'd land on her hips. Or La'Taria Stokes, a stoutly built junior who takes it as high praise when boys remark, "Your hips are screaming for twins!" "I know I'm fat," La'Taria says. "I don't care."

In a society that worships at the altar of supermodels like Claudia, Christy and Kate, white teenagers are obsessed with staying thin. But there's growing evidence that black and white girls view their bodies in dramatically different ways. The latest findings come in a study to be published in the journal *Human Organization* this spring by a team of black and white researchers at the University of Arizona. While 90 percent of the white junior-high and high-school girls studied voiced dissatisfaction with their weight, 70 percent of African-American teens were satisfied with their bodies. 2

In fact, even significantly overweight black teens described themselves as happy. That confidence may not carry over to other areas of black teens' lives, but the study suggests that, at least here, it's a lifelong source of pride. Asked to describe women as they age, two thirds of the black teens said they get more beautiful, and many cited their mothers as examples. White girls responded that their mothers may have been beautiful—back in their youth. Says anthropologist Mimi Nichter, one of the study's coauthors, "In white culture, the window of beauty is so small." 3

What is beauty? White teens defined perfection as 5 feet 7 and 100 to 110 pounds—superwaif Kate Moss's vital stats. African-American girls described the perfect size in more attainable terms—full hips, thick thighs, the sort of proportions about which Hammer ("Pumps and a Bump") and Sir Mix-Alot ("Baby Got Back") rap poetic. But they said that true beauty—"looking good"—is about more than size. Almost two thirds of the black teens defined beauty as "the right attitude." 4

The disparity in body images isn't just in kids' heads. It's reflected in fashion magazines, in ads, and it's out there, on TV, every Thursday night. On NBC, the sitcom "Friends" stars Courteney Cox, Jennifer Aniston and Lisa Kudrow, all of them white and twentysomething, classically beautiful and reed thin. Meanwhile, Fox Television's "Living Single," aimed at an African-American audience, projects a less Hollywood ideal—its stars are four twentysomething black women whose bodies are, well, *real*. Especially the big-boned, bronze-haired rapper Queen Latifah, whose size only adds to her magnetism. During a break at the Lite Nites program at the Harlem YMCA, over the squeal of sneakers on the basketball court, Brandy Wood, 14, describes Queen Latifah's appeal: "What I like about her is the way she wears her hair and the color in it and the clothes she wears." 5

6 Underlying the beauty gap are 200 years of cultural differences. "In white, middle-class America, part of the great American Dream of making it is to be able to make yourself over," says Nichter. "In the black community, there is the reality that you might not move up the ladder as easily. As one girl put it, you have to be realistic—if you think negatively about yourself, you won't get anywhere." It's no accident that Barbie has long embodied a white-adolescent ideal—in the early days, she came with her own scale (set at 110) and her own diet guide ("How to Lose Weight: Don't Eat"). Even in this postfeminist era, Barbie's tight-is-right message is stronger than ever. Before kindergarten, researchers say, white girls know that Daddy eats and Mommy diets. By high school, many have split the world into physical haves and have-nots, rivals across the beauty line. "It's not that you hate them [perfect girls]," says Sarah Immel, a junior at Evanston Township High School north of Chicago. "It's that you're kind of jealous that they have it so easy, that they're so perfect-looking."

7 In the black community, size isn't debated, it's taken for granted—a sign, some say, that after decades of preaching black-is-beautiful, black parents and educators have gotten across the message of self-respect. Indeed, black teens grow up equating a full figure with health and fertility. Black women's magazines tend to tout NOT TRYING TO BE SIZE 8, not TEN TIPS FOR THIN THIGHS. And even girls who fit the white ideal aren't necessarily comfortable there. Supermodel Tyra Banks recalls how, in high school in Los Angeles, she was the envy of her white girlfriends. "They would tell me, 'Oh, Tyra, you look so good,'" says Banks. "But I was like, 'I want a booty and thighs like my black girlfriends.'"

8 Men send some of the strongest signals. What's fat? "You got to be *real* fat for me to notice," says Muhammad Latif, a Harlem 15-year-old. White girls follow what they *think* guys want, whether guys want it or not. Sprawled across the well-worn sofas and hard-back chairs of the student lounge, boys at Evanston High scoff at the girls' idealization of Kate Moss. "Sickly," they say, "gross." Sixteen-year-old Trevis Milton, a blond swimmer, has no interest in dating Kate wanna-bes. "I don't want to feel like I'm going to break them." Here, perfection is a hardbody, like Linda Hamilton in "Terminator II." "It's not so much about eating broccoli and water as running," says senior Kevin Mack.

And if hardbodies are hot, girls often need to diet to achieve them, too. According to the Arizona study, which was funded by the National Institute of Child Health and Human Development, 62 percent of the white girls reported dieting at least once in the past year. Even those who say they'd rather be fit than thin get caught up. Sarah Martin, 16, a junior at Evanston, confesses she's tried forcing herself to throw up but couldn't. She's still frustrated: ". . . have a big appetite, and I feel so guilty when I eat." 9

Black teens don't usually go to such extremes. Anorexia and bulimia are relatively minor problems among African-American girls. And though 51 percent of the black teens in the study said they'd dieted in the last year, follow-up interviews showed that far fewer were on sustained weight-and-exercise programs. Indeed, 64 percent of the black girls thought it was better to be "a little" overweight than underweight. And while they agreed that "very overweight" girls should diet, they defined that as someone who "takes up two seats on the bus." 10

The black image of beauty may seem saner, but it's not necessarily healthy. Black women don't obsess on size, but they do worry about other white cultural ideals that black men value. "We look at Heather Locklear and see the long hair and the fair, pure skin," says *Essence* magazine senior editor Pamela Johnson. More troubling, the acceptance of fat means many girls ignore the real dangers of obesity. Dieting costs money—even if it's not a fancy commercial program; fruits, vegetables and lean meats are pricier than high-fat foods. Exercise? Only one state—Illinois—requires daily physical education for every kid. Anyway, as black teenagers complain, exercise can ruin your hair—and, if you're plunking down $35 a week at the hairdresser, you don't want to sweat out your 'do in the gym. "I don't think we should obsess about weight and fitness, but there is a middle ground," says the well-toned black actress Jada Pinkett. Maybe that's where Queen Latifah meets Kate Moss. 11

BUILDING VOCABULARY

These words have medical denotations. What are they? Check a medical dictionary.

a. anorexia (par. 10)
b. bulimia (par. 10)
c. obsess (par. 11)

THINKING CRITICALLY ABOUT THE ESSAY

Understanding the Writer's Ideas

1. What does the writer mean when she says that teenage girls generally have "no place to hide" (par. 1)?
2. What did the findings of a study by the journal *Human Organization* reveal about the way young girls see their bodies?
3. How did black and white teens view the bodies of their mothers?
4. How does superwaif Kate Moss serve as a model for teenage girls?
5. Television seems to reflect the different attitudes about body image of black and white teenage girls. How?
6. What may account for the differing views of beauty for black and white girls?
7. How are full-figured black women viewed in their community? Why?
8. Dieting is an American obsession. But is this true for black teens? Explain.
9. Are attitudes about black women's bodies potentially harmful, leading to an increase in obesity in black girls?

Understanding the Writer's Techniques

1. Where does Ingrassia state her thesis? How does the statement make the essay's plan clear?
2. How are the essay's paragraphs ordered around the comparison-contrast structure?
3. How does the writer use statistics to support the comparison-contrast paragraph technique?
4. What audience does Ingrassia have in mind? Do you think this essay is written for men or women? Explain.
5. What makes the transition sentences in paragraph 4 different from the others?
6. Do all the paragraphs (including par. 4) have a topic sentence? Give examples.
7. In the concluding paragraph of the comparison-contrast essay, it is common to bring the two subjects together for a final observation. How does Ingrassia follow that strategy?

Exploring the Writer's Ideas

1. Do you agree with the writer's premise that white girls are mostly obsessed with being thin? Why or why not?
2. Given the reported differences in the way black and white girls see their bodies, whose view do you prefer and why?
3. Do you believe, as the essay suggests, that there is a connection between how girls see their mothers' bodies and how they see their own? Why or why not?
4. Critics blame television for many of society's ills. Should television be more responsible for the body types it chooses if it influences the way young girls see their own bodies? Why or why not?
5. In the black community, "there is the reality that you might not move up the ladder as easily." How do you feel about this statement? What does it mean, and how does it relate to body image?
6. If the "black-is-beautiful" movement helped black women avoid negative body images, do white women need a similar movement? Why or why not?
7. How do men in your community communicate what they think constitutes a beautiful body? What is a beautiful man's body?
8. Despite the positive aspects of liking yourself (even if you are heavy), can an acceptance of weight lead to ill health? Why or why not? What do you propose?

IDEAS FOR WRITING

Prewriting

Make a list of your body features or those of someone you know, and explain what you like or dislike about them.

Guided Writing

Compare your attitudes about body shape to those examined in Ingrassia's essay.

1. Begin with a description that shows whether your community shares (or does not share) your attitudes about body shapes.

2. Make sure your thesis reflects the comparison your essay plans to make between your views of body image and those discussed in Ingrassia's essay.
3. Focus on how your ideas of beauty differ from (or are the same as) the ideas in the essay. Try to make at least three comparisons (paragraphs).
4. Tell how your culture has historically looked at beauty.
5. How (and what) do men make clear about feminine (or masculine) beauty in your community?
6. Conclude by evaluating what you think the ideal body type should be.

Thinking and Writing Collaboratively

Working in a group of four, use what you know about body image and the ways it can hurt some people, and do research into ways society can change to make people of all body types feel more comfortable with themselves. Then write an essay using what the group has gathered to compare ways society can change to help all people develop a positive body image.

Writing About the Text

Write an essay that probes Ingrassia's analysis by looking at how white and black women think of their bodies in similar ways. What instances can you find in Ingrassia's essay in which gender may be more important than (or at least as important as) race?

More Writing Projects

1. Watch television commercials for women's and men's products. Reflect in your journal on what beauty messages the television commercials are communicating.
2. Look at the body images of men and women in magazine ads. Then write a paragraph that compares the beauty messages you find in television commercials and magazine ads.
3. Write an essay that compares the images of men and women in television commercials and magazine ads. Take a position on which ones are acceptable or not acceptable. Consider which ones have the most harmful effects on young people or society in general.

Mixing Patterns

Mom's Unforgiving Mirror

Deborah Tannen

Deborah Tannen, who was born in 1945, is a professor of linguistics at Georgetown University in Washington, DC. Educated at Harpur College, Wayne State University, and the University of California at Berkeley (where she earned an MA and PhD in linguistics), Tannen has written prolifically and lectured widely in her field. She has also written best-selling books on gender issues and differences and also on how the language of everyday conversation affects relationships. Among her most popular books are *You Just Don't Understand: Women and Men in Conversation* (1990), *The Argument Culture: Stopping America's War of Words* (1999), and *You're Wearing THAT?: Understanding Mothers and Daughters in Conversation* (2006). A frequent guest on radio and television news and information shows, Tannen has been hailed by *The Washingtonian* as "the world's most famous linguist." In this essay from the April 10, 2007, edition of *The Washington Post*, Tannen explores a mother's tendency to focus on a daughter's slightest imperfection.

PREREADING: THINKING ABOUT THE ESSAY IN ADVANCE

What comes to mind when you think about the ways in which a parent, sibling, or relative criticizes you for some imperfection? How do you explain this behavior? What is your response?

Words to Watch

adornment (par. 1) decoration, ornamentation
asymmetry (par. 2) the condition of not being arranged equally or in a balanced way
apt (par. 3) very appropriate
component (par. 8) a part of something

I once showed my mother a photograph taken of me by a professional photographer. Instead of commenting on the glamorous pose and makeup-artist adornment, she said, "One of your eyes is smaller than the other." Then she turned to me and gripped my chin as she examined my face. "It is," she pronounced. "Your left eye is smaller." For a while after, whenever she saw me, she 1 inspected my eye and reiterated her concern. During that time, I too became preoccupied with my left eye. My mother's perspective had become my own.

2 When else does a slight imperfection—a pimple, a small asymmetry—become the most prominent feature on your face? When you're looking in a mirror. A mother who zeroes in on her daughter's appearance—often on the Big Three: hair, clothes and weight—is regarding her daughter in the same way that she looks at herself in a mirror. The more I thought about it, the more this seemed to account for some of the best and worst aspects of the mother-daughter relationship: Each tends to see the other as a reflection of herself. It's wonderful when this means caring deeply, being interested in details and truly understanding the other. But it can cause frustration when it means scrutinizing the other for flaws in the same way that you scrutinize yourself.

3 The mirror image is particularly apt during the teenage years. At this age, a girl may spend hours in front of a full-length mirror, scouring her reflection for tiny imperfections that fill her with dread. And it is typically also at this age that she is most critical of her mother. (One woman recalls how her teenage daughter summed it up: "Everything about you is wrong.") The teenage girl is critiquing her mother—and finding her wanting—just as she scans her own mirror image for imperfections.

4 Part of a mother's job is to make sure all goes well for her children; for a daughter, that often means helping her improve her appearance. But there is a double irony here. From the mother's point of view, the person you most want to help, protect and advise is often the one least likely to welcome your help, protection and advice. From the daughter's perspective, the person whom you most want to think you're perfect is the one most likely to see your flaws—and tell you about them. And when she does, your reaction is far more extreme than it would be if anyone else made the same comment, because her opinion feels like a life sentence: If she sees faults, you must, as you feared, be fatally flawed.

5 To the daughter on the receiving end of a mother's suggestion that she get a better haircut, wear a different dress or lose a few pounds, it can seem that her mother cares only about appearance, especially if the daughter expected the focus to be on something else. For example, a woman who had just been promoted to a prominent position eagerly anticipated her mother's response when her picture appeared in the newspaper; what her mother

said was, "I could see you didn't have time to cut your bangs." It's an aargh (you might say, a hair-tearing) moment: My mother dismisses my accomplishments and focuses on my appearance—even worse, how my appearance falls short.

But here's another way to look at it: Your mother may assume it goes without saying that she is proud of you. Everyone knows that. And everyone probably also notices that your bangs are obscuring your vision—and their view of your eyes. Because others won't say anything, your mother may feel it's her obligation to tell you. 6

The desire to help a daughter (or mother) look her best may be entirely selfless, but if the person you're trying to help reflects yourself, there may also be an element of self-interest. Daughters and mothers often feel that the other represents her to the world. And it's true that people tend to hold mothers (and not fathers) responsible for their children's faults. Someone who disapproves of how a young woman is dressed will often think, and maybe ask out loud, "How did her mother let her go out looking like that?" 7

Yet a mother's concern may have no selfish component at all; she may be worried about her daughter's health rather than, or in addition to, her appearance. That was true in the case of my mother and my smaller eye. She had read that thyroid problems could present themselves as a difference in eye size, and she wanted me to go to a doctor and check it out. In fact, the era of my smaller eye ended when I reported that my doctor had found that my thyroid was fine. 8

No matter how much mothers insist that their focus is health—no matter how truly that really is their motivation—remarks about how to banish pimples or lose weight are heard as criticism, not only of your appearance but more generally of you. This came out clearly in the comments by a woman who told me that when she was a child, her mother had always been at her to comb her hair. She went on to say that her mother hadn't approved of her tomboy ways; she would have preferred a more typically feminine child. 9

When a woman sees in her daughter the same worrisome characteristic that her own mother once saw in her, her reaction can be as complex and confusing as a series of fun-house minors. One woman said that because her own mother had always been after her to get her hair off her face, tie it back, smooth it down, she determined not to pester her own daughter that way. "But the not saying anything is in itself an obsession," she said. "Other people mention it all the time." The child had inherited thick curly hair from her—the same hair that she had inherited from her mother. Her impulse to help 10 her daughter gain control of her hair was intensified because she felt responsible for it—just as her mother, looking at her as a child, recalled her own struggles with the same hair.

11 I once said to my sister, "Mom always told me my hair was too long. Did she ever bug you about your hair?" "Yes," my sister replied. "She always told me it was too short." This made us laugh. Then my sister added, "The funny thing is, her hair never looked good. Remember how it always stuck out on one side?" I did indeed; we laughed some more. But then I realized with chagrin that I often told my mother that her hair didn't look good—and volunteered to fix it.

12 Then a picture came to my mind, a precious memory from my mother's last years: I am standing behind my mother facing her bedroom mirror, combing her hair and smoothing it down. She is so small compared with me—5 feet tall to my 5-9—that her vulnerability overwhelms me. The impulse to protect and care for her floods over me. Recalling that image, I understood at last that her fussing over my appearance really could have been, all along, a gesture of love.

BUILDING VOCABULARY

1. List the connotations you associate with the word *imperfection*.
2. Write definitions for the following idiomatic expressions and colloquialisms:
   - **a.** makeup-artist adornment (par. 1)
   - **b.** Big Three (par. 2)
   - **c.** mirror image (par. 3)
   - **d.** fatally flawed (par. 4)
   - **e.** receiving end (par. 5)
   - **f.** tomboy ways (par. 9)
   - **g.** realized with chagrin (par. 11)

THINKING CRITICALLY ABOUT THE ESSAY

Understanding the Writer's Ideas

1. What is the importance of the photograph that Tannen introduces at the start of her essay?
2. According to Tannen, what is the significance of "a small asymmetry" (par. 1) in relations between mothers and daughters?

3. Explain what Tannen means by the "mirror image" in this essay.
4. Summarize the key points that Tannen makes about mothers and daughters.
5. What, ultimately, is Tannen's attitude toward her own mother?

Understanding the Writer's Techniques

1. Does Tannen state her thesis or imply it? Explain.
2. Tannen wrote this essay for readers of *The Washington Post*. What aspects of style and organization would make her article appealing to this newspaper's audience?
3. Analyze the pattern of comparison and contrast that Tannen uses in this essay. Does she employ a rigid block or alternating pattern or improvise? Justify your response.
4. Trace the mirror motif that Tannen uses in this essay and explain its utility.
5. Examine and evaluate the transitional techniques that Tannen uses to move from paragraph to paragraph. Why are her topic sentences at the outset of each paragraph especially effective in unifying the essay? Cite specific examples to support your analysis.
6. What is the overall tone of Tannen's essay? Explain by reference to the text.
7. How does Tannen's concluding paragraph reinforce ideas and strategies that she presents in the beginning and the body of the essay?

✷ MIXING PATTERNS

What forms of illustration (Chapter 6) does Tannen use, and why? How does she employ causal analysis (Chapter 8) to develop her thesis? What causes and effects does she examine?

Exploring the Writer's Ideas

1. According to Tannen, mothers and daughters "see the other as a reflection of herself" (par. 2). Do you have any experience of this phenomenon or a similar phenomenon (for example, fathers and sons), either personal or by observation? Explain.

2. Your could infer from Tannen's essay that the relationship between mothers and daughters—or any relationship, for that matter—is based on fundamental conflicts. Do you agree with this assertion or not, and why?
3. Do you think that Tannen actually *likes* her mother? Refer to Tannen's essay in responding to this question.

IDEAS FOR WRITING

Prewriting

Create two lists—for example, mothers and daughters, fathers and sons, brothers and sisters—that illustrate the differences in behavior that tend to characterize this relationship.

Guided Writing

Basing your paper on the preceding prewriting exercise, write a comparative essay that illuminates the differences (and perhaps similarities) governing relationships between two family members.

1. Begin by introducing the two figures who will serve as the comparative focus for your essay.
2. Establish a thesis sentence in the first paragraph.
3. Use either a block or alternating method to develop the essay, or experiment with a combination of patterns.
4. Provide a series of personal anecdotes as well as other forms of evidence to help illustrate your thesis.
5. If you wish, create a motif or pattern (like Tannen's mirror motif) that serves to unify and enrich the parts of the essay.
6. Conclude your essay with a summary of the main issues that you raised in the introduction and body of the essay.

Thinking and Writing Collaboratively

In groups of four, discuss the personal issues raised by your essay and how personal experience influences the content of your paper. What are some of the strengths and weaknesses of relying on personal experience to build an essay? Select one member of the group to present a summary of your discussion to the class.

Writing about the Text

Write an essay in which you analyze the "mirror" motif that Tannen develops in her essay. Be certain to indicate where this pattern occurs, related uses of figurative language that Tannen employs, and the way that this motif serves to both inform and organize the essay.

More Writing Projects

1. In your journal, write about your personal response to Tannen's essay—whether you liked it or not, and why.
2. Compose an extended paragraph about an immediate family member or relative whom you like or dislike.
3. Write an essay comparing and contrasting two types of your childhood or high school friends.

SUMMING UP: CHAPTER 7

1. In the essays you have read thus far in this book, you have learned much about the personal lives of many of the authors. Select two who seem very different, and write an essay in which you contrast their lives. In your essay, use only illustrations you can cite or derive from the selections; that is, don't do any research.
2. In her essay in this chapter, Rachel Carson uses a very old fictional form: the fable. Check the Glossary for a definition of *fable* and read some fables—most are very short. Then, write an essay in which you explore Carson's use of the word.
3. Write an essay called "How to Write a Comparison-Contrast Essay" in which you analyze the reading selection you think best represents the comparison-contrast form. Indicate the techniques and strategies the writer uses. Make specific references to the essay that you have chosen as a model.
4. In the manner of Rachel Carson, write your own "Fable for Tomorrow," in which you show how today's indifference to the environment will affect the future. Remember: *Silent Spring* was written in 1962, and many scholars believe that the way people abuse the environment today is even more serious than it was then.
5. Examine the essays by Dave Barry ("Punch and Judy," pp. 267–269), and Michele Ingrassia ("The Body of the Beholder," pp. 273–276). Compare and contrast the ways in which they discuss boys and girls, men and women, and white and black Americans, respectively.
6. Michele Ingrassia and Deborah Tannen examine issues of body image in women. Write an essay that analyzes their approach to this topic.
7. Compare and contrast Elizabeth Wong's (pp. 144–146) and Dave Barry's ideas about the differences between men and women. Include in your comparison and contrast a consideration of the *tone* each writer takes in the essay.

✷ FROM SEEING TO WRITING

Write a comparative essay that focuses, as this cartoon suggests, on differences between cats and dogs—and the owners who prefer one species to the other. What do dog lovers like about their pets, and what do they dislike about cats? Similarly, what do cat fans find so appealing about felines, and why might they reject dogs as pets? Could both warring parties be in need of a psychiatrist? Use a humorous tone to develop these contrasts.

"'Bad dog, bad dog,' she said. 'We should have gotten a cat.'"

CHAPTER 8

Cause-and-Effect Analysis

WHAT IS CAUSE-AND-EFFECT ANALYSIS?

Cause-and-effect analysis answers the basic human question: *Why?* Why do events occur, such as hurricanes or the election of a new president? Why does one student do better in math than another? In addition, this form of analysis looks at the *expected* consequences of a chain of happenings. If we raise the minimum wage, what will the likely consequences be?

Basically, cause-and-effect analysis (also called causal analysis) looks for *causes* or conditions, and suggests or examines *results* or consequences (the effects).

Like most of the writing strategies you have been studying, causal analysis parallels a kind of thinking we do in everyday life. If you are a student who has returned to school after being away for several years, someone might ask you why you decided to come back. In answering, you would give causes: you needed a better job to support your children; you wanted to learn a new skill; your intellectual curiosity drove you back; and so on. These would be *causes*. Once you were attending school, a classmate might ask you what changes coming back to school have made in your life. You might consider the pride your children feel in your achievement, or the fact that you have less time to prepare meals, or that you sleep only four hours a night. Those are the *consequences* or results of your decision. In a few years' time, after graduation, the effects might be very different: a better job or a scholarship to graduate school might be one of the long-term results.

Thinking about causes can go beyond everyday life to help us understand social and political change: What were the causes of the American Civil War? What were the consequences for the nation? What caused the Great Depression? Why were women denied the vote until 1920? Why did so many Irish immigrants come to America around 1900, and what were the consequences for the growth of American industry?

In looking at such large questions, you will realize that there are different kinds of causes. First, there is the *immediate* cause that gives rise to a situation. This is the cause (or causes) most directly related, the one closest at hand. But as you can see from the historical questions in the previous paragraph, we also need to go beyond the immediate cause to the *ultimate* cause, the basic conditions that stimulated the more obvious or immediate ones.

For example, although we might identify the immediate cause of the 9/11 World Trade Center disaster of 2001 as the crashing of commercial airlines by suicide bombers, the ultimate causes for terrorism against the United States grew from long fomenting hatred and envy directed at our country by fanatics. To find the "real" causes, we have to think critically, to examine the situation deeply.

Often, a writer has to consider many causes and rank them in order of importance. Depending on the length of the essay, a writer may have to select from among many causes. If a small town begins to lose businesses to a large mall, the chamber of commerce may ask why businesses and customers prefer the mall to shopping in town. Convenience, parking, competitive pricing, and entertainment may be identified as causes: Since the town cannot solve all these problems at once, it may focus on one, and try to lure shoppers back downtown by building a larger municipal parking lot. The result, perhaps, will be that shoppers will return to Main Street.

One difficulty in working with causal analysis is that we cannot always prove that a cause or an effect is absolute. We can only do our best to offer as much evidence as possible to help the reader see the relation we wish to establish. Therefore, we have to support our causes and effects with specific details and evidence drawn from personal experience, from statistics, or from experts' statements in newspapers or books. A writer can interview people, for instance, and collect data from an online government Web site or visit the library to read articles on the post-traumatic stress disorder among Iraq War veterans.

In the essays in this chapter, you will find a variety of uses for causal analysis. Stephen King analyzes why we crave horror movies. Elie Wiesel explains the reasons for his great love for his adopted country. Bob Herbert rails against multitasking and its consequences. Finally, Katha Pollitt examines the reasons why boys and girls reveal different patterns of play and the reasons for gender-based toy selection among children. As you read each piece, keep in mind the kinds of causes the writers present and the ways in which they add support to their analysis.

HOW DO WE READ CAUSAL ANALYSIS?

Reading causal analysis requires us to ask ourselves these questions:

- What are the writer's topic and the main cause? Make an outline of the causes as you read.
- Are immediate causes or ultimate causes presented? How do you know?
- Does the author show the consequences of the event? Why or why not?
- How does the author develop the analysis? Identify the writing strategies used: narrative, description, illustration, process analysis, and so on. Which is most effective in supporting the causal analysis and why?
- What is the tone of the essay?

HOW DO WE WRITE CAUSAL ANALYSIS?

Select a topic you can manage. If you try to find the causes of psychological depression, you may need to study a great deal of Freud before you can write the essay. If, on the other hand, you decide to write about causes of suicide among college freshmen, you would narrow the scope of the essay and thus control it more easily.

Write a working thesis that tells the cause and effect you are analyzing. Why is it important?

Sample thesis statement:

> Many causes lie behind Americans' return to more healthful eating habits, but the most important are fear of disease, desire to lose weight, and curiosity about new types of food.

Make a list of the major causes and under each cause, add at least one specific example to support it.

Plan whether you want to concentrate on either causes or effects, or on a balance of the two.

Be sure that you have included all the necessary links in the chain of reasoning that you began in the thesis.

Avoid oversimplification.

Include both major and minor causes and effects.

Writing the Draft

Write an introduction that presents the thesis and your statement of the significance of the thesis.

Use transitions as you move from one cause to the next.

Use narrative, description, process analysis, and other techniques to support your causes.

Conclude by reminding your reader of the importance of understanding this chain of events.

Proofread your draft carefully. Ask a classmate to read it to see if your causes seem logical.

Make corrections and prepare a final copy.

A STUDENT PARAGRAPH: CAUSE-AND-EFFECT ANALYSIS

To focus her causal analysis, the student who wrote the following paragraph concentrated on one aspect of the thesis sentence provided earlier in this chapter's introduction. Examine the way she weaves examples as her support for an analysis of Americans' changing eating habits.

Topic sentence

Contrasting examples

Supporting examples, with definitions

The arrival of ethnic restaurants and groceries in what used to be called "white-bread" neighborhoods has transformed the eating habits of mainstream American culture—in most cases, for the better. While *chicharron de pollo* (fried chicken cracklings) and jerk pork might not be much better for you nutritionally than what you can get at McDonald's, much of the newly arrived "exotic" food is far less fatty than typical fast-food fare. Pô (a Vietnamese noodle soup), rice and beans, hummus, *chana saag* (Indian chickpeas and spinach), and similar dishes provide leaner, more healthful fuel for the body than a Philly cheese steak and fries. Many people are beginning to think they taste better, too. The positive influence of these cuisines doesn't stop at the restaurant door, either. Many Americans are beginning to bring the culinary habits of other cultures into their own kitchens, imitating their techniques (stir frying, for example), adopting their principles (using meat as a flavoring, instead of the centerpiece of the meal), and borrowing their more healthful ingredients (yogurt instead of sour cream, olive oil instead of butter, a wider range of fresh vegetables and spices). In the process, the traditions of newly arrived immigrants receive appropriate recognition, and native habits evolve in a positive direction: the effect is not only better eating, but a broadening of the American cultural horizon.

Transition "too" signals shift to related topic; examples follow

Concluding sentence establishes main effect of altered eating habits

Why We Crave Horror Movies

Stephen King

Stephen King, America's best-known writer of horror fiction, was born in 1947 in Portland, Maine. He graduated from the University of Maine at Orono. King's masterly plots and prolific output reestablished horror as a hugely popular contemporary genre. Among his widely read novels are *The Shining* (1976), which was adapted into a classic of modern horror films; *The Girl Who Loved Tom Gordon* (1999); and *Dama Key* (2008). King also writes science fiction and has published a series that features Roman Gilead, entitled *The Dark Tower.* His most recent volume in that series is *The Dark Tower VII* (2004). His short story collection *Everything's Eventual* appeared in 2002. In 2000 King became the first major author to publish his work, the story "Riding the Bullet," exclusively as an e-book. In 2010 he published *Blockade Billy*, a baseball-related suspense novella. Because he is an acknowledged master of this genre, his thoughts on why people love horror movies offer an unusual insight into this question. King also gives us a unique glimpse into why he himself creates horror. This selection originally appeared in *Playboy* in January 1982.

To learn more about King, click on **More Resources > Chapter 8 > Stephen King**

PREREADING: THINKING ABOUT THE ESSAY IN ADVANCE

Do you think that we all have a dark side to our personalities that we rarely reveal? Explain.

Words to Watch

innately (par. 4) by essential characteristic; by birth
voyeur (par. 6) a person who derives gratification from observing the acts of others
penchant (par. 7) a definite liking; a strong inclination
remonstrance (par. 10) an expression of protest
anarchistic (par. 11) active resistance and terrorism against the state
subterranean (par. 12) hidden; secret

1 I think that we're all mentally ill; those of us outside the asylums only hide it a little better—and maybe not all that much better, after all. We've all known people who talk to themselves, people who sometimes squinch their faces into horrible grimaces when they believe no one is watching, people who have some hysterical fear—of snakes, the dark, the tight place, the long drop . . . and, of course, those final worms and grubs that are waiting so patiently underground.

2 When we pay our four or five bucks and seat ourselves at tenth-row center in a theater showing a horror movie, we are daring the nightmare.

3 Why? Some of the reasons are simple and obvious. To show that we can, that we are not afraid, that we can ride this roller coaster. Which is not to say that a really good horror movie may not surprise a scream out of us at some point, the way we may scream when the roller coaster twists through a complete 360 or plows through a lake at the bottom of the drop. And horror movies, like roller coasters, have always been the special province of the young; by the time one turns 40 or 50, one's appetite for double twists or 360-degree loops may be considerably depleted.

4 We also go to re-establish our feelings of essential normality; the horror movie is innately conservative, even reactionary. Freda Jackson as the horrible melting woman in *Die, Monster, Die!* confirms for us that no matter how far we may be removed from the beauty of a Robert Redford or a Diana Ross, we are still light-years from true ugliness.

5 And we go to have fun.

6 Ah, but this is where the ground starts to slope away, isn't it? Because this is a very peculiar sort of fun indeed. The fun comes from seeing others menaced—sometimes killed. One critic has suggested that if pro football has become the voyeur's version of combat, then the horror film has become the modern version of the public lynching.

7 It is true that the mythic, "fairytale" horror film intends to take away the shades of gray. . . . It urges us to put away our more civilized and adult penchant for analysis and to become children again, seeing things in pure blacks and whites. It may be that horror movies provide psychic relief on this level because this invitation to lapse into simplicity, irrationality and even outright madness is extended so rarely. We are told we may allow our emotions a free rein . . . or no rein at all.

If we are all insane, then sanity becomes a matter of degree. If your insanity leads you to carve up women like Jack the Ripper or the Cleveland Torso Murderer, we clap you away in the funny farm (but neither of those two amateur-night surgeons was ever caught, heh-heh-heh); if, on the other hand your insanity leads you only to talk to yourself when you're under stress or to pick your nose on the morning bus, then you are left alone to go about your business . . . though it is doubtful that you will ever be invited to the best parties. 8

The potential lyncher is in almost all of us (excluding saints, past and present; but then, most saints have been crazy in their own ways), and every now and then, he has to be let loose to scream and roll around in the grass. Our emotions and our fears form their own body, and we recognize that it demands its own exercise to maintain proper muscle tone. Certain of these emotional muscles are accepted—even exalted—in civilized society; they are, of course, the emotions that tend to maintain the status quo of civilization itself. Love, friendship, loyalty, kindness—these are all the emotions that we applaud, emotions that have been immortalized in the couplets of Hallmark cards and in the verses (I don't dare call it poetry) of Leonard Nimoy. 9

When we exhibit these emotions, society showers us with positive reinforcement; we learn this even before we get out of diapers. When, as children, we hug our rotten little puke of a sister and give her a kiss, all the aunts and uncles smile and twit and cry, "Isn't he the sweetest little thing?" Such coveted treats as chocolate-covered graham crackers often follow. But if we deliberately slam the rotten little puke of a sister's fingers in the door, sanctions follow—angry remonstrance from parents, aunts and uncles; instead of a chocolate-covered graham cracker, a spanking. 10

But anticivilization emotions don't go away, and they demand periodic exercise. We have such "sick" jokes as, "What's the difference between a truckload of bowling balls and a truckload of dead babies?" (You can't unload a truckload of bowling balls with a pitchfork . . . a joke, by the way, that I heard originally from a ten-year-old.) Such a joke may surprise a laugh or a grin out of us even as we recoil, a possibility that confirms the thesis: If we share a brotherhood of man, then we also share an insanity of man. None of which is intended as a defense of either the sick joke or insanity but merely as an explanation of why the best horror films, 11 like the best fairy tales, manage to be reactionary, anarchistic, and revolutionary all at the same time.

12 The mythic horror movie, like the sick joke, has a dirty job to do. It deliberately appeals to all that is worst in us. It is morbidity unchained, our most base instincts let free, our nastiest fantasies realized . . . and it all happens, fittingly enough, in the dark. For those reasons, good liberals often shy away from horror films. For myself, I like to see the most aggressive of them—*Dawn of the Dead,* for instance—as lifting a trap door in the civilized forebrain and throwing a basket of raw meat to the hungry alligators swimming around in that subterranean river beneath.

13 Why bother? Because it keeps them from getting out, man. It keeps them down there and me up here. It was Lennon and McCartney who said that all you need is love, and I would agree with that.

14 As long as you keep the gators fed.

BUILDING VOCABULARY

King uses descriptive language in this essay to re-create some of the scary images from horror stories, such as snakes and grubs (par. 1). Make a list of his scary words (at least five). Then find a synonym for each word and use each in a sentence.

THINKING CRITICALLY ABOUT THE ESSAY

Understanding the Writer's Ideas

1. King uses the cause-and-effect method to explore why people crave horror. He says we share an "insanity of man" (par. 11). What does he mean by *insanity*?
2. For what three reasons does the writer think we dare the nightmare?
3. What does King mean when he says the "fairytale" horror films "take away the shades of gray" (par. 7)?
4. How does King explain his view on anticivilization emotions?
5. King uses the image of alligators (the gators) to make a final point. How do you interpret this?

Understanding the Writer's Techniques

1. What is the thesis? Where is it? How does the essay's title reflect the writer's thesis?
2. King uses first person narration in this essay. What other rhetorical modes does he use to develop his essay?
3. In this cause-and-effect essay, what is the cause and what is the effect?
4. King says we are all insane. What tone does this create for the reader? Is he accusing? humorous? serious?
5. King uses both specific and broad generalizations to develop his thesis. Give an example of something specific and something generalized. Which better supports the thesis and why?
6. Notice how the last and concluding sentence of the essay suddenly addresses the reader ("you"). Why? What purpose does this shift to the second person serve in this essay's conclusion?

Exploring the Writer's Ideas

1. How do you feel about the writer's bold opening statement that we are all mentally ill? Does this statement make you want to stop reading? How do you feel about his assumption?
2. Do you go to horror movies or do you avoid them? Why do you or don't you go? Explain.
3. Why do you think King chose to write out his ideas rather than discuss them with a friend? In what way is the process of writing out our ideas different from the process of thinking out loud in conversation?
4. This writer claims he isn't defending anticivilization emotions (par. 11), but he tells us that we need to "scream and roll around in the grass" (par. 9). Which side is this writer on? Which side are you on? Why?
5. Is it true that in horror tales the villains are always destroyed and good always triumphs? Should this be the case? Why or why not?

IDEAS FOR WRITING

Prewriting

Make a scratch outline of your strongest feelings for or against horror stories.

Guided Writing

Write an essay in which you analyze your reactions to horror books or movies.

1. Begin the essay by stating your feelings on why you personally like or dislike horror. Use some examples to bring to life for the reader your experience with horror.
2. Describe two or more causes for the way you react to horror.
3. Analyze some of the effects you think horror movies may have on you or others who crave them.
4. Respond to the issue of horror allowing anticivilization emotions to be exercised so they don't "get out," as King says.
5. Conclude by addressing readers, telling them why they should embrace or avoid the horror genre.

Thinking and Writing Collaboratively

Working in a group of four to five students, research what experts say about the causes and effects of television violence on children. Then write an essay that makes these causes and effects clear to an audience of parents.

Writing About the Text

If King's opening statement contains little truth, his argument in effect falls apart. Write an essay that explores the validity of his opening and then analyzes the essay's argument based on your conclusions about its opening.

More Writing Projects

1. In your journal, write about something that scares you.
2. Write a paragraph that explains what causes you to fear something.
3. In an essay, examine the causes and effects of something in your life that frightens you (for example, stage fright, test anxiety, fear of flying, and so forth).

The America I Love

Elie Wiesel

In 1943, the Nazis took fifteen-year-old Elie Wiesel and his family from their home in Romania and sent them to a concentration camp. His mother, father, and sister all died, but Elie Wiesel survived to be liberated by the Americans at Buchenwald in 1945. In 1963 he became an American citizen. His first book, *Night* (1960), told the story of his experience at Buchenwald. Since that book, he has written more than forty others, most recently, *The Sonderberg Case* (2010). For his work as a defender of victims of war and violence around the world, he was awarded the Nobel Peace Prize in 1986. In this essay, published on the Fourth of July in 2004, Wiesel answers critics of American foreign policy by taking the long view of America's record overseas.

To learn more about Wiesel, click on **More Resources > Chapter 8 > Elie Wiesel**

PREREADING: THINKING ABOUT THE ESSAY IN ADVANCE

Do you think that the United States should police the world? Many people say that America has a responsibility to fight tyranny and oppressive regimes throughout the world, while others say that our own national security is our most important objective. What is your opinion?

Words to Watch

gratitude (par. 1) thankfulness
privileged (par. 2) favored, lucky
grandiloquent (par. 4) pompous
introspection (par. 4) self-examination, reflection
throes (par. 5) struggles
sanctified (par. 6) made holy
intonation (par. 6) the way something is said
loftier (par. 10) higher in status or better
credo (par. 10) motto, statement of belief
expediency (par. 13) the way that will bring fastest results

1 The day I received American citizenship was a turning point in my life. I had ceased to be stateless. Until then, unprotected by any government and unwanted by any society, the Jew in me was overcome by a feeling of pride mixed with gratitude.

2 From that day on, I felt privileged to belong to a country which, for two centuries, has stood as a living symbol of all that is charitable and decent to victims of injustice everywhere—a country in which every person is entitled to dream of happiness, peace and liberty; where those who have are taught to give back.

3 In America, compassion for the refugee and respect for the other still have biblical connotations.

4 Grandiloquent words used for public oratory? Even now, as America is in the midst of puzzling uncertainty and understandable introspection because of tragic events in Iraq, these words reflect my personal belief. For I cannot forget another day that remains alive in my memory: April 11, 1945.

5 That day I encountered the first American soldiers in the Buchenwald concentration camp. I remember them well. Bewildered, disbelieving, they walked around the place, hell on earth, where our destiny had been played out. They looked at us, just liberated, and did not know what to do or say. Survivors snatched from the dark throes of death, we were empty of all hope—too weak, too emaciated to hug them or even speak to them. Like lost children, the American soldiers wept and wept with rage and sadness. And we received their tears as if they were heartrending offerings from a wounded and generous humanity.

6 Ever since that encounter, I cannot repress my emotion before the flag and the uniform—anything that represents American heroism in battle. That is especially true on July Fourth. I reread the Declaration of Independence, a document sanctified by the passion of a nation's thirst for justice and sovereignty, forever admiring both its moral content and majestic intonation. Opposition to oppression in all its forms, defense of all human liberties, celebration of what is right in social intercourse: All this and much more is in that text, which today has special meaning.

7 Granted, U.S. history has gone through severe trials, of which anti-black racism was the most scandalous and depressing. I happened to witness it in the late fifties, as I traveled through the South. What did I feel? Shame. Yes, shame for being white. What made it worse was the realization that, at that time, racism was the law, thus making the law itself immoral and unjust.

Still, my generation was lucky to see the downfall of prejudice in many of its forms. True, it took much pain and protest for that law to be changed, but it was. Today, while fanatically stubborn racists are still around, some of them vocal, racism as such has vanished from the American scene. That is true of anti-Semitism too. Jew-haters still exist here and there, but organized anti-Semitism does not—unlike in Europe, where it has been growing with disturbing speed. 8

As a great power, America has always seemed concerned with other people's welfare, especially in Europe. Twice in the 20th century, it saved the "Old World" from dictatorship and tyranny. 9

America understands that a nation is great not because its economy is flourishing or its army invincible but because its ideals are loftier. Hence America's desire to help those who have lost their freedom to conquer it again. America's credo might read as follows: For an individual, as for a nation, to be free is an admirable duty—but to help others become free is even more admirable. 10

Some skeptics may object: But what about Vietnam? And Cambodia? And the support some administrations gave to corrupt regimes in Africa or the Middle East? And the occupation of Iraq? Did we go wrong—and if so, where? 11

And what are we to make of the despicable, abominable "interrogation methods" used on Iraqi prisoners of war by a few soldiers (but even a few are too many) in Iraqi military prisons? 12

Well, one could say that no nation is composed of saints alone. None is sheltered from mistakes or misdeeds. All have their Cain and Abel. It takes vision and courage to undergo serious soul-searching and to favor moral conscience over political expediency. And America, in extreme situations, is endowed with both. America is always ready to learn from its mishaps. Self-criticism remains its second nature. 13

Not surprising, some Europeans do not share such views. In extreme left-wing political and intellectual circles, suspicion and distrust toward America is the order of the day. They deride America's motives for its military interventions, particularly in Iraq. They say: It's just money. As if America went to war only to please the oil-rich capitalists. 14

They are wrong. America went to war to liberate a population too long subjected to terror and death. 15

We see in newspapers and magazines and on television screens the mass graves and torture chambers imposed by Saddam 16

Hussein and his accomplices. One cannot but feel grateful to the young Americans who leave their families, some to lose their lives, in order to bring to Iraq the first rays of hope—without which no people can imagine the happiness of welcoming freedom.

17 Hope is a key word in the vocabulary of men and women like myself and so many others who discovered in America the strength to overcome cynicism and despair. Remember the legendary Pandora's box? It is filled with implacable, terrifying curses. But underneath, at the very bottom, there is hope. Now as before, now more than ever, it is waiting for us.

BUILDING VOCABULARY

1. In this essay, Wiesel uses literary and historical references that you might not know. Identify the following:
   - **a.** Buchenwald (par. 5)
   - **b.** Old World (par. 9)
   - **c.** Cambodia (par. 11)
   - **d.** Cain and Abel (par. 13)
   - **e.** Pandora's box (par. 17)
2. For each of the following words, write a definition and use it in a sentence of your own:
   - **a.** connotations (par. 3)
   - **b.** bewildered (par. 5)
   - **c.** emaciated (par. 5)
   - **d.** scandalous (par. 7)
   - **e.** abominable (par. 12)
   - **f.** implacable (par. 17)

THINKING CRITICALLY ABOUT THE ESSAY

Understanding the Writer's Ideas

1. Why was getting American citizenship a "turning point" in Wiesel's life?
2. What does Wiesel mean when he writes that he was proud and grateful because of "the Jew in me"?
3. What is it about being an American that makes Wiesel proud?
4. What has caused the "puzzling uncertainty" Wiesel refers to?

5. What happened to Wiesel on April 11, 1945?
6. What was the experience of American soldiers who discovered the Nazi concentration camps in eastern Europe, according to Wiesel?
7. What was the result for Wiesel of his liberation from Buchenwald?
8. What answer does Wiesel have for those who criticize the United States' involvement in questionable wars?
9. Why does Wiesel use the image of Pandora's box at the end of the essay?

Understanding the Writer's Techniques

1. Where is the writer's thesis statement? Is it in an effective location? Explain.
2. How does the title of the essay suggest an argument?
3. Why does Wiesel begin his essay with the emotions he felt on becoming a U.S. citizen? How does this relate to the thesis?
4. What is the effect on the reader of Wiesel's description of April 11, 1945?
5. Why does Wiesel mention the Declaration of Independence? Explain his motives, in your opinion.
6. This essay appeared in *Parade* magazine, which is included with Sunday newspapers all across the country. Who is the intended audience for this essay, and how can you tell?
7. What does Wiesel say were the causes of the war in Iraq? Is his analysis of the causes effective? Explain.
8. What do you think of Wiesel's conclusion? Is it effective or not, and why?

Exploring the Writer's Ideas

1. Wiesel provides reasons that the United States should be admired as a nation. Come up with at least three that Wiesel does not mention. Explain why these are admirable traits for a country.
2. Wiesel writes that Americans "are taught to give back." What does he mean by this, and do you agree with him? Explain your answer.

3. Wiesel contrasts his patriotic feeling about the United States with those of "skeptics." What are your own feelings about the United States as a moral force in the world?
4. What is patriotism? What are its causes?
5. Excessive patriotism is called *jingoism*. What could be some negative effects of jingoism? Do you believe that Wiesel is guilty of jingoism? Why or why not?
6. Some people say that questioning the motives of the leaders of the United States is the same as hating the country. Do you think someone can love a country and still, as Wiesel says in paragraph 14, "deride America's motives for its military interventions"?

IDEAS FOR WRITING

Prewriting

Freewrite for fifteen minutes about why you love the town or city where you grew up or where you've visited. What has led to the positive feelings you have?

Guided Writing

Using cause-and-effect analysis, write an essay titled "The ________ I Love," filling in the blank with the name of the town or city where you grew up.

1. In your introduction, recall how your positive feelings began.
2. Next, explain the origins or causes of your affection.
3. Continue by tracing how those origins led to further or more complicated admiration.
4. Emphasize why you are qualified to write about the place. What about your background lends you authority?
5. Write using emotional and/or manipulative language.
6. Mention any detractors from your town. What do they say?
7. Make it clear why the detractors are wrong, why their hearts are not in the right place.
8. Write a conclusion that points to why all people should love your town or city.

Thinking and Writing Collaboratively

Working in groups of three or four, have group members read their essays out loud. Decide as a group which essay is the strongest, and then discuss the reasons why you feel this way. Present your group's findings to the rest of the class.

Writing About the Text

Write an essay that explores whether Wiesel's own experiences influence the essay excessively. Do you think his argument remains valid despite his emotional standpoint?

More Writing Projects

1. Wiesel writes that he admires "American heroism in battle" and appreciates those American soldiers who wept over the plight of the Jewish prisoners. Still, some soldiers are sent to be heroic in the name of unheroic ideals. Is it possible to separate the soldier from the commander or from his country, to admire the soldier but not what he is doing? Write a journal entry about this topic.
2. Wiesel won the Nobel Peace Prize and several other prestigious awards. Write a paragraph or two on the influence an author's credentials have on you as a reader. Do they affect you? Why or why not?
3. Do some research on a dark part of U.S. history, such as moving Native Americans to reservations, interning Japanese Americans during World War II, oppressing blacks under Jim Crow laws, fighting what some consider an unjust war in Vietnam, and so on. Write an essay in which you argue that the action was either warranted or unwarranted, taking into account the historical context.

Mixing Patterns

Tweet Less, Kiss More

Bob Herbert

Bob Herbert began his career as a reporter with the *Star-Ledger* in Newark, New Jersey, and ultimately became its night city editor. Now a regular Op-Ed contributor for the *New York Times*, Herbert writes a twice-a-week column that comments on government, politics, urban issues, and social trends. He was a national correspondent for NBC, reporting regularly on the *Today Show* and *NBC Nightly News*, and was a founding panelist of *Sunday Edition,* a weekly television discussion program. Born in Brooklyn but reared primarily in Montclair, New Jersey, Herbert received a BS degree in journalism from the State University of New York in 1988. He has taught journalism at Brooklyn College and the Columbia University Graduate School of Journalism. He is the author of *Promises Betrayed: Waking Up from the American Dream* (2005). In this piece he reflects on the effects of our culture's demand that "we be doing, at a minimum, two or three things" during every minute that we're awake.

PREREADING: THINKING ABOUT THE ESSAY IN ADVANCE

How many tasks can you accomplish at the same time? What are some important daily activities at work or school that you can do at the same time—homework and watching television, for example, or reading a book and cooking dinner, or jogging and listening to an iPod, or driving and speaking on a cellphone? How well do you accomplish each of the simultaneous activities, do you think?

Words to Watch

swerve (par. 1) veer; turn sharply
props up (par. 3) supports; holds up
neurotic (par. 7) obsessed; irrational
gadgets (par. 12) tools; contraptions
tendency (par. 12) inclination; leaning
virtual (par. 15) simulated by computer; not completely real despite outward appearances

I was driving from Washington to New York one afternoon on Interstate 95 when a car came zooming up behind me, really flying. I could see in the rearview mirror that the driver was talking on her cellphone. 1

I was about to move to the center lane to get out of her way when she suddenly swerved into that lane herself to pass me on the right—still chatting away. She continued moving dangerously from one lane to another as she sped up the highway. 2

A few days later, I was talking to a guy who commutes every day between New York and New Jersey. He props up his laptop on the front seat so he can watch DVDs while he's driving. 3

"I only do it in traffic," he said. "It's no big deal." 4

Beyond the obvious safety issues, why does anyone want, or need, to be talking constantly on the phone or watching movies (or texting) while driving? I hate to sound so 20th century, but what's wrong with just listening to the radio? The blessed wonders of technology are overwhelming us. We don't control them; they control us. 5

We've got cellphones and BlackBerrys and Kindles and iPads, and we're e-mailing and text-messaging and chatting and tweeting—I used to call it Twittering until I was corrected by high school kids who patiently explained to me, as if I were the village idiot, that the correct term is tweeting. Twittering, tweeting—whatever it is, it sounds like a nervous disorder. 6

This is all part of what I think is one of the weirder aspects of our culture: a heightened freneticism that seems to demand that we be doing, at a minimum, two or three things every single moment of every hour that we're awake. Why is multitasking considered an admirable talent? We could just as easily think of it as a neurotic inability to concentrate for more than three seconds. 7

Why do we have to check our e-mail so many times a day, or keep our ears constantly attached, as if with Krazy Glue, to our cellphones? When you watch the news on cable television, there are often additional stories being scrolled across the bottom of the screen, stock market results blinking on the right of the screen, and promos for upcoming features on the left. These extras often block significant parts of the main item we're supposed to be watching. 8

A friend of mine told me about an engagement party that she had attended. She said it was lovely: a delicious lunch and plenty 9 of champagne toasts. But all the guests had their cellphones on the luncheon tables and had text-messaged their way through the entire event.

10 Enough already with this hyperactive behavior, this techno-tyranny and nonstop freneticism. We need to slow down and take a deep breath.

11 I'm not opposed to the remarkable technological advances of the past several years. I don't want to go back to typewriters and carbon paper and yellowing clips from the newspaper morgue. I just think that we should treat technology like any other tool. We should control it, bending it to our human purposes.

12 Let's put down at least some of these gadgets and spend a little time just being ourselves. One of the essential problems of our society is that we have a tendency, amid all the craziness that surrounds us, to lose sight of what is truly human in ourselves, and that includes our own individual needs—those very special, mostly nonmaterial things that would fulfill us, give meaning to our lives, enlarge us, and enable us to more easily embrace those around us.

13 There's a character in the August Wilson play *Joe Turner's Come and Gone* who says everyone has a song inside of him or her, and that you lose sight of that song at your peril. If you get out of touch with your song, forget how to sing it, you're bound to end up frustrated and dissatisfied.

14 As this character says, recalling a time when he was out of touch with his own song, "Something wasn't making my heart smooth and easy."

15 I don't think we can stay in touch with our song by constantly Twittering or tweeting, or thumbing out messages on our Black-Berrys, or piling up virtual friends on Facebook.

16 We need to reduce the speed limits of our lives. We need to savor the trip. Leave the cellphone at home every once in awhile. Try kissing more and tweeting less. And stop talking so much.

17 Listen.

18 Other people have something to say, too. And when they don't, that glorious silence that you hear will have more to say to you than you ever imagined. That is when you will begin to hear your song. That's when your best thoughts take hold, and you become really you.

BUILDING VOCABULARY

Identify the word parts that make up these words from the selection and write definitions based on your knowledge of the parts' meanings. Use a dictionary only if you must.

a. cellphone (par. 1)
b. rearview (par. 1)
c. overwhelming (par. 5)
d. freneticism (par. 7)
e. multitasking (par. 7)
f. inability (par. 7)
g. admirable (par. 7)
h. hyperactive (par. 10)
i. techno-tyranny (par. 10)
j. nonmaterial (par. 12)

THINKING CRITICALLY ABOUT THE ESSAY

Understanding the Writer's Ideas

1. What event does Herbert note about his drive from Washington to New York? What did the driver behind him do on Interstate 95?
2. What technological features does Herbert identify? Which one does he say sounds like a nervous disorder?
3. What is the "heightened freneticism" that Herbert sees in our culture?
4. What fault does the writer find with "extras" like scrolling messages on the bottom of the television screen? What other television extras does he complain about?
5. What does the writer identify as "one of the essential problems of our society"?
6. What does Herbert find significant in the play *Joe Turner's Come and Gone*? What line does Herbert quote from the play?
7. What, at the end of the essay, does Herbert say we should stop doing?
8. When, according to the writer, do "you become really you"?

Understanding the Writer's Techniques

1. What is Herbert's thesis? State it in your own words.

2. How do the anecdotes at the start of the essay help frame Herbert's basic point? In what ways are they effective as an introduction? Where else does the writer provide an anecdote?
3. What does the writer mean by the title "Tweet Less, Kiss More," which he repeats with slight variation in paragraph 16? Certainly he doesn't expect readers to put down the essay and begin kissing! The title is clearly *figurative* (see Glossary), not to be taken literally. What is he trying to accomplish with the title?
4. Where else in the essay does Herbert use figurative language to advantage?
5. In what ways is this selection a good example of cause-and-effect analysis? What effects does Herbert identify as a result of the behaviors he describes?
6. Herbert asks a number of rhetorical questions in the essay. Which do you find most pointed in light of the writer's thesis? Which questions would you be able to answer, do you think?
7. What is the purpose of the catalog of technological items in paragraph 6?
8. Where do you find an instance of Herbert's effort at humor in the essay? Does it work? Why or why not?
9. Who would you say is the primary audience for this essay? How do you know?
10. Who is August Wilson? Why does Herbert cite this particular writer, do you think?

Exploring the Writer's Ideas

1. What is your view of people who drive while using a cellphone? Do you ever talk on the phone while you drive? Explain.
2. Herbert is highly critical of multitasking, which many people find of great value in today's fast-paced society. Why might you agree with Herbert? With those who take the opposite position?
3. One aspect of Herbert's complaint is that we can just as well think of multitasking "as a neurotic inability to concentrate for more than three seconds." Do you find Herbert's assessment out of touch, especially harsh, completely valid—or something else?

4. Herbert says, "We need to slow down and take a deep breath." What does he mean? Would you be able to follow this advice in your life now? Why or why not?
5. What does it mean to be "out of touch with your song"? Have you ever been out of touch with your song? When?
6. Do you think that a major problem of our society is that we have lost sight of what is truly human in ourselves? Why or why not?
7. Herbert admonishes us to stop talking so much. Why might you agree or disagree with his point? Do you think that people do not listen enough? Why do you feel as you do?

IDEAS FOR WRITING

Prewriting

Make a list of the various technological elements that you use to accomplish tasks in a single day and try to estimate how much time it takes you at each task.

Guided Writing

Write a cause-and-effect essay called "Kiss Less, Tweet More" in which you essentially take the *opposite* point of view from Herbert's—that is, show how, in a fast-paced world, we take too much time with individual tasks when we should be multitasking as much as possible and using technology more, not less to accomplish our goals.

1. Open with one or two anecdotes in which you show how someone is wasting time at a single task when he or she could be doing other things at the same time.
2. Evaluate in a positive light the technological tools that are available today—Facebook, Twitter, e-mail, texting; there are many others, certainly.
3. Raise a series of rhetorical questions as Herbert does.
4. Assume that your audience is people who do not appreciate technology and its positive effects on our lives.
5. Use *figurative language* (see Glossary) where appropriate.

6. Identify the outcomes, or effects, of multitasking and the value of relying on technology to help get more done in less time.
7. Try to include a quotation that praises accomplishment or that dismisses "old-fashioned" ways of doing things.

Thinking and Writing Collaboratively

Working in groups of three or four, have members read drafts of their essays aloud. Decide on which essay is most convincing and discuss the reasons that you feel as you do. Present your group's findings to the rest of the class. How can you use the identified strengths of classmates' essays to improve your own drafts?

Writing About the Text

Write an essay about the effects that you believe would result from following Herbert's advice in some aspect of today's world.

More Writing Projects

1. Write a journal entry about how reliance on technology can be a serious problem for students.
2. Get a copy of August Wilson's *Joe Turner's Come and Gone* and write a couple of paragraphs to share your reactions to the play.
3. Write a cause-and-effect essay called "Reducing the Speed Limits of Our Lives."

✷ MIXING PATTERNS

Analyze Herbert's use of narration, illustration, and definition as rhetorical devices in the selection. How do they contribute to your understanding of the writer's thesis?

Why Boys Don't Play with Dolls

Katha Pollitt

Katha Pollitt's column, "Subject to Debate," appears in *The Nation,* a left-leaning weekly magazine of opinion. A vigorous polemicist, Pollitt is known for her provocative analyses of hot-button contemporary issues such as family values and teenage motherhood. Pollitt is a poet as well as an essayist. Her volume of poetry, *Antarctic Traveler,* won the National Book Critics Circle Award in 1982. Ten years later, a "Subject to Debate" piece on the culture wars, entitled "Why We Read: Canon to the Right of Me . . . ," received the National Magazine Award for essays and criticism. A native of New York City, she is the author of several books, including *Reasonable Creatures: Essays on Women and Feminism* (1994); *Subject to Debate: Sense and Dissents on Women, Politics, and Culture* (2001); and *Learning to Drive and Other Life Stories* (2007). In this selection, through a series of pointed causal and comparative analyses, Pollitt builds an entertaining, irritated case against recent arguments that account for gender differences by reference to "innate" biological tendencies. Notice, for example, how she uses causal analysis both to explore opposing explanations of why boys and girls behave differently and to cast a critical eye on the differences, in the matter of child rearing, between what parents preach and what they do. Consider, too, what Pollitt assumes about the values and opinions of her audience—the essay originally appeared in the *New York Times,* October 8, 1995.

PREREADING: THINKING ABOUT THE ESSAY IN ADVANCE

Gender roles are something we all know from personal experience and therefore something we may feel we know inside out. What is *your* answer to the question that the essay, according to its title, will be answering? Is your answer based just on experience? In what ways, if at all, is it based on knowledge obtained from reading or research? Are you open to hearing views other than your own on this subject?

Words to Watch

prenatal (par. 1) before birth
hormonal (par. 1) having to do with hormones, that is, those chemical substances that are created by living cells and trigger activity elsewhere in the body

cognitive (par. 2) having to do with mental processes
innate (par. 4) inborn, something we are born with
index (par. 4) indication
ambivalently (par. 7) with mixed feelings
hierarchical (par. 13) arranged in order of rank, status, or importance
determinist (par. 13) the view that acts or attributes are wholly caused by preexisting factors, such as genes
inculcating (par. 16) instilling

1 It's twenty-eight years since the founding of NOW, and boys still like trucks and girls still like dolls. Increasingly, we are told that the source of these robust preferences must lie outside society—in prenatal hormonal influences, brain chemistry, genes—and that feminism has reached its natural limits. What else could possibly explain the love of preschool girls for party dresses or the desire of toddler boys to own more guns than Mark from Michigan?

2 True, recent studies claim to show small cognitive differences between the sexes: He gets around by orienting himself in space; she does it by remembering landmarks. Time will tell if any deserve the hoopla with which each is invariably greeted, over the protests of the researchers themselves. But even if the results hold up (and the history of such research is not encouraging), we don't need studies of sex-differentiated brain activity in reading, say, to understand why boys and girls still seem so unalike.

3 The feminist movement has done much for some women, and something for every woman, but it has hardly turned America into a playground free of sex roles. It hasn't even got women to stop dieting or men to stop interrupting them.

4 Instead of looking at kids to "prove" that differences in behavior by sex are innate, we can look at the ways we raise kids as an index to how unfinished the feminist revolution really is, and how tentatively it is embraced even by adults who fully expect their daughters to enter previously male-dominated professions and their sons to change diapers.

5 I'm at a children's birthday party. "I'm sorry," one mom silently mouths to the mother of the birthday girl, who has just torn open her present—Tropical Splash Barbie. Now, you can love Barbie or you can hate Barbie, and there are feminists in both camps. But *apologize* for Barbie? Inflict Barbie, against your own convictions, on the child of a friend you know will be none too pleased?

Every mother in that room had spent years becoming a person who had to be taken seriously, not least by herself. Even the most attractive, I'm willing to bet, had suffered over her body's failure to fit the impossible American ideal. Given all that, it seems crazy to transmit Barbie to the next generation. Yet to reject her is to say that what Barbie represents—being sexy, thin, stylish—is unimportant, which is obviously not true, and children know it's not true. 6

Women's looks matter terribly in this society, and so Barbie, however ambivalently, must be passed along. After all, there are worse toys. The Cut and Style Barbie styling head, for example, a grotesque object intended to encourage "hair play." The grownups who give that probably apologize, too. 7

How happy would most parents be to have a child who flouted sex conventions? I know a lot of women, feminists, who complain in a comical, eyeball-rolling way about their sons' passion for sports: the ruined weekends, obnoxious coaches, macho values. But they would not think of discouraging their sons from participating in this activity they find so foolish. Or do they? Their husbands are sports fans, too, and they like their husbands a lot. 8

Could it be that even sports-resistant moms see athletics as part of manliness? That if their sons wanted to spend the weekend writing up their diaries, or reading, or baking, they'd find it disturbing? Too anti-social? Too lonely? Too gay? 9

Theories of innate differences in behavior are appealing. They let parents off the hook—no small recommendation in a culture that holds moms, and sometimes even dads, responsible for their children's every misstep on the road to bliss and success. 10

They allow grown-ups to take the path of least resistance to the dominant culture, which always requires less psychic effort, even if it means more actual work: Just ask the working mother who comes home exhausted and nonetheless finds it easier to pick up her son's socks than make him do it himself. They let families buy for their children, without *too* much guilt, the unbelievably sexist junk that the kids, who have been watching commercials since birth, understandably crave. 11

But the thing the theories do most of all is tell adults that the *adult* world—in which moms and dads still play by many of the old rules even as they question and fidget and chafe against them—is the way it's supposed to be. A girl with a doll and a boy with a truck "explain" why men are from Mars and women are from Venus, why wives do housework and husbands just don't understand. 12

13 The paradox is that the world of rigid and hierarchical sex roles evoked by determinist theories is already passing away. Three-year-olds may indeed insist that doctors are male and nurses female, even if their own mother is a physician. Six-year-olds know better. These days, something like half of all medical students are female, and male applications to nursing school are inching upward. When tomorrow's three-year-olds play doctor, who's to say how they'll assign the roles?

14 With sex roles, as in every area of life, people aspire to what is possible, and conform to what is necessary. But these are not fixed, especially today. Biological determinism may reassure some adults about their present, but it is feminism, the ideology of flexible and converging sex roles, that fits our children's future. And the kids, somehow, know this.

15 That's why, if you look carefully, you'll find that for every kid who fits a stereotype, there's another who's breaking one down. Sometimes it's the same kid—the boy who skateboards *and* takes cooking in his after school program; the girl who collects stuffed animals *and* A-pluses in science.

16 Feminists are often accused of imposing their "agenda" on children. Isn't that what adults always do, consciously and unconsciously? Kids aren't born religious, or polite, or kind, or able to remember where they put their sneakers. Inculcating these behaviors, and the values behind them, is a tremendous amount of work, involving many adults. We don't have a choice, really, about *whether* we should give our children messages about what it means to be male and female—they're bombarded with them from morning till night.

BUILDING VOCABULARY

The writer engaged in contemporary debate assumes that her reader will naturally understand topical allusions or other kinds of references, especially insofar as they are political. Define or identify the following topical terms or phrases:

a. NOW (par. 1)
b. feminism (par. 1), feminist revolution (par. 4)
c. the Cut and Style Barbie styling head (par. 7)
d. macho values (par. 8)
e. men are from Mars and women are from Venus (par. 12)

THINKING CRITICALLY ABOUT THE ESSAY

Understanding the Writer's Ideas

1. What is the implication of Pollitt's opening sentence?
2. What does the writer say that we are told explains the continued preference of boys for trucks and girls for dolls?
3. According to the writer, instead of innate qualities, what "index" should we look to in order to explain differences in behavior by sex?
4. Why does the writer say you should not apologize for Barbie? What does she mean by this?
5. What do you think is the writer's answer to the question that opens paragraph 8?
6. What reasons does Pollitt give to account for why innate differences in behavior are appealing?
7. Why does the writer think that the era of rigid, hierarchical sex roles is at an end?
8. "People aspire," the writer says in the opening sentence of paragraph 14, "to what is possible, and conform to what is necessary." What does this statement mean? What would you say the writer thinks is possible, and what does she think is necessary when it comes to sex roles?

Understanding the Writer's Techniques

1. What is the thesis statement of this essay? Where does it appear?
2. Pollitt attempts to answer the question *why* it seems that boys continue to prefer trucks and that girls continue to prefer dolls. In other words, she attempts to explain the *causes* of behavior. How does Pollitt explain the causes of the persistence of children's preferences in toys?
3. One provocative rhetorical device is the question that is actually a statement, either directly or by implication. Consider, for example, the question that opens paragraph 8. The question implies an argument—the argument that, while in principle most parents might reject as "sexist" our society's sex-role conventions, in practice most parents do not want their children to deviate from these conventions. Where else in the essay does Pollitt use questions to make an argument?

4. What is the *tone* of this essay? Are there places where the tone changes?
5. Explain why you find the essay's conclusion effective or ineffective.

✱ MIXING PATTERNS

What are the essential comparisons and contrasts that appear in the essay? Offer examples of how the comparative method reinforces the writer's thesis.

Exploring the Writer's Ideas

1. The "nature/nurture" debate—are we who we are because of something inborn or genetic or preprogrammed, or are we the way we are because of the society in which we are reared?—is an old one. Pollitt opens her essay by alluding to new evidence to support the deterministic (nature) side, but she clearly intends to argue against a deterministic view of sex roles. However, aside from a dismissive reference in the next paragraph, she does not tell us anything about what this new evidence might be. Why? How, if at all, does this omission affect her essay?
2. What kinds of evidence does Pollitt use to make her case? Is her evidence "scientific"? Is her evidence sufficient to refute deterministic views? Why does she never address deterministic arguments directly? Which piece of the writer's evidence do you find especially persuasive, if any? Which piece of evidence do you find least persuasive? Why?
3. What do you think Pollitt means when she says that feminism is "the ideology of flexible and converging sex roles" (par. 14)? Is feminism an ideology? What are flexible sex roles? Can you be a feminist and a determinist too? Can you be skeptical about determinist views about sex roles and yet not be a feminist? Is Pollitt's association of one position with another—antideterminism and feminism—justified and necessary, or arbitrary and opinionated?

IDEAS FOR WRITING

Prewriting

List some examples of why girls like to play with dolls *or* boys like to play with trucks. Make your examples specific.

Guided Writing

Write an essay based on the previous prewriting exercise.

1. Begin with a paragraph similar to Pollitt's that introduces primary and secondary causes and effects.
2. Indicate that this chain of causality illustrates the power of nurture over nature.
3. Provide two or three extended examples, devoting well-rounded paragraphs to each. Compare and contrast the past or present, and, using causal analysis, suggest why "nature" or conventional stereotypes might have made us doubt the emergence of the new roles you are discussing.
4. Show that these new roles are emerging despite the discomfort of adults about stepping beyond the bounds of conventional sex roles.
5. Conclude by restating your opening point, but from a future-oriented perspective.

Thinking and Writing Collaboratively

In small groups of four or five, do a Web search for new developments (one or two new findings in biological or psychological research) in the nature/nurture debate. Think about whether the evidence you discover seems to support or refute Pollitt's main argument, and share your conclusions with the rest of the class.

Writing About the Text

Write an essay based on questions 2 or 3 in Exploring the Writer's Ideas.

More Writing Projects

1. In your journal explore the ways in which, upon reflection, you can see that you have been "shaped" by parents/genes/society.
2. Write an extended paragraph that explores your personal experience of sex roles. Compare and contrast what you may have wanted to do and what you felt was expected of you.
3. Write an essay that explores the contrast between what people say and what they do. Include in your discussion a plausible defense of why people might say one thing and do another.

SUMMING UP: CHAPTER 8

1. Working in small groups, develop a questionnaire that focuses on men's and women's roles in our society. Then have each group member get at least three people outside the group to complete it. When all the questionnaires have been completed, analyze the results and present them to the class.
2. For the next week, keep a journal about something that is currently causing you to have mixed emotions. (Note: This should not be the same issue you wrote about in the Guided Writing assignment following the Stephen King essay; this should be a *current* issue.) Try to write five reasons for the emotions each day (or expand upon previous ones). At the end of the week, write an essay that analyzes how the issue is affecting your life or how you plan to deal with it in the future.
3. Some of the essays in this chapter identify inner drives that seem to function as compulsions—as things that have to be, that arise from us no matter what we would like. King writes about our anticivilization emotions, Wiesel about patriotic feelings, Herbert about multitasking, Pollitt about gender differences. Write an essay that analyzes these writers' responses to the compulsions they describe.
4. Compare and contrast Elie Wiesel's view of how cause-and-effect analysis works in feelings of patriotism with Brent Staples's view of how it operates in race relations ("Night Walker," pp. 221–223).
5. What do you think Elie Wiesel, a Holocaust survivor, would say to Stephen King's assertion that people need some insanity in their lives to stay sane? Write an essay about how Wiesel would respond to King's essay.
6. Do you think Wiesel's cause-and-effect analysis of why he loves America is right for all immigrants? Why or why not?

✶ FROM SEEING TO WRITING

Why has a police officer stopped the person in this photograph? Analyze some of the possible causal relations, moving from the obvious (the driver was speeding) to more subtle and complex causes. Offer a complete analysis in which you consider a range of possible main and secondary causes as well as possible effects.

CHAPTER 9

Classification

WHAT IS CLASSIFICATION?

Classification is the arrangement of information into groups or categories in order to make clear the relations among members of the group. In a supermarket, the soups are together in one aisle, the frozen foods in another. In a music store, all the jazz selections are in one section while rap is in another section. You wouldn't expect to find a can of tomato soup next to the butter pecan ice cream any more than you'd look for a CD of Wynton Marsalis's *Christmas Jazz Jam* in the same section as Eminem's *Recovery*.

Writers need to classify because it helps them present a mass of material by means of some orderly system. Related bits of information seem clearer when presented together as parts of a group. Unlike writing narrative, for example, developing classification requires a different level of analysis and planning. The writer not only presents a single topic or event, but also places the subject into a complex network of relations. In a narrative, we can tell the story of a single event from start to finish, such as the time we saw a Van Gogh painting in an art museum. In classification, we have to think beyond the personal experience to try to place that Van Gogh painting in a wider context. Where does Van Gogh "fit" in the history of painting? Why is he different from other painters? How does his style relate to other work of the same period? In pursuing these questions, we seek not only to *record* our experience in looking at the painting but to *understand* it more fully.

Classification, then, begins by thinking about a body of material and trying to break it down into distinct parts, or categories. Called *division* (see Glossary) or *analysis,* this first task helps split an idea or object into usable components. Then, some of the parts can serve as categories into which the writer can fit individual pieces that share some common qualities.

For example, if the writer wanted to *analyze* the Van Gogh painting, she might begin with the large subject of painting. Then she could *divide,* or break the subject down, into two groups:

traditional painting
modern painting

Then, she could further *divide* the types of modern painting:

impressionist
postimpressionist
fauvist
art nouveau
cubist
art deco
abstract expressionist
op art
minimalist art

The purpose is to determine what the parts of the whole are. If we know what the components of *modern painting* are, then we can place or locate the Van Gogh painting in relation to other paintings. We would know whether it belonged in the soup aisle or the freezer section, so to speak. In this case, we would decide that it is *not* traditional painting, so that we would separate it from that group. We would place it in the modern group. Now we know which aisle it belongs in. But is it tomato or chicken soup? Now we relate it to the other modern types of painting, and place it in the postimpressionist group. Our decision is based on an analysis of the painter's use of color, his style, and the ways he differs from painters in the other groups.

Our analysis does not mean that the Van Gogh has nothing in common with traditional painting. Van Gogh, for instance, shares an interest in landscape and self-portraits with Rembrandt. But the bright, bold colors of his *Starry Night* are so dramatically different from the somber colors of the older Dutch painter's *Nightwatch* that we are inclined to emphasize their *division.* We could, for instance, set up a supermarket on the basis of what color the food labels were: all the red labels in one aisle, all the yellow labels together. But such a system would make it much harder to find what we wanted unless we were experts in package design. Similarly, our classification of painting is based on the most sensible method of division.

In this chapter, Akbar Ahmed classifies Muslims into three groups. Jedediah Purdy explores basic types of environmentalism. Amy Rashap chronicles the changing stereotypes American magazines have used to portray ethnicity. And James T. Baker brings together a variety of writing techniques to analyze the world of education with some humor. Each writer has a different purpose for classification, but each uses the same basic system of organization.

HOW DO WE READ CLASSIFICATION?

Reading classification involves the following steps:

- Identify what the author is classifying. Find the thesis to determine what the purpose or basis of the classification is.
- Make an outline of the essay. Find the divisions and the classifications into which the author has sorted the subject.
- Determine whether the categories are clearly defined. Do they overlap?
- Be alert for stereotypes. Has the author used them in order to build the groups? If so, see if the groups are oversimplified and thus unreliable.
- Identify the intended audience. How do we know who the audience is?

HOW DO WE WRITE CLASSIFICATION?

The four essayists in this chapter should provide you with enough examples of how to classify to make your writing task easy. Classification resembles outlining. Whether the subject is personal, technical, simple, complex, or abstract, the writer can organize material into categories, and can move carefully from one category to another in developing an essay.

Select your topic and begin to separate it into categories. Try drawing a tree with branches or use a model from a biology book that shows the division of life into genus, species, phyla, and so on.

Or make lists. Think about how your library classifies books. Arranging books by the color of the covers might look attractive, but it would presume that all library users already knew what a book looked like before they came to the library. Instead, libraries divide books by type. They generally begin with two large groups: fiction and nonfiction. Within these categories, they create small ones: English fiction, Mexican fiction, Australian fiction. Within nonfiction, they divide books into history, religion, geography, mathematics, and so on. In this way, a reader can find a book based on need, and not prior knowledge. Keeping the library in mind, make a list of categories for your topic.

Make an outline and arrange the groups to avoid overlap from one group to the next.

Decide on a system of classification. Don't force objects into arbitrary slots, though. Don't ignore differences that violate your categories. Try to create a legitimate system that avoids stereotyping or oversimplification; don't classify invalidly. Be sure your categories are legitimate.

Write a thesis that identifies the purpose of your system of classification. Think of the ways in which your system can broaden a reader's understanding of the subject rather than narrow it.

Sample thesis statement:

> At least three groups of immigrants reach the United States today—political refugees seeking asylum, economic refugees looking for a better life, and religious dissidents looking for freedom to practice their chosen beliefs.

Writing the Draft

Write a rough draft. Be sure that you explain the categories and give examples for each one.

For each category, use definition, description, illustration, or narrative to help the reader see the distinct nature of the division you have created. Use transitions between each category or group.

Proofread for correctness. Make a final copy.

A STUDENT PARAGRAPH: CLASSIFICATION

The student who wrote the following paragraph considered the sample thesis statement on immigration appearing earlier, and then modified it to suit her approach to the topic. Observe her various strategies for paragraph development, especially the way she subdivides the last of her categories.

Americans have mixed feelings about immigrants; they tend to judge different categories of immigrants—illegal aliens, poor immigrants, and political or religious refugees—very differently. Illegal aliens encounter the greatest degree of hostility, despite the fact that U.S. citizens often benefit from their work as maids, gardeners, and street vendors. The second category of immigrants, poor people who are here legally but who are looking to improve their standards of living, also tend to encounter some hostility from Americans. These immigrants, according to some Americans, compete for low-level jobs, go on welfare, and strain such social services as schools and hospitals. By contrast, Americans are usually more welcoming to political and religious refugees. For one thing, political refugees and religious dissidents are fewer in number, which automatically makes them less threatening. In addition, whether from Cuba, Iran, or the former Soviet Union, they are often better educated and wealthier than the illegal aliens and economic refugees, so they are perceived as less of a drain on resources. Undoubtedly, too, they receive a warmer welcome from many Americans because of the belief that their aims are "nobler" than those of illegal aliens or economic refugees, because they flee their homelands to maintain political and religious ideals, rather than simply to make more money.

Thesis statement announces classification scheme

First category with brief examples

Second category with greater detail

Transition "By contrast" introduces third category, further subdivided into two subcategories

Evidence supports position

Mystics, Modernists, and Literalists

Akbar Ahmed

Akbar Salahuddin Ahmed is currently the Chair of Islamic Studies at American University in Washington, D.C., and a Senior Fellow at the Brookings Institution. A leading authority on contemporary Islam, he was the former Pakistani ambassador to Great Britain. He has written many books, including *Discovering Islam* (1993), which was the basis of a six-part series on BBC, the British public television service. As an anthropologist, he has written extensively on the tribal areas of Pakistan. His latest book is *Journey into America: The Challenge of Islam* (2010). In this piece for the *Wall Street Journal,* Ahmed identifies three categories of Muslims in order to clarify the distinctions among thinkers who practice Islam.

PREREADING: THINKING ABOUT THE ESSAY IN ADVANCE

What do you know about Muslims and the religion that they follow, Islam? Make a list of the qualities, characteristics, or beliefs that you identify with Muslims.

Words to Watch

moderate (par. 1) reasonable; sensible
humanism (par. 4) concern with needs, well-being, and interests of people
Islam (par. 5) Muslim religion based on the seventh-century teachings of Mohammed
nationalist (par. 6) in favor of independence and self-rule for the country
advocate (par. 7) support
delineated (par. 8) defined; outlined

In the intense discussion about Muslims today, non-Muslims often say to me: "You are a moderate, but are there others like you?" 1

Clearly, the use of the term moderate here is meant as a compliment. But the application of the term creates more problems than it solves. The term is heavy with value judgment, smacking of "good guy" versus "bad guy" categories. And it implies that while a minority of Muslims are moderate, the rest are not. 2

3 Having studied the practices of Muslims around the world today, I've come up with three broad categories: mystic, modernist and literalist. Of course, I must add the caveat that these are analytic models and aren't watertight.

4 Muslims in the mystic category reflect universal humanism, believing in "peace with all." The 13th century Sufi poet Rumi exemplifies this category. In his verses, he glorifies worshipping the same God in the synagogue, the church and the mosque.

5 The second category is the modernist Muslim who believes in trying to balance tradition and modernity. The modernist is proud of Islam and yet able to live comfortably in, and contribute to, Western society.

6 Most Muslim leaders who led nationalist movements in the first half of the 20th century were modernists—from Sultan Mohammed V, the first king of independent Morocco, to M. A. Jinnah, who founded Pakistan in 1947. But as modernists failed over time, becoming increasingly incompetent and corrupt, the literalists stepped into the breach.

7 The literalists believe that Muslim behavior must approximate that of the Prophet in seventh-century Arabia. Their belief that Islam is under attack forces many of them to adopt a defensive posture. And while not all literalists advocate violence, many do. Movements like the Muslim Brotherhood, Hamas, and the Taliban belong to this category.

8 In the Muslim world the divisions between the three categories I have delineated are real. The outcome of their struggle will define Islam's fate.

9 The West can help by understanding Muslim society in a more nuanced and sophisticated way in order to interact with it wisely and for mutual benefit. The first step is to categorize Muslims accurately.

BUILDING VOCABULARY

1. The *derivation* of a word—how it originated and where it came from—can make you more aware of meanings. Your dictionary normally lists abbreviations (for instance, L. for Latin, Fr. for French) for word origins, and sometimes explains fully the way a word came into use. Look up the following words to determine their origins.

a. watertight (par. 3)
b. humanism (par. 4)
c. modernity (par. 5)
d. nationalist (par. 6)
e. nuanced (par. 9)

2. Choose the correct meaning for each word taken from the selection and put an X in the blank space beside your choice. Be sure to check back on the context in which the words appear.
   a. **intense** (par. 1)
      ___ powerful ___ nervous ___ supportive
      ___ violent ___ gentle
   b. **caveat** (par. 3)
      ___ suggestion ___ deep cave ___ addition
      ___ sincere apology ___ caution
   c. **glorifies** (par. 4)
      ___ secures ___ adores ___ governs ___ minimizes
      ___ praises unnecessarily
   d. **incompetent** (par. 6)
      ___ ineligible ___ insecure ___ capable
      ___ bungling ___ indecent
   e. **breach** (par. 6)
      ___ shoreline ___ trouble ___ pit ___ monarchy
      ___ gap

THINKING CRITICALLY ABOUT THE ESSAY

Understanding the Writer's Ideas

1. What three categories does the writer establish?
2. What are the qualities of Muslims in the first category? What information can you find about the Sufi poet Rumi? Check your library or the Internet.
3. What characterizes the modernist Muslim? Why did modernists fail over time, according to the writer?
4. What do literalist Muslims believe? What movements belong to this category?
5. What, according to the writer, will define the fate of Islam?

6. Who are the people Ahmed names in paragraph 6? Why does he use their names in the essay? What do the names accomplish for the reader?

Understanding the Writer's Techniques

1. Which paragraphs make up the introduction to this selection, which is only nine paragraphs long? Is the introduction too short, too long, or just right, do you think? Why?
2. What is the writer's thesis? How many sentences does Ahmed take to state it?
3. Does Ahmed emphasize each of the categories equally? Why or why not, do you think? To which categories would you give more emphasis? Less?
4. Identify the uses of illustration in this brief essay. Why does Ahmed use illustration, do you think?
5. How does the writer use definition here? Are the definitions effective? Do you understand the categories better as a result of the definitions? Why or why not?
6. In paragraph 7, Ahmed says that literalists want Muslims to behave in the way Mohammed behaved in Arabia in the seventh century. However, the writer doesn't give details of what that behavior might entail. Why do you think that he omitted them? Would the essay either benefit or suffer if Ahmed had included those details? Why do you think so?

Exploring the Writer's Ideas

1. Is it possible in today's world for people to follow the teachings of the mystics as Ahmed defines them? Would it be possible today to worship "the same God in the synagogue, the church and the mosque"? Why or why not?
2. In what ways do you think that the outcome of the struggle among the three categories will determine Islam's fate? Could the three categories coexist? Why or why not?
3. Ahmed believes that to understand Muslim society we must first "categorize Muslims accurately." Why might you agree or disagree with this position? Would you argue that to understand any religion we must understand the categories of its membership? Why or why not?

IDEAS FOR WRITING

Prewriting

Identify a group of people—teachers, for example, friends, family members, churchgoers, politicians, enemies, dates you have had, or some other group of your choosing—and establish categories within the group. Make a rough outline of the qualities of each category.

Guided Writing

Using the classification method, write an essay on a specific group of individuals. Feel free to use the group that you identified in the prewriting activity above.

1. Establish your subject in the first two or three paragraphs.
2. Attempt to identify a minimum of three broad categories within the group.
3. Explain why the classification that you propose is important in understanding the whole group.
4. Identify any current term, if any exists, that you consider problematic when applied to members of the larger group. Ahmed dismisses the term "moderate," for example.
5. Label each category with a word or phrase that highlights the essential quality of the category. Ahmed uses *mystic*, *modernist*, and *literalist*. Use the words early in the essay so that readers know the names of each category in your classification scheme.
6. Attempt to balance your presentation of information in each category, but do not hesitate to present the most information about the category that you believe is the most important.
7. Use illustration and definition freely to help clarify your ideas.
8. At the end of your essay, reassert the importance of understanding the classifications you have established.
9. Give your essay a title that includes the names of the three categories.

Thinking and Writing Collaboratively

According to Ahmed, the literalists adopt a defensive posture because they feel that Islam is under attack. Form groups and discuss whether or not you believe that Islam is under attack in the

United States. Make sure that you can support your position with specifics. Ask each group to report their findings to the class.

Writing About the Text

Examine Ahmed's second paragraph carefully and write an essay about the word "moderate." Do you agree with the writer's dismissal of the term? What uses do you see for the word? Must it always establish a good-guy, bad-guy mentality? Why might you agree or disagree that the term "moderate" creates "more problems than it solves"? Is the comment accurate in understanding Muslims, do you think? Is the comment accurate in other arenas—politics, let us say, or fiscal matters, or school discipline? Explain your answer.

More Writing Projects

1. As journal practice, classify varieties of Internet services, Web sites, cellphone users, television programs—in short, classify people or objects related to some familiar technology.
2. In a paragraph or two, use classification to establish categories of people who observe the same religion or philosophy that you do.
3. Write an essay in which you expand upon one of the three categories that Ahmed identifies for Muslims. Use your library and Internet sources to research the group that interests you most. You certainly won't find the groups named as Ahmed has named them; but you should be able to find out about Arabic humanism and the poet Rumi; Muslim leaders in the twentieth century and their religious philosophies and practices; and the strict application of Mohammed's philosophy among current movements.

Shades of Green

Jedediah Purdy

Jedediah Purdy, who was born in 1975 and homeschooled until he was fourteen at his parents' farm in West Virginia, teaches law at Duke University. He has degrees from Harvard University and Yale Law School. Purdy published his first book, *For Common Things: Irony, Trust, and Commitment in America Today* (1999), when he was just twenty-four years old. His next book was *Being America: Liberty, Commerce, and Violence in an American World* (2003). His latest book is *The Meaning of Property: Freedom, Community, and the Legal Imagination* (2010). Purdy has also published articles in legal journals on ethics and international law, and contributed essays about American culture to periodicals such as the *Atlantic Monthly* and the *American Prospect,* where this essay appeared in the latter journal on June 3, 2000.

PREREADING: THINKING ABOUT THE ESSAY IN ADVANCE

How do you perceive and use *nature*? Do you consider yourself an environmentalist? Why or why not?

Words to Watch

consensus (par. 1) general agreement
divergent (par. 2) varying from the norm; different
pragmatic (par. 4) practical
carnivores (par. 4) meat-eaters
populist (par. 7) one who supports the people
pristine (par. 7) untouched, unspoiled
acrimony (par. 8) bitterness or harshness of temper, speech, or manner
visceral (par. 11) affecting or felt by the internal organs of the body

More than two-thirds of Americans call themselves environmentalists. Their rank includes every serious presidential candidate, a growing list of corporate executives, some of the country's most extreme radicals, and ordinary people from just about every region, class, and ethnic group. Even allowing for some hypocrisy, finding consensus so tightly overlaid on division is reason for a closer look. 1

2 In fact, there are several environmentalisms in this country, and there have been for a long time. They are extensions of some of the most persistent strands of American thought and political culture. They stand for different and sometimes conflicting policy agendas, and their guiding concerns are often quite widely divergent. Recently, though, they have begun to contemplate a set of issues that promises to transform each of them—and to expand environmental politics from its traditional concern with a limited number of wild places and species to a broader commitment to the environment as the place where we all live, all the time.

3 The oldest and most familiar version of environmental concern might be called romantic environmentalism. Still a guiding spirit of the Sierra Club and the soul of the Wilderness Society and many regional groups, this environmentalism arises from love of beautiful landscapes: the highest mountains, deepest canyons, and most ancient forests. As a movement, it began in the late nineteenth century when America's wealthy discovered outdoor recreation and, inspired by writers like Sierra Club founder John Muir, developed a reverence for untamed places. For these American romantics, encounters with the wild promised to restore bodies and spirits worn down by civilized life. Today's romantic environmentalists blend this ambition with a delight in whales, wolves, and distant rain forests. More than any other environmentalists, they—still disproportionately white and prosperous—feel a spiritual attachment to natural places.

4 Muir's environmentalism contains the idea that our true selves await us in the wild. Another type, managerial environmentalism, puts the wild at our service. This approach is a direct descendant of the Progressive era's hopeful reformism, specifically of Teddy Roosevelt's forestry policies; it makes its basic task the fitting together of ecology and economy to advance human ends. Pragmatic, market oriented, but respectful of public institutions, managerial environmentalists design trading schemes for pollution permits at the Natural Resources Defense Council, head up programs at the Environmental Protection Agency (EPA) to collaborate with businesses in developing clean technologies, and envision global environmental standards advancing alongside free trade accords. In their wild-eyed moments, they imagine a high-tech economy that follows nature in producing no waste or, like *The New Republic*'s senior editor Gregg Easterbrook, genetic engineering that will turn carnivores into

grass eaters and bring lion and lamb together at last. Although it began among policy makers, this managerial attitude is gaining ground in the optimistic culture of Silicon Valley and has many adherents younger than 35.

5 The environmental justice movement is another thing entirely. Only an idea a decade ago, this effort to address the relationships among race, poverty, and environmental harm has come to rapid prominence. Grassroots projects in inner cities and industrial areas around the country have drawn attention to urban air pollution, lead paint, transfer stations for municipal garbage and hazardous waste, and other environmental dangers that cluster in poor and minority neighborhoods. Eight years ago, romantic environmentalism was virtually the only movement that engaged students on college campuses; now young activists are equally likely to talk about connections between the environment and social justice or, on an international scale, the environment and human rights.

6 Environmental justice follows the tradition of social inclusion and concern for equity that had its last great triumphs during the civil rights movement and the War on Poverty. Some of its landmark moments are court cases ruling that federal projects can be challenged when they concentrate environmental harm in minority areas, which have begun to extend the principles of civil rights to environmental policy.

7 The environmental justice movement also reflects the populist streak that emerges in American politics wherever an isolated community finds itself up against big and anonymous institutions. Activists and community members tend to mistrust big business and government alike. The constituency of the environmental justice movement often perceives the gap between the prosperous and the poor, between whites and minorities, between mainstream culture and their own communities, as much more basic than the difference between the EPA and Monsanto. All outsiders are on the other side of that gap—an impression that has been reinforced where some local Sierra Club chapters have ignored community health issues and have endorsed proposals to put waste dumps in poor neighborhoods rather than in pristine valleys.

8 Environmental justice advocates have little patience for romantic environmentalism, and their culture of perpetual embattlement is worlds away from managerial optimism. When "environmentalists" of such different experiences and sensibilities address the same issue, it is no surprise that misunderstanding and acrimony

sometimes result. This tension was evident two years ago when the Sierra Club came close to endorsing strict controls on immigration to slow development and resource use in this country. The organization's justice-oriented members were outraged, as they had been over the waste-siting disputes a few years earlier. For the pure romantics, the concerns about poor communities and international equity didn't seem "environmental" at all. Meanwhile, the impassioned dispute was all rather alien to the measured rationality of the managerial environmentalists' plans for efficient resource use.

9 But our several environmentalisms are learning from their interactions, and it is possible that the lessons will be good for them all. Romantic environmentalism has long withheld itself from cities, suburbs, and factories, sometimes following Muir in treating these as fallen places where nothing beautiful will grow. The other environmentalisms have challenged this idea by insisting that "the environment" means the space where we live and work, that the built environment of Manhattan and the industrial environment of the lower Mississippi matter as much as the ecosystem of Yellowstone.

10 The change brings environmental concern home to cities and neighborhoods, where people live. This domesticated environmentalism is crystallized in the debates about sprawl, "smart growth," and the design of communities. It is powered by the recognition that the way we now pursue the things we seem to want—space, light, some trees, a little peace and quiet—can leave us feeling overcrowded and isolated, spending too much time in our cars, living and working in spaces that do not inspire our affection. Communities that decide to make walking or bicycling easy, develop dense housing in return for set-asides of open space, and foster neighborhoods where living, working, and shopping all happen on the same block, are addressing an environmental problem with an environmental solution. This is an environmentalism that urges not just setting aside a piece of wilderness for occasional visits but changing the way we live every day—the way we spend our money, build our homes, and move from place to place.

11 Attention to these domesticated environmental concerns thus corrects a huge blind spot in romantic environmentalism's sometimes exclusive commitment to wilderness. It can also help to bridge a basic gap in the policy proposals of managerial environmentalism. Those proposals concentrate on technological innovation: taxing greenhouse gases, devising permit systems for pollution,

and otherwise inventing better devices for living as we already do. The paradox that dogs the managers is that because their policy proposals generally cost money to ordinary people, big industry, or both, they stand little chance without a groundswell of popular support; yet they are just the thing to induce a fit of napping in the average citizen, whose visceral concern for the environment does not carry over into an interest in the tax code. Policies that foster, say, responsible logging, farming for stewardship, or sustainable grazing on public lands have more appeal when they come not as insights of microeconomic analysis and resource management but as part of a proposal that the work we do in nature is more appealing and honorable when it respects nature's requirements. Most of us care little about supply and demand curves, but a fair amount about where we live and how we work. Because it is close to the grain of everyday experience, the language of livable communities and environmentally responsible work can make environmental policy-designers more politically effective.

12 As for the environmental justice movement, it fits here as the Alabama bus boycotts fit into the 1964 Civil Rights Act. It fights against particular, sometimes quite outrageous, injustices. Its work is right and necessary but not usually connected with a broader agenda for sustaining dignified communities. Yet such an agenda needs not just constituents who are suburbanites upset by sprawl, but the people who suffer most from poor policies on toxics, land use, and transportation: the urban and rural poor. Moreover, a systematic response to the systematic problems those communities face is the only just way to end their thousands of brushfire struggles.

13 So one possible result of the present trends in environmental politics is a broader, more effective environmental movement. Such a movement might propose that we should need neither to withdraw our innermost selves to the woods nor to experience our neighborhoods as a species of oppression. It would make the human environment a complete and honored portion of environmental politics. Pursuing such goals would require romantics to bring some of their aspirations home from the wilderness, policy specialists to get their hands dirty in a political culture that does not yield to economists' graphs, and environmental justice activists to find reason to turn their populist anger to projects on common ground. None of our several environmentalisms will go away, and none should, but they are all better off with the recognition that the environment is very much a political, cultural, and human affair.

BUILDING VOCABULARY

1. Define the following terms—all relevant to Purdy's main subject—in the context of the essay:
   - **a.** environmentalism (par. 2)
   - **b.** policy agendas (par. 2)
   - **c.** environmental politics (par. 2)
   - **d.** free trade accords (par. 4)
   - **e.** social justice (par. 5)
   - **f.** tradition of social inclusion (par. 6)
   - **g.** culture of perpetual embattlement (par. 8)
   - **h.** ecosystem (par. 9)
   - **i.** smart growth (par. 10)
2. Explain the following *allusions* (see Glossary) in Purdy's essay:
   - **a.** Sierra Club (par. 3)
   - **b.** John Muir (par. 3)
   - **c.** Progressive era (par. 4)
   - **d.** Teddy Roosevelt (par. 4)
   - **e.** Silicon Valley (par. 4)
   - **f.** War on Poverty (par. 6)
   - **g.** Civil Rights Act (par. 12)

THINKING CRITICALLY ABOUT THE ESSAY

Understanding the Writer's Ideas

1. Explain in your own words the "several environmentalisms" that Purdy discusses in this essay.
2. Why, according to Purdy, must we be prepared to reexamine or look more closely at the environmental movement?
3. What forms of environmentalism engage students on college campuses, and why?
4. Purdy refers to the "populist streak . . . in American politics" (par. 7). What does he mean by this expression, and how does he expand the concept in the essay?
5. Why does Purdy refer not only to rural or wilderness areas but also to urban and suburban environments?
6. How do the current trends in environmentalism coincide? What advantages does Purdy see in this convergence?
7. What possible outcomes does Purdy predict for the various strands of environmentalism in the United States?

Understanding the Writer's Techniques

1. Why is "Shades of Green" an apt title for Purdy's essay?
2. Purdy's essay appeared in the *American Prospect,* a liberal magazine. Explain how you think Purdy tailors his content to his primary audience. How does Purdy's attention to his audience influence the tone that he adopts?
3. Where does Purdy's thesis statement appear? Why does he place his thesis where he does?
4. List the main categories in Purdy's essay. How does he introduce each category? What topics does he develop? Does he maintain a balance in his treatment of each category? Why or why not?
5. Where does Purdy use comparison and contrast as a rhetorical strategy? What is his purpose?
6. Purdy introduces "domesticated environmentalism" in paragraph 10. Does he set this unit up as a separate category, or do you think he violates the basic principles of division-and-classification? Justify your answer.
7. How does Purdy develop his conclusion? Do you find his conclusion optimistic or pessimistic? Explain.

Exploring the Writer's Ideas

1. Purdy grew up in rural West Virginia, where his parents were active in the "back-to-the-land" movement. How do you think Purdy's childhood tempers his approach to environmentalism as he presents it in this essay?
2. What are the values that Purdy associates with each of his several environmentalisms? Where do these values coincide, and where do they conflict? Do you think that these environmentalisms can be fully reconciled? Why or why not?
3. Does Purdy ever express a preference for one type of environmentalism over all other forms? Justify your response.

IDEAS FOR WRITING

Prewriting

Freewrite for fifteen minutes about the kinds of experiences you had with nature when you were growing up. How did these experiences influence your understanding of the natural world today?

Guided Writing

Write a classification-and-division essay entitled "Shades of _______." If you wish, you may compose your own paper on an environmental issue, but feel free to select other topics such as "shades of politics," "shades of men" or "women," "shades of pizza" or another favorite food that lends itself to classification, and so forth.

1. Begin by writing a paragraph providing an overview of the subject and the types or "shades" of meaning that you plan to develop.
2. State your thesis at the start of the second paragraph. Establish three or four categories, and clearly explain the principle of classification governing them.
3. Present each of your categories sequentially, offering equal amounts of information for each unit.
4. If you want, use comparison and contrast to distinguish between and among categories.
5. Conclude by offering an optimistic or pessimistic assessment of your subject.

Thinking and Writing Collaboratively

Go online with one or two other class members and find out more about John Muir. Then write a brief collaborative biography of Muir and present it to your instructor for evaluation.

Writing Critically About the Text

Write an analysis of Purdy's use of classification-and-division to organize his essay. Explain the benefits Purdy derives from his use of this rhetorical strategy, and evaluate his relative success in conveying information to his audience.

More Writing Projects

1. In your journal, write about the one form of environmentalism that most appeals to you.
2. Compose an extended paragraph describing the state of the environment in your hometown.
3. Use your extended paragraph as the foundation for an essay on what your town or city could do to improve its environment.

The American Dream for Sale: Ethnic Images in Magazines

Amy Rashap

Amy Rashap (b. 1955) holds a PhD in folklore from the University of Pennsylvania, and she has written about American popular culture, focusing on food, dieting, and images of the body in American society. Rashap currently teaches conversational English at the Center for American Education in Singapore. This selection appeared in the catalog published in conjunction with an exhibition at the Balch Institute for Ethnic Studies, a museum and research library in Philadelphia. Rashap classifies evolving ethnic images in U.S. popular magazines, noting how they have reflected the views and the assumed biases of readers and the society at large over the last century.

PREREADING: THINKING ABOUT THE ESSAY IN ADVANCE

One version of the American Dream conjures up the picture of boatfuls of immigrants floating by the Statue of Liberty onto the shores of the land of opportunity. How does the essay's title make use of this notion of America? What does the title imply about the role of advertising in relation to traditional notions of the American Dream?

Words to Watch

dictum (par. 1) an authoritative saying
plethora (par. 2) overabundance
subservience (par. 5) submissiveness
protagonists (par. 9) the main characters in a story
nominally (par. 9) in name only but not in fact
superficial (par. 10) shallow
impetus (par. 12) incentive, stimulus
indigenous (par. 13) from a particular region, ethnic

1 "Promise—large promise—is the soul of advertising," wrote Dr. Samuel Johnson in the eighteenth century. His dictum has remained remarkably accurate during the last two hundred and fifty years. Advertisements tell the viewer much more than the merits of a particular product. From the glossy and colorful pages

of magazines, catalogues, and newspaper supplements the reader can extract images of how to live the perfect American life. This exhibit shows how the depiction of ethnic groups has changed radically in the advertisements of nationally distributed magazines over the last century. The pictures tell a complex tale of economic power and mobility; of conflicting attitudes towards one's ethnic heritage and towards Anglo-American culture.

2 The development of modern advertising, with its sophisticated use of imagery and catchy phrases, grew hand-in-hand with the advent of the affordable monthly and weekly magazines. By the 1880's factories were churning out a plethora of ready-made goods, and the expanded system of railways and roads linked producer and consumer into a national network. During this period magazine production rose apace. Due to a variety of factors, ranging from improved typesetting techniques and low postal rates to the utilization of increasingly sophisticated photoengraving processes, publishers began to produce low-priced, profusely illustrated magazines fashioned to appeal to a national audience. The contents of the magazines, such as *Collier's, The Saturday Evening Post* and *The Ladies Home Journal*, covered a wide variety of topics: from homemaking to current events, new inventions to briskly paced fiction. By 1905 twenty general monthlies, each with a circulation of over 100,000, were in existence. Ranging in price from 10 to 15¢, easily within the budget of tens of thousands of Americans, they were an ideal vehicle for carrying the manufacturer's messages to a national audience.

3 What were the implications of advertising for the masses? As advertisers targeted their products towards a mass audience, the need arose to create an "average person," a type who embodied the qualities and attitudes of many others. Advertisers devised images that tapped into deeply held beliefs and myths of an "all-American" lifestyle—one that didn't just sell a product, but a way of life that people could buy.

4 The very nature of the advertising medium itself necessitates the use of symbols and character types that could be understood at a glance. If the advertisement was to be effective, its message had to be quickly absorbed and understood. Thus, in their depiction of ethnic groups, advertisers often used commonly held stereotypes. Within these stock images, however, one can observe various levels of complexity.

When the N.H.M. Hotels ad in figure 1 appeared in 1936, the nation was still in the midst of the Great Depression. The black railroad porter, with his knowledge of the rails and reputation for prompt and courteous service, was an effective spokesman for a hotel chain dependent for its livelihood upon Americans getting back on the move. The portrayal of the porter is interesting in this ad, for, beyond the obvious fact that the only blacks present are in service roles, the spokesman's subservience is visually reinforced by his deferential smile, slight stoop, and bent knees. As porters, blacks could assist in the resurgence of the American economy, but not fully participate in its benefits. 5

An advertisement for the Milwaukee Railroad from a 1945 *National Geographic* (figure 2) reveals another way in which ethnic groups are shown as outsiders—at the service of American culture while not actively participating in it. Here is the Noble Savage, not as the representative of any particular group of Native Americans, but as the symbol for the railroad itself, barely visible in the advertisement. In both the visuals and the copy the sale is made through stock images and associations. He is as familiar as a dime store Indian; a reassuring and time-honored part of the American landscape. However, while the Indian shown here still brandishes 6

Figure 1

Magazine advertisement, 1936

his bow and arrow, he has been tamed. He gazes mutely over the changed landscape, another symbol of technological domination.

7 In a 1949 ad in *American Home*, Chiquita Banana entices us to buy her goods. Wearing a traditional ruffled skirt and fruit-laden hat, she embodies the stereotypical, fun-loving, gay Hispanic woman. While she occasionally doffs the more demure chef's hat, her smile and pert manner never waver. Her basic message is one of festivity, tempered with the American housewife's concern for nutrition: while bananas are good for you, they can be fun, too! They make mealtimes a party. In the later television ads of the 1960s, Chiquita Banana was transformed into a more overtly sexual figure doing the rumba. Singing her famous "I'm Chiquita Banana . . ." song in a Spanish accent, the advertisement's emphasis was more on festivity than wholesomeness.

8 The use of simple external attributes to symbolize ethnic identification has long been a favorite technique of advertisers. In a Royal Crown Cola advertisement of 1938 (figure 3), the reader was

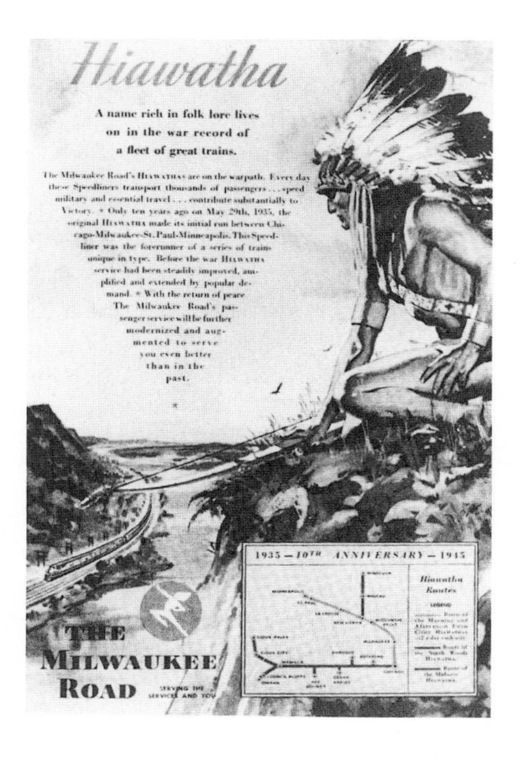

Figure 2

National Geographic *advertisement, July 1945*

urged to be like the thrifty "Scotchman" and buy the economical refreshment. Presenting its Scotsman with a broad grin and conspiratorial, chummy wink, the ad pokes gentle fun at the Scottish reputation for miserliness. Whether the character in Scottish garb is Scottish or not is incidental, for the white American can easily put on this ethnic persona without compromising or jeopardizing his identity. The Scottish stereotype can be invoked by using a few external character traits; the image does not extend beyond that initial statement. The black stereotype represented in the N.H.M. Hotel ad, however, reflects more deeply-held attitudes toward cultural differences. Compare the closeness of the two men in the RC Cola ad with the black porter and the white traveler in figure 1. Even the spacing between the characters in both ads is significant: while the men in the RC Cola ad display an easy intimacy, the black porter stands deferentially apart from the white traveler.

9 Advertisements were not the only medium that reflected the subservient role certain ethnic groups occupied within mainstream

Figure 3

Good Housekeeping *advertisement, 1938*

American culture. Magazine fiction too depicted a world in which white, Anglo-Americans were getting most of the world's material goods and occupying the more powerful roles in most human relationships. In story after story the heroes and heroines were of northern European stock, and in many cases when the protagonists were nominally foreign, their visual portrayal and characterization would belie the differences. This tendency is illustrated in a 1913 cover of the *Sunday Magazine of the Philadelphia Press,* which shows a pretty young Serbian dancer smiling languidly out at the viewer (figure 4). In her colorful native costume and dance pose, she plays her role of "old country" ethnic. But while her dress presents an image of quaint and wholesome rusticity, her features bear a reassuringly western European stamp. She satisfied an American need for foreign experience and armchair travel without really challenging any assumptions about significant cultural variation.

Figure 4

Magazine cover, November 9, 1913

Until the advent of the civil rights movement of the 1950's and 60's, American businessmen and advertisers assumed, on the whole, that the best way to sell their products was to address their advertisements to the white Anglo-American. Hence magazine stories and ads were geared towards appealing to this constituency through the use of images and symbols that were familiar and appealing to them. In recent years, however, though advertisers have become increasingly concerned with the purchasing power of the different ethnic groups, the images they use continue to reassure the consumer that the group's "foreignness" is carefully controlled. Their cultural identity is often reduced to a few superficial symbols. 10

A Sprite ad (figure 5) reveals a group of smiling Americans of all different lineages brandishing their favorite brand of soda. Yet while different ethnic groups are shown, they are all of the wholesome "all-American" type. The advertisement's point is that the "you"—the American youth, who chose Sprite, now includes Asians, Hispanics and blacks. 11

Advertisements that have appeared in nationally distributed magazines targeted at specific ethnic groups also need mentioning. 12

Figure 5

Newsweek *advertisement, 1983*

Figure 6

Ebony *advertisement, January 1955*

Until the civil rights movement gave many groups the impetus to speak out in their own voices, many of the advertisements in such magazines showed them displaying all the accoutrements and mannerisms of white, middle-class Americans. Thus the Ballantine Beer ad (figure 6) in a 1955 issue of *Ebony* portrays a group of thoroughly Anglicized and fair-complexioned black people. In black society light skin often gave a person enhanced prestige and eased acceptance into white American culture.

13 Today agencies have been formed to deal exclusively with advertisements targeted towards specific minority groups. Many of these more recent ads reveal the complex negotiations involved in attempting to reconcile indigenous cultural needs with societal acceptance: a crucial issue facing many ethnic Americans today.

BUILDING VOCABULARY

1. Advertisers necessarily work with commonly held views, powerful social myths, and broad social categories. Explain the meaning of and the common associations implied by these terms:

- **a.** mobility (par. 1)
- **b.** homemaking (par. 2)
- **c.** stock images (par. 4)
- **d.** dime store Indian (par. 6)
- **e.** "all-American" (par. 11)

THINKING CRITICALLY ABOUT THE ESSAY

Understanding the Writer's Ideas

1. According to Rashap, what can we learn from advertisements besides information on particular products?
2. What main features of ethnic life in America do magazine ads of the last century display?
3. What factors accounted for the growth of modern advertising?
4. How did the availability of a mass audience affect the nature of magazine advertisements in general? Of advertisements that depicted members of ethnic groups?
5. How do the ads the writer has selected as illustrative examples distinguish between white Americans and others?
6. In addition to advertisements, what else "reflected the subservient role" of certain ethnic groups?
7. How did the civil rights movement affect the nature of magazine advertising?
8. How do contemporary magazine ads reflect changes in American culture?

Understanding the Writer's Techniques

1. What is Rashap's thesis, and where does she state it?
2. Why does the writer provide a short history of advertising before showing the changing nature of images of ethnic groups in magazine ads?
3. Rashap notes that ethnic images in advertisements are often stereotypes, but there are "various levels of complexity" within the stereotypes. What types, or categories, of stereotypes does the author present? Which examples in each category do you find most convincing?

4. How does the writer organize her material to show "how the depiction of ethnic groups has changed"? How do her transitions help to move her essay forward in an orderly fashion?
5. The images of ethnic groups Rashap discusses are visual images. Do you think the essay would have been as effective without the illustrations, the reproductions of actual ads? If yes, why do you think the illustrations are unnecessary? If no, what do you think the illustrations add to the essay?
6. What would Rashap have had to do differently to write about images in literature? Provide some illustrative examples to support your point.
7. How does the conclusion draw the essay to an appropriate close?

Exploring the Writer's Ideas

1. Do you agree that advertising sells not just a product but a way of life (par. 3)? Support your answer with a few illustrative examples drawn from today's advertisements.
2. Could advertising, aimed naturally at large audiences, avoid stereotypes? Are the stereotypes used in advertising always "bad"—that is, somehow a distortion of the complex truth about the person or persons being depicted? Again, support your answer with illustrative examples.
3. Do you find the writer's interpretation of the ads she discusses to be fair? Look at the ads and the descriptions. On which points, if any, do you disagree? How, if at all, would your descriptions of the ads differ?
4. The essay's title implies that advertising has turned something noble—the American dream—into something for sale. Has the essay persuaded you that the advertising discussed does in fact turn something noble into a product? Why or why not?

IDEAS FOR WRITING

Prewriting

Look through a few magazines that you usually read—this time for the ads. Jot down a few of the most obvious ways in which these ads use stereotypes—ethnic or otherwise.

Guided Writing

Write an essay titled "The Image of ______ in Popular Magazine Advertising."

1. Begin with a clear statement about what you are going to classify—the image of women athletes, children, or homemakers, for example.
2. Classify the ads you have studied into at least three categories, illustrating the way magazines draw on current social stereotypes to sell their products.
3. Choose one especially useful advertisement to illustrate each of the three categories. In each case, examine the stereotype in some detail.
4. Write a paragraph that reflects on the contemporary image that you are presenting as it may differ from images ads portrayed in the past.
5. Consider whether these differences reflect a significant social shift (for example, greater equality for women) or simply a superficial change masking a persistence of an old stereotype.
6. Draw an appropriate conclusion, restating the main points of step 2.

Thinking and Writing Collaboratively

Work in small groups of four or five. Choose a well-known magazine (preferably one that none of the other groups is working on), and look through several issues, scrutinizing the advertising representations of ethnic groups. After discussing the ads as a group, report to the class on your findings, using sample ads to support your conclusions.

Writing About the Text

The writer presents several advertisements as illustrative of her theme. Do you find her analysis, ad by ad, to be impartial and persuasive? In an essay, say why. If you do not, offer a different reading of the ads. In a second part of the essay, look at the ads from a different perspective, the perspective of the advertiser. Which of these ads do you find to be especially effective? Which do you find to be least effective? What features of these ads make them effective or ineffective?

More Writing Projects

1. Choose one or two of your favorite ads—in print, on billboards, on television—and explain in your journal what you especially like about these ads.
2. Write two or three paragraphs examining one of your favorite advertisements that you feel effectively avoids stereotyping. Tell why you like the ad, and analyze what makes it work well—both text and visual elements—and how it avoids stereotyping.
3. Interview an executive at an advertising company in your community. Question the executive about the things she or he looks for in creating an ad to make it most effective. Write up your interview in an article of around 1,000 words.

Mixing Patterns

How Do We Find the Student in a World of Academic Gymnasts and Worker Ants?

James T. Baker

James T. Baker is general editor of the Creators of the American Mind series, published by Wadsworth. He has contributed several books to the series, including volumes on Nat Turner, Eleanor Roosevelt, and Abraham Lincoln. Baker received his PhD from Florida State University and is currently University Distinguished Professor at Western Kentucky University. In this witty selection from the *Chronicle of Higher Education,* Baker classifies student types that you may well recognize as you look around your classrooms, school cafeteria, lecture halls, or gymnasium. The writer enhances his unique categories by using description, definition, and colloquial language, which help make his deliberate stereotypes come alive.

PREREADING: THINKING ABOUT THE ESSAY IN ADVANCE

Before reading this essay, think about the different types of students you have encountered and the forms of behavior distinguishing one from the other. Does each type behave in a predictable way? Which category would you place yourself in? Which types do you prefer or associate with, and why?

Words to Watch

musings (par. 3) dreamy, abstract thoughts
sabbatical (par. 3) a paid leave from a job earned after a certain period of time
malaise (par. 3) uneasiness; feelings of restlessness
impaired (par. 3) made less effective
clones (par. 4) exact biological replicas, asexually produced
recuperate (par. 5) to undergo recovery from an illness
esoteric (par. 7) understood by a limited group with special knowledge
primeval (par. 7) primitive; relating to the earliest ages

mundane (par. 8) ordinary
jaded (par. 20) exhausted; bored by something from overexposure to it

1 Anatole France once wrote that "the whole art of teaching is only the art of awakening the natural curiosity of young minds." I fully agree, except I have to wonder if, by using the word "only," he thought that the art of awakening such natural curiosity was an easy job. For me, it never has been—sometimes exciting, always challenging, but definitely not easy.

2 Robert M. Hutchins used to say that a good education prepares students to go on educating themselves throughout their lives. A fine definition, to be sure, but it has at times made me doubt that my own students, who seem only too eager to graduate so they can lay down their books forever, are receiving a good education.

3 But then maybe these are merely the pessimistic musings of someone suffering from battle fatigue. I have almost qualified for my second sabbatical leave, and I am scratching a severe case of the seven-year itch. About the only power my malaise has not impaired is my eye for spotting certain "types" of students. In fact, as the rest of me declines, my eye seems to grow more acute.

4 Has anyone else noticed that the very same students people college classrooms year after year? Has anyone else found the same bodies, faces, personalities returning semester after semester? Forgive me for violating my students' individual "personhoods," but reality makes it so tempting to see them as types. Doubtless you will recognize at least some of them. They have twins, or perhaps clones, on your campus, too.

5 There is the eternal Good Time Charlie (or Charlene), who makes every party on and off the campus, who by November of his freshman year has worked his face into a case of terminal acne, who misses every set of examinations because of "mono," who finally burns himself out physically and mentally by the age of 19 and drops out to go home and recuperate, and who returns at 20 after a long talk with Dad to major in accounting.

6 There is the Young General Patton, the one who comes to college on an R.O.T.C. scholarship and for a year twirls his rifle at basketball games while loudly sniffing out pinko professors, who at midpoint takes a sudden but predictable, radical swing from far right to far left, who grows a beard and moves in with a girl who

refuses to shave her legs, who then makes the just as predictable, radical swing back to the right and ends up preaching fundamentalist sermons on the steps of the student union while the Good Time Charlies and Charlenes jeer.

7 There is the Egghead, the campus intellectual who shakes up his fellow students—and even a professor or two—with references to esoteric formulas and obscure Bulgarian poets, who is recognized by friend and foe alike as a promising young academic, someday to be a professional scholar, who disappears every summer for six weeks ostensibly to search for primeval human remains in Colorado caves, and who at 37 is shot dead by Arab terrorists while on a mission for the C.I.A.

8 There is the Performer—the music or theater major, the rock or folk singer—who spends all of his or her time working up an act, who gives barely a nod to mundane subjects like history, sociology, or physics, who dreams only of the day he or she will be on stage full time, praised by critics, cheered by audiences, who ends up either pregnant or responsible for a pregnancy and at 30 is either an insurance salesman or a housewife with a very lush garden.

9 There is the Jock, of course—the every-afternoon intramural champ, smelling of liniment and Brut, with bulging calves and a blue-eyed twinkle, the subject of untold numbers of female fantasies, the walking personification of he-manism—who upon graduation is granted managerial rank by a California bank because of his golden tan and low golf score, who is seen five years later buying the drinks at a San Francisco gay bar.

10 There is the Academic Gymnast—the guy or gal who sees college as an obstacle course, as so many stumbling blocks in the way of a great career or a perfect marriage—who strains every moment to finish and be done with "this place" forever, who toward the end of the junior year begins to slow down, to grow quieter and less eager to leave, who attends summer school, but never quite finishes those last six hours, who never leaves "this place," and who at 40 is still working at the campus laundry, still here, still a student.

11 There is the Medal Hound, the student who comes to college not to learn or expand any intellectual horizons but simply to win honors—medals, cups, plates, ribbons, scrolls—who is here because this is the best place to win the most the fastest, who plasticizes and mounts on his wall every certificate of excellence he wins, who at 39 will be a colonel in the U.S. Army and at

55 Secretary of something or other in a conservative administration in Washington.

12 There is the Worker Ant, the student (loosely rendered) who takes 21 hours a semester and works 49 hours a week at the local car wash, who sleeps only on Sundays and during classes, who will somehow graduate on time and be the owner of his own vending-machine company at 30 and be dead of a heart attack at 40, and who will be remembered for the words chiseled on his tombstone:

13 All This Was Accomplished Without Ever Having So Much As Darkened The Door Of A Library

14 There is the Lost Soul, the sad kid who is in college only because teachers, parents, and society at large said so, who hasn't a career in mind or a dream to follow, who hasn't a clue, who heads home every Friday afternoon to spend the weekend cruising the local Dairee-Freeze, who at 50 will have done all his teachers, parents, and society said to do, still without a career in mind or a dream to follow or a clue.

15 There is also the Saved Soul—the young woman who has received, through the ministry of one Gospel freak or another, a Holy Calling to save the world, or at least some special part of it—who majors in Russian studies so that she can be caught smuggling Bibles into the Soviet Union and be sent to Siberia where she can preach to souls imprisoned by the Agents of Satan in the Gulag Archipelago.

16 Then, finally, there is the Happy Child, who comes to college to find a husband or wife—and finds one—and there is the Determined Child, who comes to get a degree—and gets one.

17 Enough said.

18 All of which, I suppose, should make me throw up my hands in despair and say that education, like youth and love, is wasted on the young. Not quite.

19 For there does come along, on occasion, that one of a hundred or so who is maybe at first a bit lost, certainly puzzled; who may well start out a Good Timer, an Egghead, a Performer, a Jock, a Medal Hound, a Gymnast, a Worker Ant; who may indeed have trouble settling on a major, who will be distressed by what sometimes passes for education, who might even be a temporary dropout; but who has a vital capacity for growth and is able to fall in love with learning, who acquires a taste for intellectual pleasure, who becomes in the finest sense of the word a Student.

This is the one who keeps the most jaded of us going back to class after class, and he or she must be oh-so-carefully cultivated. He or she must be artfully awakened, given the tools needed to continue learning for a lifetime, and let grow at whatever pace and in whatever direction nature dictates. 20

For I try always to remember that this student is me, my continuing self, my immortality. This person is my only hope that my own search for Truth will continue after me, on and on, forever. 21

BUILDING VOCABULARY

1. Explain these *colloquialisms* (see Glossary) in Baker's essay.
   - **a.** someone suffering from battle fatigue (par. 3)
   - **b.** I am scratching a severe case of the seven-year itch (par. 3)
   - **c.** worked his face into a case of terminal acne (par. 5)
   - **d.** burns himself out physically and mentally (par. 5)
   - **e.** loudly sniffing out pinko professors (par. 6)
   - **f.** working up an act (par. 8)
   - **g.** gives barely a nod (par. 8)
   - **h.** the walking personification of he-manism (par. 9)
   - **i.** to spend the weekend cruising the local Dairee-Freeze (par. 14)
   - **j.** he or she must be oh-so-carefully cultivated (par. 20)
2. Identify these references.
   - **a.** R.O.T.C. (par. 6)
   - **b.** C.I.A. (par. 7)
   - **c.** Brut (par. 9)
   - **d.** Dairee-Freeze (par. 14)
   - **e.** Gospel freak (par. 15)
   - **f.** Agents of Satan (par. 15)
   - **g.** Gulag Archipelago (par. 15)

THINKING CRITICALLY ABOUT THE ESSAY

Understanding the Writer's Ideas

1. In common language, describe the various categories of college students that Baker names.

2. Who is Anatole France? What process is described in the quotation from him? Why does Baker cite it at the beginning of the essay? What is his attitude toward France's idea?
3. For how long has Baker been teaching? What is his attitude toward his work?
4. About what age do you think Baker is? Why? Explain the meaning of the sentence: "In fact, as the rest of me declines, my eye seems to grow more acute" (par. 3).
5. Choose three of Baker's categories and paraphrase each description and meaning in a serious way.
6. What does Baker feel, overall, is the contemporary college student's attitude toward studying and receiving an education? How does it differ from Baker's own attitude toward these things?
7. Although Baker's classification may seem a bit pessimistic, he refuses to "throw up . . . [his] hands in despair" (par. 18). Why?
8. Describe the characteristics that are embodied in the category of *Student*. To whom does Baker compare the "true" Student? Why?

Understanding the Writer's Techniques

1. What is Baker's thesis? Does he state it directly or not? What, in your own words, is his purpose?
2. In this essay Baker deliberately creates, rather than avoids, stereotypes. He does so to establish exaggerated representatives of types. Why?

   For paragraphs 5 to 16, prepare a paragraph-by-paragraph outline of the main groups of students classified. For each, include the following information:

   a. type represented by the stereotype
   b. motivation of type for being a student
   c. main activity as a student
   d. condition in which the type ends up
3. This article appeared in the *Chronicle of Higher Education,* a weekly newspaper for college and university teachers and administrators. How do you think this audience influenced Baker's analysis of types of students? his tone and language? How do you think his audience reacted to this essay?

4. What is Baker's tone in the essay? Give specific examples. In general, how would you characterize his attitude toward the contemporary college student? Why? Does his attitude or tone undergo any shifts in the essay? Explain.
5. Why does Baker use the term "personhoods" in paragraph 4? What attitude, about what subject, does he convey in his use of that word?
6. Why does the author capitalize the names he gives to the various categories of students? Why does he capitalize the word *Truth* in the last sentence?
7. What is the purpose of the one-sentence paragraph 13? Why does Baker set it aside from paragraph 12, since it is a logical conclusion to that paragraph? Why does he use a two-word sentence as the complete paragraph 17? In what ways do these words signal the beginning of the essay's conclusion?

✷ MIXING PATTERNS

How does Baker use description to enhance his analysis in this essay? Which descriptive details do you find most convincing? What purpose does description serve?

What is the role of *process analysis*? (Process analysis, discussed in Chapter 5, is telling how something is done or proceeds; see pages 181–184). Look especially at Baker's descriptions of each type of student. How does process analysis figure into the title of the essay?

Exploring the Writer's Ideas

1. Do you think Baker's classifications in this essay are fair? Are they representative of the whole spectrum of students? How closely do they mirror the student population at your school? The article was written in 1982: How well have Baker's classifications held up to the present conditions?
2. Into which category (or categories) would you place yourself? Why?
3. Based on your reaction to and understanding of this article, would you like to have Baker as your professor? Why or why not?

IDEAS FOR WRITING

Prewriting

Freewrite for fifteen minutes about the different types of students who are common to your campus. What are the traits or characteristics of each group? What do representatives of each group do? Where do they congregate? How many of these types can you recognize in this classroom?

Guided Writing

Write a classification of at least three "types" in a situation with which you are familiar, other than school—a certain job, social event, sport, or some such situation.

1. Begin your essay with a reference, direct or indirect, to what some well-known writer or expert said about this situation.
2. Identify your role in relation to the situation described.
3. Write about your attitude toward the particular situation and why you are less than thrilled about it at present.
4. Make sure you involve the reader as someone who would be familiar with the situation and activities described.
5. Divide your essay into exaggerated or stereotyped categories which you feel represent almost the complete range of types in these situations. In your categorization, be sure to include motivations, activities, and results for each type.
6. Use description to make your categories vivid.
7. Use satire and a bit of gentle cynicism as part of your description.
8. Select a lively title.
9. In the conclusion, identify another type that you consider the "purest" or "most truthful" representative of persons in this situation. Either by comparison with yourself or by some other means, explain why you like this type best.

Thinking and Writing Collaboratively

In groups of four to five class members, draft an article for your college newspaper in which you outline the types of students on the campus. Try to maintain a consistently lighthearted or humorous tone or point of view as you move from discussion to the drafting of the letter. Revise your paper, paying careful attention to the flow from one category to the next, before submitting the article for possible publication.

Writing About the Text

Much of the humor and energy of this essay comes from Baker's use of figurative language—from the title on. Write an essay in which you analyze the figurative language here. How does it contribute to the thesis? the tone?

More Writing Projects

1. In your journal, write your own classification of three college "types." Your entry can be serious or humorous.
2. In a 250-word paragraph, classify types of college dates.
3. Look in current magazines for advertisements directed at men or women, or both. Write an essay in which you classify current advertisements according to some logical scheme. Limit your essay to three to five categories.

SUMMING UP: CHAPTER 9

1. In groups of four, using Amy Rashap's essay on ethnic images in magazines as a model, find advertisements from today's magazines that reflect popular stereotypes. Using your work, decide what the advertisements say or imply about societal ideas about race, gender, or class. Then, write your own essay.
2. Although Ahmed's, Baker's, and Rashap's essays are classifications, they also present new ways of looking at a group of people. Ahmed has an underlying message about how to understand an ethnic group, Baker has a warning about how not to be stereotyped, and Rashap shows how easily stereotyping can dominate portrayals of people. Write a classification essay entitled "How Not to Think About________." Fill in the blank with a group of people that you believe is often misunderstood.
3. Many of the essays in this book deal with crucial experiences in the various writers' lives. Among others, Hughes and Wong tell us of coming-of-age experiences; Orwell tells of his growing dissatisfaction with his government's decisions; and Dillard and Ackerman explore their experiences with nature. Try writing an essay that classifies the personal essays that you have read in this anthology into sensible categories.
4. Several essays in this book explore childhood and the family. (See Thematic Contents for a list of those essays.) Compose a classification scheme for these essays, fitting them into three key categories.
5. Write an essay classifying views of the American Dream using the essays by Elizabeth Wong, Elie Wiesel, Amy Rashap, and Martin Luther King Jr. that appear in this book.

✷ FROM SEEING TO WRITING

The person in this cartoon obviously has an unwieldy "family" of chairs that he needs to classify or sort into categories. Write your own humorous classification essay in which you put the chairs into categories and make clear the relations among members of each group. As an alternative, write a humorous classification essay about a "family" that might be real—for example, your own extended family—or more fanciful, such as the "family" of toys in a child's room. Choose an illustration to support your classification, and organize your essay around at least three categories depicted there.

"Attention, everyone! I'd like to introduce the newest member of our family."

CHAPTER 10

Definition

WHAT IS DEFINITION?

We know that we should open a dictionary when we want to *define* a word. Often, however, the dictionary definition is brief and does not fully explain the meaning of a word as an individual writer sees it. An *extended definition* is necessary when a writer wishes to convey the full meaning of a word that is central to the writer's or a culture's thought.

When an entire essay focuses on the meaning of a key word or group of related words, extended definition becomes the primary method of organization. However, formal extended definitions typically make use of other patterns of development. Among the most useful strategies for organizing an essay of extended definition are narration, description, illustration, comparison and contrast, process analysis, and classification.

Definition can look at the *denotation* of a word, which is its literal meaning, or at the *connotations,* which are the variety of meanings associated with the word through common use (see Glossary). Denotation is generally available in the dictionary. Connotation, on the other hand, requires the writer to examine not only the denotation but also the way that a particular writer uses the word. In defining, a writer can also explore levels of *diction* (see Glossary), such as standard English, colloquial expressions, and slang. The word *red,* for example, denotes a primary color. The connotations, however, are varied: In the early twentieth century Communists were called "Reds" because of the color of the Russian flag. We also associate red with the color of Valentine's cards, with passion and romance. "Redneck" derives from the sunburned skin of a white person who works outdoors and connotes a lifestyle associated with outdoor living and conservative political views. "Redskin" was a pejorative term used by European settlers to describe Native Americans.

We need extended definition to help us fully understand the complexity of our language. Most often, we use definition when words are abstract, controversial, or complex. Terms like *freedom, pornography, affirmative action, bisexual,* and *feminism* demand extended definition because they are often confused with some other word or term; because they are so easily misunderstood; or because they are of special importance to the writer, who chooses to redefine the term for his or her own purposes.

Although writers can, of course, offer an extended definition just for the sake of definition, they usually go through the trouble of defining because they have strong opinions about complex and controversial words; consequently, they try to provide an extended definition for the purpose of illuminating a thesis for readers. Writer Alice Walker, for instance, once wrote an essay about feminism and African American women. In her extended definition, she said that the meaning of *feminism* was restricted to white, upper- and middle-class women. As a result, the word did not apply to black women. She created the term *womanist,* and wrote her essay to define it. Because of the controversial nature of her definition of *feminist,* Walker relied on extended definition to support her thesis that the women's movement needed to pay more attention to women of color.

It *is* possible to give an objective definition of *feminism,* with the writer tracing its history, explaining its historic applications, and describing its various subdivisions, such as *radical feminism.* However, most of the time, writers have strong opinions. They would want to develop a thesis about the term, perhaps covering much of the same ground as the objective account but taking care that the reader understands the word as they do. It is normal for us to have our own opinions about any word, but in all instances writers must make the reader understand fully what they mean by it.

In this chapter, fiction writer Dagoberto Gilb takes an unorthodox look at what the word *pride* means. Thomas Friedman praises today's young people, whom he terms "Generation Q." Karen Armstrong offers an extended definition of fundamentalism. Gloria Naylor, an African American woman, uses extended definition to confront the hate word *nigger.* Her many *illustrations* of how and where the word is used show how definition is often determined by context.

HOW DO WE READ DEFINITION?

Reading definition requires us to ask ourselves these questions:

- What is the writer's thesis? Determine if the definition is *objective* or *subjective* (see Glossary).
- Does the writer state the definition directly, or expect the reader to understand it from the information the writer gives? When you finish reading the essay, write out a one-sentence definition of the term the writer has defined.
- What are the various techniques the writer uses, such as illustration with examples, description, narration, comparison and contrast? The writer may also use *negation,* a technique of defining a word by what it does *not* mean. In addition, a writer may use a strategy of defining some general group to which the subject belongs (for instance, an orange is a member of the larger group of citrus), and to show how the word differs from all other words in the general group (by its color, acid content, size, and so forth).
- What is the writer's tone? Is the definition comic or serious? Does it rely on *irony* (see Glossary)?

HOW DO WE WRITE A DEFINITION?

Reading the variety of *definitions* in this chapter will prepare you to write your own. The skill required in good definition writing is to make abstract ideas concrete. Writing good definitions allows you to practice many of the other writing strategies you already know, including narration, description, and illustration.

The thesis for your definition does not have to appear in the introduction, but it is helpful to write it out for yourself before you begin.

- Select the word: for example, *multiculturalism.*
- Place it in a class: multiculturalism is a *belief,* or *system of values,* or *philosophy.*
- Distinguish it from other members of that class: multiculturalists favor recognition and celebration of differences among various social groups instead of seeking similarities.
- Use negation: multiculturalism is not the "melting pot" metaphor of how American society is constituted.

By arranging these pieces, and revising the language, you can create a working thesis.

Sample thesis statement:

> Multiculturalism supports the preservation and celebration of differences among people of diverse cultures rather than urging them to replace their ethnic identities with one single "American" identity.

Select supporting detail as evidence to illustrate, narrate, and describe the term. The selection of evidence can demonstrate the writer's *point of view* on the term. Is multiculturalism splitting the nation into separate groups, or is it affirming the identity of both minority and majority citizens? Look at how the term is used in a variety of settings, such as education, government, social services agencies, and religious institutions.

You might want to visit the library to see how a reference book's definition compares with your own. Libraries have a variety of dictionaries. Depending on the kind of word you are researching, you might want to look at a dictionary of slang, or even a dictionary of quotations to read some famous opinions about abstract words like *love, hope,* and *truth.*

What is the *purpose* of the definition? Decide whether you want to show support for the policy or argue against its effectiveness.

Who is the audience? The writer would choose different language for addressing a PTA meeting than for writing to Congress.

Plan an arrangement of the supporting evidence. Unlike comparison and contrast, for instance, definition does not require a formal method of outlining. Examples can be arranged to suit the kind of word being defined and the mood of the writer. Because so many methods can be applied effectively in an essay of extended definition, you should be able to organize and develop this type of composition easily.

Review the *transitions* you have used in other essays and see which ones apply here. You might want to focus on transitions that show addition: *another, in addition, furthermore.*

Writing and Revising the Draft

Think about where to put the thesis. What is the effect of placing it at the end rather than at the beginning?

Plan your strategy. Arrange the examples so that they most effectively create the extended definition you want. Your essay should have *coherence.* Avoid an unrelated collection of definitions.

Read your essay to a classmate who has defined a similar word. Decide whose definition is more successful, and why.

Revise. Revision may require that you reorganize, moving the examples and other supporting evidence to different sentences and paragraphs to make your argument more effective for a reader.

Proofread for correctness and make a final copy of your work.

A STUDENT PARAGRAPH: DEFINITION

Look at this introductory paragraph of a student's definition essay on multiculturalism and examine the comments in the margin to help you see the various elements of writing definitions.

Introduction of word to be defined

Comparison-contrast to aid definition: melting pot and multiculturalism

Supporting detail: dictionary citation

Detail helps reader see "melting pot" metaphor

Transition "on the other hand" signals shift to topic of multiculturalism

Essay thesis; body paragraphs will offer support

Some people these days use the term "multiculturalism" as a kind of insult, as if the idea of the American "melting pot" is the only valid way to define a culture of different peoples. The *American Heritage Dictionary* defines "melting pot" as "a place where immigrants of different cultures or races form an integrated society." "Melting pot," of course is a metaphor. The image suggests that different cultures are like different kinds of metals that meld to form a new alloy—an alloy that is stronger and more versatile than the original metals. This "alloy," of course, is the integrated society, in which everybody gives up his or her own distinctive cultural heritage to make a new (and, by implication, "better," "stronger") culture. "Multiculturalism," on the other hand, makes a very different point. Without rejecting the idea of an integrated society, it rejects the idea of a homogenous one. The idea is more along the lines of different vegetables in a big cauldron, imparting their various flavors to make the perfect soup, while still retaining much of their distinctive shape and color. Those who criticize the term "multicultural" are actually criticizing the diversity that enriches our American culture. Multiculturalism celebrates the differences among people of diverse cultures rather than urging them to replace their ethnic identities with an "American" identity.

Pride

Dagoberto Gilb

Dagoberto Gilb is a writer, teacher, and carpenter. Born in Los Angeles, he has lived in Arizona and Wyoming, and now lives in Texas. His book *The Magic of Blood* won the 1994 PEN/Hemingway Award and was a finalist for the PEN/Faulkner Award. Gilb's most recent work of fiction, a novel, is *The Flowers* (2008). His work has also appeared in the *New Yorker,* the *Threepenny Review,* and *Harper's.* A nonfiction collection, *Gritos,* appeared in 2003 and is the source of this essay, which offers an elaborately lyrical definition of a common human emotion. As you read the essay, think about why Gilb attempts to define this particular word, *pride.*

PREREADING: THINKING ABOUT THE ESSAY IN ADVANCE

What are you proud of? Think about your hometown, your job, your family. What do you take the most pride in? Is your pride always justified? From your thoughts, develop a preliminary definition of pride.

Words to Watch

asphalt (par. 1) black material used for paving roads
watts (par. 2) units of electrical power
hemline (par. 3) line formed by the bottom of a skirt
agave (par. 8) a plant native to the southwestern United States and Mexico
heritage (par. 8) culture that is passed on from generation to generation
ancestors (par. 10) earlier generations in one's family or race

It's almost time to close at the northwest corner of Altura and Copia in El Paso. That means it is so dark that it is as restful as the deepest unremembering sleep, dark as the empty space around this spinning planet, as a black star. Headlights that beam a little cross-eyed from a fatso American car are feeling around the asphalt road up the hill toward the Good Time Store, its yellow plastic smiley face bright like a sugary suck candy. The loose muffler holds only half the misfires, and, dry springs squeaking, the automobile curves slowly 1 into the establishment's lot, swerving to avoid the new self-serve gas pump island. Behind it, across the street, a Texas flag—out too late this and all the nights—pops and slaps in a summer wind that finally is cool.

2 A good man, gray on the edges, an assistant manager in a brown starched and ironed uniform, is washing the glass windows of the store, lit up by as many watts as Venus, with a roll of paper towels and the blue liquid from a spray bottle. Good night, m'ijo! he tells a young boy coming out after playing the video game, a Grande Guzzler the size of a wastebasket balanced in one hand, an open bag of Flaming Hot Cheetos, its red dye already smearing his mouth and the hand not carrying the weight of the soda, his white T-shirt, its short sleeves reaching halfway down his wrists, the whole XXL of it billowing and puffing in the outdoor gust.

3 A plump young woman steps out of that car. She's wearing a party dress, wide scoops out of the top, front, and back, its hemline way above the knees.

4 Did you get a water pump? the assistant manager asks her. Are you going to make it to Horizon City? He's still washing the glass of the storefront, his hand sweeping in small hard circles.

5 The young woman is patient and calm like a loving mother. I don't know yet, she tells him as she stops close to him, thinking. I guess I should make a call, she says, and her thick-soled shoes, the latest fashion, slap against her heels to one of the pay phones at the front of the store.

6 Pride is working a job like it's as important as art or war, is the happiness of a new high score on a video arcade game, of a pretty new black dress and shoes. Pride is the deaf and blind confidence of the good people who are too poor but don't notice.

7 A son is a long time sitting on the front porch where he played all those years with the squirmy dog who still licks his face, both puppies then, even before he played on the winning teams of Little League baseball and City League basketball. They spring down the sidewalk and across streets, side by side, until they stop to rest on the park grass, where a red ant, or a spider, bites the son's calf. It swells, but he no longer thinks to complain to his mom about it—he's too old now—when he comes home. He gets ready, putting on the shirt and pants his mom would have ironed but he wanted to iron himself. He takes the ride with his best friend since first grade. The hundreds of moms and dads, abuelos y abuelitas, the tios and primos, baby brothers and older married sisters, all

are at the Special Events Center for the son's high school graduation. His dad is a man bigger than most, and when he walks in his dress eel-skin boots down the cement stairs to get as close to the hardwood basketball-court floor and ceremony to see—m'ijo!—he feels an embarrassing sob bursting from his eyes and mouth. He holds it back, and with his hands, hides the tears that do escape, wipes them with his fingers, because the chavalitos in his aisle are playing and laughing and they are so small and he is so big next to them. And when his son walks to the stage to get his high school diploma and his dad wants to scream his name, he hears how many others, from the floor in caps and gowns and from around the arena, are already screaming it—could be any name, it could be any son's or daughter's: Alex! Vanessa! Carlos! Veronica! Ricky! Tony! Estella! Isa!—and sees his boy waving back to all of them.

8 Pride hears gritty dirt blowing against an agave whose stiff fertile stalk, so tall, will not bend—the love of land, rugged like the people who live on it. Pride sees the sunlight on the Franklin Mountains in the first light of morning and listens to a neighbor's gallo—the love of culture and history. Pride smells a sweet, musky drizzle of rain and eats huevos con chile in corn tortillas heated on a cast-iron pan—the love of heritage.

9 Pride is the fearless reaction to disrespect and disregard. It is knowing the future will prove that wrong.

10 Seeing the beauty: look out there from a height of the mountain and on the north and south of the Rio Grande, to the far away and close, the so many miles more of fuzz on the wide horizon, knowing how many years the people have passed and have stayed, the ancestors, the ones who have medaled, limped back on crutches or died or were heroes from wars in the Pacific or Europe or Korea or Vietnam or the Persian Gulf, the ones who have raised the fist and dared to defy, the ones who wash the clothes and cook and serve the meals, who stitch the factory shoes and the factory slacks, who assemble and sort, the ones who laugh and the ones who weep, the ones who care, the ones who want more, the ones who try, the ones who love, those ones with shameless courage and hardened wisdom, and the old ones still so alive, holding their grandchildren, and the young ones in their glowing prime, strong and gorgeous, holding each other, the ones who will be born from them. The desert land is rock-dry and ungreen. It is brown. Brown like the skin is brown. Beautiful brown.

BUILDING VOCABULARY

1. In this essay, Gilb uses several Spanish words without giving definitions. Locate the Spanish and look up their definitions, writing them out on a piece of paper.
2. Gilb uses some intriguing and intelligent diction to enliven his prose. Explain the meaning of the italicized words:
   a. *unremembering* sleep (par. 1)
   b. *billowing* (par. 2)
   c. *deaf and blind* confidence (par. 6)
   d. *squirmy* dog (par. 7)
   e. *stiff fertile* stalk (par. 8)
   f. *hardened* wisdom (par. 10)
   g. *rock-dry and ungreen* (par. 10)

THINKING CRITICALLY ABOUT THE ESSAY

Understanding the Writer's Ideas

1. Where is El Paso? What is at the corner of Altura and Copia?
2. What languages do the people described in this essay speak?
3. Explain the statement, "pride is working a job like it's as important as art or war."
4. What does Gilb mean by "both puppies then" (par. 7)?
5. Why does the father cry in paragraph 7?
6. Why does Gilb write, "could be any name, it could be any son's or daughter's"? What is he referring to?
7. What does the definition of pride in paragraph 8 have to do with the story of the son and father in paragraph 7?
8. Paraphrase the two sentences in paragraph 9.
9. What is "the beauty" Gilb refers to at the beginning of paragraph 10?
10. In the conclusion of his essay, how does Gilb compare the land to the people?

Understanding the Writer's Techniques

1. Does Gilb have a thesis? If so, what is it? If not, where is his main idea most clearly expressed?
2. Why does the writer begin his essay with a descriptive scene that shows what happens on a corner in El Paso?

3. What are the two most effective *images* (see Glossary) in the first two paragraphs? Why are they so effective?
4. Gilb changes strategies after paragraph 5. Describe the shift, and explain why you think he makes it.
5. What is the purpose of Gilb's offering multiple definitions of *pride*? Is this an effective technique? Explain your answer.
6. Why do you think the writer uses the present tense in paragraphs 1 to 5 and 7?
7. What example of pride in this essay do you find most effective? Explain why.
8. What is the *tone* of the essay? Cite at least three words that convey this tone.
9. Gilb disposes almost completely with *transitions* (see Glossary). Why? Explain how the essay still has *coherence* (see Glossary) without transitions.
10. Do you find Gilb's conclusion moving? Why or why not? Do you think it is his intention to move you? How can you tell?

Exploring the Writer's Ideas

1. Gilb writes about pride in the Latino community in the southwestern United States and how people's lives there connect to the land. Is the same true in all communities? in your community? Explain.
2. "Pride is working a job like it's as important as art or war" (par. 6). What is your reaction to this statement? Why? Should people take their jobs so seriously? Why or why not?
3. Have you ever felt as proud as the father who watches his son graduate? What or whom were you proud of? What does that kind of pride feel like?

IDEAS FOR WRITING

Prewriting

Freewrite for five minutes about the word *greed*. Think about the *connotations* of the word, from the physical to the emotional. Consider both positive and negative connotations of the word.

Guided Writing

Write an extended definition of the word *greed,* focusing on whichever *connotations* you think are most important but without ignoring the positive.

1. Begin with a scene in which you illustrate greed. Be as descriptive as possible, using vivid auditory, visual, and other imagery.
2. Define greed in a paragraph that includes several sentences that begin with "Greed is . . ."
3. Write another scene in which you illustrate another, conflicting aspect of greed.
4. Balance the earlier scene by being just as descriptive as before.
5. Write another paragraph in which you define greed (as shown in this second scene in step 2).
6. Conclude your essay with an extended paragraph that attempts to reconcile these two definitions of greed. Try to make your writing as lyrical and moving as possible.

Thinking and Writing Collaboratively

In groups of three, share your Guided Writing essays. Then discuss the definitions in each essay. Focus on the imagery—how well have you and the other writers in your group succeeded in bringing the illustrations to life?

Writing About the Text

Pride, traditionally one of the seven deadly sins, is often seen as the opposite of humility. Frequently, however, people are advised to take pride in their work or family. Write an essay discussing how Gilb's essay includes both connotations of pride.

More Writing Projects

1. In your journal, reflect on other human emotions that can be both constructive and destructive.
2. Write a paragraph that defines the word *desire*.
3. Consider what ties you have to the land where you live. Write an essay in which you examine what the land where you live means to you. If it means little to you, explore the reasons why.

Generation Q

Thomas L. Friedman

Thomas Lauren Friedman was born on July 20, 1953, in St. Louis Park, Minnesota, a suburb of Minneapolis. He graduated summa cum laude from Brandeis University with a degree in Mediterranean studies and received a master's degree in modern Middle East studies from Oxford University. A Pulitzer Prize–winning journalist, Friedman writes a regular column on international affairs for the *New York Times*. He has served as a visiting professor at Harvard University and has been awarded honorary degrees from several universities in the United States. He is the author of *From Beirut to Jerusalem* (1989), *The Lexus and the Olive Tree* (1999), *Longitudes and Attitudes: Exploring the World After September 11* (2002), *The World Is Flat: A Brief History of the Twenty-first Century* (2005), and *Flat, Hot, and Crowded: Why We Need a Green Revolution—and How It Can Renew America* (2008). In this essay he attempts to characterize some of the strengths and weaknesses of the current generation of college students.

PREREADING: THINKING ABOUT THE ESSAY IN ADVANCE

What world issues are most relevant on your campus today? Is it the environment, local elections, poverty—or some other important concern?

Words to Watch

impulses (par. 5) whims; sudden desires
deficit (par. 8) shortfall; shortage
subsidies (par. 11) financial support or assistance
mitigating (par. 12) making an offense seem less serious
neutrality (par. 13) impartiality; objectivity; detachment

I just spent the past week visiting several colleges—Auburn, the University of Mississippi, Lake Forest and Williams—and I can report that the more I am around this generation of college students, the more I am both baffled and impressed. 1

I am impressed because they are so much more optimistic and idealistic than they should be. I am baffled because they are so much less radical and politically engaged than they need to be. 2

3 One of the things I feared most after 9/11—that my daughters would not be able to travel the world with the same carefree attitude my wife and I did at their age—has not come to pass.

4 Whether it was at Ole Miss or Williams or my alma mater, Brandeis, college students today are not only going abroad to study in record numbers, but they are also going abroad to build homes for the poor in El Salvador in record numbers or volunteering at AIDS clinics in record numbers. Not only has terrorism not deterred them from traveling, they are rolling up their sleeves and diving in deeper than ever.

5 The Iraq war may be a mess, but I noticed at Auburn and Old Miss more than a few young men and women proudly wearing their R.O.T.C. uniforms. Many of those not going abroad have channeled their national service impulses into increasingly popular programs at home like "Teach for America," which has become to this generation what the Peace Corps was to mine.

6 It's for all these reasons that I've been calling them "Generation Q"—the Quiet Americans, in the best sense of that term, quietly pursuing their idealism, at home and abroad.

7 But Generation Q may be too quiet, too online, for its own good, and for the country's own good. When I think of the huge budget deficit, Social Security deficit and ecological deficit that our generation is leaving this generation, if they are not spitting mad, well, then they're just not paying attention. And we'll just keep piling it on them.

8 There is a good chance that members of Generation Q will spend their entire adult lives digging out from the deficits that we—the "Greediest Generation," epitomized by George W. Bush—are leaving them.

9 When I was visiting my daughter at her college, she asked me about a terrifying story that ran in this newspaper on Oct. 2, reporting that the Arctic ice cap was melting "to an extent unparalleled in a century or more"—and that the entire Arctic system appears to be "heading toward a new, more watery state" likely triggered by "human-caused global warming."

10 "What happened to that Arctic story, Dad?" my daughter asked me. How could the news media just report one day that the Arctic ice was melting far faster than any models predicted "and then the story just disappeared?" Why weren't any of the candidates talking about it? Didn't they understand: this has become the big issue on campuses?

No, they don't seem to understand. They seem to be too busy raising money or buying votes with subsidies for ethanol farmers in Iowa. The candidates could actually use a good kick in the pants on this point. But where is it going to come from? 11

Generation Q would be doing itself a favor, and America a favor, if it demanded from every candidate who comes on campus answers to three questions: What is your plan for mitigating climate change? What is your plan for reforming Social Security? What is your plan for dealing with the deficit—so we all won't be working for China in 20 years? 12

America needs a jolt of the idealism, activism and outrage (it must be in there) of Generation Q. That's what twentysomethings are for—to light a fire under the country. But they can't e-mail it in, and an online petition or a mouse click for carbon neutrality won't cut it. They have to get organized in a way that will force politicians to pay attention rather than just patronize them. 13

Martin Luther King and Bobby Kennedy didn't change the world by asking people to join their Facebook crusades or to download their platforms. Activism can only be uploaded, the old-fashioned way—by young voters speaking truth to power, face to face, in big numbers, on campuses or the Washington Mall. Virtual politics is just that—virtual. 14

Maybe that's why what impressed me most on my brief college swing was actually a statue—the life-size statue of James Meredith at the University of Mississippi. Meredith was the first African-American to be admitted to Ole Miss in 1962. The Meredith bronze is posed as if he is striding toward a tall limestone archway, re-enacting his fateful step onto the then-segregated campus—defying a violent, angry mob and protected by the National Guard. 15

Above the archway, carved into the stone, is the word "Courage." That is what real activism looks like. There is no substitute. 16

BUILDING VOCABULARY

Write definitions for these verbs, which Friedman uses in "Generation Q." Sometimes the verbs appear in the past tense. Use a dictionary to check on meanings.

1. baffle (par. 1)
2. deter (par. 4)
3. channel (par. 5)

4. epitomize (par. 8)
5. trigger (par. 9)
6. patronize (par. 13)

THINKING CRITICALLY ABOUT THE ESSAY

Understanding the Writer's Ideas

1. What is it about the current generation that baffles Friedman? What impresses him? What event led him to those conclusions?
2. Which fear that Friedman had "never came to pass"?
3. Why are students today going abroad, according to the writer?
4. What are those not going abroad doing to "channel their service impulses"?
5. Why does Friedman call the generation "Generation Q"? What does the Q stand for?
6. What issues, according to Friedman, should make Generation Q "spitting mad"? How do these issues inform the questions Friedman says Generation Q should ask candidates?
7. What questions did the writer's daughter ask him when he visited her college?
8. Why, according to Friedman, are candidates not paying attention to the big issues on campus?
9. What does Friedman believe motivates twentysomethings?
10. What impressed Friedman most on his "brief college swing"?

Understanding the Writer's Techniques

1. What is Friedman's thesis? Where does he come closest to stating it in the essay?
2. How does the title draw readers into Friedman's essay? What definition would a reader expect to find here?
3. Why does the writer tell about his visit to college campuses in the introduction? How effective a strategy is this bit of narrative detail at the start of the essay?
4. How effective is the writer's use of direct quotations from his daughter? Why would her statements matter here?
5. Friedman's paragraphs are consistently brief, usually no more than three sentences. Why has he chosen this kind of

length for his essay? How does it reflect his knowledge of his audience?

6. What would you say is the writer's tone? Is he harsh, judgmental, respectful, disappointed, gentle, or a combination of these? Or perhaps you would use some other word to characterize the tone. Explain your response.
7. What is your reaction to the label "Generation Q" that Friedman uses for today's college students? Is it just journalistic razzle-dazzle? He could have used the term the "Quiet Generation" just as well. Or is there a deeper issue at play here? Explain your response.
8. Why does Friedman name Martin Luther King and Bobby Kennedy? How do they contribute to the definition the writer is evolving?
9. How is the statue of James Meredith a *symbol* (see Glossary) of what Friedman hopes Generation Q will be like?
10. What is your reaction to the conclusion of the essay? The last paragraph has three short sentences. Why has Friedman chosen such an ending? Is he merely meeting the demands of journalistic style, or is he attempting to achieve something?

Exploring the Writer's Ideas

1. What is your view of the label "Quiet Generation" for your cohort of college students?
2. Friedman implies in paragraphs 13 and 14 that activism is absent from this generation's pursuits because of its attention to technology. Is this a valid criticism? Why or why not? What evidence could you propose to support Friedman's view? What evidence could you propose to challenge it?
3. Friedman lodges tough criticism against today's politicians, especially in paragraph 11. Is his assessment fair? Why or why not? Do you think that politicians deserve "a good kick in the pants on this point"?
4. Why does Friedman label his own generation the "Greediest Generation"? Is this a fair assessment? What acts of greed did his generation perform?
5. The last paragraph defines activism as *courage*. Is that an accurate definition? Are the two words synonyms? Can a person show courage without being an activist? Can a person be an activist without showing courage? Explain your answer.

IDEAS FOR WRITING

Prewriting

Write nonstop about how you would define a generation other than your own.

Guided Writing

Write your own essay called "Generation ______." Fill in the blank with a letter from the alphabet that is the first letter of a word you would use to highlight some generation other than your own. Choose any period in history that interests you, and, if necessary, do some research in your library. To follow Friedman's example, if you used the word *greediest* for his own generation, you'd call your essay "Generation G." Other options might be "Generation B" (for bravest), "Generation A" (for aggressive), "Generation W" (for weakest), "Generation H" (for happiest). You have many options. Then write an essay in which you define that generation—that is, identify the qualities that led you to choose the word you did.

1. Use two adjectives—other than the word you've chosen for your title—to identify how you feel about that generation. Friedman uses *baffled* and *impressed* to indicate his feelings about his daughter's generation.
2. Tell what experience led to your selection—a conversation with someone from that generation; Web sites you've examined; a book or article you have read; a film you've seen; a report you've heard on the radio or seen on TV.
3. Identify the strengths of the generation as well as the weaknesses.
4. Ultimately, tell why you chose the descriptive word that you did.
5. Make sure your thesis is clear.
6. Use a direct quote from a spoken or written resource.
7. Highlight one or two people in that generation who you think help to characterize the word you've chosen.
8. End your essay with a brief conclusion.

Thinking and Writing Collaboratively

Form groups to discuss the way your campus is reacting to the issue that Friedman's daughter finds so important: the melting of

Arctic ice in particular and global warming in general. Is this a major issue for students on your campus?

Writing About the Text

Write an analysis of Friedman's journalistic style. You might want to examine one of his books, some of which are compilations of his newspaper columns.

More Writing Projects

1. Write a journal entry about a statue on campus or in your neighborhood, a statue that represents something important for your community.
2. Write an extended paragraph in which you define the word *courage*.
3. Write an essay in which you define *twentysomethings*. Use descriptive detail, and identify the aspirations of the group as well as the problems and challenges facing twentysomethings.

Mixing Patterns

Fundamentalism Is Here to Stay

Karen Armstrong

Karen Armstrong was born in England in 1944. She joined a Catholic convent at the age of seventeen but left after seven years. Her experience as a novitiate and nun, and her departure from the Catholic Church, are recounted in her autobiography *Through the Narrow Gates* (1982). Armstrong rose to prominence with the publication of *A History of God* (1993). An internationally acclaimed author on religious topics, Armstrong asserts that "[a]ll the great traditions are saying the same thing in much the same way, despite their surface differences." What the world's religions have in common is epitomized in the Golden Rule: "Do unto others as you would have others do unto you." In the following essay, which appeared in globalagendamagazine.com, Armstrong offers an extended definition of what fundamentalism is—and is not.

PREREADING: THINKING ABOUT THE ESSAY IN ADVANCE

How would you define religious fundamentalism? Do you think that fundamentalism is a feature of all religions? Why or why not?

Words to Watch

secularism (par. 1) indifference to or rejection of religion
piety (par. 1) dutifulness in religion; devoutness
inimical (par. 4) hostile, unfriendly
sacralized (par. 8) made holy or sacred
anomie (par. 10) personal unrest, uncertainty
ethos (par. 12) guiding beliefs; moral nature
symbiotic (par. 18) living together in a mutually beneficial relationship

1 In the middle of the 20th century, it was generally assumed that secularism was the coming ideology and that religion would never again play a major role in world events. Today, religion dominates the headlines, and this is due in no small part to the militant piety that has developed in every single major world faith over the past century.

We usually call it "fundamentalism." Fundamentalist groups have staged revolutions, assassinated presidents, carried out terrorist atrocities and become an influential political force in strongly secularist nations. There has, for example, been much discussion about the role of Protestant fundamentalism in the recent American elections. It is no longer possible to dismiss fundamentalism as a passing phase. 2

FUNDAMENTALISM IS NOT . . .

We should begin by defining what fundamentalism is not. First, it should not be equated with religious conservatism. Leading American religious revivalist Billy Graham, for example, is not a fundamentalist. 3

Second, fundamentalism should not be linked automatically with violence. Only a tiny proportion of fundamentalists worldwide take part in acts of terror. The rest are simply struggling to live what they regard as a good religious life in a world that seems increasingly inimical to faith. 4

Third, fundamentalism is not an exclusively Islamic phenomenon. There are fundamentalist Jews, Christians, Hindus, Buddhists, Sikhs and Confucians, who all challenge the secular hegemony of the modern world. In fact, Islam developed a fundamentalist strain long after it had erupted in Judaism and Christianity. 5

FUNDAMENTALISM IS . . .

So what is fundamentalism? It is essentially a revolt against modern secular society. Wherever a western polity has been established that separates religion and politics, fundamentalist movements have sprung up in protest. Whatever the politicians or the pundits claim, people worldwide are demonstrating that they want to see religion reflected more prominently in public life. As part of their campaign, fundamentalists tend to withdraw from mainstream society to create enclaves of pure faith. 6

Typical examples are the Ultra-orthodox Jewish communities in New York or the fundamentalist Christianity of Bob Jones University in South Carolina. Here fundamentalists build a counterculture, in conscious defiance of the godless world that surrounds them, and from these communities some undertake a counteroffensive 7 designed to drag God or religion back to centre stage from the wings to which they have been relegated in modern secular culture.

8 This campaign is rarely violent. It usually consists of a propaganda or welfare effort. In the United States, for example, the fundamentalist riposte attempts to reform school textbooks or to get Christian candidates elected to government posts. But if warfare is endemic in a region and has become chronic—as in the Middle East or Afghanistan—fundamentalists can get sucked into the violence that pervades the whole of society. In this way, originally secular disputes such as the Arab-Israeli conflict have been sacralized, on both sides.

THE ROAD TO MODERNITY

9 The ubiquity of the fundamentalist revolt shows that there is widespread disappointment with modernity. But what is it about the modern world that has provoked such rage and distress? In the 16th century, the peoples of the west began to develop a new type of civilization unprecedented in world history. Instead of basing their economy on a surplus of agricultural produce, as did all premodern cultures, they relied increasingly on technology and the constant reinvestment of capital, which freed them from the inherent limitations of agrarian society. This demanded radical change at all levels of society—intellectual, political, social and religious. A wholly new way of thinking became essential, and new forms of government had to evolve to meet these altered conditions. It was found by trial and error that the best way of creating a productive society was to create a secular, tolerant, democratic polity.

10 It took Europe some 300 years to modernize, and the process was wrenching and traumatic, involving bloody revolutions, often succeeded by reigns of terror, brutal holy wars, dictatorships, cruel exploitation of the workforce, the despoliation of the countryside, and widespread alienation and anomie.

11 We are now witnessing the same kind of upheaval in developing countries presently undergoing modernization. But some of these countries have had to attempt this difficult process far too rapidly and are forced to follow a western programme, rather than their own.

12 This accelerated modernization has created deep divisions in developing nations. Only an elite has a western education that

enables them to understand the new modern institutions. The vast majority remains trapped in the premodern ethos. They experience the incomprehensible change as profoundly disturbing, and cling to traditional religion for support. But as modernization progresses, people find that they cannot be religious in the old way and try to find new means of expressing their piety. Fundamentalism is just one of these attempts, and it therefore develops only after a degree of modernization has been achieved.

13 The modern spirit that developed in the west had two essential characteristics: independence and innovation. Modernization in Europe and America proceeded by declarations of independence on all fronts—religious, political and intellectual—as scientists and inventors demanded the freedom to develop their ideas without interference from religious or political authorities. Further, despite the trauma of modernization, it was exciting, because the western countries were continually meeting new challenges and creating something fresh. But in some developing countries, modernization came not with independence, but with colonial dependence and subjugation, and the west was so far ahead that these could not innovate but only imitate. So they find it difficult to develop a truly modern spirit. A nation such as Japan, which was not colonized, was able to make its own distinctive contribution to the modern economy in a way that some Middle Eastern countries have not been able to do.

A FIGHT FOR SURVIVAL

14 Culture is always contested, and fundamentalists are primarily concerned with saving their own society. Protestant fundamentalists in the United States want America to be a truly Christian nation, not a secular, pluralist republic. In Palestine, Hamas began by attacking the Palestine Liberation Organization, because it wanted the Palestinian resistance to be inspired by an Islamic rather than a secular polity. Osama bin Laden started by targeting the Saudi royal family and such secularist rulers as Saddam Hussein. Only at a secondary stage—if at all—do fundamentalists begin to attack a foreign foe. Thus fundamentalism does not represent a clash between civilizations, but a clash within civilizations.

15 Perhaps the most important factor to understand about this widespread religious militancy is its rootedness in a deep fear of

annihilation. Every fundamentalist movement I have studied in Judaism, Christianity and Islam is convinced that modern secular society wants to wipe out religion—even in America. Fundamentalists, therefore, believe they are fighting for survival, and when people feel that their backs are to the wall, some can strike out violently. This profound terror of annihilation is not as paranoid as it may at first appear. Jewish fundamentalism, for example, gained fresh momentum after World War II, when Hitler had tried to exterminate European Jewry, and after the 1973 October War, when Israelis felt vulnerable and isolated in the Middle East.

16 In some Muslim countries, modernization has usually been so accelerated that secularism has been experienced as an assault. When Mustafa Kemal Ataturk created modern secular Turkey, he closed down all the madrasahs (traditional institutes for higher education in Islamic studies) and abolished the Sufi orders. He also forced all men and women to wear Western dress. Reformers such as Ataturk wanted their countries to look modern. In Iran, the shahs used to make their soldiers walk through the streets with their bayonets out, tearing off women's veils and ripping them to pieces. In 1935, shah Reza Pahlavi gave his soldiers orders to shoot at unarmed demonstrators in Mashhad (one of the holiest shrines in Iran), who were peacefully protesting against obligatory Western clothes. Hundreds of Iranians died that day. In such circumstances, secularism was not experienced as liberating and civilized, but as wicked, lethal and murderously hostile to faith.

17 The main fundamentalist ideology of Sunni Islam developed in the concentration camps in Egypt in which president Jamal Abdel Nasser had incarcerated thousands of members of the Muslim Brotherhood in the late 1950s, without trial and often for doing nothing more incriminating than attending a meeting or handing out leaflets. One of these prisoners was Sayyid Qutb, who was executed by Nasser in 1966. Qutb went into the camp as a moderate and a liberal. But in these vile prisons, watching the Brothers being executed and subjected to mental and physical torture, and hearing Nasser vowing to relegate Islam to a marginal role in Egypt, he came to regard secularism as a great evil. He developed an ideology of committed armed struggle against this threat to the faith. His chief disciple today is Osama bin Laden.

18 Thus fundamentalism usually develops in a symbiotic relationship with a secularism that is experienced as hostile and invasive. Every fundamentalist movement I have studied in each of

the three monotheistic traditions has developed in direct response to what is perceived as a secularist attack. The more vicious the assault, the more extreme the fundamentalist riposte is likely to be. Because fundamentalists fear that secularists want to destroy them, aggressive and military action will only serve to confirm this conviction and exacerbate their fear, which can spill over into ungovernable rage.

19 Thus membership of al-Qaeda has increased since the recent Gulf War. The offensive has convinced many Muslims that the West has really inaugurated a new crusade against the Islamic world. In the United States, Protestant fundamentalists in the smaller towns and rural areas often feel "colonized" by the alien ethos of Harvard, Yale and Washington DC. They feel that the liberal establishment despises them, and this has resulted in a fundamentalism that has gone way beyond Jerry Falwell and the Moral Majority of the 1970s. (Falwell is an American fundamentalist Baptist pastor, televangelist and founder of the Moral Majority—a group dedicated to promoting its conservative and religious Christian-centric beliefs via support of political candidates.) Some groups, such as the Christian Reconstructionists, look forward to the imminent destruction of the federal government; the blazing towers of the World Trade Center would not be alien to their ideology. When liberals deplore the development and persistence of fundamentalism in their own societies and worldwide, they should be aware that the excesses of secularists have all too often been responsible for this radical alienation.

HERE TO STAY

20 Fundamentalism is not going to disappear, as secularists once imagined that religion would modestly retreat to the sidelines and confine itself to private life. Fundamentalism is here to stay, and in Judaism, Christianity and Islam, at least, it is becoming more extreme. Fundamentalism is not confined to the "other" civilizations. A dangerous gulf has appeared, dividing many societies against themselves. In the Middle East, India, Pakistan, Israel and the United States, for example, fundamentalists and secular liberals form two distinct camps, neither of which can understand the other.

21 In the past, these movements were often dismissed with patrician disdain. This has proved to be short-sighted. We have to take fundamentalism very seriously. Had the United States made a greater effort to understand Shiite Islam, for example, it might have avoided unnecessary errors in the lead-up to the Iranian Revolution of 1978 to 79. The first step must be to look beneath the bizarre and often repulsive ideology of these movements to discern the disquiet and anger that lie at their roots. We must no longer deride these theologies as the fantasies of a lunatic fringe, but learn to decode their ideas and imagery. Only then can we deal creatively with fears and anxieties that, as we have seen to our cost, no society can safely ignore.

BUILDING VOCABULARY

1. Write one- or two-sentence definitions for the following religions that Armstrong mentions in her essay: Judaism, Christianity, Islam, Hinduism, Buddhism, Sikhism, Confucianism.
2. Compose a list of all the words in this essay that you do not know, and then find definitions for them. Use five of these words in sentences.

THINKING CRITICALLY ABOUT THE ESSAY

Understanding the Writer's Ideas

1. What do you expect from Armstrong's title? Does she satisfy your expectations? Why or why not?
2. What does Armstrong mean by "militant piety" (par. 1)? Do you find this term to be contradictory? Why or why not?
3. According to Armstrong, what are the main historical and economic factors that gave rise to modernity?
4. Why is fundamentalism a response to modernity?
5. What does Armstrong mean when she writes that fundamentalism "does not represent a clash between civilizations, but a clash within civilizations" (par. 14)? What examples does she provide to support this statement?
6. What conclusions does Armstrong draw concerning fundamentalism?

Understanding the Writer's Techniques

1. Does this essay have a thesis statement or claim? If so, where is it located? If not, how does the essay succeed without one?
2. How would you characterize Armstrong's introduction?
3. Where does Armstrong use negative definition? What is the writer's purpose here?
4. What types of evidence does Armstrong use to support her definition? From what branches of knowledge do these examples come? What does Armstrong's selection of these illustrations suggest about her audience?
5. Why does Armstrong divide her essay into sections? Do you find this strategy to be effective? Why or why not?

✷ MIXING PATTERNS

Where does Armstrong use comparison and contrast (Chapter 7) to support her definition of fundamentalism? Where does she shift from definition to process analysis (Chapter 5)?

6. How would you characterize the tone of the essay? Does Armstrong present herself as argumentative, opinionated, objective, fair-minded, or what? Identify sentences and passages that support your response to the writer's voice.
7. What, in Armstrong's opinion, is the answer to fundamentalism? How does her conclusion reflect this viewpoint?

Exploring the Writer's Ideas

1. Armstrong asserts that fundamentalism "is not an exclusively Islamic phenomenon" (par. 5). Do you agree? Why or why not? Why is there a tendency in today's media to associate fundamentalism with Islam rather than other religions?
2. What do you think Armstrong means when she asserts that culture "is always contested" (par. 14)? Provide examples to support your response.
3. As noted earlier, Armstrong refers to the "clash of civilizations." Go online to discover the origin of the term and how various writers have responded to it.

IDEAS FOR WRITING

Prewriting

Make a list of all the forms of fundamentalism that you detect in the world today.

Guided Writing

Write your own extended definition of fundamentalism.

1. Compose a three-paragraph introduction in which you present your topic and state your main idea or argument.
2. Next, use negative definition to explain in your own words what your definition is *not*.
3. Develop at least three examples to support and amplify your definition.
4. Link your definition to the "clash of civilizations."
5. Use at least one other rhetorical strategy—for example, comparison and contrast or causal analysis—to help organize and develop your essay.
6. Conclude the essay by stating your answer to the problem of fundamentalism.

Thinking and Writing Collaboratively

Form groups to discuss the many complicated issues raised by Armstrong's essay. Focus on the strategies that she uses to develop her extended definition. Provide a summary of your discussion to the class.

Writing about the Text

Write an analysis of Armstrong's style—her level of diction, tone, sentence structure, allusions, and the like. Explain how her style reflects the expectations that Armstrong holds for her audience.

More Writing Projects

1. Write a journal entry explaining your own attitude toward fundamentalism.
2. Compose an extended paragraph defining "militant piety."
3. Write an essay defining the "clash of civilizations."

Mixing Patterns

A Word's Meaning

Gloria Naylor

Gloria Naylor was born in New York City on January 25, 1950. When she was thirteen, her mother joined Jehovah's Witnesses; Naylor herself was baptized and became a Jehovah's Witnesses minister in 1968. She proselytized for Jehovah's Witnesses in New York, North Carolina, and Florida over a period of years, supporting herself as a switchboard operator. In 1975 she left Jehovah's Witnesses, suffered a nervous breakdown, and entered Medgar Evers College to study nursing. After reading Toni Morrison's *The Bluest Eye,* Naylor began to think of writing herself. In 1981 she graduated from Brooklyn College with a BA in English. The following year she published *The Women of Brewster Place,* still her best-known novel. She has also published *Bailey's Cafe* (1992), *The Men of Brewster Place* (1998), and *1996* (2005). In 1990 Naylor established One Way Productions, her own multimedia production company. As an African American woman and a writer, Naylor has found that words can change their meaning, depending on who defines them. Telling of a confrontation with an angry classmate who called her a "nigger" in the third grade, Naylor develops an extended definition of the word and its multiple meanings. As you read, what other words can you identify that depend on context for their meaning?

To learn more about Naylor, click on **More Resources > Chapter 10 > Gloria Naylor**

PREREADING: THINKING ABOUT THE ESSAY IN ADVANCE

Naylor suggests that even offensive words mean different things to different people. Would you agree? Can you think of a word that you find offensive but that others might find acceptable?

Words to Watch

transcendent (par. 1) rising above
fleeting (par. 1) moving quickly
intermittent (par. 2) alternate; repeated
consensus (par. 2) agreement

verified (par. 3) confirmed
gravitated (par. 4) moved toward
inflections (par. 5) pitch or tone of voice
endearment (par. 9) expression of affection
disembodied (par. 9) separated from the body
unkempt (par. 10) messy
social stratum (par. 14) status

1 Language is the subject. It is the written form with which I've managed to keep the wolf away from the door and, in diaries, to keep my sanity. In spite of this, I consider the written word inferior to the spoken, and much of the frustration experienced by novelists is the awareness that whatever we manage to capture in even the most transcendent passages falls far short of the richness of life. Dialogue achieves its power in the dynamics of a fleeting moment of sight, sound, smell and touch.

2 I'm not going to enter the debate here about whether it is language that shapes reality or vice versa. That battle is doomed to be waged whenever we seek intermittent reprieve from the chicken and egg dispute. I will simply take the position that the spoken word, like the written word, amounts to a nonsensical arrangement of sounds or letters without a consensus that assigns "meaning." And building from the meanings of what we hear, we order reality. Words themselves are innocuous; it is the consensus that gives them true power.

3 I remember the first time I heard the word nigger. In my third-grade class, our math tests were being passed down the rows, and as I handed the papers to a little boy in back of me, I remarked that once again he had received a much lower mark than I did. He snatched his test from me and spit out that word. Had he called me a nymphomaniac or a necrophiliac, I couldn't have been more puzzled. I didn't know what a nigger was, but I knew that whatever it meant, it was something he shouldn't have called me. This was verified when I raised my hand, and in a loud voice repeated what he had said and watched the teacher scold him for using a "bad" word. I was later to go home and ask the inevitable questions that every black parent must face—"Mommy, what does 'nigger' mean?"

4 And what exactly did it mean? Thinking back, I realize that this could not have been the first time the word was used in my presence. I was part of a large extended family that had migrated from the rural South after World War II and formed a close-knit

network that gravitated around my maternal grandparents. Their ground-floor apartment in one of the buildings they owned in Harlem was a weekend mecca for my immediate family, along with countless aunts, uncles and cousins who brought along assorted friends. It was a bustling and open house with assorted neighbors and tenants popping in and out to exchange bits of gossip, pick up an old quarrel or referee the ongoing checkers game in which my grandmother cheated shamelessly. They were all there to let down their hair and put up their feet after a week of labor in the factories, laundries and shipyards of New York.

Amid the clamor, which could reach deafening proportions—two or three conversations going on simultaneously, punctuated by the sound of a baby's crying somewhere in the back rooms or out on the street—there was still a rigid set of rules about what was said and how. Older children were sent out of the living room when it was time to get into the juicy details about "you-know-who" up on the third floor who had gone and gotten herself "p-r-e-g-n-a-n-t!" But my parents, knowing that I could spell well beyond my years, always demanded that I follow the others out to play. Beyond sexual misconduct and death, everything else was considered harmless for our young ears. And so among the anecdotes of the triumphs and disappointments in the various workings of their lives, the word nigger was used in my presence, but it was set within contexts and inflections that caused it to register in my mind as something else. 5

In the singular, the word was always applied to a man who had distinguished himself in some situation that brought their approval for his strength, intelligence or drive: 6

"Did Johnny *really* do that?" 7

"I'm telling you, that nigger pulled in $6,000 of overtime last year. Said he got enough for a down payment on a house." 8

When used with a possessive adjective by a woman—"my nigger"—it became a term of endearment for husband or boyfriend. But it could be more than just a term applied to a man. In their mouths it became the pure essence of manhood—a disembodied force that channeled their past history of struggle and present survival against the odds into a victorious statement of being: "Yeah, that old foreman found out quick enough—you don't mess with a nigger." 9

In the plural, it became a description of some group within the community that had overstepped the bounds of decency as my 10 family defined it: Parents who neglected their children, a drunken couple who fought in public, people who simply refused to look for work, those with excessively dirty mouths or unkempt households were all "trifling niggers." This particular circle could forgive hard times, unemployment, the occasional bout of depression—they had gone through all of that themselves—but the unforgivable sin was a lack of self-respect.

11 A woman could never be a "nigger" in the singular, with its connotation of confirming worth. The noun "girl" was its closest equivalent in that sense, but only when used in direct address and regardless of the gender doing the addressing. "Girl" was a token of respect for a woman. The one-syllable word was drawn out to sound like three in recognition of the extra ounce of wit, nerve or daring that the woman had shown in the situation under discussion.

12 "G-i-r-l, stop. You mean you said that to his face?"

13 But if the word was used in a third-person reference or shortened so that it almost snapped out of the mouth, it always involved some element of communal disapproval. And age became an important factor in these exchanges. It was only between individuals of the same generation, or from an older person to a younger (but never the other way around), that "girl" would be considered a compliment.

14 I don't agree with the argument that use of the word nigger at this social stratum of the black community was an internalization of racism. The dynamics were the exact opposite: the people in my grandmother's living room took a word that whites used to signify worthlessness or degradation and rendered it impotent. Gathering there together, they transformed "nigger" to signify the varied and complex human beings they knew themselves to be. If the word was to disappear totally from the mouths of even the most liberal of white society, no one in that room was naïve enough to believe it would disappear from white minds. Meeting the word head-on, they proved it had absolutely nothing to do with the way they were determined to live their lives.

15 So there must have been dozens of times that the "nigger" was spoken in front of me before I reached the third grade. But I didn't "hear" it until it was said by a small pair of lips that had already learned it could be a way to humiliate me. That was the word I went home and asked my mother about. And since she knew that I had to grow up in America, she took me in her lap and explained.

A note from Gloria Naylor: The author wants it understood that the use of the word "nigger" is reprehensible in today's society. This essay speaks to a specific time and place when that word was utilized to empower African Americans; today, it is used to degrade them even if spoken from their own mouths. 16

BUILDING VOCABULARY

1. In paragraph 3, Naylor says the word *nigger* is as puzzling to her as *nymphomaniac* and *necrophiliac*. Using a dictionary, find both meanings of these two terms and their etymology, or roots.
2. In paragraph 14, Naylor writes, "I don't agree with the argument that use of the word nigger at this social stratum of the black community was an internalization of racism." Put Naylor's idea into your own words. Use the context of the sentence to understand key terms such as "social stratum" and "internalization."

THINKING CRITICALLY ABOUT THE ESSAY

Understanding the Writer's Ideas

1. What is the original situation in which Naylor recognizes that *nigger* can be a hate word? What clues from outside the dictionary meaning of the word help her to recognize this meaning? What confirms her suspicion that the word is "bad"?
2. In paragraph 4, Naylor gives us information about her family and background. In your own words, what kind of family did Naylor come from? Where did she grow up? What economic and social class did her family come from? How do you know?
3. In paragraph 5, Naylor explains the values of her group. What was considered appropriate and what was inappropriate for children to hear? What kind of behavior did the group condemn?
4. Naylor defines at least five contexts in which the word *nigger* might be used. Make a list giving the five contexts, and write a sentence putting the use of the word into your own definition.

5. Explain one context in which Naylor says *nigger* was never used (par. 11). How are age and gender important in determining how the word was used?
6. When Naylor says in paragraph 14 that blacks' use of the word *nigger* about themselves rendered the word "impotent," what does she mean? How do they "transform" the meaning of the word?
7. In the last paragraph, Naylor recalls her mother's reaction to the experience of hearing a third-grade classmate use the word to humiliate her. What do you think the mother explained?

Understanding the Writer's Techniques

1. Where is the thesis statement of Naylor's essay? How do you know?
2. Why does Naylor begin with two paragraphs about language, in a very general or theoretical way? Explain what these two paragraphs tell us about the writer's authority to define words. How does she use her introduction to make herself sound like an expert on the problem of defining words?
3. In paragraph 3, the writer shifts tone. She moves from the formal language of the introduction to the personal voice as she retells her childhood experience. What is the effect of this transition on the reader? Why?
4. Look closely at the examples of usage Naylor provides in paragraphs 8, 9, 10, and 11. Why does she provide dialogue to illustrate the various contexts in which she heard the word *nigger* used? In what way is this variety of speakers related to her thesis statement?
5. Naylor uses grammatical terms to clarify differences in meaning, such as "in the singular" (par. 6), "possessive adjective" (par. 9), "plural" (par. 10), and "third-person reference" (par. 13). Why does she use these technical terms? What does it reveal about the audience for whom she is writing? What does it reveal about Naylor's understanding of that audience?
6. What do you think about the last sentence of the essay? Why does the writer return to the simple and direct language of her childhood experience in order to conclude rather than using the theoretical and technical language of other parts of the essay?

✷ MIXING PATTERNS

Why does Naylor use narration to organize her extended definition? What other rhetorical strategies does she rely on, and why?

Exploring the Writer's Ideas

1. Naylor chooses to define a difficult and controversial word in her essay. How does the way that she defines it make you think again about the meaning of the word *nigger*? Have you used the word in any of the ways she defines? How have contemporary rap musicians used the word in ways to suggest that Naylor's definition is accurate?
2. Naylor argues that the definition of words emerges from consensus. So, if the third-grader used *nigger* to humiliate his classmate, we must draw the conclusion that little boy's society consented to the racism he intended by using the word. How does Naylor reinforce this idea in the last paragraph of the essay? What attitude toward racism does the mother seem to reveal when she picks up her daughter? Does Naylor's definition essay offer any solutions to the negative meaning the word carries? in what ways?
3. The classic American novel *The Adventures of Huckleberry Finn,* by Mark Twain, uses the word *nigger* almost 200 times. For this reason, some school libraries want to ban the book. In what ways does Naylor's definition essay engage in this censorship debate?

IDEAS FOR WRITING

Prewriting

Select an objectionable or offensive word, and for five minutes freewrite on the subject, trying to cover as many ways in which the word is used as possible.

Guided Writing

Choose a word that you have recently heard used that offended you because it was sexist, racist, anti-Semitic, homophobic, or otherwise objectionable. Write a definition essay in which you define the word, show examples of its power to offend, and conclude by offering alternate words.

1. Use an anecdote to show whom you heard using the word, where it was used, and how you felt when you heard it used. In your introduction, explain who you are and who the other speaker was.
2. In your thesis, give the word and give an expanded definition of what the word means to you.
3. Explain the background of the word's negative use. Who uses it? What is the dictionary meaning of the word? How do you think the word got corrupted?
4. Give examples to expand your thesis that the word has negative meanings. Show who uses it and for what purpose. Draw your examples from people at work, the media, or historical figures.
5. Use another example to show how the word can change meaning if the speaker deliberately uses it in order to mock its usual meaning or "render it impotent" as Naylor says.
6. If possible, try to define the word by negation—that is, by what it does not mean.
7. Connect your paragraphs with transitions that relate one idea thoughtfully to the next.
8. In your conclusion, place the term in a broader perspective, one that goes beyond the specific word to the power of language to shape reality or control behavior.

Thinking and Writing Collaboratively

Many colleges and universities are trying to find ways to discourage or prevent hate speech by writing codes of conduct. In groups of five or six, discuss possible approaches to this issue, and then draft a policy statement that defines what unacceptable language is and how your campus will respond to it.

Writing About the Text

In what way does Naylor's discussion of language raise issues similar to those discussed by Amy Tan in "Mother Tongue" (pages 39–45)? Although Tan is dealing with language among immigrants and Naylor is addressing the varieties of meaning of words to native speakers of English, both writers deal with the politics of language. How does each writer define the relationship between language and power?

More Writing Projects

1. In your journal, record an incident in which someone addressed you or someone you know with an offensive word. Explain how you reacted and why.
2. Write a one-paragraph definition of a word or phrase by which you would feel comfortable being labeled. Are you a single parent? an Italian American? an honor student? Write a sharp thesis to define the term, and then expand the definition with examples.
3. Read the following poem by Countee Cullen (1903–1946). Then write an essay in which you compare and contrast his approach to the use of offensive language to Naylor's. How do the two works converge? diverge? What is the effect of each work on the reader?

INCIDENT

Once riding in old Baltimore
Heart-filled, head-filled with glee,
I saw a Baltimorean
Keep looking straight at me.
Now I was eight and very small,
And he was no whit bigger,
And so I smiled, but he poked out
His tongue, and called me, "Nigger."
I saw the whole of Baltimore
From May until December
Of all the things that happened there
That's all that I remember.

SUMMING UP: CHAPTER 10

1. In her essay on the N-word, Gloria Naylor defines a term we all understand but might have difficulty defining. One way she approaches this definition is through negation—that is, by explaining what the word is *not*. Write an essay that defines by negation another term that is understood but difficult to explain—for example, *privacy, the blues, class, happiness,* or *success.*
2. Gilb's essay attempts a complicated definition of a complicated concept, pride. In what way do you disagree with his definition? Write your own definition of pride, referring to Gilb's essay in forging your own definition.
3. Gloria Naylor argues that a word is defined by "consensus." That is, the members of a community agree about how to use a word, despite outside definitions. On your campus find examples of words defined by "consensus." Choose a word whose meaning on campus might surprise people like your parents, and write an essay defining that word.
4. Look back over the titles of all the essays in this and previous chapters of this book. Choose one word or phrase from any title (for example, "The Struggle to Be an All-American Girl," "Salvation," "Night Walker," "In the Jungle"), and write an essay defining that term *subjectively* (from your personal viewpoint).
5. Imagine a conversation between Akbar Ahmed (328–329) and Karen Armstrong. Remember that the writers are attempting to identify the impact of religion on life today. Write an essay in which you explore what each writer would say to the other.
6. Compare and contrast Gloria Naylor's treatment of race with Dagoberto Gilb's. What do you think is the difference between their definitions?

✷ FROM SEEING TO WRITING

Examine this 1934 photograph of a street scene in Harlem, the section of New York City that is famous as a center of African American culture. Use the photograph as the basis for an extended definition of a key term or concept—for example, *community, culture, city,* or *race*. In writing your essay, refer specifically to elements in the photograph that support your thesis. Use those writing strategies that serve best to develop your extended definition.

CHAPTER 11

Argumentation and Persuasion

WHAT ARE ARGUMENTATION AND PERSUASION?

When we use *argumentation,* we aim to convince someone to join our side of an issue. We want the readers to change their views and adopt ours. We also use *persuasion* when we want a person to take action that will advance our cause. Both argumentation, which appeals to reason, and persuasion, which appeals to emotions, aim to convince an audience to agree with your position. Argument and persuasion often work hand in hand.

In everyday life we hear the word *argument* used as a synonym for *fight*. In writing, however, an argument is not a brawl but a train of thought directed toward a well-focused goal. Usually an argument has a topic that can be debated, and an argument should reflect the ethical and critical standards that apply to debate. Although argument naturally includes emotion and even passion, a good argument avoids mere emotional appeals. A good argument appeals to reason. Consequently, argument relies on logic more than do other kinds of writing. At the same time, all writing—analysis, narrative, even description—can be said to be a form of argument. Whatever we write, we want the reader to get our point, and if possible to see it our way. This proposition can be reversed, as well. Just as all writing includes some form of argument, so, too, argumentation draws on all the writers' tools that you have learned so far. In preparing your argumentative essay, you will be able to rehearse and refine the skills you have learned to this point.

The first step in arguing successfully is to state your position clearly. This means that a good thesis is crucial to your essay. For argumentative or persuasive essays, the thesis is sometimes called a *major proposition,* or a *claim.* Through your major proposition, you take a definite position in a debate, and by taking a strong position, you give your essay its argumentative edge. Your readers must know what your position is and must see that you have supported your main idea with convincing minor points. The weakest arguments are those in which the writer tries to take both sides and as a result persuades no one. As you will see in the reading selections, writers often concede or yield a point to the opposition, but they do so only to strengthen the side that they favor.

Writing arguments should make you even more aware of the need to think about audience. In particular, in writing you need to think about the people who will make up their minds on the basis of your evidence. As you consider how to present your case, think about what kind of language, what kinds of examples, and what general tone will speak most persuasively to your audience. As well, keep in mind that readers are rarely persuaded simply by assertion; you can't just tell them something is true. You need to show them through well-organized support of the main and minor points that support your major proposition or claim. In this respect you might say that there are two audiences for an argumentative essay: the actual, living audience of readers; and something that you might see as the "court of standards"—the rules of logic and of evidence. The actual audience is in fact more likely to be convinced of your case if it follows these rules and meets the standards for debate. Moreover, an essential feature of argument is credibility. An excellent way to establish and sustain your credibility is to follow the rules of logic and of evidence faithfully.

Evidence or support can come from many sources. Among the most powerful forms of evidence are facts, whether these are drawn from the historical record, from reliable statistical sources, or from personal experience. Another common form of evidence is expert opinion. If, for example, you are writing an essay about cleaning up pollution in a river, you may want to rely on statements from scientists or environmental engineers to support your point. Indeed, you may have come to your own conclusions on the basis of authoritative information or opinion.

In addition to evidence, writers often depend on analysis of the opponent's points to advance the writer's own arguments. Finally, a writer can of course use narrative, description, comparison and contrast, illustration, process, cause and effect, classification, and definition to persuade.

Because we use argument in everyday life, we may think it is easy to argue in writing—but just the opposite is true. If we are arguing with someone in person, we can *see* our opponent's response and quickly change our direction. In writing, we can only imagine the opponent and so must carefully prepare evidence for all possible responses. Moreover, although the evening news may expose us to arguments, about abortion clinics, increasing the minimum wage, or accusations of sexual harassment, we often see only what media experts call "sound bites," tiny fragments of information. We may see just a slogan as a picket sign passes a camera. We may hear only a few sentences out of hours of testimony. We seldom see or hear the entire argument. When we turn to writing arguments ourselves, we need to remember to develop a complete and detailed and *rational* argument.

This does not mean that written arguments lack emotion. Rather, written argument channels that emotion into a powerful eloquence that can endure much longer than a shouting match. The writer states the major proposition, or point he or she wants to make, and keeps it firmly in front of the reader. To do this, a writer must have a clear sense of purpose and audience and plan the argument accordingly.

A wide range of topics—and of purposes and intended audiences—is possible. For example, a writer may want to argue that the U.S. government should grant amnesty to illegal aliens who have been in the country for at least two years. He may write to his member of Congress to persuade her to take action on a proposed bill. Or the writer may want to convince a group of readers, such as readers of the local newspaper, that something is true—that single fathers make excellent parents, for example, or that wife abuse is an increasingly serious crime in our society.

Whatever the writer's topic, the keys to a good argument are

- a clear and effective major proposition or claim
- a reasonable tone
- an abundance of evidence
- an avoidance of personal attacks

ORGANIZATION OF THE CHAPTER

Because of the nature of argumentation, we have organized this chapter differently from the others so as to highlight more than usual the issues—the claims, ideas, techniques—raised in the selections. Since argument typically implies an opposing or differing viewpoint, we start by providing a set of pro and con essays on a topic of current interest: social networking. However, in order to help readers understand that issues are often complex and lend themselves to multiple viewpoints, we have grouped additional essays under two sets of perspectives: ethnicity, and rights and responsibilities.

Here are the selections you find in this chapter:

Arguments Pro and Con: Facebook: Friend or Foe?

John Lemuel, "*Why I Registered on Facebook*"
Ryan Singel, "*Facebook's Gone Rogue; It's Time for an Open Alternative*"

Perspectives on Ethnicity: Who Are We, and How Are We Formed?

John Edgar Wideman, "*The Seat Not Taken*"
Manuel Muñoz, "*Leave Your Name at the Border*"
Richard Rodriguez, "*The Great Wall of America*"
Ronald Takaki, "*The Harmful Myth of Asian Superiority*"

Perspectives on Rights and Responsibilities: Are We Truly Free?

Molly Ivins, "*Get a Knife, Get a Dog, but Get Rid of Guns*"
Martin Luther King Jr., "*I Have a Dream*"
Susan Cheever, "*Baby Battle*"

HOW DO WE READ ARGUMENTS?

Try to find out something about the background and credentials of the writer. In what way is he or she an expert on the topic?

Is the proposition presented in a rational and logical way? Is it credible and presented accurately and fairly? What reasons (or minor propositions) are used to support the writer's claim, and are they convincing?

Has the writer presented ample reliable evidence to back up the proposition? (If you look at the headlines on supermarket tabloid newspapers that try to persuade us that aliens have been keeping Elvis Presley alive on Mars, you will see why it is important to be able to evaluate a writer's evidence before accepting the proposition!)

Does the writer consider the counterarguments and deal effectively with the opposition?

HOW DO WE WRITE ARGUMENTS?

State a clear major proposition, and stick to it.

Convince readers of the validity of your thesis by making an essay plan that introduces *minor propositions*. These are assertions that help clarify the reasons you offer to support your main idea.

Use *refutation*. This is a technique in which you anticipate what an opponent will say and answer the objection ahead of time. Another technique is *concession*. You yield a small point to your opponent but at the same time claim a larger point on your own side. Using these techniques makes your argument seem fairer. You acknowledge that there *are* at least two sides to the issue. Moreover, these devices help you make your own point more effectively.

Be aware of these pitfalls:

- Avoid personal attacks on your opponent, and don't let excessive appeals to emotion damage the tone of your argument.
- Avoid hasty generalization—that is, using a general statement about a subject without properly supporting it.
- Avoid drawing a conclusion that does not follow from the evidence in your argument.
- Avoid faulty analogies—that is, comparing two things or situations that are not really comparable.

Writing the Draft

Begin the rough draft. State your thesis or main proposition boldly.

Back up all minor propositions with

- statistics
- facts
- testimony from authorities
- personal experience

Find a reliable listener and read your essay aloud. Encourage your listener to refute your points as strongly as possible.

Revise the essay, taking into account your listener's refutations. Find better support for your weakest points. Write a new draft.

Revise the essay carefully. Read it aloud again if possible. Prepare a final copy.

A STUDENT PARAGRAPH: ARGUMENTATION AND PERSUASION

In the following paragraph, the student begins quite forcibly by stating his position on custody battles during divorce cases—in other words, in an argumentative mode. Examine the simple but effective way he provides evidence for his position.

Main proposition; "outrageous" a cue for sympathy

Cites authority to support main proposition

Case study provides evidence

The outcomes of custody battles during divorce proceedings exemplify the outrageous prejudice against fathers in our culture. Recently, the *Houston Chronicle* reported on the outcome of a child custody case the paper had followed for nearly six months. In the case, both father and mother wanted sole custody of their only child. The mother, a defense attorney at a high-flying Houston firm, worked 60–70 hours a week; she had maintained this schedule from the time the child, now six, was two months old. She frequently spent at least one weekend day at the office; she traveled on business as many as 10 weeks out of the year. The father, a freelance writer who worked at home, was acknowledged by both spouses to be the child's primary caretaker, and to have filled this role from the time the child was two months old and the wife returned to work. He typically woke the child, prepared breakfast, helped her choose clothing to wear, packed her a lunch, and walked her to school. He picked her up from school, accompanied her on playdates or took her to play in the park, made dinner for them both, helped the child with her homework, bathed her, read her a story, and put her to sleep. The mother ordinarily arrived home from work after the child was already asleep, and often left for work before the child was awake. Guess who got custody? The mother, of course. Sadly, judges persist in assuming that mothers are always the better—the more "natural"—caretaker. This assumption leads them all too often to award custody to the mother, despite evidence in many cases that the child has been raised primarily by the father, and would be better off continuing in his care.

Identification of opposition: conservative judges

Refutation and conclusion that reinforces main proposition

ARGUMENTS PRO AND CON

Facebook: Friend or Foe?

Among the great achievements that historians of the twenty-first century surely will record is the new form of rapid communication among citizens of the world. Social networking has spread over the globe like brushfire, linking friends, relatives, voyeurs, stargazers, serious filmmakers and pornographers, scientists and quacks, financiers and crooks, politicians and terrorists. Launched in 2004 exclusively for college men and women by Harvard University students Mark Zuckerberg (now heralded as the youngest billionaire in the world) and his then friend and schoolmate Eduardo Saverin, and given great public notoriety in the film *The Social Network* (2010—an admittedly fictional account—Facebook is now as popular worldwide as old-fashioned e-mailing and really old-fashioned telephoning once were. As of January 2011, Facebook had more than 600 million active users. Six hundred million! The number is staggering—and growing.

You probably already know how to use Facebook, named after the colloquially labeled book of photos and brief biographies that colleges and universities often distribute at the start of an academic year to help students get to know each other better. Users on Facebook create a personal profile and add other users as "friends" who can have access to this profile and exchange messages, photographs, music, videos, games, and other cyber entities with any approved person who is interested. In addition, users may establish or join interest user groups or communities, organized by profession, workplace, educational institution, or any other characteristic deemed worthy of a following. Through Facebook, you can make your life a widely opened book.

Despite the incredible numbers of Facebook users, and despite the many advantages that the service offers, critics call attention to an endless stream of negative outcomes of its use. Friends and family can find out more about your life than you may want to reveal. Requests to be a "friend" will bombard you. Your photographs can be misused. Your privacy is no longer assured. You may become addicted to Facebook, and it will eat away your time like a hungry wolf.

We present here two arguments, with elements clearly pro and con, for the uses of Facebook. The first essay is by a professor who joined Facebook early in its history because his students encouraged him, and he comes to see the advantages of his joining. The second essay is a strong attack against Facebook's shifting ideas of privacy. Which argument convinces you most? Why? How do you feel about Facebook after you finish reading the two selections?

Why I Registered on Facebook

John Lemuel

There's not much to offer here in the way of biographical information for John Lemuel. The writer has used a pseudonym—a fictitious or pen name—to indicate his authorship. He has revealed to the publisher of this piece, the *Chronicle of Higher Education*, only that he is a professor at a small liberal-arts college in the Midwest. The essay appeared in 2006, just two years after Facebook's historic entry into the cyber communications realm. The essay itself, as you will see even from the title, tries to present the advantages of joining the social network. As you read, keep in mind the status of anonymity that the writer has claimed. Just why has he chosen to use a pseudonym? What hints in the selection help you understand the writer's choice? Do you think he was justified? Why or why not?

PREREADING: THINKING ABOUT THE ESSAY IN ADVANCE

In your view, what does Facebook contribute to the world we live in?

Words to Watch

misgivings (par. 2) doubts; suspicions
far-flung (par. 3) distant
reassurance (par. 7) guarantee; support
urgency (par. 8) importance; hurry
trolling (par. 10) looking for; attempting to find something
persona (par. 11) character; personality
recalcitrant (par. 14) stubborn
shoddy (par. 17) careless; sloppy
callous (par. 18) cruel; heartless
cavorting (par. 22) frolicking; fooling around

Yeah, I did it. I registered for an account on Facebook.com. I'm sure I protest too much when I say it went against my instincts and better judgment to do so. Nothing's more embarrassing than a grown-up trying to be one of the kids. But we can't let the students have all the fun, now, can we? 1

A few of my graduate-school colleagues, now working at other campuses where I rarely hear from them, had already signed 2 up and pestered me to get in the loop. They had misgivings about it, too, they assured me, but quickly found that joining led to easy networking and positive interactions with students.

3 And for what it's worth, I've had more contact with those far-flung former colleagues through Facebook these last few months than I'd had in years before via e-mail and phone.

4 Facebook allows users to search for other users on their own campus and elsewhere. Some users allow anyone to look at their profiles, while others restrict access to those on their list of friends. Inviting a fellow Facebook user to become your "friend" allows that user to view your profile. Accepting an invitation to become friends puts you on your friend's list of friends, and vice versa. Then users can form groups of friends around a common theme and post messages to each other.

5 I started off slow, reluctant to get too chummy online with students I would still have in my classes next term. I found it easier to banter freely with those who had transferred to other campuses. But it seemed hardly worth the effort to cultivate those relationships. At best, what? They might ask me for a recommendation letter? "Sally was an above-average student in my intro course, but she's been a terrific Facebook friend since she left this campus!"

6 The site tracks the number of Facebook friends I have made, which is into double digits, but still well below the typical student user's average. The friend count sounds like an innocent tally, but at times it feels like Facebook is keeping score.

7 Adolescence was a long time ago. Grad school taught me to relate to others more as colleagues than as friends. If I need reassurance of my students' esteem, I need look no further than my course evaluations (Ha!). So my sparse friend count doesn't normally bother me.

8 But when I first opened my account, it read "You have no friends" at my institution. Such a bold declarative statement has the power of persuasion. The blunt words dug in like spurs, producing a momentary sense of urgency that I do something, anything, to rack up some friends. The moment passed and an adult perspective returned, but for a moment there I was 13 again and on the fringes of social isolation.

9 Some student users seem to be competing for the highest score. One of my first friend invitations came from a student I scarcely recall from one of my intro classes. Her performance in the class was not particularly memorable. I'm not sure what

constitutes online friendship, but I don't think I've exchanged 10 words with her in person. I accepted the invitation and haven't heard a peep since.

10 That's one approach: Trolling for new friends to invite, on the faintest glimmer of acquaintance, to raise your score. That student boasts several hundred Facebook friends—some, I hope, on a more genuine basis.

11 As in a personal ad, choosing the right photo for your profile matters. Unlike a personal ad, you can't fake much. Readers of my profile may have me for a class, pass me daily on the sidewalk, or hear about me through the grapevine. So I can present things they might not know about me, but a phony persona would be a ticket to Poserville.

12 There's a lot of potential to use a profile as a publicity organ. My photo features me in an exotic locale where I recently led an overseas study trip. Other students have seen the photo and started asking when the next trip would be. The more students ask, the greater my inclination to pull together another study trip.

13 I've also posted pictures of our student majors on research trips and departmental outings. That promotes not only our program, but (I like to think) a sense of the intellectual culture of college in general. It doesn't hurt to put more photos of our students being studious into circulation, since the vast majority of Facebook photos highlight their decidedly nonacademic activities.

14 Students post ample contact information on their Facebook pages, which has me contemplating other uses, such as tracking down recalcitrant advisees and frequent absentees from my classes. In a pinch, it might help scare up a last-minute babysitter, housesitter, or moving crew. Another means of contacting students can't be a bad thing.

15 Unexpectedly I found recent alumni of our program on Facebook. They had profiles through graduate school or secondary schools where they work now. I was delighted, because I had no other current contact information for them, and this saved the hassle of going through the alumni office, where records may not be up to date anyway. We want our students to network with recent graduates, and I hope Facebook might facilitate that.

16 But it can be odd to associate with others through the indirect means of online profile pages.

17 Some would-be online friends make you think twice. One student failed the same class with me two years in a row, the second

time by turning in the same shoddy papers submitted the year before. So I was pleasantly surprised when he issued me a friend invitation. The invite allowed me to view his profile before accepting. A quick glance through his beer-soaked, obscenity-laden profile convinced me I didn't want him showing up in my Friends column. Mama always warned about hanging out with the wrong crowd.

18 To minimize rejection, Facebook does not tell inviters when their invitation has been declined. But it still felt callous to reject the guy, this being the only invitation I had turned down. Suddenly I'm 13 again, only this time as the snooty Mr. Popular: "Friends? With you? I don't think so."

19 The lessons of after-school specials replay in my mind. If the decent kid (DK) befriended the troubled kid (TK), which way did it go? Was DK a good influence on TK, or did TK lead DK astray? I'm sure I saw both plots play out, on television and in junior high.

20 It's frankly absurd to imagine Facebook friends exercising much of a good or bad influence on each other's real lives through their online profiles. I'm sure having this fellow as my online friend would look neither good nor bad, but simply absurd—assuming anyone cared. So I made peace with my decision on grounds of avoiding absurdity.

21 But I could have just as easily embraced the absurdity to declare it for what it is. One of my students seems to have taken this tack: His profile lacks all detail except his membership in one group, "Facebook is dumb." Other students have formed a group to satirize the shallowness of online friendship, called, "You're my friend on Facebook, but in public you act like you don't know me."

22 There is such a thing as knowing too much about your students. One of my Facebook friends is a first-year student who married her boyfriend right after high-school graduation. He went to boot camp and got shipped to Iraq, while she went to college. She's bright in the classroom, but pictures on Facebook show her cavorting like an unmarried woman. I don't know them as a couple, and it's none of my business, but I can't help wondering if hubby's ever had a glimpse of her profile.

23 Is it wrong for the grown-ups to intrude on this student-centered forum?

24 The designers of Facebook apparently didn't think so, granting access to anyone with an e-mail address in an ".edu" domain. That includes faculty and staff members, even college alumni at a growing number of institutions. That means plenty of parents of students on Facebook.

A lot depends on the reasons for gate-crashing. "Grown-ups" mingling with the "kids" online have to find a balance between staying hip and embarrassing themselves. It's not worth keeping score, or sinking lots of time into your profile or anyone else's. 25

But Facebook can be a medium for faculty and staff members and even administrators to be in contact with students, and maybe provide a little adult guidance. Individually one faculty Facebooker might not have much influence, but a collective presence could raise the tone and dial down the antics on this increasingly public student venue. 26

BUILDING VOCABULARY

Determine the meaning of each word in italics and then provide an *antonym* (a word that means the opposite of the given word).

1. pester (par. 2)
2. cultivate (par. 5)
3. chummy (par. 5)
4. esteem (par. 7)
5. sparse (par. 7)
6. decidedly (par. 13)
7. facilitate (par. 15)
8. snooty (par. 18)
9. absurd (par. 20)
10. shallowness (par. 21)

THINKING CRITICALLY ABOUT THE ESSAY

Understanding the Writer's Ideas

1. Why has the writer chosen to open a Facebook account? What do the writer's graduate students tell him about joining the network?
2. How does the writer compare Facebook with telephoning and e-mailing?
3. With whom does the writer say he has difficulty in making friends? With whom does he find it easier to banter?
4. What did his account read when Lemuel first opened it? How did he feel about it?

5. What questions does the writer receive from some students who see his online photo?
6. Why does he post photos of students on research trips?
7. What other uses does the writer see for Facebook?
8. Why does he reject one particular student who wants to be his Facebook friend?
9. About which student does the writer feel he knows too much? Why does he feel that way?
10. How, according to the writer, can Facebook facilitate contact among students, faculty, and administrators?

Understanding the Writer's Techniques

1. From the very first word, the writer has assumed a highly colloquial style for the essay. Which colloquial expressions other than "Yeah" can you identify? Why has the writer chosen such a style, particularly since the piece appeared in a weekly newspaper for college and university professors, administrators, and staff?
2. Why does the writer explain in paragraph 4 how Facebook works? Does the analysis help readers? Why would he include it so close to the beginning of the essay?
3. Writers often use rhetorical questions to prompt the reader to pay special attention to an issue. Lemuel asks a number of questions throughout the piece. Identify some of them. Why does he include questions in this essay? Are they meant to be answered, or do you consider them simply rhetorical?
4. What is the writer's major proposition? Has he convinced you of his argumentative position? Why or why not?
5. What minor propositions does the writer introduce to support his thesis?
6. What is Lemuel's purpose in writing this piece, do you think?
7. The writer provides anecdotes to illustrate his point. What does he attempt to achieve with the anecdote about the returning student (par. 17)? About the married student (par. 22)?
8. How has the writer dealt with opposing arguments to his thesis? Has he treated the opposition fairly? Find instances in the essay to support your position.
9. The reasons a writer uses a pseudonym are certainly complex and often very private. Yet it's worth speculating on why a

writer of an essay about Facebook in a college-oriented publication would choose not to use his actual name. Why do you think that Lemuel has used a pen name? What issues might the use of his real name have raised on his campus, do you think? Remember that the piece appeared early in Facebook's public history. If Lemuel were writing today, do you think he would use a pseudonym? Why or why not?

10. What rhetorical modes do you identify here in the service of argumentation? Where has the writer used narrative? Process? Cause and effect? Definition?

Exploring the Writer's Ideas

1. Why do you think that joining Facebook initially went against the writer's "instincts and better judgment"?
2. Lemuel says, "Nothing's more embarrassing than a grown-up trying to be one of the kids." Where else does he establish a contrast between "grown-ups" and "kids"? Who do you think he means by "kids"? Why might you agree or disagree with his observations? Do you find the word *kids* appropriate, condescending, silly, unfortunate—or something else?
3. Facebook clearly has grown beyond some of the limited observations the writer has made about it in 2006, when users were essentially students and young people. What elements or statements need correcting, given the passage of time since Lemuel wrote the essay? Look, for example, at the title of the essay and paragraph 24.
4. Of the people you know who use Facebook, is there a competition for the highest score, that is, to see who can accumulate the most friends? Why should numbers of friends be important? Are numbers important to you? Why or why not?
5. Lemuel says "it can be odd to associate with others through the indirect means of online profile pages." Do you agree with the statement? Why or why not?

IDEAS FOR WRITING

Prewriting

Write nonstop for 10–15 minutes on this topic: Why I Have (or Do Not Have) a Facebook Account.

Guided Writing

Write an argumentative essay about the advantages of having a Facebook, Twitter, or some other social networking account. Hundred of networking sites exist including those that provide dating services, health care connections, artistic linkages, and many others. Choose one of your interests.

1. State your major proposition as your thesis early in the essay.
2. Consider the reasons that someone might be reluctant to have such an account.
3. Provide lively examples drawn from your own experience or from what you've read to show the advantages of social networking.
4. Introduce opposing arguments thoughtfully—that is, explain why people disapprove of Facebook or others of its type.
5. Write in an informal and colloquial style.
6. Raise rhetorical questions to engage the reader.

Thinking and Writing Collaboratively

Form groups and discuss this point from the essay: "'Grown-ups' mingling with the 'kids' online have to find a balance between staying hip and embarrassing themselves." Lemuel wrote this before Facebook became available to anyone, not just college students. But does the statement still have validity? Why or why not? Would you say that the statement is applicable to offline mingling as well as online? Why or why not? What examples can group members provide to support or oppose the point?

Writing About the Text

Write a brief essay on the style of this selection with particular attention to its informal language.

More Writing Projects

1. Write a journal entry about why students should (or should not) have Internet accounts unknown to their parents.
2. View the film *The Social Network* and write an essay about its effectiveness as a historical account of Facebook's beginnings. Examine newspaper articles and reviews of the film to help you gain perspective on the issue.

3. Consider the use of Facebook or other social networks in politics and government (President Obama's 2008 election campaign and the 2011 demonstrations in Egypt come to mind) and write an argumentative essay on how social networking can become (or is already) a force for good or evil (your choice!) in the world.

Facebook's Gone Rogue; It's Time for an Open Alternative

Ryan Singel

Ryan Singel is a San Francisco–based writer and journalist with a wide range of interests. As a blogger, he covers policy issues regarding technology, privacy, and civil liberties. He writes the Epicenter blog for Wired.com, an online extension of *Wired Magazine,* published by the magazine conglomerate Condé-Nast. Singel does not shrink from controversy: he co-founded the Threat Level blog with convicted hacker (now turned journalist) Kevin Lee Poulsen. Singel has a Facebook account, but as you can see from this entry posted on his blog on May 7, 2010, he has many complaints about how the social network behaves toward its members, and he argues convincingly about Facebook's missteps.

PREREADING: THINKING ABOUT THE ESSAY IN ADVANCE

Internet use, and especially use of social networking sites, has raised many questions about individual privacy. What are some privacy issues that Internet users should consider? Have you or anyone you know faced privacy challenges online or in any other context?

Words to Watch

rogue (par. 1) unpredictable, dangerous
default (par. 6) preset option; failure to meet an obligation
preemptively (par. 8) done before others can act
opt out (par. 8) choose not to do something
mores (par. 16) customs; ways of life
coercing (par. 22) forcing; compelling
shenanigans (par. 24) questionable acts; pranks

1 Facebook has gone rogue, drunk on founder Mark Zuckerberg's dreams of world domination. It's time the rest of the Web ecosystem recognizes this and works to replace it with something open and distributed.

2 Facebook used to be a place to share photos and thoughts with friends and family and maybe play a few stupid games that let you pretend you were a mafia don or a homesteader. It became a very

useful way to connect with your friends, long-lost friends and family members. Even if you didn't really want to keep up with them.

3 Soon everybody—including your uncle Louie and that guy you hated from your last job—had a profile.

4 And Facebook realized it owned the network.

5 Then Facebook decided to turn "your" profile page into your identity online—figuring, rightly, that there's money and power in being the place where people define themselves. But to do that, the folks at Facebook had to make sure that the information you give it was public.

6 So in December, with the help of newly hired Beltway privacy experts, it reneged on its privacy promises and made much of your profile information public by default. That includes the city that you live in, your name, your photo, the names of your friends and the causes you've signed onto. This spring Facebook took that even further. All the items you list as things you like must become public and linked to public profile pages. If you don't want them linked and made public, then you don't get them—though Facebook nicely hangs onto them in its database in order to let advertisers target you.

7 This includes your music preferences, employment information, reading preferences, schools, etc. All the things that make up your profile. They all must be public—and linked to public pages for each of those bits of info—or you don't get them at all. That's hardly a choice, and the whole system is *maddeningly complex*.

8 Simultaneously, the company began shipping your profile information off preemptively to Yelp, Pandora and Microsoft—so that if you show up there while already logged into Facebook, the sites can "personalize" your experience when you show up. You can try to opt out after the fact, but you'll need a master's in Facebook bureaucracy to stop it permanently.

9 Care to write a status update to your friends? Facebook sets the default for those messages to be published to the entire Internet through direct funnels to the Net's top search engines. You can use a dropdown field to restrict your publishing, but it's seemingly too hard for Facebook to actually remember that's what you do. (Google Buzz, for all the criticism it has taken, remembers your setting from your last post and uses that as the new default.)

10 Now, say you you write a public update, saying, "My boss had a crazy great idea for a new product!" Now, you might not know it, but there is a Facebook page for "My Crazy Boss" and because your post had all the right words, your post now shows up on that

page. Include the words "FBI" or "CIA," and you show up on the FBI or CIA page.

11 Then there's the new Facebook "Like" button littering the Internet. It's a great idea, in theory—but it's completely tied to your Facebook account, and you have no control over how it is used. (No, you can't like something and not have it be totally public.)

12 Then there's Facebook's campaign against outside services. There was the Web 2.0 suicide machine that let you delete your profile by giving it your password. Facebook shut it down.

13 Another company has an application that will collect all your updates from services around the Web into a central portal—including from Facebook—after you give the site your password to log in to Facebook. Facebook is suing the company and alleging it is breaking *criminal* law by not complying with its terms of service.

14 No wonder *14 privacy groups filed an unfair-trade complaint* with the FTC against Facebook on Wednesday.

15 Mathew Ingram at GigaOm wrote a post entitled "The Relationship Between Facebook and Privacy: It's Really Complicated."

16 No, that's just wrong. The relationship is simple: Facebook thinks that your notions of privacy—meaning your ability to control information about yourself—are just plain old-fashioned. Head honcho Zuckerberg told a live audience in January that Facebook is simply *responding to changes in privacy mores,* not changing them—a convenient, but frankly untrue, statement.

17 In Facebook's view, everything (save perhaps your e-mail address) should be public. Funny too about that e-mail address, for Facebook would prefer you to use its e-mail–like system that *censors the messages sent between users.*

18 Ingram goes onto say, "And perhaps Facebook doesn't make it as clear as it could what is involved, or how to fine-tune its privacy controls—but at the same time, some of the onus for doing these things has to fall to users."

19 What? How can it fall to users when most of the choices don't' actually exist? I'd like to make my friend list private. Cannot.

20 I'd like to have my profile visible only to my friends, not my boss. Cannot.

21 I'd like to support an anti-abortion group without my mother or the world knowing. Cannot.

22 Setting up a decent system for controlling your privacy on a Web service shouldn't be hard. And if multiple blogs are writing posts explaining how to use your privacy system, you can take

that as a sign you aren't treating your users with respect. It means you are coercing them into choices they don't want using design principles. That's creepy.

23 Facebook could start with a very simple page of choices: I'm a private person, I like sharing some things, I like living my life in public. Each of those would have different settings for the myriad of choices, and all of those users could then later dive into the control panel to tweak their choices. That would be respectful design—but Facebook isn't about respect—it's about re-configuring the world's notion of what's public and private.

24 So what that you might be a teenager and don't get that college-admissions offices will use your e-mail address to find possibly embarrassing information about you. Just because Facebook got to be the world's platform for identity by promising you privacy and then later ripping it out from under you, that's your problem. At least, according to the bevy of privacy hired guns the company brought in at high salaries to provide cover for its shenanigans.

25 Clearly Facebook has taught us some lessons. We want easier ways to share photos, links and short updates with friends, family, co-workers and even, sometimes, the world.

26 But that doesn't mean the company has earned the right to own and define our identities. It's time for the best of the tech community to find a way to let people control what and how they'd like to share. Facebook's basic functions can be turned into protocols, and a whole set of interoperating software and services can flourish.

27 Think of being able to buy your own domain name and use simple software such as Posterous to build a profile page in the style of your liking. You'd get to control what unknown people get to see, while the people you befriend see a different, more intimate page. They could be using a free service that's ad-supported, which could be offered by Yahoo, Google, Microsoft, a bevy of startups or Web-hosting services like Dreamhost.

28 "Like" buttons around the Web could be configured to do exactly what you want them to—add them to a protected profile or get added to a wish list on your site or broadcast by your micro-blogging service of choice. You'd be able to control your presentation of self—and as in the real world, compartmentalize your life.

29 People who just don't want to leave Facebook could play along as well—so long as Facebook doesn't continue creepy data practices like turning your info over to third parties, just because one of your contacts takes the "Which Gilligan's Island character are you?"

quiz. (Yes, that currently happens.) Now, it might not be likely that a loose confederation of software companies and engineers can turn Facebook's core services into shared protocols, nor would it be easy for that loose coupling of various online services to compete with Facebook, given that it has 500 million users. Many of them may be fine having Facebook redefine their cultural norms, or just be too busy or lazy to leave. But in the Internet I'd like to live in, we'd have that option, instead of being left with the choice of letting Facebook use us, or being left out of the conversation altogether.

BUILDING VOCABULARY

1. For each word in italics below, choose the letter of the word or expression that most clearly matches its meaning. Go back to the indicated paragraphs to check on the *context* (see Glossary) in which the word appears.

a. **reneged** on (par. 6)
___ supported ___ went back on ___ reviewed ___ built on

b. **database** (par. 6)
___ home office ___ plans ___ files ___ exclusions

c. **maddeningly** (par. 7)
___ happily ___ hopelessly ___ dramatically ___ annoyingly

d. **notions** (par. 17)
___ concepts ___ proposals ___ notes ___ supports

e. **honcho** (par. 17)
___ thinker ___ lawyer ___ chief ___ owner

f. **onus** (par. 18)
___ mistakes ___ registration ___ helplessness ___ responsibility

g. **bevy** (par. 24)
___ selection ___ strong men ___ users ___ large number

h. **protocols** (par. 26)
___ efforts ___ procedures ___ proposals ___ lists of complex activities

i. **flourish** (par. 26)
___ flee ___ thrive ___ identify ___ relegate

j. **confederation** (par. 29)
___ alliance ___ confection ___ opposing forces ___ opening

2. Identify these names that appear in the selection.
   a. Mark Zuckerberg (par. 1)
   b. Yelp, Pandora, and Microsoft (par. 8)
   c. Google (par. 9)
   d. FBI or CIA (par. 10)
   e. FTC (par. 14)
   f. Mathew Ingram at GigaOM (par. 15)
   g. Yahoo (par. 27)
   h. Dreamhost (par. 27)
   i. Gilligan's Island (par. 29)

THINKING CRITICALLY ABOUT THE ESSAY

Understanding the Writer's Ideas

1. What did Singel like about Facebook in its early days?
2. What, according to the writer, did Facebook do with its members' profile pages?
3. What are some of the elements of a person's profile that Facebook first turned into public information?
4. How, according to the writer, did Facebook take that step further?
5. How could someone appear innocently on the FBI or CIA page?
6. What does the Facebook "Like button" accomplish?
7. How did Facebook limit outside services, according to the writer?
8. What does the writer say that Facebook is trying to accomplish about users' notions of privacy? What did Zuckerberg say about privacy mores?
9. What would Singel like to do that Facebook prevents him from doing?
10. What are some of the steps that the writer recommends to improve a person's control over his or her own privacy?

Understanding the Writer's Techniques

1. What is Singel's major premise? Where does he come closest to stating it exactly?
2. The very first sentence is quite bold in its assertion. Why does the writer open with such a dramatic statement? What does it accomplish for the essay?

3. Who is the audience for this piece? How can you tell?
4. The writer uses many informal expressions here, such as "stupid games" (par. 2) and "including your Uncle Louie" (par. 3). Make a list of some other informal or colloquial words or expressions. Why has Singel used them in the selection?
5. Where does Singel use testimony from outside sources? What are the sources that he cites?
6. What rhetorical strategies does the writer use to advance his argument? Where does he use process, for example? Cause and effect?
7. In paragraphs 19–21, Singel uses three one-word sentences—and they're all the same word, "Cannot." Why does he use such a repetitive, one-word sentence structure? What does he hope to accomplish with it, do you think?
8. How has Singel used *refutation* (see Glossary) here?
9. What is your view of the title? What does it mean to "go rogue"? Is Singel being fair in using this expression? How well does it serve the purpose of his essay?
10. What is your opinion of the last paragraph? In what ways is it a fitting conclusion to this selection?

Understanding the Writer's Ideas

1. Do you agree with Singel's assertions that Facebook had some useful purposes at the outset? Do you believe that it still provides valuable services for its members? Why or why not?
2. Singel is most upset with what he sees as Facebook's violation of the privacy pledged to its members—"promising you privacy and then ripping it out from under you." Why might you agree or disagree with the statement that Facebook is about "reconfiguring the world's notion of what's public and private"?
3. How do you feel about Facebook's use of private information? Do you share Singel's point of view? Do you worry that too much of the private information in someone's Facebook profile can become public? Do you believe, for example, as Singel does, that for teenagers "college admissions offices will use your e-mail address to find possibly embarrassing information about you"? Why or why not?
4. How does Facebook "own and define our identities" according to Singel? Do you agree with his point? Why or why not?

5. The writer believes that it would be easy to correct the violations he identifies in Facebook's behavior. Why might you agree or disagree with him? What other steps could you recommend?

IDEAS FOR WRITING

Prewriting

Brainstorm in writing on the topic of Internet privacy. What is your position on the matter?

Guided Writing

Write an argumentative essay about something that failed to live up to its promise or that once provided a service you expected but then stopped providing it. You might use another Internet source—YouTube, Twitter, Google, or even one of the dating services you've heard about or may have used. You might select politics—the Democratic or Republican Party's not fulfilling promises to voters; video games—the undelivered potential after much success of your favorite game's latest edition; television—sudden poor approaches in a show that you watch regularly; personal events—your boyfriend or girlfriend or husband or wife "going rogue." These are just suggestions: many possibilities exist for a good paper.

1. Open your essay with a bold, dramatic assertion that you intend to support throughout your essay.
2. Develop a major premise and include it as a clear thesis statement in an early paragraph.
3. Use a conversational style, as if you are writing for the same kind of audience Singel is aiming for.
4. Be sure to state the kind of service you once had from the entity you are writing about.
5. Identify the ways in which the entity has changed for the worse. Give specific examples.
6. Try to write one or two one-word sentences for dramatic effect.
7. Where possible, bring in and name outside sources who support (or challenge) your point of view.
8. Recommend ways in which the entity could change to satisfy you and others.

Thinking and Writing Collaboratively

Form groups and discuss what you would say to Mark Zuckerberg about privacy (or any other important matter) if he were a guest in your classroom.

Writing About the Text

Write an essay about the changes you would make in this essay (and why you would make them) if you intended to submit it to a mainstream periodical, such as the *New York Times, Newsweek,* or the *Atlantic,* for example. If you wouldn't make any changes, explain why the essay is appropriate for a non-Internet audience.

More Writing Projects

1. Write a journal entry on your last use of the Internet and how well you fared with it.
2. Write an extended paragraph on the issue of privacy beyond the Internet.
3. Write an argumentative essay about an Internet service other than Facebook. Identify pros and cons as you see them, but choose only one side of the argument. Readers should know whether or not you approve of the service.

PERSPECTIVES ON ETHNICITY: WHO ARE WE, AND HOW ARE WE FORMED?

Whether we've been in the United States for weeks or for generations, our origins are elsewhere in the world. As such, we contain in ourselves multiple cultural identities based on race, ethnicity, gender, social and national backgrounds, and more. How others see us—and how we see ourselves—often provokes debate over the nature of the American experience and our place within it.

The writers in this section—John Edgar Wideman, Manuel Muñoz, Richard Rodriguez, and Ronald Takaki—represent distinct ethnic and racial branches of the national experience. They pose provocative questions: Who am I? Am I a unique individual, with certain physical and emotional traits and with the habits and tastes that I myself have chosen to develop? Or am I the product of a certain group, community, nation, race, religion? Am I my own person or the person others perceive me to be?

These are among the most charged issues about which we, as Americans, must contend with. But how can we discuss issues of identity fairly and reasonably? How can we persuade others of the rightness of our views and the limitations of theirs? As you read the following selections, pause to reflect not only about what the writers have to say but also about how they present their claim. All writers composing arguments will try to persuade you to accept their viewpoint. As critical readers of such essays, you must evaluate the relative success of the rhetorical strategies Wideman, Muñoz, Rodriguez, and Takaki use to make their case.

The Seat Not Taken

John Edgar Wideman

John Edgar Wideman was born in Washington, D.C., and grew up in Pittsburgh, Pennsylvania, he attended the University of Pennsylvania, where he became an all–Ivy League forward on the basketball team. Wideman was the second African American to win a Rhodes Scholarship. The winner of many literary awards, he is the first to win the International PEN/Faulkner Award twice. His nonfiction book *Brothers and Keepers* (1984) received a National Book Critics Circle nomination, and his memoir *Fatheralong* (1994) was a finalist for the National Book Award. In 1997, his novel *The Cattle Killing* won the James Fenimore Cooper Prize for Best Historical Fiction. He has taught at the University of Wyoming; the University of Pennsylvania, where he founded and chaired the African American Studies Department; and the University of Massachusetts Amherst's MFA Program for Poets & Writers. In this essay for the *New York Times'* Op-Ed page, he explores the reasons that the seat next to him on a train he takes regularly is always empty for the several hours it takes to make the journey.

PREREADING: THINKING ABOUT THE ESSAY IN ADVANCE

When you enter a bus or train, do you take the first available seat or do you consider the person in the seat next to the empty one before you sit down? Why or why not?

Words to Watch

disquieting (par. 2) disturbing
deformity (par. 5) defect; abnormality
savor (par. 6) enjoy; delight in
appealing (par. 6) attractive; pleasing
assurance (par. 7) confidence
bounty (par. 7) reward; prize

1 At least twice a week I ride Amtrak's high-speed Acela train from my home in New York City to my teaching job in Providence, R.I. The route passes through a region of the country populated by, statistics tell us, a significant segment of its most educated, affluent, sophisticated and enlightened citizens.

2 Over the last four years, excluding summers, I have conducted a casual sociological experiment in which I am both participant

and observer. It's a survey I began not because I had some specific point to prove by gathering data to support it, but because I couldn't avoid becoming aware of an obvious, disquieting truth.

3 Almost invariably, after I have hustled aboard early and occupied one-half of a vacant double seat in the usually crowded quiet car, the empty place next to me will remain empty for the entire trip.

4 I'm a man of color, one of the few on the train and often the only one in the quiet car, and I've concluded that color explains a lot about my experience. Unless the car is nearly full, color will determine, even if it doesn't exactly clarify, why 9 times out of 10 people will shun a free seat if it means sitting beside me.

5 Giving them and myself the benefit of the doubt, I can rule out excessive body odor or bad breath; a hateful, intimidating scowl; hip-hop clothing; or a hideous deformity as possible objections to my person. Considering also the cost of an Acela ticket, the fact that I display no visible indications of religious preference and, finally, the numerous external signs of middle-class membership I share with the majority of the passengers, color appears to be a sufficient reason for the behavior I have recorded.

6 Of course, I'm not registering a complaint about the privilege, conferred upon me by color, to enjoy the luxury of an extra seat to myself. I relish the opportunity to spread out, savor the privacy and quiet and work or gaze at the scenic New England woods and coast. It's a particularly appealing perk if I compare the train to air travel or any other mode of transportation, besides walking or bicycling, for negotiating the mercilessly congested Northeast Corridor. Still, in the year 2010, with an African-descended, brown president in the White House and a nation confidently asserting its passage into a postracial era, it strikes me as odd to ride beside a vacant seat, just about every time I embark on a three-hour journey each way, from home to work and back.

7 I admit I look forward to the moment when other passengers, searching for a good seat, or any seat at all on the busiest days, stop anxiously prowling the quiet-car aisle, the moment when they have all settled elsewhere, including the ones who willfully blinded themselves to the open seat beside me or were unconvinced of its availability when they passed by. I savor that precise moment when the train sighs and begins to glide away from Penn or Providence Station, and I'm able to say to myself, with relative assurance, that the vacant place beside me is free, free at last, or at least free until the next station. I can relax, prop open my briefcase or rest papers, snacks or my arm in the unoccupied seat.

8 But the very pleasing moment of anticipation casts a shadow, because I can't accept the bounty of an extra seat without remembering why it's empty, without wondering if its emptiness isn't something quite sad. And quite dangerous, also, if left unexamined. Posters in the train, the station, the subway warn: if you see something, say something.

BUILDING VOCABULARY

Explain in your own words the meanings of the following phrases, with special attention to the words in italics. Use clues from the surrounding text to help you understand the definitions.

1. "*affluent, sophisticated,* and *enlightened* citizens" (par. 1)
2. "*invariably*, after I have *hustled* aboard" (par. 3)
3. "9 out of 10 people will *shun* a free seat" (par. 4)
4. "a hateful, *intimidating scowl*" (par. 5)
5. "the privilege, *conferred* upon me by color" (par. 6)
6. "a particularly *appealing perk*" (par. 6)
7. "stop anxiously *prowling*" (par. 7)
8. "pleasing moment of *anticipation*" (par. 8)

THINKING CRITICALLY ABOUT THE ESSAY

Understanding the Writer's Ideas

1. Why does Wideman take Amtrak at least twice a week?
2. What sociological experiment has he conducted?
3. What information does his casual experiment yield?
4. How does he explain the phenomenon he observes?
5. What does he rule out as possible reasons for people not taking the seat next to him?
6. What does he savor about having an empty seat beside him? And yet he is not truly happy about it. Why?

Understanding the Writer's Techniques

1. What is the thesis of this selection?
2. Where has the writer used concrete sensory details to advantage?

3. The paragraphs here are short, and the sentence style fairly simple. Why has the writer chosen to approach his topic in such a simple manner? How does the fact that he's writing an opinion piece for a daily newspaper affect his style, do you think?
4. In paragraph 5, the writer identifies traits that most people would agree might be enough to make them choose another seat. What other traits can you imagine that might prevent someone from sitting next to another person on a train or bus?
5. What elements of the rhetorical strategy of argumentation do you find in this piece?
6. Does Wideman's argument convince you? Why or why not?
7. In what ways does the last paragraph serve as a fitting conclusion to the piece? Where did the saying, "If you see something, say something" originate? What is its intended purpose? Why has Wideman used it here?
8. The title "The Seat Not Taken" is an obvious reference to Robert Frost's poem "The Road Not Taken." Why has Wideman chosen to echo Frost here?

Exploring the Writer's Ideas

1. Do you agree that color is solely responsible for someone not sitting beside the writer? Why or why not? What other reason, if any, might a person have for not sitting beside Wideman? If there are other reasons in your opinion, does that fact invalidate the writer's conclusions about the empty seat beside him? Why or why not?
2. The writer calls attention to the privilege conferred upon him by color. Do you agree that the color of a person's skin brings certain privileges? What are they?
3. Why does Wideman mention the White House? Do you agree that our country is "asserting its passage into a postracial era"? Why or why not? What in fact is a postracial era, in your opinion?
4. The writer says that the emptiness of the seat is quite sad. "And quite dangerous." Why does he think it dangerous? Why might you agree or disagree with his observation?

IDEAS FOR WRITING

Prewriting

Make a list of the factors that you think people weigh in choosing to sit in an empty seat when someone is occupying the seat next to the empty one.

Guided Writing

Write an essay called "The Seat Taken" in which you identify the factors that people consider in choosing to sit in an empty seat when someone is sitting in the seat next to the empty one.

1. Conduct a "casual sociological experiment" by asking friends, classmates, and relatives what factors enter their decision to sit beside someone on a train, subway, or bus.
2. Write a thesis that shows your conclusion about people's responses and how you feel about them.
3. Using the results of your experiment, identify and explain the factors that you have discovered.
4. Identify any negative qualities that people have listed about the person they might be sitting next to. In paragraph 5 Wideman rejects a number of negative qualities about himself.
5. If you can identify positive features that your respondents have indicated, discuss them as well.
6. Analyze the results in an effort to argue in support of or as a challenge to people's preferences.
7. Write in a simple, direct style.

Thinking and Writing Collaboratively

Divide into groups and discuss how much race and skin color enter people's decisions about forming friendships and acquaintanceships.

Writing About the Text

Reread Robert Frost's brief but powerful poem "The Road Not Taken." Write an essay comparing the poem to the essay by Wideman. What similarities do you note? What differences?

More Writing Projects

1. In your journal, freewrite about how you would feel and behave if you had to share an office with someone of a different racial background from your own.
2. Write a paragraph on what we should expect from the "most educated, affluent, sophisticated, and enlightened citizens" in regard to their behavior toward ethnic groups other than their own.
3. On December 1, 1955, Rosa Parks refused to follow the orders of a bus driver to give up her seat to a white passenger in a Montgomery, Alabama, bus and sparked the Montgomery Bus Boycott. Parks's act of defiance became an important symbol of the modern civil rights movement and Parks became an international symbol of resistance to segregation. Write an argumentative essay in which you consider Parks's and Wideman's experiences, separated by more than a half-century, as part of the same racial realities in today's world.

Leave Your Name at the Border

Manuel Muñoz

Mixing Patterns

Manuel Muñoz was born in a small town in California in 1972. The son of farm workers, Muñoz was the first member of his family to attend college, an experience that he alludes to in the essay that follows. He received a BA from Harvard College and an MFA from Cornell University. Muñoz has published two collections of short stories, *Zigzagger* (2003) and *The Faith Healer of Olive Avenue* (2007), on the San Joaquin Valley of his childhood. Muñoz has also contributed stories and essays to major newspapers and magazines. In this essay, first published in 2007 in the *New York Times,* Muñoz ponders the contradictions arising from his Latino name and his American upbringing.

PREREADING: THINKING ABOUT THE ESSAY IN ADVANCE

How does your family name reflect your ancestry, general background, ethnicity, perhaps even religion? How do others respond to your name?

Words to Watch

well-coiffed (par. 2) with nicely arranged hair
siblings (par. 6) brothers and sisters
incongruity (par. 7) incompatible, inconsistent, lacking in harmony
deference (par. 14) courteous respect
acculturation (par. 17) the process by which people adjust to the culture of a particular society
alliteration (par. 21) the repetition of the same sounds at the beginning of words

1 At the Fresno airport, as I made my way to the gate, I heard a name over the intercom. The way the name was pronounced by the gate agent made me want to see what she looked like. That is, I wanted to see whether she was Mexican. Around Fresno, identity politics rarely deepen into exacting terms, so to say "Mexican" means, essentially, "not white." The slivered self-identifications Chicano,

Hispanic, Mexican-American and Latino are not part of everyday life in the Valley. You're either Mexican or you're not. If someone wants to know if you were born in Mexico, they'll ask. Then you're From Over There—de alla. And leave it at that.

The gate agent, it turned out, was Mexican. Well-coiffed, in her 30s, she wore foundation that was several shades lighter than the rest of her skin. It was the kind of makeup job I've learned to silently identify at the mall when I'm with my mother, who will say nothing about it until we're back in the car. Then she'll stretch her neck like an ostrich and point to the darkness of her own skin, wondering aloud why women try to camouflage who they are.

I watched the Mexican gate agent busy herself at the counter, professional and studied. Once again, she picked up the microphone and, with authority, announced the name of the missing customer: "Eugenio Reyes, please come to the front desk."

You can probably guess how she said it. Her Anglicized pro nunciation wouldn't be unusual in a place like California's Centra Valley. I didn't have a Mexican name there either: I was an instruc tion guide.

When people ask me where I'm from, I say Fresno because don't expect them to know little Dinuba. Fresno is a booming ci of nearly 500,000 these days, with a diversity—white, Mexica African-American, Armenian, Hmong and Middle Eastern peop are all well represented—that shouldn't surprise anyone. It's in t small towns like Dinuba that surround Fresno that the awareness cultural difference is stripped down to the interactions between t only two groups that tend to live there: whites and Mexicans. Wh you hear a Mexican name spoken in these towns, regardless of speaker's background, it's no wonder that there's an "English w of pronouncing it."

I was born in 1972, part of a generation that learned b English and Spanish. Many of my cousins and siblings are bi gual, serving as translators for those in the family whose Eng is barely functional. Others have no way of following the Span banter at family gatherings. You can tell who falls into which gro Estella, Eric, Delia, Dubina, Melanie.

It's intriguing to watch "American" names begin to domin among my nieces and nephews and second cousins, as well with the children of my hometown friends. I am not surprised meet 5-year-old Brandon or Kaitlyn. Hardly anyone questions t incongruity of matching these names with last names like Truji or Zepeda. The English-only way of life partly explains the quiet erasure of cultural difference that assimilation has attempted to accomplish. A name like Kaitlyn Zepeda doesn't completely obscure her ethnicity, but the half-step of her name, as a gesture, is almost understandable.

8 Spanish was and still is viewed with suspicion: always the language of the vilified illegal immigrant, it segregated schoolchildren into English-only and bilingual programs; it defined you, above all else, as part of a lower class. Learning English, though, brought its own complications with identity. It was simultaneously the language of the white population and a path toward the richer, expansive identity of "American." But it took getting out of the Valley for me to understand that "white" and "American" were two very different things.

9 Something as simple as saying our names "in English" was our unwittingly complicit gesture of trying to blend in. Pronouncing Mexican names correctly was never encouraged. Names like Daniel, Olivia and Marco slipped right into the mutability of the English language.

10 I remember a school ceremony at which the mathematics teacher, a white man, announced the names of Mexican students correctly and caused some confusion, if not embarrassment. Years later we recognized that he spoke in deference to our Spanish-speaking parents in the audience, caring teacher that he was.

11 These were difficult names for a non-Spanish speaker: Araceli, Nadira, Luis (a beautiful name when you glide the u and the i as you're supposed to). We had been accustomed to having our birth names altered for convenience. Concepcion was Connie. Ramon was Raymond. My cousin Esperanza was Hope—but her name was pronounced "Hopie" because any Spanish speaker would automatically pronounce the e at the end.

12 Ours, then, were names that stood as barriers to a complete embrace of an American identity, simply because their pronunciations required a slip into Spanish, the otherness that assimilation was supposed to erase. What to do with names like Amado, Lucio or Elida? There are no English "equivalents," no answer when white teachers asked, "What does your name mean?" when what they really wanted to know was "What's the English one?" So what you heard was a name butchered beyond recognition, a pronunciation that pointed the finger at the Spanish language as the source of clunky sound and ugly rhythm.

My stepfather, from Ojos de Agua, Mexico, jokes when I ask him about the names of Mexicans born here. He deliberately stumbles over pronunciations, imitating our elders who have difficulty with Bradley and Madelyn. "Ashley Sanchez. Tu crees?" He wonders aloud what has happened to the "nombres del rancho"—traditional Mexican names that are hardly given anymore to children born in the States: Heraclio, Madaleno, Otilia, Dominga. 13

My stepfather's experience with the Anglicization of his name—Antonio to Tony—ties into something bigger than learning English. For him, the erasure of his name was about deference and subservience. Becoming Tony gave him a measure of access as he struggled to learn English and get more fieldwork. 14

This isn't to say that my stepfather welcomed the change, only that he could not put up much resistance. Not changing put him at risk of being passed over for work. English was a world of power and decisions, of smooth, uninterrupted negotiation. There was no time to search for the right word while a shop clerk waited for him to come up with the English name of the correct part needed out in the field. Clear communication meant you could go unsupervised, or that you were even able to read instructions directly off a piece of paper. Every gesture made toward convincing an employer that English was on its way to being mastered had the potential to make a season of fieldwork profitable. 15

It's curious that many of us growing up in Dinuba adhered to the same rules. Although as children of farm workers we worked in the fields at an early age, we'd also had the opportunity to stay in one town long enough to finish school. Most of us had learned English early and splintered off into a dual existence of English at school, Spanish at home. But instead of recognizing the need for fluency in both languages, we turned it into a peculiar kind of battle. English was for public display. Spanish was for privacy—and privacy quickly turned to shame. 16

The corrosive effect of assimilation is the displacement of one culture over another, the inability to sustain more than one way of being. It isn't a code word for racial and ethnic acculturation only. It applies to needing and wanting to belong, of seeing from the outside and wondering how to get in and then, once inside, realizing there are always those still on the fringe. 17

When I went to college on the East Coast, I was confronted for the first time by people who said my name correctly without prompting; if they stumbled, there was a quick apology and 18 an honest plea to help with the pronunciation. But introducing myself was painful: already shy, I avoided meeting people because I didn't want to say my name, felt burdened by my own history. I knew that my small-town upbringing and its limitations on Spanish would not have been tolerated by any of the students of color who had grown up in large cities, in places where the sheer force of their native languages made them dominant in their neighborhoods.

19 It didn't take long for me to assert the power of code-switching in public, the transferring of words from one language to another, regardless of who might be listening. I was learning that the English language composed new meanings when its constrictions were ignored, crossed over or crossed out. Language is all about manipulation, or not listening to the rules.

20 When I come back to Dinuba, I have a hard time hearing my name said incorrectly, but I have an even harder time beginning a conversation with others about why the pronunciation of our names matters. Leaving a small town requires an embrace of a larger point of view, but a town like Dinuba remains forever embedded in an either/or way of life. My stepfather still answers to Tony and, as the United States-born children grow older, their Anglicized names begin to signify who does and who does not "belong"—who was born here and who is de alla.

21 My name is Manuel. To this day, most people cannot say it correctly, the way it was intended to be said. But I can live with that because I love the alliteration of my full name. It wasn't the name my mother, Esmeralda, was going to give me. At the last minute, my father named me after an uncle I would never meet. My name was to have been Ricardo. Growing up in Dinuba, I'm certain I would have become Ricky or even Richard, and the journey toward the discovery of the English language's extraordinary power in even the most ordinary of circumstances would probably have gone unlearned.

22 I count on a collective sense of cultural loss to once again swing the names back to our native language. The Mexican gate agent announced Eugenio Reyes, but I never got a chance to see who appeared. I pictured an older man, cowboy hat in hand, but I made the assumption on his name alone, the clash of privileges I imagined between someone de alla and a Mexican woman with a good job in the United States. Would she speak to him in Spanish? Or would she raise her voice to him as if he were hard of hearing?

But who was I to imagine this man being from anywhere, based on his name alone? At a place of arrivals and departures, it sank into me that the currency of our names is a stroke of luck: because mine was not an easy name, it forced me to consider how language would rule me if I allowed it. Yet I discovered that only by leaving. My stepfather must live in the Valley, a place that does not allow that choice, every day. And Eugenio Reyes—I do not know if he was coming or going. 23

BUILDING VOCABULARY

1. Use the words in Words to Watch in sentences of your own.
2. Define the following words. Consult a Spanish-English dictionary or ask a friend who knows Spanish if you need help.
   a. de alla (par. 1)
   b. Chicano (par. 1)
   c. Latino (par. 1)
   d. Tu crees (par. 13)
   e. nombres del rancho (par. 13)

THINKING CRITICALLY ABOUT THE ESSAY

Understanding the Writer's Ideas

1. What does the title of Muñoz's essay mean to you?
2. Where does the action take place in Muñoz's essay? Why is this sense of place important, according to Muñoz?
3. Who are the major and minor characters in the essay? How are they related and interrelated?
4. What do we learn about Muñoz? What details stand out?
5. What is Muñoz's key observation about Spanish and English, and about Latino and Anglo culture?
6. In the context of the paragraph and the essay, what does Muñoz mean by "code-switching" (par. 19)?
7. Which paragraph best explains Muñoz's attitude toward assimilation?

Understanding the Writer's Techniques

1. Does Muñoz state his claim or imply it? Justify your response with reference to the text?

2. What is the tone of this essay? Cite at least two passages to support your response to the writer's voice.
3. Explain the importance of narration and description in this essay. Why does Muñoz use these strategies? Are these patterns of development effective in the development of an argument? Why or why not?
4. Where in the essay does Muñoz use causal analysis? What is his purpose here?
5. Why does Muñoz introduce and even list so many names in his essay? What is the overall effect of this strategy?
6. How do the introduction and conclusion function as a framing device for the essay?

✷ MIXING PATTERNS

How does Muñoz use comparison and contrast to organize and develop his essay?

Exploring the Writer's Ideas

1. Muñoz asserts that names define our identity. Names also create problems for us. Why might you agree or disagree with him?
2. The writer states, "Language is all about manipulation, or not listening to the rules" (par. 19). How do you interpret this statement? Can you think of examples that support Muñoz's thinking?
3. Do you sense that Muñoz essentially does not think that Anglos totally accept Latinos in the national culture? Why or why not?

IDEAS FOR WRITING

Prewriting

Freewrite on the following topic: Should everyone in American society be fully assimilated? Why or why not?

Guided Writing

Argue for or against the claim that assimilation can produce—in the words of Manuel Muñoz—"corrosive effects."

1. Make this argument a personal one in which you discuss your own process of assimilation or that of someone you know; or perhaps your experience with a particular group that does or does not acculturate fully.
2. Feel free to mix rhetorical patterns, using narrative, descriptive, analytical, and argumentative strategies.
3. State your claim at the outset.
4. Organize your essay around a series of comparisons and contrasts—for example, people who fully assimilate into the dominant culture and those who don't.
5. Maintain a consistent tone throughout the essay.
6. End your essay by returning to the content of your introductory paragraph.

Thinking and Writing Collaboratively

In small groups, list all the names Muñoz weaves into his essay. Then discuss the relevance of these names to his argument. Finally, have one member of the group present your evaluation to the class.

Writing About the Text

Write an essay exploring the ways in which Muñoz mixes rhetorical patterns in his essay. Evaluate the desirability of mixing patterns in an argumentative essay.

More Writing Projects

1. In your journal, tell about your name—first and last—and how you think people respond to it.
2. Develop your journal entry into an extended paragraph.
3. Write an argumentative essay on the topic of code-switching in public, attempting to convince the reader that this behavior either enriches or degrades American culture.

Mixing Patterns

The Great Wall of America

Richard Rodriguez

Richard Rodriguez, the son of Mexican immigrants, was born in San Francisco in 1944. When he was a young boy, he moved to a white neighborhood in California's capital, Sacramento. His first book, *Hunger of Memory: The Education of Richard Rodriguez* (1982), is based on his childhood experiences. Rodriguez also has written *Days of Obligation: My Argument with My Mexican Father* (1992) and *Brown: The Last Discovery of America* (2002). He has published widely in popular magazines and journals, including *American Scholar, Harper's, Mother Jones,* and *Time*. Rodriguez also appears frequently on National Public Radio and the News Hour. Rodriguez has degrees from Stanford and Columbia universities. In this essay, published in the *Los Angeles Times* in 2010, Rodriguez explores life on both sides of the U.S.-Mexico border—and other borders as well.

PREREADING: THINKING ABOUT THE ESSAY IN ADVANCE

How would you deal with the 2,000-mile U.S.-Mexico border and the thousands of undocumented immigrants who cross it every month? Do borders—all kinds of borders and barriers—actually make you safe? Justify your response.

Words to Watch

cynicism (par. 1) the quality of thinking that human behavior is motivated by self-interest
palisade (par. 3) a high barrier for defense
cul-de-sac (par. 6) a dead end
scrub (par. 7) a stunted tree or bush
ramparts (par. 14) broad walls or mounds raised as fortifications
precedent (par. 15) an earlier occurrence or something similar that could serve as an example or rule
nativism (par. 19) a policy of favoring established citizens over immigrants

1 Between cynicism and hypocrisy lies the 2,000-mile U.S.-Mexico border. America is raising a wall in the desert to separate Mexican drug exporters from American drug consumers, to separate Latin American peasants who will work for low wages from the Americans who would hire them.

The Great Wall of America, straddling less than half the length of the border, descends into canyons and across the desert floor. For the Mexican, it represents a high hurdle. For the American, it is an attempt to stop the Roadrunner's progress with an Acme Border Sealing Kit. 2

In some places the wall is made of tennis-court-style cyclone fencing or dark mesh of the sort used for barbeque grills in public parks. In other places the wall is a palisade of 20-foot-tall bars that make a cage of both sides. The most emphatic segments are constructed of graffiti-ready slabs of steel. 3

On the Mexican side, if you stand with your back to the wall, you will see the poorest neighborhoods, built right up to the line. These frayed, weedy streets have become the killing fields in an international drug war; they are more daunting than the dangers of climbing the wall. 4

The traditional Mexican accommodation to moral failure—the bribed policeman—has degenerated to lawlessness in places such as Juarez and Tijuana, where police kill federal soldiers who kill police who kill drug gangsters who kill other gangsters of the sort who did kill, apparently with impunity, at least 15 teenagers celebrating a soccer victory. Punch 911 and you may get the devil. 5

On the American side, if you stand with your back to the wall, you will see distance, as the United States recedes from the border. There is a shopping mall with big-box stores half a mile away. There is a highway that eventually leads to suburban streets laid out in uniform blocks, and cul-de-sacs where Mexican gardeners are the only ambulatory human life. 6

The suburban grid belies America's disorder. Grandma's knockoff Louis Vuitton handbag is so full of meds it sounds like a snake rattle. Grandma shares a secret addiction with her drug-addled dude of a grandson, whose dad prowls the Home Depot parking lot in his Japanese pickup, looking to hire a couple of Mexicans to clear out some dry scrub. 7

From a distant height, America's wall might seem a wonderful stunt, like Christo and Jeanne-Claude's "Running Fence" of 1976—a 24-mile-long curtain that ran over the Northern California foothills to the sea. Before it was dismantled, "Running Fence" rippled and swelled with breezes off the Pacific. 8

David Tomb, an artist known for his studio portrait paintings, has for several years been hiking the Southwestern borderlands, drawing the birds of the region. Tomb tells me he has noticed 9 how often the American wall interferes with the movement of the many animals that inhabit the desert and canyons—wolves, coyotes, mountain lions, even snakes. His bird subjects are able to fly over the wall, as are butterflies, as are Piper Cub cocaine consignments.

10 In the remotest regions of northern Mexico, the terrain is so treacherous that nature itself forms the wall against America. Desperation moves migrants to attempt ever-more-treacherous terrain to achieve U.S. soil.

11 In recession America 2010, the lament most often heard is that the middle class is losing its grip on the American dream. (We have redefined the American dream as the ability of a succeeding generation to earn more than its preceding generation.)

12 On patriotism-for-profit talk radio and television, the illegal immigrant is, by definition, criminal. She comes to steal the American dream. But in my understanding, the dream belongs to the desperation of the poor and always has. The goddess of liberty in New York harbor still advertises for the tired and the poor, the wretched refuse. I tell you, there is an unlucky man in the Sonoran Desert today who will die for a chance to pluck dead chickens in Georgia or change diapers in a rest home in Nevada.

13 Great empires expand beyond their own borders. Empires in decline build walls.

14 As it stands, the Great Wall of America is a fraction of the length of the Great Wall of China. China's dragon-spined ramparts, once a wonder of isolation, are now a draw for tourists, even while China trespasses its own borders to forge the Chinese century. The dragon flies to Africa and to Latin America. While American soldiers die in Afghanistan, the Chinese venture to Kabul to negotiate mineral rights.

15 The nearer precedent to the American Wall may be Israel's wall in the West Bank. More than 400 miles long, the Israeli "barrier"—in some places a fence, in others a concrete mass nearly twice the height of the Berlin Wall—was constructed, according to Israeli officials, to deter terrorists. After Sept. 11, the fear one heard in America was that agents of violence from the Middle East might easily disguise themselves as Latin American peasants and trespass into our midst.

16 What more obvious reason is there for a wall than protection? Any nation should police those who come and go across its borders. But in the United States, as in Israel, the wall has created a

new anxiety. Once the wall is in place, anxiety about the coming outsider changes to an anxiety about who belongs within.

The question that has lately been debated in the Knesset is bluntly stated: Who is a Jew? In Israel, the answer to the question concerns religion and citizenship. But it entails further practical considerations. Israel has decided to rid itself of 400 children of illegal foreign workers (some of whom built the West Bank wall), children who were born in Israel, speak Hebrew as their mother tongue and know no other country. 17

The question that has lately been taken up by U.S. senators is bluntly stated: Who is an American? Republicans have proposed excising the part of the 14th Amendment that guarantees citizenship to anyone born on U.S. soil. GOP Sen. Lindsey Graham of South Carolina refers to foreign women who come to this country to "drop" their babies. Graham chooses diction that describes inhuman beasts of burden. 18

I cannot guess whether this new nativism—though it overrules nativity—is serious business or merely a play for reelection. The irony remains: The land of the free that the wall was built to protect—the literal "homeland," soil so infused with sacred legend it was deemed by the makers of the Constitution more important than blood in determining citizenship—is threatened from within. And the wall that is supposed to proscribe the beginning of America becomes the place where America ends. 19

BUILDING VOCABULARY

Explain in your own words the meanings of the following phrases. Use clues from the surrounding text to help you understand.

a. high hurdle (par. 2)
b. graffiti-ready (par. 3)
c. killing fields (par. 4)
d. big-box stores (par. 6)
e. suburban grid (par. 7)
f. treacherous terrain (par. 10)
g. bluntly stated (par. 18)
h. sacred legend (par. 19)

THINKING CRITICALLY ABOUT THE ESSAY

Understanding the Writer's Ideas

1. What is the significance of Rodriguez's title?
2. Explain what Rodriguez means when he writes at the start of the essay, "Between cynicism and hypocrisy lies the 2,000-mile U.S. border" (par. 1). Do you think that Rodriguez is cynical in this essay? Why or why not?
3. How does Rodriguez characterize the U.S.-Mexico border?
4. According to Rodriguez, what is life like on the Mexican side of the border? on the U.S. side?
5. What does Rodriguez mean by the statement, "The suburban grid belies America's disorder" (par. 7)?
6. Aside from the wall separating the United States and Mexico, what other walls does Rodriguez mention? How does he characterize them?
7. What, finally, does Rodriguez think about walls, borders, immigration, and the future of the United States?

Understanding the Writer's Techniques

1. What is Rodriguez's argument in this essay, and where does he come closest to stating it?
2. How important is Rodriguez's use of description in this essay? Is it justified? Effective? Cite examples to support your response.
3. Characterize the tone of this essay. Is Rodriguez objective, angry, ironic, sympathetic, or what? Justify your answer by citing specific passages from the text.
4. How does the image of the "great wall" function symbolically? Might there be other symbols in the essay? Explain.
5. Identify and explain the many allusions that appear in the essay. Why, for example, does Rodriguez refer to artists in paragraphs 8–9?
6. Where does Rodriguez introduce rhetorical questions? What is his purpose?
7. In what ways does this essay reflect periodical style and organization?

8. Evaluate Rodriquez's concluding paragraph. How does this end paragraph both capture preceding argumentative elements and introduce a new one?

✷ MIXING PATTERNS

Rodriguez draws on several rhetorical patterns to advance his argument. Where does he use *comparison and contrast, illustration,* and *classification,* and how effective are these strategies?

Exploring the Writer's Ideas

1. Do you agree that "for-profit" talk radio and television promote the idea that the illegal immigrant is "by definition, criminal" (par. 12)? Why or why not?
2. Do you accept Rodriguez's proposition that walls historically have not kept "others" out? Why or why not?
3. What is your reaction to Rodriguez's assertion that we are now in an era of "new nativism" (par. 19)?

IDEAS FOR WRITING

Guided Writing

Write an argumentative essay in which you present your viewpoint on the wall currently being built along the U.S.-Mexican border.

1. Title your essay "The Case for the Wall" or "The Case Against the Wall."
2. State your claim or main proposition early in the essay.
3. Develop at least three minor propositions to reinforce your claim.
4. Provide solid evidence in the form of facts, data, and statistics to support your major and minor propositions.
5. Employ comparison and contrast to organize your argument.
6. Use a consistent tone to guide your overall purpose.
7. Conclude your essay with an evaluation of current Hispanic immigration and the future of the American dream.

Thinking and Writing Collaboratively

In groups of four or five, try to refute Rodriguez's claims about immigration, walls, the American dream, nativism, and any other issues that you consider important in the text. Jot down these ideas and present them to the class.

Writing about the Text

Write an essay evaluating Rodriguez's use of imagery, symbolism, and irony to develop his argument.

More Writing Projects

1. In your journal, freewrite for ten minutes about this topic: Hispanic immigration. When you finish, exchange your journal entry with another student. How do your responses compare? contrast?
2. Do you think that fences and walls make good neighbors? Write a paragraph in which you state and defend your response to this question.
3. Write an argumentative essay in the form of a letter to a local newspaper in which you take a position on Rodriguez's claim, "Empires in decline build walls" (par. 13).

The Harmful Myth of Asian Superiority

Ronald Takaki

Mixing Patterns

Ronald Takaki, whose grandparents were Japanese plantation workers in Hawaii, is Professor of Ethnic Studies at the University of California, Berkeley. He received his PhD from Berkeley in 1967 and has since published widely in the area of ethnic studies. His works include *Pau Hana: Plantation Life and Labor in Hawaii* (1983) and *Strangers from a Different Shore: A History of Asian Americans* (1989). His most recent publication is *Debating Diversity: Clashing Perspectives on Race and Ethnicity in America* (2002). In this selection, written in 1990, Takaki argues that stereotyping Asian Americans as uniformly successful not only belies the facts but also is a veiled form of racist attack on other American ethnic groups, in particular African Americans.

PREREADING: THINKING ABOUT THE ESSAY IN ADVANCE

How are we to gauge whether the American dream is truly available to all Americans? Is race a factor? How do you account for the success of some recent immigrants in the face of the poverty of many who have lived in the United States for generations? Is the success of some immigrants used unfairly to bolster racial stereotyping, for example, by appealing to the argument: if they can do it, why can't you?

Words to Watch

ubiquity (par. 2) presence everywhere
pundits (par. 3) authoritative opinion-shapers
superfluous (par. 3) unnecessary
acquiring (par. 5) obtaining
median (par. 12) a number or value in a set (say, the set of all incomes) such that there are an equal number of greater and lesser numbers or values
paragons (par. 12) models of excellence
exacerbates (par. 15) worsens

1 Asian Americans have increasingly come to be viewed as a "model minority." But are they as successful as claimed? And for whom are they supposed to be a model?

2 Asian Americans have been described in the media as "excessively, even provocatively" successful in gaining admission to universities. Asian American shopkeepers have been congratulated, as well as criticized, for their ubiquity and entrepreneurial effectiveness.

3 If Asian Americans can make it, many politicians and pundits ask, why can't African Americans? Such comparisons pit minorities against each other and generate African American resentment toward Asian Americans. The victims are blamed for their plight, rather than racism and an economy that has made many young African American workers superfluous.

4 The celebration of Asian Americans has obscured reality. For example, figures on the high earnings of Asian Americans relative to Caucasians are misleading. Most Asian Americans live in California, Hawaii, and New York—states with higher incomes and higher costs of living than the national average.

5 Even Japanese Americans, often touted for their upward mobility, have not reached equality. While Japanese American men in California earned an average income comparable to Caucasian men in 1980, they did so only by acquiring more education and working more hours.

6 Comparing family incomes is even more deceptive. Some Asian American groups do have higher family incomes than Caucasians. But they have more workers per family.

7 The "model minority" image homogenizes Asian Americans and hides their differences. For example, while thousands of Vietnamese American young people attend universities, others are on the streets. They live in motels and hang out in pool halls in places like East Los Angeles; some join gangs.

8 Twenty-five percent of the people in New York City's Chinatown lived below the poverty level in 1980, compared with 17 percent of the city's population. Some 60 percent of the workers in the Chinatowns of Los Angeles and San Francisco are crowded into low-paying jobs in garment factories and restaurants.

9 "Most immigrants coming into Chinatown with a language barrier cannot go outside this confined area into the mainstream of American industry," a Chinese immigrant said. "Before, I was a painter in Hong Kong, but I can't do it here. I got no license, no education. I want a living; so it's dishwasher, janitor, or cook."

10 Hmong and Mien refugees from Laos have unemployment rates that reach as high as 80 percent. A 1987 California study

showed that three out of ten Southeast Asian refugee families had been on welfare for four to ten years.

Although college-educated Asian Americans are entering the professions and earning good salaries, many hit the "glass ceiling"—the barrier through which high management positions can be seen but not reached. In 1988, only 8 percent of Asian Americans were "officials" and "managers," compared with 12 percent for all groups. 11

Finally, the triumph of Korean immigrants has been exaggerated. In 1988, Koreans in the New York metropolitan area earned only 68 percent of the median income of non-Asians. More than three-quarters of Korean greengrocers, those so-called paragons of bootstrap entrepreneurialism, came to America with a college education. Engineers, teachers, or administrators while in Korea, they became shopkeepers after their arrival. For many of them, the greengrocery represents dashed dreams, a step downward in status. 12

For all their hard work and long hours, most Korean shopkeepers do not actually earn very much: $17,000 to $35,000 a year, usually representing the income from the labor of an entire family. 13

But most Korean immigrants do not become shopkeepers. Instead, many find themselves trapped as clerks in grocery stores, service workers in restaurants, seamstresses in garment factories, and janitors in hotels. 14

Most Asian Americans know their "success" is largely a myth. They also see how the celebration of Asian Americans as a "model minority" perpetuates their inequality and exacerbates relations between them and African Americans. 15

BUILDING VOCABULARY

This selection draws on concepts from economics and sociology. Define the terms below:

a. cost(s) of living (par. 4)
b. the national average (par. 4)
c. the poverty level (par. 8)
d. unemployment rates (par. 10)
e. welfare (par. 10)

THINKING CRITICALLY ABOUT THE ESSAY

Understanding the Writer's Ideas

1. Why have Asian Americans been viewed as a "model minority"?
2. What's wrong with such a categorization, according to Takaki?
3. How has the "celebration of Asian Americans . . . obscured reality" (par. 4)?
4. How does the "model minority" image homogenize Asian Americans?
5. What is the consequence of the language barrier faced by Chinese immigrants?
6. How has the "triumph" of Korean immigrants been "exaggerated" (par. 12)?

Understanding the Writer's Techniques

1. What is the writer's thesis statement?
2. The writer begins by stating the view he is going to oppose, and asks two questions to probe the opposing view. How does he answer these two questions? What evidence does he use in each case?
3. Categorize the examples the writer uses to show that the "celebration of Asian Americans has obscured reality" (par. 4).
4. Much of Takaki's supporting evidence is in the form of examples. How does he develop his essay and maintain coherence?
5. What do you think is the writer's strongest piece of evidence for his point of view? What is the weakest? What is his strongest argument? His weakest?
6. Takaki saves the word *myth* for last. Does that decision strengthen his use of the word to sum up his essay? Is the conclusion effective?

✷ MIXING PATTERNS

How does the writer solve the problem of definition that his essay involves, that is, the definition of "Asian American"? How do comparison and contrast and classification operate as strategies in Takaki's essay?

Exploring the Writer's Ideas

1. Is the writer's reliance on example excessive? Are some of his examples more persuasive than others? Are some of his examples liable to other interpretations? Is it a problem for his argument that he does *not* give certain examples, such as the statistics on Asian American admissions to universities? What other strategies might the writer have considered as alternatives to the one he chose? Explain your answers.
2. African Americans often identify themselves as a coherent group. Why is it appropriate (or inappropriate) to do the same with Asian Americans?
3. Takaki cites examples and statistics about Asian Americans that seem, unintentionally, to be very positive. He says, for example, that Asian Americans work long hours, cooperate as families, have entered the professions, and have higher family incomes than whites. Are these examples a contradiction of his thesis? Why or why not?

IDEAS FOR WRITING

Prewriting

Is it fair to make any generalizations about "groups," or do groups simply consist of individuals who should be judged on their own merits? Write down ideas about the two sides of this question.

Guided Writing

Write an essay titled "The Harmful Myth of ______." Make your myth a positive perception that nonetheless can have negative repercussions for those inside or outside the group. For example, the myth that all Ivy League students are brainy might be a positive perception that leads people to undervalue the academic achievements of other students or, say, the athletic achievements of Ivy League students.

1. Begin by stating the myth. Raise two questions that expose the myth as distorting the reality.
2. Indicate kinds of negative repercussions the myth can have.
3. Use four examples to demonstrate that the reality is more complex than the myth allows. In discussing these examples, and elsewhere in your essay, draw on strategies of definition,

comparison and contrast, and classification—as needed—to advance your thesis.

4. End by restating how the myth obscures the reality and can be used negatively.

Thinking and Writing Collaboratively

Debate the question of whether a focus on ethnic or racial identification is a positive or negative phenomenon in the context of our multiethnic society. One half of the class should prepare the case that such a focus is harmful because, for example, it obscures differences within the group and discourages the appreciation of individuals as individuals. The other half should make the case that such a focus is beneficial because, for example, solidarity within a group can promote the economic and political progress of the individuals within the group.

Writing About the Text

Write an essay that explores the question of success as Takaki sees it. What is "success"? What are the main factors that make a person successful in America today? How important is the individual's race or ethnicity in success? How does race or ethnicity play a role?

More Writing Projects

1. Many essays in *The Short Prose Reader* are by members of minority ethnic or racial groups. How do these essays influence your reading of Takaki? How does your reading of Takaki affect your appreciation for these other essays? Write journal entries that answer these questions.
2. Write a one-paragraph portrait of a city street, either your own street or one you have visited recently. Choose one with a clear ethnic identity. What ethnic groups are represented? What effect has each group had on the life of this street?
3. Interview Asian American immigrants in your community, town, or city about their notion of the American Dream. Did they have an idea of the American Dream before they arrived in the United States? What do they think of the American Dream now? Has being part of the American Dream changed their identity? Write an essay based on the interviews.

PERSPECTIVES ON RIGHTS AND RESPONSIBILITIES: ARE WE TRULY FREE?

Issues of political rights arise from conflicting conceptions of freedom, government, progress, and human welfare. Men and women over the centuries have argued passionately about politics. Is freedom the freedom to be left to my own devices—and thus, freedom from government interference in my life (individual rights)? Or is freedom being treated fairly and equally—and thus, freedom sustained by government so I can run my life as I please (civil rights)? What is the appropriate balance between the individual and the state? In the United States these issues often arise in the context of the law, specifically the Bill of Rights and in the Constitution in general. In the selections that follow, look carefully at the arguments and how they draw on American law and American tradition even as they attempt to change that tradition or to apply it to unprecedented situations. Broadly speaking, these essays use irony, reason, and rhetorical insights to advance their views. Which do you find most persuasive, and why? What can you take from these essays for use in your own essays?

Organizations like the ACLU work to extend and defend civil rights. How does this screenshot from their Web site support this position?

American Civil Liberties Union, Inc. Used with permission.

Get a Knife, Get a Dog, but Get Rid of Guns

Molly Ivins

Born in Monterey, California, in 1944, political columnist Molly Ivins grew up in Houston, Texas. She graduated from Smith College and from the prestigious Columbia University School of Journalism. Ivins's column for the Fort Worth *Star-Telegram* was syndicated in 113 newspapers. Author of the best-selling *Molly Ivins Can't Say That Can She?* (1990), Ivins is known for her brash, amusing writing. Her titles alone are provocative. Consider her 2004 work *Who Let the Dogs In?: Incredible Political Animals I Have Known*. In addition to appearing regularly in major American publications, she wrote about press issues for the American Civil Liberties Union. Ivins died in 2007; that year, her last book, *Bill of Wrongs: The Executive Branch's Assault on America's Fundamental Rights* was published. This selection from her *Nothin' but Good Times Ahead* (1993) attacks "gun nuts" in a spirited, wry, and sometimes angry tone. As a professional writer for popular audiences, Ivins is alert to the need to be both persuasive and entertaining. Keep an eye out for how she manages to achieve these goals.

To learn more about Ivins, click on
More Resources > Chapter 11 > Molly Ivins

PREREADING: THINKING ABOUT THE ESSAY IN ADVANCE

Stop a moment to explore your attitudes toward guns. Can you say *why* you think what you do? Are your opinions based on reliable evidence? Are your opinions well reasoned?

Words to Watch

ricochet (par. 3) bounce off a surface
civil libertarian (par. 4) a person who believes strongly in freedom of speech and action
infringed (par. 5) violated
perforating (par. 6) making holes in
lethal (par. 8) deadly
wreak . . . carnage (par. 8) cause great bloodshed

martial (par. 12) warlike
literally (par. 13) actually
psychosexual (par. 13) having to do with the emotional aspects of sexuality
psyches (par. 14) emotional makeup

1 Guns. Everywhere guns.

2 Let me start this discussion by pointing out that I am not anti-gun. I'm pro-knife. Consider the merits of the knife.

3 In the first place, you have to catch up with someone in order to stab him. A general substitution of knives for guns would promote physical fitness. We'd turn into a whole nation of great runners. Plus, knives don't ricochet. And people are seldom killed while cleaning their knives.

4 As a civil libertarian, I, of course, support the Second Amendment. And I believe it means exactly what it says:

5 *A well-regulated militia being necessary to the security of a free state, the right of the people to keep and bear arms shall not be infringed.* Fourteen-year-old boys are not part of a well-regulated militia. Members of wacky religious cults are not part of a well-regulated militia. Permitting unregulated citizens to have guns is destroying the security of this free state.

6 I am intrigued by the arguments of those who claim to follow the judicial doctrine of original intent. How do they know it was the dearest wish of Thomas Jefferson's heart that teenage drug dealers should cruise the cities of this nation perforating their fellow citizens with assault rifles? Channeling?

7 There is more hooey spread about the Second Amendment. It says quite clearly that guns are for those who form part of a well-regulated militia, that is, the armed forces, including the National Guard. The reasons for keeping them away from everyone else get clearer by the day.

8 The comparison most often used is that of the automobile, another lethal object that is regularly used to wreak great carnage. Obviously, this society is full of people who haven't enough common sense to use an automobile properly. But we haven't outlawed cars yet.

9 We do, however, license them and their owners, restrict their use to presumably sane and sober adults, and keep track of who sells them to whom. At a minimum, we should do the same with guns.

In truth, there is no rational argument for guns in this society. This is no longer a frontier nation in which people hunt their own food. It is a crowded, overwhelmingly urban country in which letting people have access to guns is a continuing disaster. Those who want guns—whether for target shooting, hunting, or potting rattlesnakes (get a hoe)—should be subject to the same restrictions placed on gun owners in England, a nation in which liberty has survived nicely without an armed populace. 10

The argument that "guns don't kill people" is patent nonsense. Anyone who has ever worked in a cop shop knows how many family arguments end in murder because there was a gun in the house. Did the gun kill someone? No. But if there had been no gun, no one would have died. At least not without a good foot race first. Guns do kill. Unlike cars, that is all they do. 11

Michael Crichton makes an interesting argument about technology in his thriller *Jurassic Park*. He points out that power without discipline is making this society into a wreckage. By the time someone who studies the martial arts becomes a master—literally able to kill with bare hands—that person has also undergone years of training and discipline. But any fool can pick up a gun and kill with it. 12

"A well-regulated militia" surely implies both long training and long discipline. That is the least, the very least, that should be required of those who are permitted to have guns, because a gun is literally the power to kill. For years I used to enjoy taunting my gun-nut friends about their psychosexual hang-ups—always in a spirit of good cheer, you understand. But letting the noisy minority in the NRA force us to allow this carnage to continue is just plain insane. 13

I do think gun nuts have a power hang-up. I don't know what is missing in their psyches that they need to feel they have the power to kill. But no sane society would allow this to continue. 14

Ban the damn things. Ban them all. 15

You want protection? Get a dog. 16

BUILDING VOCABULARY

1. Identify the following:
   a. the Second Amendment (par. 4)
   b. the judicial doctrine of original intent (par. 6)

c. Michael Crichton's *Jurassic Park* (par. 12)
d. NRA (par. 13)

2. This is an essay that argues a certain point of view. It therefore wishes to undermine opposing ideas. List five words or phrases in this essay that aim to strengthen the writer's position by making fun of or otherwise undermining the opposition.

THINKING CRITICALLY ABOUT THE ESSAY

Understanding the Writer's Ideas

1. Why does the writer devote her first three paragraphs to the knife?
2. In your own words, state the writer's interpretation of the Second Amendment.
3. What is the point of comparing guns and cars?
4. In the view of the writer, was there ever an argument for the unlimited access to firearms?
5. What is the writer's response to the argument that "guns don't kill people," it is people using guns who do?
6. Why does the writer allude to *Jurassic Park*?

Understanding the Writer's Techniques

1. What is the *tone* (see Glossary) of this essay? How does the tone support the writer's argument?
2. What is the rhetorical effect of beginning the essay by a discussion of knives? How does the first sentence frame this discussion?
3. This essay lists and responds to the main arguments in *favor* of unlimited sale and possession of guns. Identify these positive arguments in the order they are presented.
4. Why does Ivins present the arguments for guns in the order that she does?
5. In addition to responding to arguments by the opposition, the writer puts forward her own arguments against guns. Identify these in the order that she presents them.
6. How does the concluding paragraph reinforce the writer's argument?

Exploring the Writer's Ideas

1. Is the writer too "argumentative"? That is, does she overstep credibility by mocking those who oppose her views? Explain your opinion.
2. Meddling with amendments to the Constitution is a serious matter, for these provisions have governed the nation well for hundreds of years. Does the writer do justice to the gravity of the documents whose meaning she is interpreting? Could she advance her argument in a less provocative way? Explain.
3. Do Ivins's arguments regarding militias persuade you? If so, explain why. If not, explain why not.
4. Write a response to the writer's taunt that progun advocates must have something "missing in their psyches."

IDEAS FOR WRITING

Prewriting

Using the same tone as the writer, write a few sentences in support of guns.

Guided Writing

Write an essay in which you mock a well-established but controversial position, such as the advocacy of unlimited access to pornography on the grounds of free speech or the appropriateness of sex education in elementary schools.

1. Begin the essay with a bold mocking statement that puts those opposed to your view on the defensive. Make sure you can usefully return to the example or tactic of your opening at other points in your essay.
2. State the main argument for the opposition point of view, preferably one referring to its basis in law.
3. Refute this argument by short, dismissive sentences and examples.
4. State two or three other arguments for the opposing point of view, again using short, pointed, and mocking retorts.
5. End your essay by a return, in the form of a pithy summary, to the ploy of your opening paragraph.

Thinking and Writing Collaboratively

Divide the class arbitrarily in two. Assign one group the progun position, and the other the antigun position. Have each group take the writer's main points and amplify or refute them.

Writing About the Text

Ivins states in paragraph 10, "In truth, there is no rational argument for guns in this society." How well has she supported this argument? What examples or details best support it? Has the essay convinced you to accept her argument? Why or why not? Address these questions in an essay that analyzes "Get a Knife, Get a Dog, but Get Rid of Guns."

More Writing Projects

1. Visit a firing range and interview some people there about their views on guns. Write an outline for an essay about your visit.
2. Read the debates that led to the original adoption of the Second Amendment. Write an extended paragraph that reflects on the relevance or irrelevance of the arguments of that time to our own.
3. Write an essay that argues for a favored solution of your own to the problem of violence in our society.

I Have a Dream

Martin Luther King Jr.

Martin Luther King Jr. (1929–1968), American clergyman and Nobel Prize winner, was one of the main leaders of the civil rights movement of the 1960s and a passionate advocate of nonviolent protest. His assassination in 1968 became an international rallying cry in the struggle for racial justice. A native of Atlanta, Georgia, King was educated at Morehouse College and Boston University. In 1957 King helped to found the Southern Christian Leadership Conference, and he soon led a series of protests throughout the South to desegregate the society. In 1963 King organized the now-legendary March on Washington, at the conclusion of which, standing before the Lincoln Memorial, he delivered the "I Have a Dream" speech, printed below, to an audience of more than 200,000 people. Immediately adopted into the canon of great American oratory, King's speech, with its distinctive use of religious language and emotional allusion to American images of freedom, merits careful attention as an example of powerful and historic argument.

To learn more about King, click on **More Resources > Chapter 11 > Martin Luther King Jr.**

PREREADING: THINKING ABOUT THE ESSAY IN ADVANCE

The essay's title is in the present tense: the speaker *has* a dream. How would the essay be different if King's title used the past tense? It's unlikely that you have not heard of Martin Luther King Jr., or of this essay. But it was originally not an essay: it was a speech on a highly public occasion. What expectations does King raise by speaking of a dream rather than, say, a goal, or an ambition, or a purpose?

Words to Watch

symbolic (par. 1) representative
emancipation (par. 1) liberation
proclamation (par. 1) official publication

unalienable (par. 3) incapable of being surrendered or taken away
interposition (par. 16) interference
nullification (par. 16) the impeding by a state of federal law
prodigious (par. 21) vast

1 Five score years ago, a great American, in whose symbolic shadow we stand, signed the Emancipation Proclamation. This momentous decree came as a great beacon light of hope to millions of Negro slaves who had been seared in the flames of withering injustice. It came as a joyous daybreak to end the long night of captivity.

2 But one hundred years later, we must face the tragic fact that the Negro is still not free. One hundred years later, the life of the Negro is still sadly crippled by the manacles of segregation and the chains of discrimination. One hundred years later, the Negro lives on a lonely island of poverty in the midst of a vast ocean of material prosperity. One hundred years later, the Negro is still languishing in the corners of American society and finds himself an exile in his own land. So we have come here today to dramatize an appalling condition.

3 In a sense we have come to our nation's capital to cash a check. When the architects of our republic wrote the magnificent words of the Constitution and the Declaration of Independence, they were signing a promissory note to which every American was to fall heir. This note was a promise that all men would be guaranteed the unalienable rights of life, liberty, and the pursuit of happiness.

4 It is obvious today that America has defaulted on this promissory note insofar as her citizens of color are concerned. Instead of honoring this sacred obligation, America has given the Negro people a bad check; a check which has come back marked "insufficient funds." But we refuse to believe that the bank of justice is bankrupt. We refuse to believe that there are insufficient funds in the great vaults of opportunity of this nation. So we have come to cash this check—a check that will give us upon demand the riches of freedom and the security of justice. We have also come to this hallowed spot to remind America of the fierce urgency of *now*. This is no time to engage in the luxury of cooling off or to take the tranquilizing drugs of gradualism. *Now* is the time to make real the promises of Democracy. *Now* is the time to rise from the dark and desolate valley of segregation to the sunlit path of racial justice. *Now* is the time to open the doors of opportunity to all of God's

children. *Now* is the time to lift our nation from the quicksands of racial injustice to the solid rock of brotherhood.

It would be fatal for the nation to overlook the urgency of the moment and to underestimate the determination of the Negro. This sweltering summer of the Negro's legitimate discontent will not pass until there is an invigorating autumn of freedom and equality. 1963 is not an end, but a beginning. Those who hope that the Negro needed to blow off steam and will now be content will have a rude awakening if the nation returns to business as usual. There will be neither rest nor tranquility in America until the Negro is granted his citizenship rights. The whirlwinds of revolt will continue to shake the foundations of our nation until the bright day of justice emerges. 5

But there is something that I must say to my people who stand on the warm threshold which leads into the palace of justice. In the process of gaining our rightful place we must not be guilty of wrongful deeds. Let us not seek to satisfy our thirst for freedom by drinking from the cup of bitterness and hatred. We must forever conduct our struggle on the high plane of dignity and discipline. We must not allow our creative protest to degenerate into physical violence. Again and again we must rise to the majestic heights of meeting physical force with soul force. The marvelous new militancy which has engulfed the Negro community must not lead us to a distrust of all white people, for many of our white brothers, as evidenced by their presence here today, have come to realize that their destiny is tied up with our destiny and their freedom is inextricably bound to our freedom. We cannot walk alone. 6

And as we walk, we must make the pledge that we shall march ahead. We cannot turn back. There are those who are asking the devotees of civil rights, "When will you be satisfied?" We can never be satisfied as long as the Negro is the victim of the unspeakable horrors of police brutality. We can never be satisfied as long as our bodies, heavy with the fatigue of travel, cannot gain lodging in the motels of the highways and the hotels of the cities. We cannot be satisfied as long as the Negro's basic mobility is from a smaller ghetto to a larger one. We can never be satisfied as long as a Negro in Mississippi cannot vote and a Negro in New York believes he has nothing for which to vote. No, no, we are not satisfied, and will not be satisfied until justice rolls down like waters and righteousness like a mighty stream. 7

I am not unmindful that some of you have come here out of great trials and tribulations. Some of you have come fresh from 8 narrow jail cells. Some of you have come from areas where your quest for freedom left you battered by the storms of persecution and staggered by the winds of police brutality. You have been the veterans of creative suffering. Continue to work with the faith that unearned suffering is redemptive.

9 Go back to Mississippi, go back to Alabama, go back to South Carolina, go back to Georgia, go back to Louisiana, go back to the slums and ghettos of our northern cities, knowing that somehow this situation can and will be changed. Let us not wallow in the valley of despair.

10 I say to you today, my friends, that in spite of the difficulties and frustrations of the moment I still have a dream. It is a dream deeply rooted in the American dream.

11 I have a dream that one day this nation will rise up and live out the true meaning of its creed: "We hold these truths to be self-evident; that all men are created equal."

12 I have a dream that one day on the red hills of Georgia the sons of former slaves and the sons of former slaveowners will be able to sit down together at the table of brotherhood.

13 I have a dream that one day even the state of Mississippi, a desert state sweltering with the heat of injustice and oppression, will be transformed into an oasis of freedom and justice.

14 I have a dream that my four little children will one day live in a nation where they will not be judged by the color of their skin but by the content of their character.

15 I have a dream today.

16 I have a dream that one day the state of Alabama, whose governor's lips are presently dripping with the words of interposition and nullification, will be transformed into a situation where little black boys and black girls will be able to join hands with little white boys and white girls and walk together as sisters and brothers.

17 I have a dream today.

18 I have a dream that one day every valley shall be exalted, every hill and mountain shall be made low, the rough places will be made plain, and the crooked places will be made straight, and the glory of the Lord shall be revealed, and all flesh shall see it together.

19 This is our hope. This is the faith with which I return to the South. With this faith we will be able to hew out of the mountain of despair a stone of hope. With this faith we will be able to transform the jangling discords of our nation into a beautiful symphony

of brotherhood. With this faith we will be able to work together, to pray together, to struggle together, to go to jail together, to stand up for freedom together, knowing that we will be free one day.

This will be the day when all of God's children will be able to sing with new meaning 20

My country, 'tis of thee,
Sweet land of liberty,
Of thee I sing:
Land where my fathers died,
Land of the pilgrims' pride,
From every mountain-side
Let freedom ring.

And if America is to be a great nation this must become true. So let freedom ring from the prodigious hilltops of New Hampshire. Let freedom ring from the mighty mountains of New York. Let freedom ring from the heightening Alleghenies of Pennsylvania! 21

Let freedom ring from the snowcapped Rockies of Colorado! 22

Let freedom ring from the curvaceous peaks of California! 23

But not only that; let freedom ring from Stone Mountain of Georgia! 24

Let freedom ring from Lookout Mountain of Tennessee! 25

Let freedom ring from every hill and molehill of Mississippi. From every mountainside, let freedom ring. 26

When we let freedom ring, when we let it ring from every village and every hamlet, from every state and every city, we will be able to speed up that day when all of God's children, black men and white men, Jews and Gentiles, Protestants and Catholics, will be able to join hands and sing in the words of the old Negro spiritual, "Free at last! free at last! thank God almighty, we are free at last!" 27

BUILDING VOCABULARY

King's speech is highly metaphorical. Rewrite the words in italics below in simple declarative language:

a. "slaves who had been *seared in the flames of withering* injustice" (par. 1).

b. "the Negro *lives on a lonely island of poverty in the midst of a vast ocean of material prosperity*" (par. 2).

c. "We refuse to believe that *there are insufficient funds in the great vaults of opportunity* of this nation" (par. 4).
d. *"from the quicksands of racial injustice to the solid rock of brotherhood"* (par. 4).

THINKING CRITICALLY ABOUT THE ESSAY

Understanding the Writer's Ideas

1. Who is the "great American" King speaks about in the first sentence of his essay?
2. What is the "appalling condition" that King says he and his followers have come to Washington to dramatize?
3. What does King mean when he says "we have come to our nation's capital to cash a check" (par. 3)?
4. Why does King emphasize the word *now* in par. 4?
5. What does King advise as proper for his followers as they stand "on the warm threshold" of justice?
6. How does King respond to the charge that his demands are insatiable?
7. Summarize in one sentence the point King makes in paragraphs 10–18.
8. How does King connect his faith and hope with the tradition of American patriotism?
9. Why does King end his speech with a passage from a Negro spiritual?

Understanding the Writer's Techniques

1. What aspects of King's address illustrate that it is a speech and not an essay? What is the purpose of King's speech?
2. King casts the purpose of the March on Washington in surprisingly monetary terms. The Constitution and Declaration of Independence were, he says, a "promissory note" on which America has "defaulted." But King has come to Washington "to cash this check." In what ways is this extended metaphor appropriate to advance King's cause? Or do you think it is too much to do with money and demeans his cause?
3. King, a preacher, makes abundant use of biblical allusion and biblical language to make his points. In paragraph 2, for

example, King speaks of the Negro as being an "exile in his own land." How does this analogy appeal to Judeo-Christian tradition? What other examples of biblical allusion or biblical language do you find especially effective?

4. What is King's thesis? Where does he state it?
5. To whom do you think King addressed this speech? Support your answer by quoting pertinent passages.
6. How does King, as an orator, seek to move his audience? Why, for example, does he open his speech with the words "Five score" instead of "One hundred"?
7. Why does King include the opening of "My Country, 'Tis of Thee"? Why does he refer to so many different places in his final paragraphs? What is especially significant in his choice of Mississippi for his final geographical reference?
8. What argumentative strategies does King use? Which do you find most effective?
9. How does repetition affect the essay? Cite some examples and explain why you think King used repetition as he did.
10. How do the final words of the speech form an especially effective conclusion?

Exploring the Writer's Ideas

1. In the opening paragraphs of his speech, King uses metaphors related to money and payment in explaining the reason for his speech. Later in the speech, however, he calls upon a whole new set of references as he talks about his dream, a dream that doesn't seem to have much to do with money at all. Explain why you think that these two parts of his speech do or do not fit well together.
2. Do you think that King would today advocate the kind of nonviolent protest, known as "passive resistance," that he advocated in 1963 (par. 6)? Do you think that passive resistance would succeed in obtaining justice for people struggling for their rights today, within the United States or outside of it? Explain your answers.
3. Few ideas in American life are more powerful than the idea that "all men are created equal" (par. 11). But how does King intend us to understand that phrase? Does he mean that all people are entitled to the same things? Why does he not mention women? And can we achieve this entitlement? Does King

mean that we are all equal in the eyes of God? If so, what does that imply for political equality? economic equality? Should the government of the United States ensure that all people in the nation enjoy economic equality? Explain your thinking.

4. Do you find King's intensely religious way of speaking, with its echoes of biblical language and its heavy use of biblical metaphors, a strength or a weakness of his speech? Explain your answer.

IDEAS FOR WRITING

Prewriting

How should our democracy settle social or political grievances? Jot down some ideas about how you would go about changing some common practice or law that many people find oppressive—say, the laws that establish the age at which young people can drink; or the laws about marriage between people of the same sex; or . . . .

Guided Writing

Write a speech intended to stir your classmates to conduct a sit-in or other protest at the college administration building, the mayor's or governor's offices, or a similar location to call attention to an injustice that you think affects many people.

1. Begin by making an allusion to a famous American or famous alumnus or alumna, with the purpose of showing that this person acted to correct an injustice.
2. Then note that many years have passed and yet today injustices remain.
3. In metaphorical language, indicate the injustice that you want to rouse your audience to oppose.
4. Say that the moral high ground demands action—but action that avoids violence.
5. Emphasize King's notion that "unearned suffering is redemptive" (par. 8).
6. In your concluding paragraph or paragraphs, paint a picture of what you dream will come to pass.
7. Conclude the essay with an emotional sentence or phrase from a hymn or spiritual or popular patriotic or protest song.

Thinking and Writing Collaboratively

Almost half a century has passed since King delivered this famous speech. In small groups discuss whether his dream has been realized. Jot down the evidence for and against the view. Compare the conclusion arrived at by your group with the conclusions of the other groups in the class.

Writing About the Text

Argument depends mainly on reason. But clearly King does not mainly rely on reason. He often appeals directly to emotion. Is there then an inherent conflict between the fairly cool and objective standards of argument and the inevitably emotional methods of persuasion? Write an essay that considers whether in King's speech, his rational arguments support or undermine his more emotional writing, his methods of persuasion; and whether, on the other hand, the emotional passages of the essay tend to support or undermine the passages that rely more on reason.

More Writing Projects

1. Will social inequality always exist, or can we eliminate it? In your journal, record your responses to this question.
2. Write a paragraph about King's conception of justice based on what you can reasonably conclude from the references and metaphors of his speech.
3. On the basis of some research, write an essay in which you describe the picture of America in 1963 that emerges from King's speech, and do research to determine whether that picture was or was not accurate.

Mixing Patterns

Baby Battle

Susan Cheever

Susan Cheever was born July 31, 1943, in New York City. She is the daughter of John Cheever, the Pulitzer Prize–winning short story writer and novelist. Cheever graduated from Brown University and was a Guggenheim Fellow. She teaches in the Bennington College MFA program and at the New School. Her books include *My Name is Bill—Bill Wilson: His Life and the Creation of Alcoholics Anonymous* (2004); *Home Before Dark* (1999), a memoir about her father; *American Bloomsbury: Louisa May Alcott, Ralph Waldo Emerson, Margaret Fuller, Nathaniel Hawthorne, and Henry David Thoreau: Their Lives, Their Loves, Their Work* (2006); and five novels, including *Looking for Work* (1981) and *Doctors and Women* (1987). Her most recent book is *Louisa May Alcott: A Personal Biography* (2001), about the author of the enduring classic *Little Women*. In this selection Cheever explores the phenomena of what she calls Stay-at-Home Mothers as opposed to Working Mothers and Women Without Children.

PREREADING: THINKING ABOUT THE ESSAY IN ADVANCE

Before you read, consider the title of this essay, "Baby Battle." What does the title make you think of? What do you think the essay will be about based on the title?

Words to Watch

entitlement (par. 4) right or privilege
slalom (par. 10) zigzag
encumbered (par. 13) burdened; hindered
progeny (par. 14) children; offspring
fatuous (par. 18) silly; pointless
Lamaze (par. 18) an instructional program in birthing for mothers and fathers expecting a child
burgeoning (par. 18) growing; rapidly increasing
hapless (par. 23) unfortunate; unlucky
effusively (par. 27) overly enthusiastic and expressive in emotions
caul (par. 29) membrane, usually the membrane surrounding the amniotic fluid that protects the child in the womb
patriarchal (par. 31) characteristic of rule by men

1 There is a war going on in the streets of New York City.

2 Platoons of mothers in bicycle shoes and designer sweats wheel divisions of gleaming, clanking strollers down the sidewalks, chattering into their cell phones and blocking the passage of other pedestrians. These are the Stay-at-Home Mothers.

3 Their adversaries, the Working Mothers and the Women Without Children, straighten their sleek success suits and try to stay out of the way.

4 "It's not just the strollers," said a Working Mother friend recently as we barely escaped being mowed down by a squadron of juice-cup-wielding Stay-at-Home Mothers. "It's the stroller *entitlement*."

5 The Stay-at-Homes hang together as if they are from a different planet than the mothers who chose to go on working, or the mothers who *have* to go on working. They regroup in the playgrounds, brushing the crumbs off their strollers, Björns, and tricycles. If a toddler under a nanny's care has an accident or a tantrum, the Stay-at-Homes cluck and shake their heads knowingly. *That child needs a mother.*

6 Women without children are whipsawed by hostility from both camps. The Working Moms look down on the Stay-at-Home Moms: *What on earth do they do all day? How can they be so dependent?* The Stay-at-Home Moms feel sorry for the Working Moms: *Do they know what they're missing?*

7 Why are children such a divisive force between women?

8 What happened to the good old days when women used to fight with men?

9 Last week, a mother and her toddler were in my local supermarket in the evening, at a time when few children are there. The toddler was mounted on a tricycle with a metal handle protruding about three feet at a forty-five-degree angle from the seat. The purpose of the handle—parental control—had apparently been forgotten. As the toddler sped down the aisles, the handle brought down a paper-towel display and threatened the eggs. "Gabby! *Gabby!* GAB-RI-ELLE!!" the mother's voice escalated as she looked the other way and manically loaded her cart with an assortment of Lunchables, Dunkaroos, and other junk foods manufactured to temporarily pacify and ultimately enrage our country's children.

10 As little Gabby approached my shopping cart, she began to slalom, sending the handle zooming from side to side and

knocking loaves of freshly baked bread into the aisle. Clouds of choking flour rose around us as I dodged flying baguettes. I was about to grab little Gabby and summon her irresponsible mother.

11 *Flashback.*

12 Only a few years ago, I *was* that mother.

13 Before that, as a single woman twenty-five years ago, I fiercely protected my single rights. I had a great job and I did what I pleased. I was thrilled not to be encumbered by a family. When the people in the apartment next door bought a piano for their little girl, and her endless practices bothered me, *I hired a lawyer to limit her practice time.* Why should families have more rights than single people? I chose to be single. They chose to have children. Therefore I was as entitled to my silence and freedom as they were entitled to their family.

14 I looked down on women with children as fools, dupes who had fallen for a myth created for the purpose of their own oppression. Women with children were trapped, dependent on their husbands for money and for whatever else they still had the brains to need. Just the presence of a child seemed to reduce intelligent women to blithering idiots. Once at the gynecologist's office I watched as a group of chic, smart, professional women kicked off their Chanel sling-backs, left their briefcases unattended, and crawled around on the filthy floor making goo-goo faces at someone's sluglike progeny.

15 "Ohhh, she's so adooorable," cooed a real estate tycoon.

16 "And look at that face!" squawked a Citibank vice president.

17 I was appalled. Even if I ever had a child—and for most of my twenties and thirties it was the last thing I imagined doing—I would never, ever, behave like that.

18 Marriage and pregnancy at the age of thirty-eight didn't change me. I was amazed at the fatuous way people spoke about childbirth in my Lamaze class. "I want to share Cathy's pain," one of the husbands intoned. The leader nodded approvingly while I burst out laughing. Even my husband smiled. We flunked Lamaze. When strangers cooed at me and reached out for my burgeoning stomach, I wanted to bite them.

19 "Oh, it's such a celebration," gushed one friend with a new baby, a woman who had formerly been a brilliant journalist. She and I had once spent two hours searching for the perfect lip gloss—a pale pink called *Prrr.* She used to be *fun.* Now she appeared to

be drooling. As I watched her change her baby, exclaiming over its small green excrement, I took a vow. I would have the baby—there was no way to avoid that now—but I would never lose my mind. I planned for full-time help. I signed a contract for a new book. I rented an office.

Then I had my baby, my Sarah. 20

The moment I held her in my arms, I became a different person. You could say that I joined the human race. For the first time in my life, my connection with someone else sliced through the web of defenses, fear, and pride that had separated me from the world. I had been married twice, but holding Sarah was my first experience of love. My heart seemed to melt. My mind no longer interested me. This tiny baby became the center of my world. I crossed over. 21

As soon as I got home from the hospital I went out and bought the biggest, most expensive stroller I could find. I wanted my precious girl to be safe. With her tucked into the stroller, I resented anyone else on the sidewalk. Everything seemed like a threat to the only being I had ever loved. I took Sarah everywhere with me, even in places where she wasn't allowed. To me it seemed criminal that my baby wasn't supposed to be with me at all times. Why should she have to be alone with a strange babysitter instead of at the movies with me? I took her to expensive restaurants and delighted when she threw the foie gras on the floor and smeared her adorable face with *quenelles de brocket*. Other diners frowned at us; I ignored them. 22

On airplanes, where baby Sarah was particularly fussy, I demanded extra help from the staff and often threw enough of a tantrum to get an extra seat—no one wanted to be close to us anyway, not even my husband. I personally took the time to explain to hapless complainers that my child was a *child,* and that people who were not enchanted by the noise of children were uptight, intolerant puritans who had probably never had an orgasm. *Weren't you ever a child yourself?* I would hiss. If someone suggested that I might think about controlling my daughter, I would lean over them menacingly. *So you think I'm a bad mother?* These confrontations never ended well. 23

As a mother I felt like the keeper of the flame, a woman who had been entrusted with something infinitely sacred. I had done nothing to earn the gift of this child. Watching her sleep I sometimes felt enveloped in a golden cloud of unconditional grace. 24

I kept on working—I had signed the book contract—but I slowed way down, and my old Armani success suits are still gathering dust in the back of the closet. Suddenly, I looked with pity on people who had never had children. How sad. They had never loved. They didn't know what they were missing.

25 My baby daughter is twenty-two now, and although she remains at the center of my life she has also developed a life of her own. My beloved son is fourteen. I've had decades of being a mother first and a writer second. I kept on working when my children were born, partly because I didn't have the luxury of having to decide whether to be a stay-at-home or a working mother. I took a professional hit and lost a lot of the sharpness and brashness that were my trademarks. I spent hours on the floor oohing and aahing over tiny hands and feet. I wrote and edited among the blocks and plastic castles in the pediatrician's waiting room and missed deadlines to attend parents' meetings. My lip gloss was whatever I could find at the bottom of a bag filled with lunch passes, old homework papers, and half-empty juice boxes.

26 Lately though, as my children become adults, I am noticing a change. I have become dependent on getting eight hours of sleep a night. I get regular haircuts and spend more money than I should on clothes. For the first time in a long time I'm annoyed by children like little Gabby and the way their mothers defend them. I'm crossing back over. I can almost feel it. I'm changing sides again.

27 Why does having children, while bringing out our most loving, effusively maternal selves, simultaneously ignite our fears and turn us against one another? After all, women with children—whether they work or stay at home—might get together to make this world a better place for all women with children.

28 What's all this anger really about?

29 For one thing, we're too sleep-deprived to be tolerant or temperate. I remember the caul of exhaustion I lived in as the mother of young children. In those days the most erotic thing a man could say to me was "Why don't you just go back to sleep." My idea of lingerie was earplugs and a sleep mask—neither of which blocked out my children clamoring for my attention.

30 Women do the lion's share—perhaps it should be called the woman's share—of the child care and household work in this country. A recent National Labor Bureau study shows that

women who work still spend twice as much time as men on child care and housework. We live with the results of half a revolution: Women have earned the right to work as hard as men do, but men did not take over half the work at home. Every woman knows her pediatrician's telephone number; I have yet to meet a man who does.

31 What worsens our predicament is that women lack core representation in our government. Photographs of the Senate still look like "Class of 1970" men's college-reunion photos. One of the great mysteries of modern politics is that women, who comprise more than half the population, still comprise less than 20 percent of the government. More women vote than men, but we don't vote for one another. Certainly gender is not the defining reason to vote for or against anyone, but if more women voted for women, at least we would be governed by those who have walked in our flip-flops and pushed our strollers and hunched over our changing tables at 4 A.M. Have we been so indoctrinated by a patriarchal society that we secretly think men are more fit to govern? Are we so hardwired by advertising and fairy tales that we assume the best child care always comes from a mother even if she's a resentful nervous wreck?

32 Working and stay-at-home moms today are like the famous psychology experiment in which too many rats are put in a cage with too little food. The rats *have* had enough sleep, nevertheless, they kill one another. The stakes in the baby battle are high—nothing is more precious than our children and being able to provide for them and ourselves. The level of resources is low. There isn't much support for women who work—support like office child care, flexible hours, and reasonable maternity leaves. There isn't much support for women who stay home—like tax breaks, financial protection in case of divorce, subsidized medical care, or even licensed child care. Kennels are more strictly regulated than child-care agencies; veterinarians get paid more than pediatricians; men who can hire better lawyers tend to walk away with more advantageous divorce decrees than their ex-wives who have spent two decades with zeros on their income tax forms.

33 No wonder every woman who has made a different choice seems like an enemy. What if you are right? What if I am wrong? What if in working we are damaging our children by being absent and preoccupied? What if by staying home we are sacrificing our

independence and our ability to financially take care of our children and hurting them in another way?

34 And so we fight.

BUILDING VOCABULARY

Cheever uses a number of words that connote offensive action. Write definitions for each of the words. Then explain why Cheever has chosen this language for her essay. (Look again at the title of the essay as well.)

1. platoons (par. 2)
2. adversaries (par. 3)
3. squadron (par. 4)
4. whipsawed (par. 6)
5. hostility (par. 6)
6. divisive force (par. 7)
7. oppression (par. 14)
8. brashness (par. 25)
9. ignite (par. 27)
10. indoctrinated (par. 31)

THINKING CRITICALLY ABOUT THE ESSAY

Understanding the Writer's Ideas

1. Who are the women in the "war on the streets"? How does Cheever distinguish them from each other?
2. Which women does the writer initially identify as the aggressors? Who are the victims?
3. Who is Gabby? Why does Cheever mention her?
4. How did Cheever feel about families when she was a single woman? when she was married and pregnant? after she had her child?
5. What specific actions for her child did the writer take after her daughter Sarah was born?
6. Now that her children are adults, what changes does Cheever note about her own behavior?
7. How does the writer explain the anger of women who turn against each other?

8. How do men figure into the equation of anger?
9. In what ways does the government represent a roadblock to women?
10. What kind of support does Cheever see as absent in the "opt-out" revolution?

Understanding the Writer's Techniques

1. The first paragraph is just one sentence long. What is your reaction to it? Why has Cheever chosen to write such a brief opening? How does the second paragraph in the essay explain the point she has made in this introductory paragraph? How does the opening paragraph interact with the essay's title? the very last paragraph?
2. Cheever builds to her main argument. In the first part of the essay she argues about the relations among different groups of women. Later, she proposes ways to improve women's predicament. Where in the essay does she state the first part of the argument? the second? What would you say, then, was her major proposition? State it in your own words.
3. Where does Cheever provide evidence for her argument? How do you feel about the details drawn from her own life experiences? What other kinds of supporting detail does she offer?
4. Like other writers throughout this book, Cheever uses questions as strategies for engaging readers' attention. But by any measure, the questions here seem quite numerous. In fact, in the next to the last paragraph (par. 33) we read four consecutive questions. What is your reaction to these and other questions throughout the essay? Identify them by checking them off in the margin or by making a list. How does Cheever answer the questions that she raises, if at all? How would you answer them?
5. Whom would you say is Cheever's audience for this piece? How do you know?
6. Cheever uses humor throughout the essay. Which examples of humor do you think best serve her argument?
7. The writer presents several direct quotes uttered by various people. What do the quotes add to the essay—Gabby's mother's statement, for example, or the statement from the Citibank vice president?

8. Cheever says that after the birth of her children, she "took a hit and lost the sharpness and brashness" that were her "trademarks." Would you agree that this essay lacks sharpness and brashness? Why or why not? Support your opinion with direct references to the text.

✷ MIXING PATTERNS

Cheever draws on several rhetorical patterns to build her argument. Where and how does she use classification? narrative? comparison and contrast? Do you find her cause-and-effect reasoning valid? What is your reaction to these various modes in a single essay?

Exploring the Writer's Ideas

1. In regard to the war that Cheever sees in the streets: is this a war found only in New York City? Why? Where else might you find similar conflict? Is the conflict exclusively an urban phenomenon? Explain your response.
2. Discuss your responses to this question that Cheever raises: "Why should families have more rights than single people?"
3. Cheever argues that "there isn't much support for women who work." Why might you agree or disagree with this statement?

IDEAS FOR WRITING

Prewriting

Make two columns on a sheet of paper, and make a numbered list to indicate under each the value for women of joining the workforce and the value of staying at home to rear their children.

Guided Writing

Write an argumentative essay in which you weigh the options for women after they have children: returning to work or being stay-at-home moms. Be sure to take a position on the matter.

1. Open and close your essay with an attention-getting one-sentence paragraph.

2. Clearly state your major proposition, or claim, at a key point in your essay.
3. Draw on your personal experience or the experience of people you know.
4. Provide relevant data and any other details to support your argument.
5. Use humor to advance your position.
6. Draw on at least two other patterns as you develop your argument—for example, you could choose from narration, comparison and contrast, classification, or cause or effect.
7. Raise questions in your essay and attempt to answer them.
8. Give your essay a provocative title.

Thinking and Writing Collaboratively

Bring to class your draft in response to the Guided Writing activity. In small groups, read each other's essays. What suggestions can you make to help improve your classmates' efforts?

Writing About the Text

Write an essay about the language Cheever uses in this essay. She makes many references to popular culture (the references to designer products, for example) and relies on many colloquial and informal expressions to advance her position. How effective are these strategies? If you could speak with the writer, what would you tell her about your response to her language?

More Writing Projects

1. Write a journal entry about how our society addresses the needs of single people in a world more focused on families.
2. Write a well-developed paragraph on the responsibilities of parents to supervise their children in public settings like restaurants, supermarkets, doctors' offices, and airplanes.
3. Write an essay to address this question from Cheever's essay: "Why are children such a divisive force between women?"

SUMMING UP: CHAPTER 11

1. Write an essay in which you compare and contrast the three essays included in the section Perspectives on Rights and Responsibilities: Are We Truly Free? Which of the writers makes the strongest argument?
2. Invite a local expert to class to speak on a current controversial issue. You might want to think about inviting a scholar from your school, a legislator (local, state, or federal), or a newspaper reporter. Then, write an essay in support of, or in opposition to, the speaker's opinion.
3. Justify the inclusion of the essays by Ivins, Rodriguez, Cheever, and Singel under the category "Argumentation and Persuasion." Treat the major issues they raise, their positions on these issues, their minor propositions, their use of evidence, and their tone. Finally, establish the degree to which you are persuaded by their arguments.
4. Exchange with a classmate an essay that you've each written for one of the Guided Writing exercises in this chapter. Even if you agree with your partner's opinion, write a strongly worded response opposing it. Be sure you touch on the same, or similar, major and minor propositions.
5. Fill in the blanks in the following essay topic as you please, and use it as the major proposition in a well-developed argumentation–persuasion paper. Draw on the expository writing skills you have studied throughout the book. "I am very concerned about ________, and I believe it's necessary to ________."
6. What are the similarities and differences that you detect in the essays by Wideman, Muñoz, and Takaki?
7. Write an essay that seeks to reconcile the views of Richard Rodriguez.
8. The United States was once known as a "melting pot," meaning that the great thing about American life was that everyone could be assimilated into one nation regardless of race, creed, or religion. Today, we talk about diversity instead. Write an essay that explores the implications of this change in attitudes, using the selections in this and other chapters as resources for your argument.
9. Some readers consider John Edgar Wideman and Molly Ivins "liberal" or "progressive" writers. Argue for or against the

proposition that their liberalism prevents them from arguing in a fair or accurate way.

10. Reread the essays by Lemuel, Takaki, and Quindlen, and then select your favorite. Write about why you think your choice is the best essay about identity in this chapter.
11. John Lemuel and Ryan Singel take opposite points of view on the matter of Facebook's role. How do their writing styles compare? In what ways are they similar? In what ways are they different? Write an essay to explore these questions.

✷ FROM SEEING TO WRITING

What is the protestor's argument, and how does he advocate it? Do you support or oppose his decision to engage in civil disobedience? Take your own stand on a specific environmental issue, and state your main proposition. Offer three reasons to support your position, and supply evidence for each. Deal with the opposing viewpoints. In your conclusion, either support or reject the use of civil disobedience as a way of advancing your viewpoint.

Earth First!
EARTH FIRST!

APPENDIX:
A Guide to Research and Documentation

WHAT ARE RESEARCH AND DOCUMENTATION?

A *research* paper grows out of careful investigation of books, periodicals, online resources, and other documents and texts to support a thesis. Research writing can be a form of problem-solving or a careful investigation of a subject. You may identify a problem, form a hypothesis (an unproven thesis, theory, or argument), gather and organize information from various sources, assess and interpret data, evaluate alternatives, reach conclusions, and provide documentation. Other research writing projects may involve the discovery or revision of facts, theories, or applications. In either kind of research paper, your purpose is to demonstrate how other researchers approach a problem and how you treat that problem. A good research paper subtly blends your ideas and the ideas or discoveries of others. In research writing, you become part of a larger academic, social, or cultural conversation. You synthesize ideas that have already been made public—carefully documenting the sources of those ideas—and you contribute your own unique insights and conclusions.

Documentation refers to the rules and conventions by which academic researchers acknowledge the sources on which they base their work. As you research your subject, you will use documentation to note carefully where you find your information so that readers of your work can retrace your sources. Documentation also allows you to give proper credit to the work of other writers. Not providing full and accurate documentation can leave you open to charges of plagiarism.

THE RESEARCH PROCESS

The research process involves thinking, searching, reading, writing, and rewriting. The final product—the research paper—is the result of your discoveries about your topic as well as your contribution to the ongoing academic conversation about your topic. More than any other form of college writing, the research paper evolves gradually through a series of stages. As you develop as a writer and researcher, you will probably adapt this process according to your own strengths and style. As a beginning researcher and writer, however, you may find that a more methodical approach to this process will help you structure your library work as well as your writing.

PHASE I: CHOOSING AND LIMITING A TOPIC

- Browsing
- Limiting the topic

PHASE II: GATHERING AND ORGANIZING DATA

- Developing a working bibliography
- Assessing and evaluating sources
- Taking notes
- Developing a thesis
- Organizing your notes and writing an outline

PHASE III: WRITING THE PAPER

- Drafting
- Incorporating sources
- Revising your draft
- Preparing the final manuscript

PHASE IV: DOCUMENTING SOURCES

PHASE I: CHOOSING AND LIMITING A TOPIC

Although you may receive a very specific research topic from your professor, you are far more likely to meet your first research challenge before you even set foot in the library: what will you write about? One of the great challenges of academic research is learning how to ask the kind of question that will lead to a terrific research topic. You can save time, effort, and anxiety if you approach your research project as a problem to be investigated and solved, a controversy to take a position on, or a specific question to be answered. As a basis for your research, you need at least a hunch or a calculated guess—an idea that will lead to a strong hypothesis or working thesis.

- Before you can formulate a hypothesis, you need to start with a general idea of what subject you want to explore, what your purpose is going to be, and how you plan to select and limit a topic from your larger subject area.

To find and limit that topic, you'll want to begin with some preliminary browsing in the library.

Browsing

When you *browse,* you inspect, informally, Web sites, books and articles in your general area of interest. These points will help you browse in the library as you explore a topic idea:

- *Search engines* online can help you find a broad range of information about your general topic—but that very broadness of information can be overwhelming. Your instructor may be able to recommend useful sites, as can your reference librarian. Search engines such as Google, Firefox, Dogpile, and HotBot hunt through vast numbers of pages at Web sites, seeking those that mention key words that you specify. Browsing through the "hits" you get through such a search engine can give you a spectrum of ideas about your topic. However, you will probably want to check with your instructor about any Web sites you may wish to use as a basis for your research. Print out the first page of the Web site, which will give you the URL (the site's address); you can then ask your instructor to visit the Web site and evaluate its reliability as a source.

- The *library reference section* provides encyclopedias, almanacs, and other reference books for an overview of your area of interest. These resources may be print, online, or on CD-ROM. General reference resources can be useful for background reading and an introduction to your topic. However, these general resources should only be the beginning of your research—do not rely exclusively on these sources, which may not be the most up-to-date or in-depth.
- The *library catalog* lists information by author, title, subject, and key word. It will suggest possible subtopics under the general topic heading and also give you an idea of how many books have been written about your topic. Your library may have both a card catalog and an online catalog; if so, your browsing will be more fruitful if you use both. Ask your reference librarian for guidance on using both the online and card catalogs.
- In your catalog browsing, you will notice that books on your topic most likely share a *call number,* or have call numbers within the same range. Go to that area of your library where books with these call numbers are shelved. Because library classification systems group all books on similar topics near one another, you have many approaches to your topic at your fingertips. Select books that have the most recent copyright dates, which you'll find on the first few pages of the book (ten years is a good boundary). Examine the table of contents, the index, the glossary, and the appendices. Look at the illustrations, if there are any. Read a paragraph or two from the preface or introduction.
- A *periodical index* is an alphabetical listing (usually annual) of authors, titles, and subjects of articles in magazines, journals, or newspapers. Some *databases,* which your library may have on CD-ROM or online, may also provide summaries or complete texts of articles. Indexes are both general (covering major newspapers, journals, and magazines, and a wide range of topics) and very subject-specific. Ask your reference librarian for indexes specific to your subject. Like a library catalog, an index or database shows you at a glance the kinds of subtopics current writers have addressed as parts of larger topics. Reading over the titles of current articles, you can see a variety of approaches to your topic.

For more help with locating sources, click on
Research > Using the Library
Research > Using the Internet
Research > Discipline-Specific Resources

Limiting the Topic

The first step in research writing is to *limit* your research to a *researchable topic*. Such a topic is appropriate in scope for your assignment, promises an adventure for you in the realm of ideas, and interests your audience. Developing a hypothesis, or a question that requires more than a simplistic answer, will lead to a researchable topic. The following chart shows examples of general topics narrowed to researchable topics.

NARROWING THE TOPIC

Too General	*Still Broad*	*Less Broad*	*Narrow Enough*
Teaching	teaching number concepts	teaching number concepts to children	teaching number concepts at home to children under five
Religion	religious customs	ancient religious customs in North America	Anasazi religious customs in America's Midwest
Pollution	fighting air pollution	fighting air pollution in California	the government's role in fighting air pollution in Los Angeles
World War II	effects of WWII	effects of WWII in the United States	economic effects of WWII in Detroit

After your first effort to limit your topic as a result of browsing and of some preliminary thinking, you should expect to limit your topic even further. A further strategy for narrowing your topic is *freewriting*. Try the following freewriting exercise:

1. Why does this topic interest me so strongly?
2. What do I already know about this topic?

3. What three or four questions do I have about this topic, based on my preliminary browsing?
4. What are my opinions about problems related to this topic?

Sharing your freewriting with other students in a discussion group, with your instructor, or with some other friendly reader will give you additional insight into your topic.

PHASE II: GATHERING AND ORGANIZING MATERIAL

Developing a Working Bibliography

The purpose of compiling a working bibliography is to keep an accurate record of all the sources you consulted with all the critical information about them. If you are required to do so, you can prepare a list of works cited (see pages A-19 to A-24) from the data in your working bibliography. Although you may wish to keep your working bibliography as a computer document, you may find it useful to use 4 by 6-inch index cards. Index cards allow you to do the following:

- Arrange the cards easily in alphabetical order as sources are added or deleted (your final bibliography will be alphabetically organized)
- Make quick notes to yourself about your first impressions of the materials to help you decide later whether to return to the source for closer study
- Carry them easily to the library for quick notes, where a computer is not always convenient

Use a standard form for your working bibliography, whether you use cards or computer entries, to simplify the task of preparing your final Works Cited or References section.

INFORMATION FOR A WORKING BIBLIOGRAPHY

Record the following information for a book:

1. Name(s) of author(s)
2. Title of book, underlined
3. Place of publication

(continued)

4. Publisher's name
5. Date of publication
6. Call number or location in library

Record the following information for an article in a periodical:

1. Name(s) of author(s)
2. Title of article, in quotation marks
3. Title of periodical, underlined
4. Volume number or issue number
5. Date of publication
6. Page numbers on which article appears
7. Call number or location in library

For online sources, record all of the above information as well as the complete URL (site address) and date of access online.

Sample working bibliography card: Article

Gladwell, Malcolm. "Examined Life." The New Yorker 17 Dec. 2001: 86–92.

Assessing and Evaluating Sources

At this phase in the research process, you will have amassed a variety of sources and perspectives. Your task now is to revisit those Web sites, articles, books, and other sources—using your working bibliography as a constant guide. Begin by *skimming* your sources. Skimming is not random or casual reading, but a careful examination of the material to sort out the useful sources from those that aren't helpful. For a book, check the table of contents and index for information on your topic; then determine whether the information is relevant to your topic (your hypothesis, question, or problem). For an article, see if the abstract or topic sentences in the body of the essay apply to your topic.

Online sources require careful and critical evaluation on your part. In general, librarians have recommended or chosen the books that you find in your school library. In addition, editors and experts in the field have for the most part reviewed books and articles in print. To the contrary, unbiased or authoritative experts may or may not have examined materials located on the Web. When in doubt, ask your instructor or a reference librarian.

EVALUATING PRINT AND ONLINE SOURCES

1. Is the source directly relevant to your topic? Does it confirm your hypothesis, answer your question, or propose a solution to your problem?
2. Does the source present relatively current information, especially for research in the social and natural sciences?
3. Does the source indicate the author's expertise (background, education, other publications)? Do other writers refer to this author as a reliable expert?
4. Does the source provide information comparable to that in other reputable sources?
5. Does the source supply notes, a bibliography, or other information to document its own sources?
6. Does an online source identify its author? Is the site sponsored by a particular business, agency, or organization? Is contact information provided for the author or sponsor?
7. Does an online source supply useful, appropriate links? Are the links current and relevant? Are many of the links broken? (Many broken links indicate that the site has not been recently updated.)

For more help with assessing and evaluating sources, click on **Research > CARS Source Evaluation Tutor**

Taking Notes

Once you have assembled relevant, useful sources, you can begin to read these sources more closely and take detailed notes. Accurate, well-chosen notes will help you build your research essay. You want to select and summarize the general ideas that will form the outline of your paper, to record specific evidence to support your ideas, and to copy exact statements you plan to quote for evidence or interest.

Online applications (such as UberNote, NoodleBib, and Evernote) are available for note taking and have many valuable features, such as Web searching, organizing methods, and online collaboration with fellow students. Some researchers still find it useful to take notes on 4 by 6-inch cards. By keeping your notes on cards, you can easily rearrange information from different sources; compare ideas from different sources; and build a visual outline when it's time to draft your research essay.

There are three kinds of notes that you can take as you do your research:

- *Summaries* of material keep track of specific facts, overall perspectives, reminders of what particular sources provide.
- *Paraphrases* of material compel you to think carefully about what you read so that you can express it in your own words. Paraphrase helps you to summarize specific ideas and arguments without having to copy out, word for word, a particular source.
- *Direct quotations* are exact copies of an author's own words. Use direct quotations for ideas and concepts that are concise, specific, and that state the author's opinion or conclusion.

GUIDELINES FOR TAKING NOTES ON YOUR TOPIC

1. Write down the author's last name, the title of the book or article, and the page number. Be sure that you also have an entry for this source in your working bibliography. This will help you accurately document your sources and save you time later.
2. Copy only one idea, group of closely related facts, or quote for each entry you make. This will make it easier for you to organize the information when you begin to draft your research essay.

(*continued*)

3. Identity subtopics for your notes. This will help you to arrange your notes into groups, which can then serve as the basis of your outline. Keep a separate list of these subtopics.
4. If applicable, add your own ideas to each card—perhaps using a different color ink, or on the reverse side of the card.

The sample entries below illustrate each of these note-taking strategies.

1: Sample note entry: Summary

Subtopic	S.A.T./college admissions
Author/title	Gladwell, "Examined Life"
Page number(s)	86–88
Summary	The University of California in 2001 proposed using measures other than the S.A.T. when considering students for admission, because a study of UC students found that the S.A.T. was the least reliable measure of potential student success.

2: Sample note entry: Paraphrase

Subtopic	S.A.T./college admissions
Author/title	Gladwell, "Examined Life"
Page number(s)	86–88
Paraphrase	A University of California study showed that achievement tests like the S.A.T. II were far more likely than the S.A.T. in predicting student success. High school grade point averages were also found by the study to be a more reliable way to determine student success. The study was based on the records of UC students from 1996–1999. Achievement tests were found, overall, to be more fair to students because they measure what students have already learned.

3: Sample note entry: Direct Quotation

Subtopic	S.A.T./college admissions
Author/title	Gladwell, "Examined Life"
Page number(s)	86–88
Direct quotation	Gladwell quotes Richard Atkinson, the president of the University of California: "Achievement tests are fairer to students because they measure accomplishment rather than promise . . . they tell students that a college education is within the reach of anyone with the talent and determination to succeed."

Developing a Thesis

As you read your material and take notes, you should start developing ideas for your proposal or thesis. You began your research with a *hypothesis*—an unproven idea, hunch, or question that guided your reading and helped you to narrow your topic. Your *thesis* is the main idea of your research essay. Although your thesis may change a bit as you draft your research paper and continue to think about different ideas and perspectives, writing your thesis down before you begin your outline will give you a solid foundation for your outline and draft.

HYPOTHESIS	THESIS
Fashion magazines promote an unrealistic body image.	The self-esteem of adolescent girls determines how they respond to unreal images of women in fashion magazines.

Organizing Your Notes and Writing an Outline

Because you must organize all of this material you have gathered in a clear, logical way, an outline is especially valuable for a research essay. Plan to spend as much time as you can in drafting your outline and organizing your evidence, as this will make the actual writing of your research essay much more efficient. Your instructor may require you to submit an outline at some stage of writing the research essay; be sure that you understand the required format. You may also find it useful to ask your instructor, or fellow students, to review your outline and make suggestions. A good outline should allow a reader to follow easily the lines of your argument and see how each piece of evidence will fit in to the final essay.

THE ORGANIZING PROCESS

1. Review all your notes. Be sure they include source information (p. A-9).
2. Group your notes by subtopic. Can any subtopics be combined? Are any subtopics so large that you can divide them further?
3. Do any notes duplicate each other? Set aside any notes which, within a subtopic grouping, duplicate information.
4. Are there any subtopics that include just one or two ideas or that don't seem to "fit" anywhere? Set those aside.
5. Number your notes within each subtopic. This will help you save time as you write your rough draft.
6. Do not discard any notes. Even if you don't see an obvious place for a note or subtopic in your outline, you never know what might prove useful as you write.
7. Do not feel obliged to use every note when you write your paper. You may be overwhelmed by the number of notes that you have—but you probably won't use every single quotation, paraphrase, and piece of information in your final paper.

This grouping of notes by subtopic should provide you with the basic structure of an outline. If your instructor requires a formal outline, follow the guidelines provided. If not, follow these basic principles as you arrange your notes within each subgrouping:

I. (Most important points)
  A.
  B. (Next most important point)
    1.
    2.
    3. (Supporting points)
      a.
      b. (Relevant details, minor points)

For more help with outlining, click on
Writing > Outlines
Writing > Outlining Tutor

PHASE III: WRITING THE PAPER

As you begin the third phase of the research process, keep in mind that your research paper will be a formal essay, not a collection of notes. You should be prepared to take your research effort through multiple drafts, each time reconsidering the relevance and "fit" of your evidence.

Drafting

For your rough draft, concentrate on filling in the shape of your outline. Take the time to organize your notes in the topic order of your outline. In this way you will be able to integrate notes and writing more efficiently.

Remember that your outline is a *guide* for your writing—you are not obliged to adhere to it. As you write, you may find subtle points taking on new importance, or additional evidence that needs to be included. Your purpose in writing a rough draft is to work out the shape and content of your research essay, and you should expect to make many changes and adjustments as you write.

You may choose to incorporate direct quotations from your notes into the rough draft. Some writers prefer to save time by indicating in the draft which notes to return to later in order to copy out the entire paraphrase or quote. If you have numbered your notes as suggested above, you might find this a valuable time-saving strategy.

As you work through your outline, organizing your sources, you must contribute your own commentary. You will arrange details in an effective order, sort out conflicting claims and interpretations, and solve problems. Writing the rough draft of a research paper is much more complex than a mere transcription of facts and quotations. The process of writing is an effort to work in a logical way from the introduction and the statement of your thesis, through the evidence, to the outcome or conclusion that supports everything that has come before.

You may not use every note in your rough draft. Again, set aside those that you do not use, or that do not seem to fit. *Do not throw away any notes!* At the same time, you may find as you write that you need further information on a particular point. Try to phrase that "missing" information in the form of questions. Consult your working bibliography and all of your notes (those you are using as well as those you have set aside). Can you answer your questions from sources you already have? If not, what sources will you consult (or return to) in order to get the information you need?

For more help with drafting, click on
Writing > Drafting and Revising

Incorporating Sources

As you draft, you will refer to your notes for ideas as well as information. Introducing that information—hard facts, paraphrases, or direct quotations—into the flow of your own writing requires that you make it clear to your reader that the following information or words come from a different source. At the same time, you do not want to interrupt the flow of your own argument by randomly dropping in chunks of outside information. Your basic challenge is gracefully incorporating research sources into your essay in order to support your own ideas without confusing the reader. Think of this as a kind of conversational skill; by including other voices in your research essay and clearly identifying each of those voices, you are allowing your "listener"—your reader—to take part in the ongoing academic "conversation" about your research topic. For example:

> Recently, some colleges and universities have reconsidered the importance of S.A.T. scores in admissions decisions. "Seventy-five years ago, the S.A.T. was instituted because we were more interested, as a society, in what a student was capable of learning than in what he had already learned. Now, apparently, we have changed our minds . . ." (Gladwell 88).

In revision, this writer used paraphrase to help make the transition from her argument to Gladwell's observation:

> Discussing the recent decision by the University of California to use measures other than the S.A.T. in admissions decisions,

> Malcolm Gladwell points out that "seventy-five years ago, the S.A.T. was instituted because we were more interested, as a society, in what a student was capable of learning than in what he had already learned" (Gladwell 88), whereas today's educators realize that it is more fair to assess what students have already accomplished.

Using conversational verbs rather than simply "says" or "writes" can enliven your introduction of sources without confusing your reader. The writer above uses the verb phrase "points out." Other possibilities include:

> Malcolm X forcefully argues that . . .
> Annie Dillard vividly describes . . .
> Katha Pollitt admits that . . .

You will notice that this system does not rely on footnotes or end notes to give credit to the source of information. When you write your research essay and incorporate outside sources, be sure to include the author's last name and the page number on which you found the ideas to which you are referring. You must provide this information for paraphrases and factual information as well as direct quotations. For more information on in-text citation, see p. A-18 of this appendix.

For more help with paraphrasing, summarizing, and quoting, click on

Research > Avoiding Plagiarism > Summarize/Paraphrase
Research > Avoiding Plagiarism > Using Quotations
Research > Incorporating Source Information
Research > Using Sources Accurately

Revising Your Draft

In your rough draft you thought and wrote your way through your problem or hypothesis, considering different kinds of evidence and various points of view. In revision, you rethink and rewrite in order to give better form and expression to your ideas. Your instructor may ask you to share your rough draft with other students, which allows you to test the structure of your argument and the strength of your evidence. Even if you are not required to share your paper in class, you might find it very helpful to exchange drafts with another student for comment and feedback at this stage.

GUIDELINES FOR REVISING YOUR RESEARCH WRITING

1. Does my title clearly indicate the topic of my essay? Does it capture my reader's interest?
2. Does my opening paragraph clearly establish and limit my topic?
3. Is my thesis statement clear, limited, and interesting?
4. Do all my body paragraphs support the thesis? Is there a single topic and main idea for each paragraph? Is there sufficient evidence in each paragraph to support the main idea?
5. Are there clear and effective transitions linking my ideas within and between paragraphs?
6. Do I incorporate evidence gracefully and logically? Do I acknowledge other people's ideas properly? Do I clearly indicate the sources of facts and evidence?
7. Is my conclusion strong and effective? Does it clearly and obviously echo my thesis statement?
8. If I share my paper with a student reader, does that reader have any questions about my argument or my evidence? What further information would my reader suggest I add?
9. Are my sentences grammatically correct and complete? Have I varied my sentences effectively?
10. Is my use of punctuation correct?
11. Are all words spelled correctly? Have I printed out and read through my paper to catch any spelling errors that a computerized "spell-check" function might miss?

For more help with revising your essay, click on

Writing > Drafting and Revising

Preparing the Final Manuscript

Leave time in your research writing to prepare a neat, clean manuscript. Consult your instructor for the required format, and carefully follow those guidelines for your final manuscript. Store your word processor file on a backup disk, and print or duplicate an extra copy for your own records.

PHASE IV: DOCUMENTING SOURCES

Documenting your sources throughout your paper and in a section called Works Cited tells your audience just how well you have conducted your research. It offers readers the opportunity to check and review the same sources you used in writing your paper. Failure to provide proper documentation for your paper can have very serious consequences, including charges of *plagiarism.* Plagiarism, or the use of material without giving proper credit to the source, is considered a kind of intellectual theft. The disciplinary consequences of plagiarism in academic writing can range from a failing grade for that assignment to dismissal from the college. The consequences for plagiarism in the workplace are even more severe, ranging from dismissal from a job to criminal charges.

MATERIALS THAT REQUIRE DOCUMENTATION

1. Direct quotations
2. Paraphrased material
3. Summarized material
4. Any key idea or opinion adapted and incorporated into your paper
5. Specific data (whether quoted, paraphrased, or tabulated)
6. Disputed facts
7. Illustrations (maps, charts, graphs, photographs, etc.)

For more help with documenting sources, click on

Research > Avoiding Plagiarism > Using Copyrighted Materials

Research > Bibliomaker

In-Text Citations, in the Style of the Modern Language Association (MLA), Seventh Edition (2009)

Briefly identifying sources in the text of your paper, either as part of your sentence or within parentheses, is the most common method of indicating sources. In MLA style, include the author's name and the page number of the source. Then list complete information alphabetically by author or title (if the source has no specific author) in the Works Cited section.

GUIDELINES FOR PARENTHETICAL (IN-TEXT) DOCUMENTATION

1. Give enough information so that the reader can readily identify the source in the Works Cited section of your paper.
2. Give the citation information in parentheses placed where the material occurs in your text.
3. Make certain that the complete sentence containing the parenthetical documentation is readable and grammatically correct.

The following examples illustrate how to cite a source in the text. The MLA guidelines require you to include the author's last name and the page number where the quotation or information is located. If you state the author's name in the text, do not repeat it in the citation. Other professional organizations, such as the American Psychological Association (APA), require alternate citation styles.

Page Number(s) for a Book

The play offers what many audiences have found a satisfying conclusion (Hansberry 265–76).

Garcia Marquez uses another particularly appealing passage as the opening of the story (105).

Page Number(s) for an Article in a Journal or Magazine

Barlow's description of the family members includes "their most notable strengths and weaknesses" (18).

Section and Page Number(s) for a Newspaper Article

A report on achievement standards for high school courses found "significant variation among schools" (Mallory B1).

Page Number(s) for a Work Without an Author

Computerworld has developed a thoughtful editorial on the issue of government and technology ("Uneasy Silence" 54).

Works Cited List

To prepare your Works Cited list of sources, simply transcribe those bibliography cards or entries that you actually used to write the paper. The Works Cited page is a separate page at the end of your research paper (see p. A-31 for an example).

GUIDELINES FOR THE WORKS CITED LIST

1. Use the title Works Cited. Center this title at the top of the page. Do not underline this title, type it in an italic font, or place it in quotation marks. Use upper and lower case.
2. Arrange the list of sources alphabetically according to the author's last name or according to the title of the work if there is no author. Ignore *A, An,* or *The*. Use italics for the titles of books and periodicals.
3. List alphabetically according to title other works by the same author directly under the first entry for the author's name.
4. For works by more than one author, list the entry under the last name of the first author, giving other writers' names in regular order (first name, middle, last).
5. Begin each entry at the left margin. Indent everything in an entry that comes after the first line by one-half inch or five spaces. Use the hanging indent feature of your software to achieve this.
6. Double-space every line.
7. Punctuate with periods after the three main divisions in most entries: author, title, and publishing information.
8. All print entries require the word *Print* after the source information. All online entries require the word *Web* after the source information.

For more help with documenting sources, click on

Research > Avoiding Plagiarism > Using Copyrighted Materials
Research > Bibliomaker
Research > Links to Documentation Sites

PERIODICAL PRINT PUBLICATIONS

Article in a Journal with Pagination Continuing Through Each Volume

Columb, Gregory G. "Franchising the Future." *College Composition and Communication* 62 (2010): 11–30. Print.

Article in a Journal with Pagination Continuing Only Through Each Issue

Add the issue number after the volume number.

Pinkowski, Jennifer. "A City by the Sea." *Archaeology* 59.1 (2006): 46–49. Print.

Article in a Weekly or Biweekly Periodical

Seabrook, John. "How to Make It." *New Yorker* 20 Sept. 2010: 66–73. Print.

Article in a Monthly or Bimonthly Periodical

If an article in a magazine or a newspaper does not continue on consecutive pages, follow the page number on which it begins with a plus sign.

Leslie, Jacques. "The Last Empire." *Mother Jones* Jan.–Feb. 2008: 28+. Print.

Article in a Daily Newspaper

Walkin, Daniel J. "Mahler Said What to Whom?" *New York Times* 4 Feb. 2011: C1+. Print.

Article with No Author

"Spanish Customs." *The Economist* 1–7 March 2008: 55. Print.
"People in the News." *US News and World Report* 11 Jan. 1999: 16. Print.

Editorial in a Periodical

Gannon, Mary. "Studies in Writing." Editorial. *Poets and Writers* Nov.–Dec. 2007: 6. Print.

Letter Written to the Editor of a Periodical

West, Bing. "Securing Iraq." Letter. *Foreign Affairs* Jan.–Feb. 2008: 199. Print.

NONPERIODICAL PRINT PUBLICATIONS

Book by One Author

Notice the punctuation and italics in the basic entry for a book.

Grisham, John. *The Confession.* New York: Doubleday, 2010. Print.
Michaelis, David. *Schulz and Peanuts: A Biography.* New York: Harper, 2007. Print.

Several Books by One Author

If you use several books by one author, list the author's name in the initial entry. In the next entry or entries, arranged alphabetically by title, replace the name with three hyphens.

Friedman, Thomas L. *Hot, Flat, and Crowded: Why We Need a Green Revolution and How It Can Renew America.* New York: Farrar, 2008. Print.
---. *The World Is Flat: A Brief History of the Twenty-first Century.* New York: Farrar, 2006. Print.

Book with Two or Three Authors or Editors

List the names of several authors in the sequence in which they appear in the book. Begin with the last name of the author listed first because it is used to determine the alphabetical order for entries. Then identify the other authors by first and last names.

Baghai, Mehrdad, and James Quigley. *As One: Individual Action, Collective Power.* New York: Penguin, 2011. Print.

Work with More than Three Authors or Editors

Name all those involved, or list only the first author or editor followed by *et al.*, for "and others."

Nordhus, Inger, Gary R. VandenBos, Stig Berg, and Pia Fromholt, eds. *Clinical Geropsychology*. Washington: APA, 1998. Print.

Nordhus, Inger, et al., eds. *Clinical Geropsychology.* Washington: APA, 1998. Print.

Work with Group or an Organization as Author

American Heart Association. *The New American Heart Association Cookbook*, *8th ed.* New York: Crown, 2010. Print.

Work Without an Author

The New York Times Guide to Essential Knowledge. New York: St. Martins, 2004. Print.

Work in a Collection of Pieces All by the Same Author

Coetzee, J. M. "Nadine Gordimer." *Inner Workings: Literary Essays 2000–2005.* New York: Viking, 2007. 244–56. Print.

Work in an Anthology

Kolbert, Elizabeth. "Butterfly Lessons." *The Best American Science Writing* 2007. Ed. Gina Kolata. New York: Harper, 2007. 234–51. Print.

Work Translated from Another Language

Keilson, Hans. *Comedy in a Minor Key.* Trans. Damion Searls. New York: Farrar, 2010. Print.

New Edition of an Older Book

Wharton, Edith. *The Custom of the Country*. 1913. NY Public Library Collector's Edition. New York: Doubleday, 1998. Print.

Entry from a Reference Volume

Treat less common reference books like other books, including place of publication, publisher, and date. For encyclopedias, dictionaries, and other familiar references, simply note the edition and its date. No page numbers are needed if the entries appear in alphabetical order in the reference volume.

"Civil War." *World Book:* 2008 ed. Print.

Minton, John. "Worksong." *American Folklore: An Encyclopedia.* Ed. Jan Harold Brunvand. New York: Garland, 1996. Print.

ONLINE PUBLICATIONS

Book, Article, or Other Source Available Online

Besides author and title, add any translator or editor, the publisher or sponsor of the site, the date of electronic publication or last update, and the medium of publication (Web). Conclude with the date on which you visited the electronic site where the source is located.

Land-Webber, Ellen. *To Save a Life: Stories of Jewish Rescue.* 1999. Web. 15 Mar. 2011.

Latham, Ernest. "Conducting Research at the National Archives into Art Looting, Recovery, and Restitution." *National Archives Library.* National Archives and Records Administration. 4 Dec. 1998. Web. 27 Apr. 2011.

Marvell, Andrew. "Last Instructions to a Painter." Ed. Bob Blair, Jon Lachelt, Nelson Miller, and Steve Spanoudis. *Poet's Corner.* 31 Aug. 2003. Web. 27 Feb. 2010.

Wollstonecraft, Mary. "A Vindication of the Rights of Women: With Strictures on Political and Moral Subjects." Ed. Steven van Leeuwen. *Bartleby.com.* Columbia U. Jan. 1996. Web. 5 May 2010.

Magazine Article Available Online

Sivy, Michael. "Three Bargains for Uncertain Times." *money.cnn.com. Money.* 21 Apr. 2005. Web. 27 May 2010.

Database Available Online

Van Leeuwen, Steven, Ed. *Bartleby Library. Bartleby.com.* 1999. Web. 27 Apr. 2011.

Newspaper Article Available Online

Meyer, Jeremy P. "Kids Eating Up Chef's Classes." *denverpost.com.* 17 Oct. 2008. Web. 22 Jan. 2011.

Article from an Electronic Journal

Warren, W. L. "Church and State in Angevin Ireland." *Chronicon: An Electronic History Journal* 1 (1997): 6 pars. Web. 27 Apr. 2010.

Electronic Posting to a Group

Faris, Tommy L. "Tiger Woods." *H-Net: Humanities & Social Sciences Online Posting.* 3 Sept. 1996. Web. 5 Oct. 2011.

ADDITIONAL COMMON SOURCES

Film, Videotape

Start with the title, italicized. Then include any actor, producer, director, or other person whose work you wish to emphasize. Or simply list the italicized title of the recording. Note the form cited—videocassette, film, and so forth.

No End in Sight. Ferguson, Charles, writer, dir. and prod. Magnolia Home Entertainment, 2007. DVD.

Black Swan. Dir. Darren Aronofsky. Perf. Natalie Portman. Fox Searchlight, 2010. Film.

Programs on Radio or Television

"Greek Tragedy Now." *What's the Word.* WBGC, New York, 27 Apr. 2005. Radio.

CD or Other Recording

Identify the format of the recording.

Basie, Count. "Sunday at the Savoy." Rec. 11–12 May 1983. *88 Basie Street.* Pablo Records, 1984. LP.

Groban, Josh. *Illuminations.* Reprise/WEA, 2010. CD.

Published or Personal Interview

Doctorow, E. L. Personal interview. 16 May 2010.

Previn, Andre. Interview with Jed Distler. "A Knight at the Keyboard." *Piano and Keyboard.* Jan.–Feb. 1999: 241–29. Print.

SAMPLE STUDENT RESEARCH PAPER

Yeager 1

Frances Yeager
Professor Richard Kelaher
Expository Writing
June 3, 2011.

Who Wants to Be a Cover Girl?: Media and Adolescent Body Image

Title clearly defines topic.

In our consumer-focused society, the average American encounters between 400 and 600 advertisements per day. One in every 11 of those advertisements contains a message directly related to beauty (Wolf 35). And yet many Americans—especially adolescents—are not critical about the power that the advertising media holds. For so many young people, advertisements are the ultimate determining judgment of what is *chic* and what is *passé*. This holds especially true for women. Research has shown that girls are more inclined to become vulnerable to the ideal body images projected by the media than boys are. Many studies conducted on this issue have concluded that our culture places more importance on physical beauty in the assessment of women and girls than it does on boys or men. According to Naomi Wolf, females of all ages have been "consistently taught from an early age that their self-worth is largely dependent on how they look. The fact that women earn more money than men in only two job categories, those of modeling and prostitution, serves to illustrate this point" (50). Writers like Hargreaves make the point very clear: Unrealistic images of the female body in advertising and the media can lead to distorted body image and eating disorders in young women immersed in our media culture.

All lines double-spaced.

Opening establishes common audience experience and interests.

Last sentence of paragraph is the thesis statement.

Yeager 2

Specific evidence to support thesis is introduced.

Summarized information is cited correctly.

Certainly, the print media geared towards young women seems to confirm this argument. A study of five popular fashion and beauty magazines geared variously towards women between the ages of 13 and 40 (*Seventeen, Cosmopolitan, Glamour,* and *Teen Vogue*), found that approximately 65 percent of their advertising consisted of products and services directly related to beauty (Stice and Shaw 289). Most of these advertisements used one or more of the following in their ads: models, sexual images, celebrities or other iconic figures, and images of happiness, popularity, success, and love.

Advertisements—print and other media—also require citation. All illustrations require credit lines, unless you provide all information in the text or take photo yourself (as here).

Consider, for example, two typical advertisements (shown below) that appeared in the women's magazines *Cosmopolitan* and *Allure* in April 2005. Both ads use popular singers in sexy poses to sell products. The ad on the left, featuring Christina Aguilera, shows the singer in tight jeans draped in a titillating manner across a police car; except for the text at the bottom, it's not clear that readers would know the ad was for Skechers footwear. The ad on the right, featuring Britney Spears, emphasizes romance; note the barely visible man in the background, which suggests that women who "dare" to wear Curious, Britney's new fragrance, will find love.

Yeager 3

In a study comparing forty-eight issues of the four most popular women's magazines with the four most popular men's magazines, there was a total of sixty three diet food ads for women and one diet food ad for men (Mellin, Scully, and Irwin). What is even more disconcerting is that in the magazines geared more towards teens and young adults (*Seventeen, Teen Vogue*), this same study found that the average of sexual images and ads related to sex was much higher than in magazines geared for older women (*Cosmopolitan, Paper, Glamour*). The magazines targeted to adolescent girls and young women also used icons and celebrities more often to sell products, as well as popularity gimmicks, implying that "popular" people buy *this* product and people who have fun use *that* product.

Online source does not need a page number for in-text citation.

A typical advertisement from the May 2001 issue of the teen magazine *Seventeen* is for the shampoo "Herbal Essence" (15). The ad features a picture of the popular singer Britney Spears, with a caption reading: "Does this look like a girl who stays home on Friday nights to wash her hair? YES!" The clear implication is that even famous—and famously sexy—young girls clear their calendar to shampoo with "Herbal Essence," and therefore young girls who idolize Britney Spears should do so as well. (Of course, the older sisters of *Seventeen* readers are targeted by a much more explicit television campaign for "Herbal Essence," implying that washing with the shampoo is an "organic" experience—but with a blatant implication that it's really "orgasmic." One commercial even featured "sex expert" Dr. Ruth Westheimer praising the "organic" pleasures of the shampoo.)

Television, magazines, and other popular media seem at once to create and perpetuate our culture's values for beauty, and what is currently found acceptable for body shape and size, style, and attitude. Magazines, television ads, billboards, music videos, and movies all reveal images of tall, thin, tanned, and beautiful young people, linking them smoothly to other images of love, success, happiness, prestige, popularity, and wealth for women. It has been found that "repeated exposure to the thin ideal via the various media can lead to the internalization of this ideal" (Richins 75), and Stice and Shaw find that, to women who have internalized these ideals, the fantasy begins to seem an attainable goal. Studies also suggest that exposure to the idealized images lowered women's satisfaction with their own attractiveness; and that immediately after viewing these images women began to experience shame, guilt, body dissatisfaction, depression, and stress (Richins 83). These results leave women even more vulnerable to ever-enticing advertisements selling them happiness, beauty and confidence in a bottle of shampoo or tube of lipstick.

The direct quote, from a print source, is immediately cited with a page number. The paraphrased online study is identified by the authors' names in the text.

For many young women, the effort to remake themselves in the idealized images perpetuated by the media becomes life-threatening. They affect "five times as many people as schizophrenia and twice as many people who have Alzheimer's disease" (Grohol). A 1991 study that tracked the incidents of anorexia nervosa over a fifty-year period found that the incidents of the disease among American females aged 10 to 19 reflected directly changes in fashion and its ideal body image. Many of the subjects also stated that they felt the greatest pressure of body weight ideals primarily from the media, with additional but lesser influence from peers and family. Even more devastating is that these results of the media's influence do not only affect adolescents and adults, but also children (Lucas et al.). A study conducted by the American Association of University Women (1990) found that girls who had a negative body image were three times as likely as boys to believe that others perceived them negatively. The study also established that a negative body image has been directly linked to a higher risk of suicide for girls, and not boys.

This paragraph summarizes the conclusions of two studies, demonstrating the *cause* and *effect* of the author's thesis (unreal media images—the "cause"—can lead to eating disorders—the "effect.").

The direct quote comes from a Web source, "National Eating Disorders Week 2010."

A 1997 study by the Kaiser Family Foundation finds that young women are receiving conflicting views and reflections of their bodies and social roles. In some circumstances, "women are shown being self-reliant and using intelligence, honesty and efficiency to achieve their goals," and magazines "reinforce these messages by encouraging their readers to rely on themselves and resolve situations in honest and direct ways." However, many other television shows targeted to adolescent females broadcast "stereotypical messages about appearance, relationships and careers, as well as more subtle signals about girls' value and importance" (Signorelli). Commenting on these findings, a study for the Vanier Institute of the Family notes that the more television girls and young women watch, the more likely they would be to create a hypothetical female television character "who is rich and thin, concerned about popularity, clothes, money, and looking attractive, and who wants to be a model or a famous actress" (Moscovitch). These conflicting messages can have a powerful and confusing influence on young women at a vulnerable stage of their development.

The study, published electronically, does not require a page number for in-text citation.

Moscovitch's article is also published electronically.

Young women—and young men, too—want to be popular. But an increasing body of evidence suggests that young women in particular believe that the route to popularity and success depends on their physical beauty, and their ability to meet rigid definitions of "beauty" perpetuated by the media. Cynical advertising campaigns exploit this anxiety among young women, encouraging them to buy beauty-related products to make them as popular, beautiful, and successful as Britney Spears or the latest supermodel. Most people want to look in the mirror and be happy with what they see, but the fact is few young women are happy when they are comparing themselves to the covers of *Teen Vogue* or *In Style.* The fashion world knows this, the advertising companies know this, and they also know that most women will pay a large price for a temporary fix of their shame and self-dissatisfaction. Women are sold on a quick pick-me-up with the latest lipstick, or the new and trendy jeans.

Paragraph reminds readers of author's thesis and key points.

Yeager 6

Conclusion makes a prediction based on assembled evidence. The author's language is strong, but she has amassed enough evidence to support her opinion.

The research cited above suggests that the media's strong influence on women and girls wreaks havoc on the mental, physical, and emotional condition of America's female population. As the media and advertising companies continue to sell to the insecurities that the media itself created, the cycle of distorted body image and associated eating disorders will continue.

Yeager 7

Pagination continues from body of paper.

Works Cited

Title centered.

All entries double-spaced.

All entries in alphabetical order by author.

First line at left margin; subsequent lines indented 5 spaces or one-half inch (one hit on "tab" key).

American Association of University Women. *Shortchanging Girls, Shortchanging America: Full Data Report.* Washington, D.C.: American Association of University Women, 1990. Print.

Curious, Britney's New Fragrance. Advertisement. *Allure* April 2005: 27. Print.

Grohol, John M. "National Eating Disorders Awareness Week 2010." *Psych Central.* 2010. Web. 28 April 2011.

Hargreaves, D. "Idealized Women in TV Ads Make Girls Feel Bad." *Journal of Social and Clinical Psychology* 21 (2002): 287–308. Print.

Herbal Essences by Clairol. Advertisement. *Seventeen* May 2001: 15. Print.

Lucas, A. R., C. M. Beard, W. M. O'Fallon, and L. T. Kurland. "50-Year Trends in the Incidence of Anorexia Nervosa in Rochester, Minn.: A Population-Based Study." *American Journal of Psychiatry* 148:7 (1991): 917–922. Print.

Mellin, L. M., S. Scully, and C. E. Irwin. "Disordered Eating Characteristics in Preadolescent Girls: Meeting of the American Dietetic Association." Las Vegas: 1986. Abstract. *About-Face.org.* 1996–2001. Web. 15 May 2008.

Moscovitch, Arlene. "Electronic Media and the Family." The Vanier Institute of the Family. 1998. Web. 20 May 2010.

Richins, M. L. "Social Comparison and the Idealized Images of Advertising." *Journal of Consumer Research* 18 (1991): 71–83. Print.

Signorelli, Nancy. "A Content Analysis: Reflections of Girls in the Media." *The Kaiser Family Foundation.* April 1997. Web. 20 May 2010.

Yeager 8

Skechers Footwear. Advertisement. *Cosmopolitan* April 2005: 65. Print.

Stice, E., and H. E. Shaw. "Adverse Effects of the Media-Portrayed Thin Ideal on Women and Linkages to Bulimic Symptomatology." *Journal of Social and Clinical Psychology* 13 (1994): 288–308. Print.

Wolf, Naomi. *The Beauty Myth*. New York: Doubleday, 1992. Print.

For another sample research essay using MLA-style documentation, click on

Research > Sample Research Paper > Sample Paper in MLA Style

For additional sample research essays using other documentation styles, click on

Research > Sample Research Paper > Sample Paper in APA Style

Research > Sample Research Paper > Sample Paper in CMS Style

Research > Sample Research Paper > Sample Paper in CSE Style

Glossary

Abstract and concrete are ways of describing important qualities of language. Abstract words are not associated with real, material objects that are related directly to the five senses. Such words as *love, wisdom, patriotism,* and *power* are abstract because they refer to ideas rather than to things. Concrete language, on the other hand, names things that can be perceived by the five senses. Words like *table, smoke, lemon,* and *half-back* are concrete. Generally you should not be too abstract in writing. It is best to employ concrete words naming things that can be seen, touched, smelled, heard, or tasted in order to support your more abstract ideas.

Allusion is a reference to some literary, biographical, or historical event. It is a "figure of speech" (a fresh, useful comparison) used to illuminate an idea. For instance, if you want to state that a certain national ruler is insane, you might refer to him as a "Nero"—an allusion to the emperor who burned Rome.

Alternating method in comparison and contrast involves a point-by-point treatment of the two subjects that you have selected to discuss. Assume that you have chosen five points to examine in a comparison of the Volkswagen Jetta (subject A) and the Honda Accord (subject B): cost, comfort, gas mileage, road handling, and frequency of repair. In applying the alternating method, you would begin by discussing cost in relation to A + B; then comfort in relation to A + B; and so on. The alternating method permits you to isolate points for a balanced discussion.

Ambiguity means uncertainty. A writer is ambiguous when using a word, phrase, or sentence that is not clear. Ambiguity usually results in misunderstanding, and should be avoided in essay writing. Always strive for clarity in your compositions.

Analogy is a form of figurative comparison that uses a clear illustration to explain a difficult idea or function. It is unlike a formal comparison in that its subjects of comparison are from different categories or areas. For example, an analogy likening "division of labor" to the activity of bees in a hive makes the first concept more concrete by showing it to the reader through the figurative comparison with the bees.

Antonym is a word that is opposite in meaning to that of another word: *hot* is an antonym of *cold; fat* is an antonym of *thin; large* is an antonym of *small.*

Argumentation is a type of writing in which you offer reasons in favor of or against something (see Chapter 11).

Audience refers to the writer's intended readership. Many essays (including most in this book) are designed for a general audience, but a writer may also try to reach a special group. For example, William Zinsser in his essay "Simplicity" (pp. 29–34) might expect to appeal more to potential writers than to the general reading public. Similarly, Elizabeth Wong's "The Struggle to Be an All-American Girl" (pp. 144–146) could mean something particularly special to young Chinese Americans. The intended audience affects many of the writer's choices, including level of diction, range of allusions, types of figurative language, and so on. (See also, "Purpose.")

Block method in comparison and contrast involves the presentation of all information about the first subject (A), followed by all information about the second subject (B). Thus, using the objects of comparison explained in the discussion of the "alternating method," you would for the block method first present all five points about the Volkswagen. Then you would present all five points about the Honda. When using the block method, remember to present the same points for each subject, and to provide an effective transition in moving from subject A to subject B.

Causal analysis is a form of writing that examines causes and effects of events or conditions as they relate to a specific subject (see Chapter 8).

Characterization is the description of people. As a particular type of description in an essay, characterization attempts to capture as vividly as possible the features, qualities, traits, speech, actions, and personality of individuals.

Chronological order is the arrangement of events in the order that they happened. You might use chronological order to trace the history of the Vietnam War, to explain a scientific process, or to present the biography of a close relative or friend. When you order an essay by chronology, you are moving from one step to the next in time.

Classification is a pattern of writing in which the author divides a subject into categories and then groups elements in each of those categories according to their relation to each other (see Chapter 9).

Clichés are expressions that were once fresh and vivid, but have become tired and worn from overuse. "I'm so hungry that I could eat a horse" is a typical cliché. People use clichés in conversation, but writers generally should avoid them.

Closings or "conclusions" are endings for your essay. Without a closing, your essay is incomplete, leaving the reader with the feeling that something important has been left out. There are numerous closing possibilities available to writers: summarizing main points in the essay; restating the main idea; using an effective quotation to bring the essay to an end; offering the reader the climax to a series of events; returning to the introduction and echoing it; offering a solution to a problem; emphasizing the topic's significance; or setting a new frame of reference by generalizing from the main thesis. Whatever type of closing you use, make certain that it ends the essay in a firm and emphatic way.

Coherence is a quality in effective writing that results from the careful ordering of each sentence in a paragraph, and each paragraph in the essay. If an essay is coherent, each part will grow naturally and logically from those parts that come before it. Coherence depends on the writer's ability to organize materials in a logical way, and to order segments so that the reader is carried along easily from start to finish. The main devices used in achieving coherence are transitions, which help to connect one thought with another.

Colloquial language is language used in conversation and in certain types of informal writing, but rarely in essays, business writing, or research papers. There is nothing wrong with colloquialisms like *gross, scam,* or *rap* when used in conversational settings. However, they are often unacceptable in essay writing—except when used sparingly for special effects.

Comparison/contrast is a pattern of essay writing treating similarities and differences between two subjects (see Chapter 7).

Composition is a term used for an essay or for any piece of writing that reveals a careful plan.

Conclusion (See *Closings*)

Concrete (See *Abstract and concrete*)

Connotation/denotation are terms specifying the way a word has meaning. Connotation refers to the "shades of meaning" that a word might have because of various emotional associations it calls up for writers and readers alike. Words like *American, physician, mother, pig,* and *San Francisco* have strong connotative overtones to them. With denotation, however, we are concerned not with the suggestive meaning of a word but with its exact, literal meaning. Denotation refers to the "dictionary definition" of a word—its exact meaning. Writers must understand the connotative and denotative value of words, and must control the shades of meaning that many words possess.

Context clues are hints provided about the meaning of a word by another word or words, or by the sentence or sentences coming before or after it. Thus in the sentence, "Mr. Rome, a true *raconteur,* told a story that thrilled the guests," we should be able to guess at the meaning of the italicized word by the context clues coming both before and after it. (A *raconteur* is a person who tells good stories.)

Definition is a method of explaining a word so that the reader knows what you mean by it (see Chapter 10).

Denotation (See *Connotation/denotation*)

Derivation is how a word originated and where it came from. Knowing the origin of a word can make you more aware of its meaning, and more able to use it effectively in writing. Your dictionary normally lists abbreviations (for example, O.E. for Old English, G. for Greek) for word origins and sometimes explains fully how they came about.

Description is a type of writing that uses details of sight, color, sound, smell, and touch to create a word picture and to explain or illustrate an idea (see Chapter 3).

Dialogue is the exact duplication in writing of something people say to each other. Dialogue is the reproduction of speech or conversation; it can add concreteness and vividness to an essay, and can also help to reveal character. When using dialogue, writers must be careful to use correct punctuation. Moreover, to use dialogue effectively in essay writing, you must develop an ear for the way other people talk, and an ability to create it accurately.

Diction refers to the writer's choice or use of words. Good diction reflects the topic of the writing. Malcolm X's diction, for example, is varied, including subtle descriptions in standard diction and conversational sarcasms (see Chapter 2). Levels of diction refer both to the purpose of the essay and to the writer's audience. Skillful choice of the level of diction keeps the reader intimately involved with the topic.

Division is that aspect of classification (see Chapter 9) in which the writer divides some large subject into categories. For example, you might divide *fish* into saltwater and freshwater fish; or *sports* into team and individual sports. Division helps writers to split large and potentially complicated subjects into parts for orderly presentation and discussion.

Effect is a term used in causal analysis (see Chapter 8) to indicate the outcome or expected result of a chain of happenings. When dealing with the analysis of effects, writers should determine whether they want to work with immediate or final effects, or both. Thus, a writer analyzing the effects of an accidental nuclear explosion might choose to analyze effects immediately after the blast, as well as effects that still linger.

Emphasis suggests the placement of the most important ideas in key positions in the essay. Writers can emphasize ideas simply by placing important ones at the beginning or at the end of the paragraph or essay. But several other techniques help writers to emphasize important ideas: (1) key words and ideas can be stressed by repetition; (2) ideas can be presented in climactic order, by building from lesser ideas at the beginning to the main idea at the end; (3) figurative language (for instance, a vivid simile) can call attention to a main idea; (4) the relative propor-tion of detail offered to support an idea can emphasize its importance; (5) comparison and contrast of an idea with other ideas can emphasize its importance; and (6) mechanical devices like underlining, capitalizing, and using exclamation points (all of which should be used sparingly) can stress significance.

Essay is the name given to a short prose work on a limited topic. Essays take many forms, ranging from a familiar narrative account of an event in your life to explanatory, argumentative, or critical investigations of a subject. Normally, in one way or the other, an essay will convey the writer's personal ideas about the subject.

Euphemism is the use of a word or phrase simply because it seems less distasteful or less offensive than another word. For instance, *mortician* is a euphemism for *undertaker; sanitation worker* for *garbage collector.*

Fable is a story with a moral. The story from which the writer draws the moral can be either true or imaginary. When writing a fable, a writer must clearly present the moral to be derived from the narrative, as Rachel Carson does in "A Fable for Tomorrow" (see pp. 260–262).

Figurative language, as opposed to *literal,* is a special approach to writing that departs from what is typically a concrete, straightforward style. It involves a vivid, imaginative comparison that goes beyond plain or ordinary statements. For instance, instead of saying that "Joan is wonderful," you could write that "Joan is like a summer's rose" (a *simile*); "Joan's hair is wheat, pale and soft and yellow" (a *metaphor*); "Joan is my Helen of Troy" (an *allusion*); or use a number of other comparative approaches. Note that Joan is not a rose, her hair is not wheat, nor is she some other person named Helen. Figurative language is not logical; instead, it requires an ability on the part of the writer to create an imaginative comparison in order to make an idea more striking.

Flashback is a narrative technique in which the writer begins at some point in the action and then moves into the past in order to provide necessary background information. Flashback adds variety to the narrative method, enabling writers to approach a story not only in terms of straight chronology, but in terms of a back-and-forth movement. However, it is at best a very difficult technique and should be used with great care.

General/specific words are necessary in writing, although it is wise to keep your vocabulary as specific as possible. General words refer to broad categories and groups, while specific words capture with more force and clarity the nature of a term. The distinction between general and specific language is always a matter of degree. "A woman walked down the street" is more general than "Mrs. Walker walked down Fifth Avenue," while "Mrs. Webster, elegantly dressed in a muslin suit, strolled down Fifth Avenue" is more specific than the first two examples. Our ability to use specific language depends on the extent of our vocabulary. The more words we know, the more specific we can be in choosing words.

Hyperbole is obvious and intentional exaggeration.

Illustration is the use of several examples to support an idea (see Chapter 6).

Imagery is clear, vivid description that appeals to our sense of sight, smell, touch, sound, or taste. Much imagery exists for its own sake, adding descriptive flavor to an essay, as when Suzanne Berne in "My Ticket to the Disaster" writes, "Light reflecting off the Hudson River vaults into the site, soaking everything—especially on an overcast morning—with a watery glow." However, imagery can also add meaning to an essay. For example, when Orwell writes at the start of "A Hanging," "It was in Burma, a sodden morning of the rains. A sickly light, like yellow tinfoil, was slanting over the high walls into the jail yard," we see that the author uses imagery to prepare us for the somber and terrifying event to follow. Writers can use imagery to contribute to any type of wording, or they can rely on it to structure an entire essay. It is always difficult to invent fresh, vivid description, but it is an effort that writers must make if they wish to improve the quality of their prose.

Introductions are the beginning or openings of essays. Introductions should perform a number of functions. They should alert the reader to the subject, set the limits of the essay, and indicate what the *thesis* (or main idea) will be. Moreover, they should arouse the reader's interest in the subject, so that the reader will want to continue reading into the essay. There are several devices available to writers that aid in the development of sound introductions.

1. Simply state the subject and establish the thesis. See the essay by Zinsser (pp. 29–34).
2. Open with a clear, vivid description that will become important as your essay advances. Save your thesis for a later stage, but indicate what your subject is. See the essay by Orwell (pp. 167–172).
3. Ask a question or a series of questions, which you might answer in the introduction or in another part of the essay. See the Takaki essay (pp. 452–454).
4. Tell an anecdote (a short, self-contained story of an entertaining nature) that serves to illuminate your subject. See the Staples essay (pp. 220–223).
5. Use comparison or contrast to frame your subject and to present the thesis. See the Pollitt essay (pp. 314–317).
6. Establish a definitional context for your subject. See the Ingrassia essay (pp. 273– 276).
7. Begin by stating your personal attitude toward a controversial issue. See the Ivins essay (pp. 460–462).

These are only some of the devices that appear in the introductions to essays in this book. Writers can also ask questions, give definitions, or provide personal accounts—there are many techniques that can be used to develop introductions. The important thing to remember is that you *need* an introduction to an essay. It can be a single sentence or a much longer paragraph, but it must accomplish its purpose—to introduce readers to the subject, and to engage them so that they want to explore the essay further.

Irony is the use of language to suggest the opposite of what is stated. Writers use irony to reveal unpleasant or troublesome realities that exist in life, or to poke fun at human weaknesses and foolish attitudes. For instance, in Orwell's "A Hanging," the men who are in charge of the execution engage in laughter and lighthearted conversation after the event. There is irony in the situation and in their speech because we sense that they are actually very tense—almost unnerved—by the hanging; their laughter is the opposite of what their true emotional state actually is. Many situations and conditions lend themselves to ironic treatment.

Jargon is the use of special words associated with a specific area of knowledge or a specific profession. It is similar to "shop talk" that members of a certain trade might know, but not necessarily people outside it. For example, the technology jargon in Singel's essay helps him talk to an audience of tech-savvy readers. Use jargon sparingly in your writing, and be certain to define all specialized terms that you think your readers might not know.

Journalese is a level of writing associated with prose types normally found in newspapers and popular magazines. A typical newspaper article tends to present information factually or objectively; to use simple language and simple sentence structure; and to rely on relatively short paragraphs. It also stays close to the level of conversational English without becoming chatty or colloquial.

Metaphor is a type of figurative language in which an item from one category is compared briefly and imaginatively with an item from another area. Writers create metaphors to assign meaning to a word in an original way.

Narration is telling a story in order to illustrate an important idea (see Chapter 4).

Objective/subjective writing refers to the attitude that writers take toward their subject. When writers are objective, they try not to report their own personal feelings about their subject. They attempt to control, if not eliminate, their own attitude toward the topic. Thus in the essay by Jared Diamond (see pp. 245–249) we read about globalization, but he doesn't try to convince us that globalization is good or bad. Many essays, on the other hand, reveal the authors' personal attitudes and emotions. In the essay, by

Jennifer Lee the author's personal approach to the process of reading seems clear. She takes a highly subjective approach to the topic. Other essays, such as "Thumbs on the Wheel" (see pp. 185–186), blend the two approaches to help balance the author's expression of a strong opinion. For some kinds of college writing, such as business or laboratory reports, research papers, or literary analyses, it is best to be as objective as possible. But for many of the essays in composition courses, the subjective touch is fine.

Order is the manner in which you arrange information or materials in an essay. The most common ordering techniques are *chronological order* (involving time sequence); *spatial order* (involving the arrangement of descriptive details); *process order* (involving a step-by-step approach to an activity); *deductive order* (in which you offer a thesis and then the evidence to support it); and *inductive order* (in which you present evidence first and build toward the thesis). Some rhetorical patterns such as comparison and contrast, classification, and argumentation require other ordering techniques. Writers should select those ordering principles that permit them to present materials clearly.

Paradox is a statement that *seems* to be contradictory but actually contains an element of truth. Writers use it in order to call attention to their subject.

Parallelism is a variety of sentence structure in which there is "balance" or coordination in the presentation of elements. "I came, I saw, I conquered" is a good example of parallelism, presenting both pronouns and verbs in a coordinated manner. Parallelism can also be applied to several sentences and to entire paragraphs. It can be an effective way to emphasize ideas.

Personification is giving an object, thing, or idea lifelike or human qualities. Like all forms of figurative writing, personification adds freshness to description, and makes ideas vivid by setting up striking comparisons.

Point of view is the angle from which a writer tells a story. Many personal or informal essays take the *first-person* (or "I") point of view, as the essays by Malcolm X, Hughes, Orwell, and others reveal. The first-person "I" point of view is natural and fitting for essays when the writer wants to speak in a familiar and intimate way to the reader. On the other hand, the *third-person* point of view ("he," "she," "it," "they") distances the reader somewhat from the writer. The third-person point of view is useful in essays where writers are not talking exclusively about themselves, but about other people, things, and events, as in the essays by Ahmed and Carson. Occasionally, the *second-person* ("you") point of view will appear in essays, notably in essays involving process analysis where the writer directs the reader to do something; part of Ernest Hemingway's essay (which also uses a third-person point of view) uses this strategy. Other point-of-view combinations are possible when a writer wants to achieve a special effect—for example, combining *first-* and *second-person* points of view. The position that you take as a writer depends largely on the type of essay you write.

Prefix is one or more syllables attached to the front of another word in order to influence its meaning or to create a new word. A knowledge of prefixes and their meanings aids in establishing the meanings of words and in increasing the vocabulary that we use in writing. Common prefixes and their meanings include *bi-* (two), *ex-* (out, out of), *per-* (through), *pre-* (before), *re-* (again), *tele-* (distant), and *trans-* (across, beyond).

Process analysis is a pattern of writing that explains in a step-by-step way the methods for doing something or reaching a desired end (see Chapter 5).

Proposition is the main point in an argumentative essay. It is like a *thesis,* except that it usually presents an idea that is debatable or can be disputed.

Purpose refers to what a writer hopes to accomplish in a piece of writing. For example, the purpose may be *to convince* the reader to adopt a certain viewpoint (as in Herbert's "Tweet Less, Kiss More," pp. 307–309), *to explain* a process (as in Hemingway's "Camping Out," pp. 195–199), or to allow the reader *to feel a dominant impression* (as in Lopez's "Apologia," pp. 105–110). Purpose helps a writer to determine which expository technique will dominate the essay's form, as well as what kinds of supporting examples will be used. Purpose and *audience* are often closely related.

Refutation is a technique in argumentative writing in which you recognize and deal effectively with the arguments of your opponents. Your own argument will be stronger if you can refute—prove false or wrong—all opposing arguments.

Root is the basic part of a word. It sometimes aids us in knowing what the larger word means. Thus if we know that the root *doc-* means "teach," we might be able to figure out a word like *doctrine. Prefixes* and *suffixes* are attached to roots to create words.

Sarcasm is a sneering or taunting attitude in writing. It is designed to hurt by ridiculing or criticizing. Basically, sarcasm is a heavy-handed form of irony, as when an individual says, "Well, you're exactly on time, aren't you" to someone who is an hour late, and says it with a sharpness in the voice, designed to hurt. Writers should try to avoid sarcastic writing and to use more acceptable varieties of irony and satire to criticize their subject.

Satire is the humorous or critical treatment of a subject in order to expose the subject's vices, follies, stupidities, and so forth. Barry, for instance, satirizes stereotyped ideas of men and women, exposing them as empty concepts. Satire is a better weapon than sarcasm in the hands of the writer because satire is used to correct, whereas sarcasm merely hurts.

Sentimentality is the excessive display of emotion in writing, whether it is intended or unintended. Because sentimentality can distort the true nature of a situation, writers should use it cautiously, or not at all. They should be especially careful when dealing with certain subjects, for example the death of a loved one, the remembrance of a mother or father, a ruined romance, the loss of something valued, that lend themselves to sentimental treatment. Only the best writers—like Hughes and others in this text—can avoid the sentimental traps rooted in their subjects.

Simile is an imaginative comparison using *like* or *as*. When Orwell writes, "A sickly light, like yellow tinfoil, was slanting over the high walls into the jail yard," he uses a vivid simile in order to reinforce the dullness of the scene.

Slang is a level of language that uses racy and colorful expressions associated more often with speech than with writing. Slang expressions like "Mike's such a dude" or "She's a real fox" should not be used in essay writing, except when the writer is reproducing dialogue or striving for a special effect. Hughes is one writer in this collection who uses slang effectively to convey his message to the reader.

Subjective (See *Objective/subjective*)

Suffix is a syllable or syllables appearing at the end of a word and influencing its meaning. As with prefixes and roots, you can build vocabulary and establish meanings by knowing about suffixes. Some typical suffixes are *-able* (capable of), *-al* (relating to), *-ic* (characteristic of), *-ion* (state of), *-er* (one who), which appear often in standard writing.

Symbol is something that exists in itself but also stands for something else. As a type of figurative language, the symbol can be a strong feature in an essay, operating to add depth of meaning, and even to unify entire essays.

Synonym is a word that means roughly the same as another word. In practice, few words are exactly alike in meaning. Careful writers use synonyms to vary word choice, without ever moving too far from the shade of meaning intended.

Theme is the central idea in an essay; it is also often termed the *thesis*. Everything in an essay should support the theme in one way or another.

Thesis is the main idea in an essay. The *thesis sentence,* appearing early in the essay, and normally somewhere in the first paragraph, serves to convey the main idea to the reader in a clear way. It is always useful to state your central idea as soon as possible, and before you introduce other supporting ideas.

Title for an essay should be a short, simple indication of the contents of your essay. Titles like "Salvation" (pp. 152–155) and "Pride" (pp. 370–372) convey the central subjects of these essays in brief, effective ways. Others, such as "I Have a Dream" (pp. 466–470) and "Night Walker" (pp. 220–223), also convey the central idea, but more abstractly. Always provide titles for your essays.

Tone is the writer's attitude toward his or her subject or material. An essay writer's tone may be objective, ironic, comic, nostalgic, or a reflection of numerous other attitudes. Tone is the "voice" that you give to an essay; every writer should strive to create a "personal voice," or tone, that will be distinctive throughout any type of essay under development.

Transition is the linking of one idea to the next in order to achieve essay *coherence*. Transitions are words that connect these ideas. Among the most common techniques to achieve smooth transition are (1) repeating a key word or phrase; (2) using a pronoun to refer back to a key word or phrase; (3) relying on traditional connectives like *thus, for example, moreover, therefore, however, finally, likewise, afterward,* and *in conclusion;* (4) using parallel structure (see *Parallelism*); and (5) creating a sentence or an entire paragraph that serves as a bridge from one part of your essay to the next. Transition is best achieved when the writer presents ideas and details carefully and in logical order. Try not to lose the reader by failing to provide adequate transition from idea to idea.

Unity is that feature in an essay where all material relates to a central concept and contributes to the meaning of the whole. To achieve a unified effect in an essay, the writer must design an introduction and conclusion, maintain a consistent tone and point of view, develop middle paragraphs in a coherent manner, and always stick to the subject, never permitting unimportant elements to enter. Thus, unity involves a successful blending of all elements that go into the creation of a sound essay.

Vulgarisms are words that exist below conventional vocabulary, and are not accepted in polite conversation. Always avoid vulgarisms in your own writing, unless they serve an illustrative purpose.

Credits

PHOTOS

Figure 2.2: © Jacob A. Riis/Getty Images; **2.3:** © Mary Kate Denny/PhotoEdit; **2.4:** © Getty Images; **3.1:** © James Marshall/The Image Works; **4.1:** Getty Images RF; **6.1:** © M. Bradley/US Navy; **8.1:** © Kim Kulish/Corbis; **9.1–9.6:** © Courtesy of Balch Institute of Collections/Historical Society of Pennsylvania; **10.1:** © Culver Pictures, Inc.; **11.2:** © Scott Daemmrich/Stock, Boston; App. 1: © Brooke Pleasanton.

COLOR INSERT PHOTOS

Page 1: © Brand X/Jupiter Images RF; **p. 2:** © Brand X/Fotosearch RF; **p. 3:** © Kevin Fleming/Corbis; **p. 5:** © Comstock/Punchstock RF; **p. 7:** © Rick Gayle/Corbis; **p. 8:** © Getty Images.

TEXT

Ahmed, Akbar. "Mystics, Modernists, and Literalists." Reprinted from *The Wall Street Journal*, September 1, 2010, © 2010 Dow Jones & Company. All rights reserved.

Bader, Eleanor J. "Homeless on Campus," *The Progressive*, vol. 68, no. 7 (July 2004), pp. 29–31. This piece was originally written for *The Progressive* magazine, 409 E. Main St., Madison, WI 53703. www.progressivemediaproject.org. Reprinted by permission of The Progressive.

Baker, James T. "How Do We Find the Student in a World of Academic Gymnasts and Worker Ants?" *Chronicle of Higher Education*, 1982. Reprinted by permission of the author.

Barry, Dave. "Neither Man Nor Rat Can Properly Fold Laundry," *Miami Herald*, July 2, 2000. Reprinted by permission of Dave Barry.

Carson, Rachel. "A Fable for Tomorrow" from *Silent Spring* by Rachel Carson. Copyright © 1962 by Rachel L. Carson, renewed 1990 by

Roger Christie. Reprinted by permission of Houghton Mifflin Harcourt Publishing Company and Frances Collin, Trustee. All rights reserved.

Cheever, Susan. "Baby Battle" by Susan Cheever, copyright © 2006 by Susan Cheever, from *Mommy Wars*, edited by Leslie Morgan Steiner, copyright 2006. Used by permission of Random House, Inc. and The Martell Agency.

Cofer, Judith Ortiz. "Volar" is reprinted with permission from the publisher of *The Year of Our Revolution: New and Selected Stories and Poems* by Judith Ortiz Cofer (© 1998 Arte Público Press–University of Houston).

Cullen, Countee. "Incident" from *Color* by Countee Cullen. Copyright 1925 Harper & Bros., NY. Renewed 1952 Ida M. Cullen. Copyrights held by Amistad Research Center, Tulane University. Administered by Thompson and Thompson, Brooklyn, NY.

Diamond, Jared. "Globalization Rocked the Ancient World Too" by Jared Diamond from *Los Angeles Times*, September 14, 2003. Used with permission of the author.

Dillard, Annie. "In the Jungle" (pp. 71–77) from *Teaching a Stone to Talk: Expeditions and Encounters* by Annie Dillard. Copyright © 1982 by Annie Dillard. Reprinted by permission of HarperCollins Publishers and Russell & Volkening as agents for the author.

Ehrenreich, Barbara. "What I've Learned from Men," *Ms.* magazine (1985). Reprinted by permission of *Ms.* magazine, © 1985.

Ephron, Nora. "How to Foil a Terrorist Plot in Seven Simple Steps," *Huffington Post*, June 4, 2007. Reprinted by permission of International Creative Management, Inc. Copyright © 2007 by Nora Ephron.

Gates, Henry Louis, Jr. "In the Kitchen" from *Colored People: A Memoir* by Henry Louis Gates, Jr., copyright © 1994 by Henry Louis Gates, Jr. Used by permission of Alfred A. Knopf, a division of Random House, Inc. and the author.

Gilb, Dagoberto. "Pride" from *Gritos*. Grove/Atlantic, 2003. Copyright © 2003 by Dagoberto Gilb. Reprinted by permission of the author.

Hughes, Langston. "Salvation" from *The Big Sea* by Langston Hughes. Copyright © 1940 by Langston Hughes. Copyright renewed 1968 by Arna Bontemps and George Houston Bass. Reprinted by permission of Hill and Wang, a division of Farrar, Straus and Giroux, LLC, and Harold Ober Associates Incorporated.

Ingrassia, Michele. "The Body of the Beholder" by Michele Ingrassia. *Newsweek*, April 24, 1995, pp. 66–67. © 1995.

Ivins, Molly. "Get a Knife, Get a Dog, but Get Rid of Guns" from *Nothin' But Good Times Ahead* by Molly Ivins, copyright © 1993 by Molly Ivins. Used by permission of Random House, Inc.

King, Martin Luther Jr. "I Have a Dream." Reprinted by arrangement with The Heirs to the Estate of Martin Luther King Jr., c/o Writers House as agent for the proprietor New York, NY. Copyright 1963 Dr. Martin Luther King Jr; copyright renewed 1991 Coretta Scott King.

King, Stephen. "Why We Crave Horror Movies." Reprinted With Permission. © Stephen King. All rights reserved. Originally appeared in *Playboy* (1982).

Kingston, Maxine Hong. "Catfish in the Bathtub" from *The Woman Warrior* by Maxine Hong Kingston, copyright © 1975, 1976 by Maxine Hong Kingston. Used by permission of Alfred A. Knopf, a division of Random House, Inc., and Pan Macmillan, London.

Lam, Andrew. "Waterloo" from *East Eats West: Writing in Two Hemispheres* by Andrew Lam. Berkeley, CA: Heyday Books, 2010. Copyright © 2010 by Andrew Lam. Reprinted by permission of the author. Andrew Lam is editor of New America Media.

Lemuel, John. "Why I Registered on Facebook," *Chronicle of Higher Education*, September 1, 2006. Reprinted with permission.

Lopez, Barry. "Apologia" from *About This Life: Journeys on the Threshold of Memory*. New York: Knopf, 1998. Reprinted by permission of SLL/Sterling Lord Literistic, Inc. Copyright by Barry Holstun Lopez.

Malcolm X. From *The Autobiography of Malcolm X* by Malcolm X and Alex Haley, copyright © 1964 by Alex Haley and Malcolm X. Copyright © 1965 by Alex Haley and Betty Shabazz. Published by Random House, and in the UK by Hutchinson. Used by permission of Random House, Inc. and the Random House Group Ltd.

Naylor, Gloria. "A Word's Meaning Can Often Depend on Who Says It," *The New York Times Magazine*. Reprinted by permission of SLL/Sterling Lord Literistic, Inc. Copyright by Gloria Naylor.

Orwell, George. "A Hanging" from *Shooting an Elephant and Other Essays* by George Orwell, copyright © George Orwell, 1931, copyright 1950 by Sonia Brownell Orwell and renewed 1978 by Sonia Pitt-Rivers, reprinted by permission of Houghton Mifflin Harcourt Publishing Company and Bill Hamilton as the Literary

Executor of the Estate of the Late Sonia Brownell Orwell and Secker & Warburg Ltd.

Pollitt, Katha. "Why Boys Don't Play with Dolls," *The New York Times Magazine*, October 8, 1995. © 1995 by Katha Pollitt. Reprinted by permission of the author.

Purdy, Jedediah. Reprinted with permission from Jedediah Purdy, "Shades of Green," *The American Prospect*: January 2000. Volume 11, Issue 4. http://www.prospect.org. *The American Prospect*, 1710 Rhode Island Avenue, NW, 12th floor, Washington, DC 20036. All rights reserved.

Quindlen, Anna. "Turning the Page," *Newsweek*, March 26, 2010. Reprinted by permission of International Creative Management, Inc. Copyright © 2010 by Anna Quindlen.

Rashap, Amy. "The American Dream for Sale: Ethnic Images in Magazines" by Amy Rashap, written for a catalog published in conjunction with an exhibition at the Balch Institute for Ethnic Studies. Reprinted by permission of the author.

Rodriguez, Richard. "The 'Great Wall of America' and the Threat from Within" by Richard Rodriguez. Copyright © 2010 by Richard Rodriguez. Originally appeared in the *Los Angeles Times* (September 5, 2010). Reprinted by permission of Georges Borchardt, Inc., on behalf of the author.

Staples, Brent. "Just Walk on By: A Black Man Ponders His Power to Alter Public Space" by Brent Staples as appeared in *Ms.* Magazine. Reprinted by permission of the author.

Takaki, Ronald. "The Harmful Myth of Asian Superiority," *The New York Times*, June 16, 1990. Reprinted by permission of the author.

Tan, Amy. "Mother Tongue." Copyright © 1989. First appeared in *Threepenny Review*. Reprinted by permission of the author and the Sandra Dijkstra Literary Agency.

Tannen, Deborah. "Mom's Unforgiving Mirror," *Washington Post*, April 10, 2007, pp. F1, F7. Copyright Deborah Tannen. Reprinted by permission. This article is adapted from *You're Wearing THAT? Understanding Mothers and Daughters in Conversation*. New York: Random House, 2006; paperback; Ballantine.

Welty, Eudora. Reprinted by permission of the publisher from *One Writer's Beginnings* by Eudora Welty, pp. 5–11, Cambridge, Mass.: Harvard University Press, Copyright © 1983, 1984 by Eudora Welty.

Index of Authors and Titles